BTEC
Level 3

D0510412

PUBLIC
SERVICES LEVEL 3

Book 1 BTEC National

Debra Gray | Tracey Lilley | John Vause

A PEARSON COMPANY

Published by Pearson Education Limited, a company incorporated in England and Wales, having its registered office at Edinburgh Gate, Harlow, Essex, CM20 2JE. Registered company number: 872828

www.pearsonschoolsandfecolleges.co.uk

Edexcel is a registered trademark of Edexcel Limited
Text © Pearson Education Limited 2010

First published 2010

14
10 9 8 7

British Library Cataloguing in Publication Data
A catalogue record for this book is available from the British Library.

ISBN 978 1 846907197

Edited by Priscilla Goldby
Designed by Tony Richardson (Wooden Ark)
Typeset by Tek-Art
Original illustrations © Pearson Education Limited 2010
Cover design by Visual Philosophy, created by eMC Design
Picture Research by Pearson Education Limited
Front cover photo by Monkey Business Images/Shutterstock and back cover photos (from left to right) by Frances Twitty/iStockphoto and Graham Taylor/Shutterstock
Printed in Malaysia, CTP-PJB

Disclaimer
This material has been published on behalf of Edexcel and offers high-quality support for the delivery of Edexcel qualifications.

This does not mean that the material is essential to achieve any Edexcel qualification, nor does it mean that it is the only suitable material available to support any Edexcel qualification. Edexcel material will not be used verbatim in setting any Edexcel examination or assessment. Any resource lists produced by Edexcel shall include this and other appropriate resources.

Copies of official specifications for all Edexcel qualifications may be found on the Edexcel website: www.edexcel.com

Contents

Credits

Debra Gray would like to thank the following:

From Pearson Education: Amanda Hamilton, Lewis Birchon, Alexandra Clayton and Priscilla Goldby whose editing, patience and support have been invaluable.

From Dearne Valley College: A big thank you to the entire public services team for their humour, patience and resilience in the face of the challenging FE sector and having me as a boss, John Vause, Barry Pinches, Paul Meares, Charlotte Baker, Boris Lockyer, Kelly Ellery, Nick Lawton, Mick Blythe, Jean Tinnion and Debbie. Thanks also to my boss Julie – you are one in a million.

From the Services: Lance Corporal Kelly Stevens 38 Signals, South Yorkshire Police, South Yorkshire Fire and Rescue Service, South Yorkshire Ambulance Service.

My family: Ben, India, Sam and Genevieve who make every day brighter. And to Jin who started me on this path.

The authors and publisher would also like to thank the following.

For their contribution to this publication: Abingdon Fire Station (Oxfordshire Fire and Rescue Service): Graham Turner, Gary Walker, Steve Barclay Dean Goddard, Julian Bradwell, Neil Priestley

For permission to reproduce photographs: **p.1** Photodisc/Photolink, **p.17** and **p.122** Derek Blair/Rex Features, **p.3** and **p.229** Photos. com, **p.35** James Boulette/iStockphoto, **p.36** Pearson Education Ltd/Arnos Design, **p.37** Graham Taylor/Shutterstock, **p.39** and **p.205** Pearson Education Ltd/Studio 8/Clark Wiseman, **p.46** and **295** The Illustrated London News Picture Library, **p.56, p.81, p.218** and **p.223** AFP/Getty Images, **p.63** and **p.144** National Archives and Records Administration, **p.73, p.125** and **p.317** Janine Wiedel Photolibrary/Alamy, **p. 75** Gregory Wrona/Alamy, **p.77** Shutterstock/Sorin Popa, **p.79** Graham Jepson/Alamy, **p.82** Andrew Parsons/ epa/Corbis, **p. 83, p.126** and **309** Kevin Britland/Shutterstock, **p.86** and **p.260** Photodisc/Getty Images, **p.90** Sonia Birch, **p.92** Kelly Stevens/Debra Gray, **p.104** , **p.263** and **p.278** Pearson Education Ltd/Naki Kouyioumtzis, **p.109** Dean Mitchell/Shutterstock, **p.106** Trinity Mirror/Mirrorpix/Alamy, **p.111** John Gomez/iStockphoto, **p.113** Nik Taylor Photography/Alamy, **p.119, p.162** and **p.314** Stefan Hamilton, **p.120** and **p.203** Jae C Hong/AP/Press Association Images, **p.130** Chris Parker, **p.132** Pearson Education Ltd/ MindStudio, **p.138** Corbis, **p.139** Imagesource.com, **p.145** and **296** AMAR AMAR/Rex Features, **p.149** Dave Bartruff/Corbis, **p.151** Paul David Drabble/Alamy, **p.153** LWA-Dann Tardif/Corbis, **p.155** and **p.190** Christopher Futcher/Shutterstock, **p.156, p.192** and **p.196** Photodisc/Karl Weatherly , **p.176** Medical-on-Line/Alamy, **p.177** Jupiter Images/Brand X/Alamy, **p.184** Imagestate/John Foxx Collection, **p.185** and **p.321** Yuri Arcurs/Shutterstock, **p.187** Frances Twitty/iStockphoto, **p.189** and **p.265** Pearson Education Ltd/ Jules Selmes, **p.201** Laura Lezza/Getty Images, **p.225** Pearson Education Ltd/Gareth Boden, **p.233** PA/PA Archive/Press Association Images, **p.230** Mel Stoutsenberger/iStockphoto, **p.240** Sipa Press/Rex Features, **p.246** and **305** Rex Features, **p.247** Peter Byrne/ PA Wire/Press Association Images, **p.227** Oleg Popov/Reuters/Corbis, **p.249** and **p.251** Ian Miles-Flashpoint Pictures/Alamy, **p.253** Shutterstock/Paul Matthew Photography, **p.256** Toby Melville/Reuters/Corbis, **p.261** and **p.328** Shutterstock/Monkey Business Images, **p.268** Blend Images/John Lund/Marc Romanelli/Getty Images, **p.269** Photofusion Picture Library/Alamy, **p.272** Peter Evans, **p.275** Pearson Education Ltd/Lord and Leverett, **p.279** Shutterstock/Dmitriy Shironosov, **p.281** Art Directors & TRIP/Alamy, **p.283** Desha Cam/Shutterstock, **p.285** Shutterstock/Phil Date, **p.289** Nils Jorgensen/Rex Features, **p.294** Thierry Dosogne /Getty, **p.298** Creatas, **p.299** TopFoto.co.uk, **p.311** Owen Humphreys/PA Wire/Press Association Images, **p.315** Tandem/Shutterstock, **p.319** Steve Cole/iStockphoto, **p.332** iStockphoto, **p.334** Shutterstock/Sean Prior, **p.343** Golden Pixels LLC/Shutterstock

For permission to reproduce copyright material: **p.16** Independent Police Complaints Commission statistics 2008-9, **p.20** Getty Images/The Conservative Party Archive, **p.85** Population of the UK by ethnic group, National Census data 2001 **p.100** Equal Opportunities Policy for the Army 2000 **p.117** HM Prison Service Mission Statement **p.124** Code of Professional Standards for Police Officers 2006: Crown copyright data and information is reproduced under the terms of the Click-Use Licence (C2010000590).

For cited texts: Abrams, D, Hogg M A *Social Identification, Self-Categorization and Social Influence* European Review of Social Psychology, 21, pp.131 (1990), Asch, S E *Effects of Group Pressure Upon the Modification and Distortion of Judgments in Perspectives in Consumer Behaviour* (3rd edition) E. Kassarjian and T. Robertson (eds.), Glenview, Ill: Scott, Foresman and Company, 343-349, pp.136 (1981), Crutchfield, R *Conformity and Character*, American Psychologist, 10, 191-198 pp.129 (1955), Deutsch, M and Gerard, H B *A Study of Normative and Informational Social Influences Upon Individual Judgment* Journal of Abnormal and Social Psychology, 54, 629-636 pp.131 (1955), Ericson, R, Baranek, P, and Chan, J *Visualizing Deviance* (University of Toronto Press, 1987), Glueck, S and Glueck, E *Unravelling juvenile delinquency* (Harvard University Press, 1988), Goring, C. *The English Convict: A Statistical Study*. London: HMSO. (1913), Gross, R and McIlveen, R *Psychology A New Introduction* (Hodder & Stoughton, 1988), Hewitt, J P *The Myth of Self-Esteem: Finding Happiness and Solving Problems in America* (St Martin's Press, 1998), Hofling, C K *An Experimental Study of Nurse-Physician Relationships* Journal of Nervous and Mental Disease 141, 171-180, pp.139 (1966), Hough, M *Anxiety About Crime: Findings from the 1994 British Crime Survey*, Home Office Research Study No. 147 (Home Office, London, 1995), Linton, R (ed.), The Science of Man in the World Crisis (Columbia University Press, 1945), Milgram, S. *Obedience to Authority: An Experimental View* (Harper Collins, 1974), Newburn T, *Criminology* (Willan Publishing, 2007), Raven, B H *Social Influence and Power* in Steiner, D, Fishbein, M (eds), Current Studies in Social Psychology, Holt, Rinehart & Winston, pp.142 (1965), Sheldon, W H *The varieties of human physique: An introduction to constitutional psychology* (Harper & Brothers, 1940), Simmons, J *Crime in England and Wales 2001/2002*. Home Office Statistical Bulletin Issue 7/02 (Home Office. London, 2002), Williams, P and Dickinson, J *Fear of Crime: Read all About It? The Relationship Between Newspaper Crime Reporting and Fear of Crime*, British Journal of Criminology, 33, 1, pp.33-56. (1993), Zimbardo P G, Lieppe M R *The Psychology of Attitude Change and Social Influence* (Temple University Press, 1991),

About the authors

Debra Gray has taught public services in the Further Education sector for 13 years. She has a degree in Criminology and master's degrees in Criminal Justice and Education Management. She has written numerous publications for both learners and tutors on public services and other issues, such as the new diplomas. Debra also served as an External Verifier for three years.

Tracey Lilley has worked as a Senior Verifier and External Verifier and is involved in the development of new BTEC Public Services specifications. She served as a special constable and, more recently, as a teacher and lecturer delivering and assessing programmes from level 1 to level 6. A member of the Institute of Educational Assessors and the Institute for Learning, Tracey is also a Senior Assessment Associate for the Principal Learning Public Services.

John Vause has taught public services for the past 10 years. He studied Philosophy after his career in the West Yorkshire and then the South Yorkshire Police. During this period he was involved in planning, organising and taking part in numerous outdoor activities and exhibitions while training Police Cadets. He has also attended several major incidents, including multiple-vehicle road traffic collisions and fire incidents. As a detective in the Criminal Investigation Department, John investigated hundreds of crimes, including murder.

About BTEC Level 3 National Public Services

There are many different optional units in your BTEC Level 3 Public Services qualification, which you may use to focus on specific services or to build a broader programme of learning. This student book covers enough units for the Edexcel BTEC Level 3 Subsidiary Diploma in Public Services (uniformed or non-uniformed), but if you want a bigger choice of optional units or if you are completing the Edexcel BTEC Level 3 Diploma or Extended Diploma in Public Services, you may be interested in Student Book 2.

Written in the same accessible style with the same useful features to support you through your learning and assessment, *BTEC Level 3 National Public Services Student Book 2* (ISBN: 9781846907203) covers the following units:

Unit	Credit value	Unit name
9	10	Outdoor and adventurous expeditions
14	10	Responding to emergency service incidents
15	15	Planning and management of major incidents
17	5	Police powers in the public services
18	5	Behaviour in public sector employment
20	10	Communication and technology in the uniformed public services
21	10	Custodial care services
22	10	Aspects of the legal system and the law making process
24	10	Current and media affairs in public services
34	10	Environmental policies and practices

Available direct from www.pearsonfe.co.uk/btec2010 and can be ordered from all good bookshops.

About your BTEC Level 3 National Public Services book

BTEC Level 3 Public Services will give you an insight into the different uniformed and non-uniformed public services, from firefighters, the army and the police to mountain rescue, teaching and custodial care. Your qualification will help you to understand the importance of teamwork and effective communication within the public services as well as the entry requirements and working environment for the services you are most interested in.

Your BTEC Level 3 National Public Services is a **vocational** or **work-related** qualification. This doesn't mean that it will give you *all* the skills you need to do a job, but it does mean that you'll have the opportunity to gain specific knowledge, understanding and skills that are relevant to your chosen subject or area of work.

What will you be doing?

The qualification is structured into **mandatory units** (ones that you must do) and **optional units** (ones that you can choose to do). How many units you do and which ones you cover depend on the type of qualification you are working towards.

Qualifications	Credits from mandatory units	Credits from optional units	Total credits
Edexcel BTEC Level 3 Certificate	10	20	30
Edexcel BTEC Level 3 Subsidiary Diploma	40	20	60
Edexcel BTEC Level 3 Diploma	50	70	120
Edexcel BTEC Level 3 Extended Diploma	60	120	180

How the books cover the qualifications

This table shows how the units covered by the books in this series cover the different types of BTEC qualification.

Unit	Credit value		Cert.	Sub. Dip.	Uniformed pathway		Non-uniformed pathway	
					Dip.	Ex. Dip.	Dip.	Ex. Dip.*
1	10	Government, policies and the public services	M	M	M	M	M	M
2	15	Leadership and teamwork in the public services	O	M	M	M	M	M
3	15	Citizenship, diversity and the public services	O	M	M	M	M	M
4	10	Understanding discipline in the uniformed public services	O	O	M	M		
5	10	Physical preparation, health and lifestyle for the public services	O	O	O	O	O	O
6	10	Fitness testing and training for the uniformed public services			O	M		
7	5	International institutions and human rights	O	O	O	O	O	O
8	5	Understand the impact of war, conflict and terrorism on public services	O	O	O	O	O	O
9	10	Outdoor and adventurous expeditions	O	O	O	O	O	O
12	10	Crime and its effects on society	O	O	O	O	O	O
13	10	Command and control in the uniformed public services	O	O	O	O		
14	10	Responding to emergency service incidents			O	O		
15	10	Planning and management of major incidents	O	O	O	O	O	O
17	5	Police powers in the public services	O	O	O	O	O	O
18	5	Behaviour in public sector employment	O	O	O	O	O	O
20	10	Communication and technology in the uniformed public services			O	O		
21	10	Custodial care services			O	O	O	O
22	10	Aspects of the legal system and the law making process			O	O	O	O
24	10	Current and media affairs in public services			O	O	O	O
25	10	Public service data interpretation					M	M
34	10	Environmental policies and practices	O	O	O	O	O	O

* The Non-uniformed Extended Diploma also requires Unit 26: Enhancing public service delivery through the use of ICT, which is not covered here.

Units in yellow are covered in this book. Units in green are covered in *BTEC Level 3 National Public Services Student Book 2* (ISBN: 9781846907203).

How to use this book

This book is designed to help you through your BTEC Level 3 National Public Services course.

It contains many features that will help you to use your skills and knowledge in work-related situations and assist you in getting the most from your course.

Introduction ●

These introductions give you a snapshot of what to expect from each unit – and what you should be aiming for by the time you finish it!

Credit value: 10

1 Government, policies and the public services

Much of our interaction with others is political, even if we don't realise it. Every time you have an argument or come to an agreement about how things should be run or shared out, you are engaging in a political process. The only difference between this and national politics is the scale and influence the opinions, disagreements and decisions have. Although many people think they are not interested in politics and that it's not connected with their lives or that it's boring, they are, in fact, engaging in politics every day. Political decisions affect everyone.

This unit provides you with an introduction to the political structure of the UK, including the levels of government and the roles and responsibilities each level has. Through it you will examine different government departments, especially the departments that have a direct effect on the public services such as the Ministry of Defence and the Ministry of Justice. You will also look at the accountability of the services.

This unit is essential in providing you with an understanding of the policies and influences that impact on the work of the services every day of their working lives. It is important that you have a clear grasp of the political issues that the public services deal with. Remember that the business of government is your business as well. You live and work under the policies the government creates, whether you agree with them or not.

You will also have the opportunity to find out how political representatives are elected to power and what their main roles and responsibilities are. You will also look at how government policies are developed, the external factors that influence public policy and the impact that these policies can have on the work of the services.

Learning outcomes

After completing this unit you should:

1. know the different levels of government in the UK
2. understand the democratic election process for each level of government in the UK
3. know the impact of UK government policies on the public services
4. be able to demonstrate how government policies are developed.

Assessment and grading criteria ●

This table explains what you must do in order to achieve each of the assessment criteria for each unit. For each assessment criterion, shown by the grade button **P1**, there is an assessment activity.

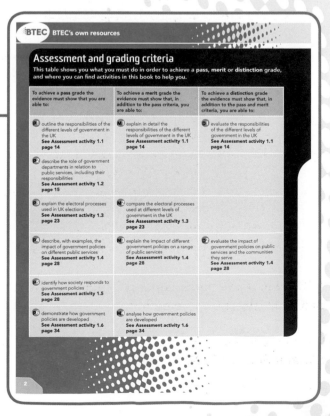

BTEC BTEC's own resources

Assessment and grading criteria

This table shows you what you must do in order to achieve a pass, merit or distinction grade, and where you can find activities in this book to help you.

To achieve a pass grade the evidence must show that you are able to:	To achieve a merit grade the evidence must show that, in addition to the pass criteria, you are able to:	To achieve a distinction grade the evidence must show that, in addition to the pass and merit criteria, you are able to:
P1 outline the responsibilities of the different levels of government in the UK **See Assessment activity 1.1 page 14**	**M1** explain in detail the responsibilities of the different levels of government in the UK **See Assessment activity 1.1 page 14**	**D1** evaluate the responsibilities of the different levels of government in the UK **See Assessment activity 1.1 page 14**
P2 describe the role of government departments in relation to public services, including their responsibilities **See Assessment activity 1.2 page 15**		
P3 explain the electoral processes used in UK elections **See Assessment activity 1.3 page 23**	**M2** compare the electoral processes used at different levels of government in the UK **See Assessment activity 1.3 page 23**	
P4 describe, with examples, the impact of government policies on different public services **See Assessment activity 1.4 page 28**	**M3** explain the impact of different government policies on a range of public services **See Assessment activity 1.4 page 28**	**D2** evaluate the impact of government policies on public services and the communities they serve **See Assessment activity 1.4 page 28**
P5 identify how society responds to government policies **See Assessment activity 1.5 page 28**		
P6 demonstrate how government policies are developed **See Assessment activity 1.6 page 34**	**M4** analyse how government policies are developed **See Assessment activity 1.6 page 34**	

i

Assessment

Your tutor will set assignments throughout your course for you to complete. These may take a variety of forms. The important thing is that you evidence your skills and knowledge to date.

How you will be assessed

This unit will be assessed by an internal assignment that will be devised and marked by the staff at your centre. The assignment is designed to allow you to show your understanding of the learning outcomes for government, policies and the public services. These relate to what you should be able to do after completing this unit. Assessments can be quite varied and can take the form of:

- reports
- leaflets
- presentations
- posters
- practical tasks
- case studies
- simulations.

Maneno looks at the layers of government in the UK

I didn't expect to like this unit as politics isn't really my thing and I've always thought it was really boring. It turns out that everything we do or decide can be influenced by politics. Because I am quite outspoken and have an opinion on lots of things, it turns out I am very political without even realising it!

One of the things I enjoyed most was looking at the different levels of government in the UK. I hadn't realised how all the responsibility in the country is divided up and shared by the different levels. I particularly liked looking at what my local council does, as they are the ones who control the facilities and standards in the place I live. If they don't do their job properly it shows on the streets and housing estates near my home.

I also liked looking at the different views the political parties have. It's interesting to see how they come up with their policies and why. I'm not old enough to vote yet, but when I am I think I will have a much better idea of who I agree with and who I want to vote for.

My tutor also recommended that we started to read a broadsheet newspaper at least once a week or read the BBC News website in our lunch hour. I'm much better informed since I've started doing this and I've found it really helps to be up to date with the news in my other units as well.

Over to you!

- What areas of government might you find interesting?
- Have you ever been involved in politics before?
- Do you have strong opinions on current issues?
- What preparation could you do to get ready for your assessments?

Learner experience

Stuck for ideas? Daunted by your first assignment? These learners have all been through it before…

Activities

There are different types of activities for you to do: Assessment activities are suggestions for tasks that you might do as part of your assignment and will help you develop your knowledge, skills and understanding. Grading tips clearly explain what you need to do in order to achieve a pass, merit or distinction grade.

Assessment activity 1.1

The public services must abide by the policies created at the various levels of government in the UK. This means you should be able to describe the responsibilities each level of government has. In the form of a presentation answer the following questions:

1 Outline the responsibilities of the levels of government in the UK **P1**

2 Explain in detail the responsibilities of the different levels of government in the UK **M1**

3 Evaluate the responsibilities of the different levels of government in the UK **D1**

Grading tips

For **P1** a simple outline is required, so you do not have to go into detail in order to pass. When you are delivering your presentation you can explain the responsibilities in more detail and this should be enough to help you gain **M1**. To get **D1** you should supply a set of supporting notes to your tutor which goes into much greater detail about the responsibilities.

There are also suggestions for activities that will give you a broader grasp of the sector, stretch your understanding and deepen your skills.

Activity: Examples of the use of different types of authority

- A squad of new recruits in the British Army are about to have their first session of drill and they only have three months before their passing out parade. Which type of authority do you think would be applicable here, and why?
- Consider the huge exercise involved in the recovery operation following the London bombings in July 2005. The Commissioner of the Metropolitan Police Service at that time, Sir Ian Blair, was in charge of coordinating the operation – which style of authority do you think he would have used?
- The station manager has attended a multi-vehicle accident where people are trapped inside vehicles. There is a strong risk that leaking fuel could ignite, but there is an equal risk that people will die if they are left trapped in their vehicles without medical care. Which type of authority do you think would be applicable for the station manager to use, and why?
- Can you think of a situation where dictatorial authority is used in the uniformed public services? If not, explain why not.

Personal, learning and thinking skills

Throughout your BTEC Level 3 National Public Services course, there are lots of opportunities to develop your personal, learning and thinking skills. Look out for these as you progress.

PLTS

Completing this assessment will help you develop your self manager skills.

Functional skills

It's important that you have good English, Mathematics and ICT skills – they're important for communicating information effectively and accurately, which could be the difference between life and death. Use these activities to help develop and stretch your skills.

Functional skills

By producing a slideshow presentation you are practising your ICT functional skills.

Key terms

Technical words and phrases are easy to spot. You can also use the glossary at the back of the book.

Key term

Reserve forces are volunteer troops who may be called up in time of conflict, but have a normal civilian life and do their military training in their spare time.

WorkSpace

WorkSpace provides snapshots of life in the public services and shows you how the knowledge and skills you are developing through your course can be applied in your future career.

WorkSpace Linda McLoughlin
Local Councillor

I work as a local councillor in the town where I live. My job is to make sure that local money is spent on the right things and to make sure that the people of my community are represented and their views get heard by the council. I also have to work closely with lots of other agencies to make sure that the people of my town get all the high quality services they are entitled to and sometimes I represent the people of my town at national or regional events.

A typical day

I wish I could say what a typical day for a councillor might be but the tasks are so varied there's no such thing. It's not a full time job so I juggle my responsibilities with working full time and raising my family. Usually I will be required to attend meetings and respond to council business and the correspondence of my constituents.

Most councillors spend around 15 hours a week on their role unless they have extra responsibilities in the council.

The best thing about the job

This is when I get to see my constituents and help them with their problems. They elected me to serve them and represent their interests so helping them when they are in difficulties is a really big part of my job. It might involve matters of housing or refuse collection or even lobbying for community facilities such as a bike track or footpath to be created. All of this goes to making my community a better place to live for everyone.

Think about it!

What topics have you covered in this unit that might give you the background to work in local or national government?

What knowledge and skills do you think you need to develop further if you want to be involved in policy creation in the future?

25

Just checking

When you see this sort of activity, take stock! These quick activities and questions are there to check your knowledge. You can use them to see how much progress you've made and to identify any areas where you need to refresh your knowledge.

Edexcel's assignment tips

At the end of each unit, you'll find hints and tips to help you get the best mark you can, such as the best websites to go to, checklists to help you remember processes and useful reminders to avoid common mistakes. You might want to read this information before starting your assignment…

Link

In the margin, alongside a topic in the main text, you will find cross references that guide you to other parts of the book where the topic is covered in more detail or where you will be able to find relevant information.

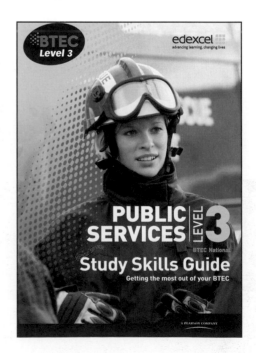

Have you read your **BTEC Level 3 National Study Skills Guide?** It's full of advice on study skills, putting your assignments together and making the most of being a BTEC Public Services student.

 Ask your tutor about extra materials to help you through the course. The **Teaching Resource Pack** which accompanies this book contains interesting activities, presentations and information about the Public Services sector.

Your book is just part of the exciting resources from Edexcel to help you succeed in your BTEC course.

Visit:

- www.edexcel.com/BTEC or
- www.pearsonfe.co.uk/BTEC 2010

1 Government, policies and the public services

Much of our interaction with others is political, even if we don't realise it. Every time you have an argument or come to an agreement about how things should be run or shared out, you are engaging in a political process. The only difference between this and national politics is the scale and influence the opinions, disagreements and decisions have. Although many people think they are not interested in politics and that it's not connected with their lives or that it's boring, they are, in fact, engaging in politics every day. Political decisions affect everyone.

This unit provides you with an introduction to the political structure of the UK, including the levels of government and the roles and responsibilities each level has. Through it you will examine different government departments, especially the departments that have a direct effect on the public services such as the Ministry of Defence and the Ministry of Justice. You will also look at the accountability of the services.

This unit is essential in providing you with an understanding of the policies and influences that impact on the work of the services every day of their working lives. It is important that you have a clear grasp of the political issues that the public services deal with. Remember that the business of government is your business as well. You live and work under the policies the government creates, whether you agree with them or not.

You will also have the opportunity to find out how political representatives are elected to power and what their main roles and responsibilities are. You will also look at how government policies are developed, the external factors that influence public policy and the impact that these policies can have on the work of the services.

Learning outcomes

After completing this unit you should:

1. know the different levels of government in the UK
2. understand the democratic election process for each level of government in the UK
3. know the impact of UK government policies on the public services
4. be able to demonstrate how government policies are developed.

Assessment and grading criteria

This table shows you what you must do in order to achieve a **pass**, **merit** or **distinction** grade, and where you can find activities in this book to help you.

To achieve a pass grade the evidence must show that you are able to:	To achieve a merit grade the evidence must show that, in addition to the pass criteria, you are able to:	To achieve a distinction grade the evidence must show that, in addition to the pass and merit criteria, you are able to:
P1 outline the responsibilities of the different levels of government in the UK **See Assessment activity 1.1 page 14**	**M1** explain in detail the responsibilities of the different levels of government in the UK **See Assessment activity 1.1 page 14**	**D1** evaluate the responsibilities of the different levels of government in the UK **See Assessment activity 1.1 page 14**
P2 describe the role of government departments in relation to public services, including their responsibilities **See Assessment activity 1.2 page 15**		
P3 explain the electoral processes used in UK elections **See Assessment activity 1.3 page 23**	**M2** compare the electoral processes used at different levels of government in the UK **See Assessment activity 1.3 page 23**	
P4 describe, with examples, the impact of government policies on different public services **See Assessment activity 1.4 page 28**	**M3** explain the impact of different government policies on a range of public services **See Assessment activity 1.4 page 28**	**D2** evaluate the impact of government policies on public services and the communities they serve **See Assessment activity 1.4 page 28**
P5 identify how society is affected by government policies **See Assessment activity 1.5 page 28**		
P6 demonstrate how government policies are developed **See Assessment activity 1.6 page 34**	**M4** analyse how government policies are developed **See Assessment activity 1.6 page 34**	

How you will be assessed

This unit will be assessed by an internal assignment that will be devised and marked by the staff at your centre. The assignment is designed to allow you to show your understanding of the learning outcomes for government, policies and the public services. These relate to what you should be able to do after completing this unit. Assessments can be quite varied and can take the form of:

- reports
- leaflets
- presentations
- posters
- practical tasks
- case studies
- simulations.

Maneno looks at the layers of government in the UK

I didn't expect to like this unit as politics isn't really my thing and I've always thought it was really boring. It turns out that everything we do or decide can be influenced by politics. Because I am quite outspoken and have an opinion on lots of things, it turns out I am very political without even realising it!

One of the things I enjoyed most was looking at the different levels of government in the UK. I hadn't realised how all the responsibility in the country is divided up and shared by the different levels. I particularly liked looking at what my local council does, as they are the ones who control the facilities and standards in the place I live. If they don't do their job properly it shows on the streets and housing estates near my home.

I also liked looking at the different views the political parties have. It's interesting to see how they come up with their policies and why. I'm not old enough to vote yet, but when I am I think I will have a much better idea of who I agree with and who I want to vote for.

My tutor also recommended that we started to read a broadsheet newspaper at least once a week or read the BBC News website in our lunch hour. I'm much better informed since I've started doing this and I've found it really helps to be up to date with the news in my other units as well.

Over to you!

- What areas of government might you find interesting?
- Have you ever been involved in politics before?
- Do you have strong opinions on current issues?
- What preparation could you do to get ready for your assessments?

1. The different levels of government in the UK

Thinking about government

Disagreeing with a government policy can be a very dangerous thing to do in some parts of the world. Can you think of a country where political dissent might cost you your life?

In the UK, every citizen is allowed to disagree with government decisions and protest peacefully against them if they choose. However, people working in the public services, especially the armed forces, have an obligation to obey lawful orders. How does this affect the role of the public services? What would happen if you disagreed with a government decision to go to war, but you were a serving British soldier? Write down your thoughts and share them with the rest of your class.

There are many different levels of government in the UK that have a direct or indirect impact on our lives as well as the work of the uniformed services. This part of the unit looks at these levels in detail.

1.1 Levels of government and their responsibilities

European Parliament

Although the European Parliament is not strictly part of the UK levels of government, it has a significant impact on EU (European Union) citizens and their public services. The parliament has 736 members who represent all 27 member states of the EU. There are 72 that are directly elected from the UK and are there to represent the interests of our country. The role of the Parliament is to draft **legislation** that has an impact across all the EU states on issues such as:

- the environment
- equal opportunities
- transport
- consumer rights
- movement of workers and goods.

Activity: The European Parliament

What are your thoughts on the European Parliament? Go to their website at www.europa.eu and research the role of the Parliament. Do you think it represents the interests of the member states fairly? Do you think the decisions are beneficial for all EU citizens? What is the impact of these decisions on the public services of the member states? Make notes on what you find and feedback to your tutor.

Central government

Central government is the layer of government that operates across the whole country. It is usually located in the country's capital city and it has very specific responsibilities that no other level of government is able to carry out. For example:

- signing treaties or agreements with other nations
- making laws
- defending the nation.

Key term

Legislation refers to the laws that have been made. To legislate means to make laws.

Activity: Laws

Why are responsibilities such as signing treaties and making laws the role of central government? What would happen if all levels of government had those powers?

The central government of the UK is based at the Palace of Westminster in London. It contains the major central political institutions of the UK: the House of Commons and the House of Lords. Together with the ruling monarch these institutions are known as Parliament which passes legislation.

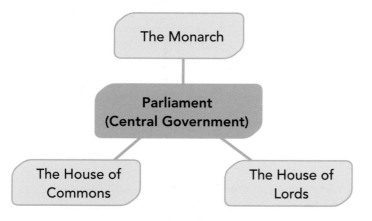

Figure 1.1: These institutions make up the UK Parliament.

Devolved parliaments

Devolution is a process whereby power is transferred from a centralised governmental organisation to a regional organisation. Devolution consists of three elements:

- The transfer of power to another elected body that is lower down the chain of authority.
- The geographical move of power from the capital to another city or town.
- The transfer of roles and responsibilities of government from central to regional assemblies.

Key term

Devolution means to pass governmental powers to a lower-level elected body.

In the UK there are three main regional assemblies that have devolved power:

- the Scottish Parliament
- the Welsh Assembly
- the Northern Ireland Assembly.

Did you know?

A problem with the present arrangements for devolution is that Scottish and Northern Irish MPs can vote on issues affecting England but English MPs cannot vote on issues affecting Scotland and Northern Ireland that are dealt with by their devolved governments. This is called the 'West Lothian Question', after the imbalance was pointed out by Tam Dalyell, MP for West Lothian in Scotland.

Table 1.1: The advantages and disadvantages of devolution.

Devolution	
Advantages	**Disadvantages**
• Regional assemblies can reflect and take into account cultural and linguistic differences between the region and central government. • Regional assemblies are more in touch with the needs of their people; laws will be fairer and more readily accepted by the people. • Reduces the burden on central government. • Because regional assemblies only deal with the work of the region they are more efficient. • Central government can concentrate on issues of national importance rather than being concerned about the regions. • The combative politics seen in centralised government may be reduced in regional assemblies where, despite opposing each other, the parties share a common concern for their local area.	• Establishing regional assemblies is very expensive. Why create an organisation to do what central government already does? • Regional assemblies lack the decision-making experience of central government. • Regional assemblies may conflict with central government. • Regional assemblies may lead to the break up of the UK. • Low voter turn out in devolution referendums suggests a lack of popular support for regional assemblies. • Being distant from local rivalries and resentments may help central government be more impartial than regional assemblies.

Table 1.2: The main regional assemblies in the UK.

Assemblies	Description
The Scottish Parliament	The Scottish Parliament was established by the Scotland Act 1998. The Scottish Parliament is empowered to deal with devolved matters such as education, health, civil and criminal law, environment, housing and local government. The Scottish Parliament is self-contained, which means it can pass laws without having to go through the UK Parliament in Westminster first. The UK Parliament has reserved powers, which means it still has jurisdiction on matters that affect the UK as a whole or that have an international impact, such as declarations of war. The Scottish Parliament is made up of 129 elected members of the Scottish Parliament (MSP). As with the UK Parliament, the party that has the most representatives forms the government, which is also referred to as the Scottish Executive. The majority party selects a representative from their ranks who is appointed as First Minister by the Queen.
The Welsh Assembly	The Welsh Assembly was established by the Government of Wales Act 1998, after a Welsh **referendum** showed a narrow majority of public support for the idea. The Welsh Assembly has 60 members. Like the Scottish Parliament, the Welsh Assembly has considerable scope to deal with regional issues such as transport, health, education and the environment. Wales also has a First Minister who is elected by the whole executive and is usually the leader of the largest political party. One substantial difference between the Scottish Parliament and the Welsh Assembly is that Wales does not have jurisdiction over its own criminal and civil law; it is subject to English law in this area.
The Northern Ireland Assembly	The Northern Ireland Assembly was created by the Northern Ireland Act 1998. This act was based on a referendum of the Belfast Agreement (more often referred to as the Good Friday Agreement). There are 108 members, six representatives from each of the 18 constituencies in Northern Ireland. As with Scotland and Wales, the Northern Ireland Assembly has responsibility for education, health, agriculture, housing and so on. The Assembly is based at Stormont and there are around eight political parties represented within it. Like the other regional assemblies it has a first minister who is elected by all members and is usually a member of the dominant party. The conflict between the different parties in the Northern Ireland Assembly has in the past led to an unstable assembly.

Key term

Referendum is a public vote on whether to pass a law. Usually laws are made and passed in Parliament, but in a referendum the public make a direct decision.

Activity: Devolution

What are the implications of allowing devolution to continue to other regions that have a distinctive culture and language, such as Cornwall? What would be the impact on the citizens of the area, their public services and the country as a whole?

Regional governments

There are eight regional assemblies in England, which were created by the Regional Development Agencies Act 1998. They are as follows:

- East of England Regional Assembly
- North East Assembly
- South East England Regional Assembly
- West Midlands Regional Assembly
- East Midlands Regional Assembly
- South West Regional Assembly
- North West Regional Assembly
- Yorkshire and Humber Assembly

London has its own regional system that works differently from those listed above and is discussed in the case study.

Key

North East Assembly

Yorkshire and Humber Assembly

East Midlands Regional Assembly

East of England Regional Assembly

South East England Regional Assembly

South West Regional Assembly

West Midlands Regional Assembly

North West Regional Assembly

N

Figure 1.2: Map of the regional areas of local government in England.

The membership of regional assemblies varies from region to region, about 70 per cent of the members are elected local authority councillors and 30 per cent are drawn from businesses, voluntary groups, religious groups and environmental organisations. Regional

assemblies are funded through central government although some also receive money from local authorities (see below).

Key term

Regional government is a form of government where the decisions about what happens in a particular region are made at local level.

Role of regional assemblies

Regional assemblies perform four main roles and these are shown in Figure 1.3.

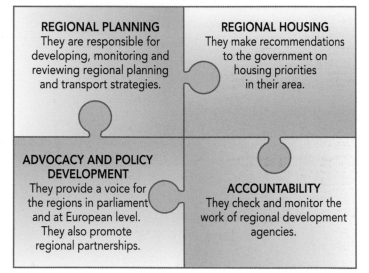

REGIONAL PLANNING
They are responsible for developing, monitoring and reviewing regional planning and transport strategies.

REGIONAL HOUSING
They make recommendations to the government on housing priorities in their area.

ADVOCACY AND POLICY DEVELOPMENT
They provide a voice for the regions in parliament and at European level. They also promote regional partnerships.

ACCOUNTABILITY
They check and monitor the work of regional development agencies.

Figure 1.3: Regional assembly roles.

Case study: The London region

Arrangements for regional governance are different in London from the other eight regions. London has the Greater London Authority (GLA), which is a city-wide form of government with an elected mayor and separately elected assembly. The Mayor of London plays a key role in the development of the city's policies on a variety of issues, such as transport, emergency planning, budgets for key public services (e.g. the Metropolitan Police Authority and the London Fire and Emergency Planning Authority), and so on. The assembly acts as a form of scrutiny on the actions of the mayor to ensure what they are doing is correct and in the best interests of London. To this end they must approve all of the Mayor's budgets, they have

the opportunity to question the Mayor at a monthly question time, and they investigate and publish reports on issues that affect Londoners.

1   Why do you think that the London region needs a different form of regional assembly from the other eight regions?

2   Is it important to have a Mayor of London who acts a spokesperson for the capital?

3   Why would the activities of the Mayor require scrutiny?

4   Are there issues that affect Londoners that don't affect the rest of the country?

Table 1.3: The main forms of local government.

Type of council	Roles and responsibilities
County	• Education • Emergency Planning • Highways and Traffic • Libraries • Planning and Development • Public Transport • Refuse Disposal • Social Services • Trading Standards
District (part of a county and several district councils come under each county council)	• Registration of Births, Deaths and Marriages • Cemeteries and Crematoria • Education • Environmental Health • Housing • Planning and Development • Recreation and Amenities • Refuse Collection • Registration of Electors • Tax and Council Tax Collection
Parish (a single village or part of a town)	• Street Lighting • Local Transport and Traffic Services • Allotments • Cemeteries • Recreation Grounds • War Memorials • Seating and Shelters • Rights of Way • Tourist information centres

Type of council	Roles and responsibilities
Metropolitan district (part of a very large city)	• Registration of Births, Deaths and Marriages • Cemeteries and Crematoria • Education • Emergency Planning • Environmental Health • Highways and Traffic • Housing • Libraries • Planning and Development • Public Transport • Recreation and Amenities • Refuse Collection • Refuse Disposal • Registration of Electors • Social Services • Tax and Council Tax Collection • Trading Standards
Unitary authorities (a city that is large enough to need its own local authority dealing with just that city)	• Registration of Births, Deaths and Marriages • Cemeteries and Crematoria • Education • Emergency Planning • Environmental Health • Highways and Traffic • Housing • Libraries • Planning and Development • Public Transport • Recreation and Amenities • Refuse Collection • Refuse Disposal • Registration of Electors • Social Services • Tax and Council Tax Collection • Trading Standards

Local authorities

There are many forms of local government, such as county councils, metropolitan councils, parish and district councils. Many of the roles and responsibilities they perform overlap, but they all focus on the services and facilities needed in local areas.

Monarch

The UK is a constitutional monarchy, which means that our head of state is the current reigning monarch, although laws are generated and approved by an elected body – for us this is the Houses of

Parliament. The monarch is currently Her Majesty Queen Elizabeth II who has reigned since 1952, and her formal title in the UK is 'Elizabeth the Second, by the Grace of God of the United Kingdom of Great Britain and Northern Ireland and of Her other Realms and Territories Queen, Head of the Commonwealth, Defender of the Faith'.

The Queen has several important formal and ceremonial governmental roles, including:

- opening each new session of Parliament
- disinterment of peers
- advice and guidance to the Prime Minister.

House of Commons

The House of Commons consists of 646 elected members of parliament (MPs) who represent a broad spectrum of political parties. Each of the MPs represents a localised geographical area, called a **constituency**. All constituencies should have approximately the same population so that all votes are equally important. That means constituencies in densely populated cities have a much smaller area than rural constituencies, where the people are spread out. Constituencies can change boundaries to become bigger or smaller or sometimes disappear altogether.

There are two ways in which an individual can be elected to the House of Commons. The first is through a **general election**, which is when representatives from all 646 constituencies are elected simultaneously, and the second is via a by-election. A **by-election** happens when the current representative of a constituency dies, retires or resigns and a new representative is needed for that constituency only. A general election happens every five years or so, but a by-election can occur at any time.

Activity: The House of Commons

Using the parliament website research the current breakdown of MPs from different parties at www.parliament.uk. Who has a majority? Who is in opposition? Are there any very small parties? Draw a pie chart to show your findings.

Did you know?

The five elected members of Sinn Fein are not allowed to take their seats in Parliament or use their vote until they swear allegiance to the Queen – something all MPs must do. The oath reads: *I swear by Almighty God that I will be faithful and bear true allegiance to Her Majesty Queen Elizabeth, her heirs and successors, according to law. So help me God.*

Sinn Fein representatives are from a party that believes Northern Ireland should leave the UK and become part of the Irish Republic. This means that they refuse to swear allegiance to the Queen, as they don't want Northern Ireland to remain part of the country of which she is monarch. Yet they do take part in the Northern Ireland government. Do you think they should have to swear allegiance before taking part in government?

A range of political views and interests are represented in the House of Commons. This enables the House to ensure that legislation and decisions are well debated by a variety of individuals holding different political views. The majority party is called upon to form the government and this party sits to the right of the Speaker while the main **opposition** party and smaller parties sit on the left of the Speaker.

Key terms

Constituency is a geographical area that has an elected representative in Parliament.

General election is where all of the seats in the House of Commons come up for election at the same time. General elections are called by the serving Prime minister and must happen five years and three weeks apart or less.

By-election is an election that happens in a specific constituency due to the retirement, death or resignation of the current MP for that area. They can happen at any time.

Sinn Fein is a political movement and party seeking a united republican Ireland.

Opposition refers to the members of parliament from those parties who do not form the current government.

Table 1.4: Duties of the House of Commons.

Function	Explanation
Making laws	Nearly 50% of the work in the House of Commons involves making new laws. These laws can have an extremely wide impact on the country and public services alike.
Controlling finance	The House of Commons controls the raising of finances through taxation and the selling of government assets. It must also give its approval to any plans the government has to spend money. The House can also check up on the spending of government departments through the Public Accounts' Committee.
Scrutiny	The House of Commons scrutinises the work of the government. The government must explain its policies to the House and be prepared to accept criticism and questioning. This ensures that all decisions have been examined by a variety of individuals before they are implemented.
Delegated legislation	The House does not have the time it needs to debate, discuss and pass all the laws needed by the country. It overcomes this problem through delegated legislation The House creates the parent law and then monitors how delegated legislation is implemented by local authorities and councils.
Examining European Union proposals	The House of Commons must examine all proposed European Union laws in order to assess their likely impact on the UK, its population and its public services.
Protecting the individual	The members of the House of Commons are often contacted by individuals with difficulties or petitioned on a variety of issues of importance to individuals or groups, such as road building, reducing taxes and changes to the law.

House of Lords

The House of Lords dates back to the fourteenth century and it has a long, distinguished and, more recently, controversial history. The House of Lords can have a variable number of members, currently there are around 737, and a number of different types of Lords, for example:

- **Life Peers.** This title is for a lifetime only and not able to be passed on to the next generation. Life Peers are appointed by the Queen on the advice of the Prime Minister and they make up the majority of the Lords. There are currently around 600 of them.

- **Bishops and Archbishops**. This title is for those who represent the Church of England. There are currently 25 sitting in the House of Lords. They pass their title onto the next most senior Bishop when they retire.

The House of Lords carries out a variety of roles, some of which are similar to the Commons, but some of which are quite different (see Table 1.4). The House of Lords used to be the highest level of court in the UK, but its role as a court have been taken over by the Supreme Court.

Table 1.5: Duties of the House of Lords.

Role	Description
Law creation	The process by which a bill is created is detailed in later in this unit. The House of Lords plays a large part in this. The Lords spend around 60% of their time on this kind of work.
Scrutiny	The House of Lords performs the same function as the Commons in that they act as a form of scrutiny on the government, using questioning and criticism as a form of control on government.
Independent expertise	The Lords conduct a variety of investigations and inquiries. They have a range of expertise, which can be used on government business.

Branches of government

The UK is a liberal democracy. This means that we encourage competition and plurality and the minimal interference of the state. There are three forms of power involved in the running of a liberal democracy.

Legislative. This is the power to make laws. In the UK the body with legislative power is Parliament. Parliament makes laws through a multi-stage process, which is outlined in Figure 1.9 (page 32). In addition to the power to make new laws, Parliament also has the legislative power to reform old laws.

Executive. This is the power to suggest new laws and ensure existing laws are implemented. This power is invested in government departments and the civil service who deal with the day to day running of the country. Laws are suggested via green papers, which open discussion about potential new laws and white papers, which set out blueprints for potential laws.

Judicial. This is the power to interpret the laws that have been made and make unbiased judgements on whether laws have been broken. This power is given to the court system and is implemented by judges in all courts in the UK.

These three powers work together to ensure the smooth running and stability of the nation.

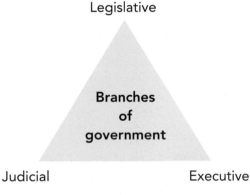

Figure 1.4: Branches of government in the UK.

1.2 Main roles at government level

The government in its current form could not work effectively without people who fulfil the main roles needed to ensure the country works effectively and decisions are made and implemented. The key roles you are required to examine are as follows:

- Prime Minister
- Government Ministers
- MPs
- Mayors
- Council Members

Prime Minister (PM)

A bill of rights was passed in 1689, which restricted the power of the ruling monarch by making it illegal for them to act on a variety of matters without the consent of parliament. This was in response to unscrupulous monarchs who raised taxes and executed laws to suit their own financial and political purposes. The monarch remained as head of the executive branch of the government and was, therefore, still able to propose and create law. However, the monarch did not rule alone as had been the case previously, instead they appointed a **cabinet** of **ministers** who were able to take on many of the duties of government with the support of the House of Commons. This situation continued for around 30 years or so until the early 1700s when the monarch of the time, George I, stopped attending cabinet meetings. In his absence a minister was deputised to act on his behalf and called the 'First Lord of the Treasury'. The role of First Lord gradually evolved into the role of **Prime Minister** over the next 150 years.

Key terms

Prime Minister the leader of the political party with most seats in the House of Commons.

Minister usually an MP appointed by the Prime Minister to take charge of a government office such as defence, or the Home Office.

Cabinet a committee of the 20 or so most senior government ministers who meet once a week to support the Prime Minister in running the country.

The individual who is appointed to the office of PM is usually the leader of the political party with the highest number of representatives in the House of Commons. The role of PM is complex and difficult, involving a variety of administrative, bureaucratic and public duties such as:

- allocation of duties to ministers
- appointment and dismissal of ministers
- appointment of chairs of national industries
- to give out honours
- setting agendas for government business
- control of information released to the government ministers, Parliament and the public.

The power of the government is distributed throughout the government ministers but the PM is extremely influential and dominant. The PM also plays a significant role on the European and world stage, meeting with other heads of state to discuss foreign and financial policies, which can have far reaching implications well past our own borders. However, it is important to note that as a public servant the PM is answerable to the Queen, their own political party and the public. When appointing to ministerial posts, they must take account of advice from senior advisors and ensure that individuals appointed are competent to do the job and do not create substantial political imbalance.

The increased concentration of the media on high profile politicians such as government ministers and the Prime Minister means that their activities are closely scrutinised and the majority of their choices are in the public domain. This means that PMs must balance their own conscience with the demands of the public, who often favour or disfavour issues based on biased media campaigns rather than a real analysis of the facts. Leaders must be aware of this and sometimes be prepared to take a political stance which is in opposition to the wishes of the public. Yet if a leader's views become too different from the views of the public, he or she will be voted out.

Activity: Ministerial decisions

Can you think of a recent issue where the Prime Minister has made a decision that the majority of the population didn't agree with? What are the political implications of doing this?

Government minister

There are many government ministers, but the 20 or so most important ministers are called 'the **cabinet**', which operates as the central committee of the British government. Cabinet members are selected by the Prime Minister; the majority are elected MPs from the House of Commons who have been selected by virtue of their expertise and loyalty to head up particular

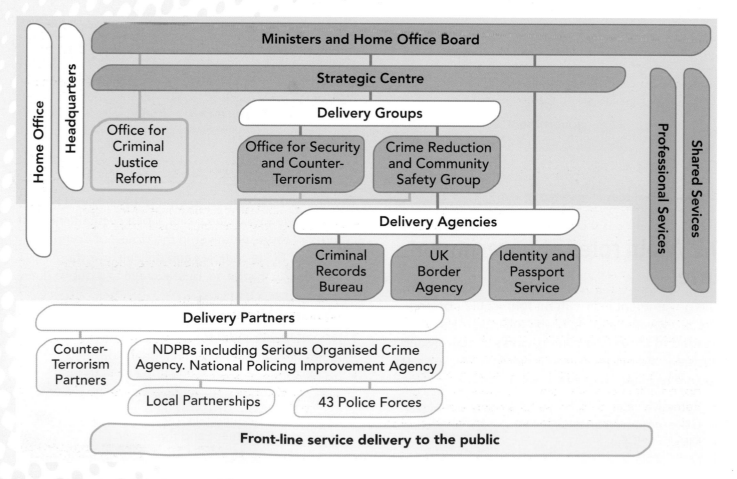

Figure 1.5 Structure within the Home Office.

ministries such as the Ministry of Defence or the Home Office (see Figure 1.5). The cabinet also consists of a few members of the House of Lords and so it is representative of both chambers of Parliament.

There are some issues that overlap many government departments, such as terrorism. On issues such as these ministries try to work in close coordination to ensure that the overall government response to a situation is sensible and provides a good service to the citizens they serve. All government departments are headed up by a Secretary of State (Senior Minister), who may or may not be part of the cabinet. The Secretary of State usually has several junior ministers who are responsible for specific areas of the ministries' responsibilities.

Members of Parliament (MPs)

The duties of an MP are split between working in the constituency where they are elected and working in the House of Commons itself. The current split is shown in Figure 1.6.

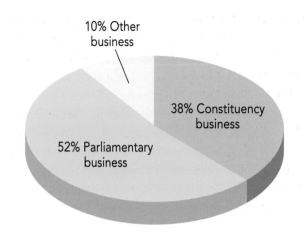

Figure 1.6: Pie chart of the relative time spent by an MP in their consituency and in Parliament.

Although the role of an MP is largely decided by the individual themselves there are several key functions which they should perform. Many MPs spend a great deal of time in their **constituency** listening to and acting upon the concerns of their constituents. This is particularly true of MPs who do not have an official role in the government.

Did you know?

That the 646 elected members of parliament cannot run an effective government by themselves. The actual machinery of government, which implements decisions, lies with the 500,000 or so civil servants employed by the government.

Key term

Constituency a body of voters in a specific area who elect a member of parliament.

Case study: MPs' expenses

In May 2009 the *Telegraph* newspaper obtained a full list of the expenses claimed by Members of Parliament and released the information to the public over a period of a few weeks. The public were shocked and disgusted at the expense claims, which included paying for mortgages that no longer existed, switching the property identified as the main home to claim more money and refurbishing properties at the taxpayers' expense in order to sell them for profit.

There were also allegations about MPs employing family members on high salaries for work that could not be evidenced, spending taxpayers' money on items such as a duck house for a pond, clearing debris from a moat and cleaning a swimming pool at a country home.

After the scandal became public many MPs were forced to step down from their jobs or pay back significant amounts of money.

1 Why do you think the public were angry at the expenses scandal?

2 What harm do you think the scandal did to the reputations of MPs?

3 Why do public servants like MPs have to be careful about their public conduct?

4 Research the expenses of your own MP. What did they claim for? In your opinion are the claims justified?

One of the benefits of our current voting system is that MPs are strongly tied to a particular geographical area and a particular local population. This means that they cannot ignore constituency duties if they want to be re-elected. However MPs are often powerless to address the local concerns that constituents are likely to raise, such as rubbish collection or poor repair of council houses, since these concerns are the business of local councillors. MPs also spend a great deal of time on public business. This includes the creation of legislation and membership of committees, which evaluate potential law.

Activity: Your MP

Conduct some research to find out who your local MP is and what role they play in politics in your local area and whether they have any specific responsibilities in the House of Commons.

Mayors

A mayor can have a variety of roles, they are normally appointed or elected for a period of one year and their role is often largely ceremonial.

The main duties of a mayor are:

- representing the council in civic and ceremonial occasions

- chair meetings of the full council
- promoting the area and being the council's spokesperson
- teaching civic pride to young people
- supporting charities and community groups.

Remember!

The role of the Mayor of London is different as you will have noted from the previous detail on the London assembly and its Mayor.

Council members

Councillors are elected by the local community to conduct the business of the council. They try to improve the quality of life in their area where they are elected by making decisions about local issues such as transport, education and public services. They are often community leaders and promote community groups and charities in their area, they may also act as advocates by speaking on behalf of individuals or groups who are in need. One of their most important roles is to decide on the policies that will be implemented by the council. These policies have far reaching effects both on ordinary citizens and the work of the public services.

Assessment activity 1.1

 **P1** **M1** **D1** **BTEC**

The public services must abide by the policies created at the various levels of government in the UK. This means you should be able to describe the responsibilities each level of government has. In the form of a presentation answer the following questions:

1 Outline the responsibilities of the levels of government in the UK **P1**

2 Explain in detail the responsibilities of the different levels of government in the UK **M1**

3 Evaluate the responsibilities of the different levels of government in the UK **D1**

Grading tips

For **P1** a simple outline is required, so you do not have to go into detail in order to pass. When you are delivering your presentation you can explain the responsibilities in more detail and this should

be enough to help you gain **M1**. To get **D1** you should supply a set of supporting notes to your tutor which goes into much greater detail about the responsibilities.

1.3 Responsibilities government departments and other levels of government have for specific public services

Many government departments have responsibility for one or more public services. Table 1.6 highlights the main government departments and their responsibilities to the uniformed public services. The uniformed public services fall into several different ministries, this is one of the reasons why they are subject to different terms and conditions of employment.

Assessment activity 1.2

You have been asked by a local charity to produce a leaflet which can be given out free to the public which describes the role of government departments in relation to the public services, including their responsibilities **P2**

Grading tip

Your leaflet should cover the main public service responsibilities of the Ministry of Justice, Home Office, Ministry of Defence and Department of Communities and Local Government.

Table 1.6: Responsibilities of the main government departments (find out more at the relevant government department website).

Government department	Responsibilities for the public services
Ministry of Defence (MOD) www.mod.gov.uk	The Ministry of Defence has responsibility for the British Army, the Royal Navy and the Royal Air Force. It is headed by the Secretary of State for Defence and three junior ministers, namely the Minister of State for the Armed Forces, the Under Secretary of State and Minister for Defence Procurement and the Under Secretary of State for Defence and Minister for Veterans. The MOD decides on budgets, policy and procurement for all three armed services. This means it has a tremendous amount of influence on the armed services, deciding everything from pay and conditions to equipment to locations of service.
Ministry of Justice www.justice.gov.uk	This ministry has responsibility for the courts, prisons and Probation Service, which means it is involved in offender management from charge to release.
The Home Office www.homeoffice.gov.uk	The Home Office has primary responsibility for many of the UK civilian public services such as the police, passports and immigration service and drugs policies. It contains the Immigration and Nationality Directorate, the Passport Office and it has responsibility for homeland counter-terrorism. The ministerial responsibility chart for the Home Office is shown in Figure 1.5.
Department of Communities and Local Government www.communities.gov.uk	This is where primary responsibility for the UK's Fire and Rescue Services lies. It is headed by the Secretary of State for Communities and Local Government and several junior ministers. It has responsibility for allocating local governments with resources to fund their Fire and Rescue Services and it also develops Fire and Rescue national policies and priorities. This ministry also has responsibility for local government which while non-uniformed is still an essential public service.
Department for Health www.dh.gov.uk	This department has overall responsibility for the healthcare of the nation by running the National Health Service (NHS). From a uniformed public service point of view, this gives the department responsibility for the Ambulance Service.
HM Revenue and Customs www.hmrc.gov.uk	This government department has responsibility for the collection of taxes. From a public service point of view, it has responsibility for the Customs and Excise Service.

Accountability of uniformed public services

Since the uniformed public services are funded with public money and are designed to serve the needs of the public, it is important that there are checks and balances on their behaviour. Some of the public services have tremendous power over the lives of individuals and it is essential that they are seen to act in a fair and consistent manner. Equally, it is important to note that our public services cost billions of pounds of taxpayers' money each year and the taxpayer has a right to know if that money is being used effectively.

The government recognises this and has set up a variety of inspectorates and monitoring commissions that are designed to establish whether the public services offer value for money and if they are effective in the job they are supposed to do. These inspectorates may also offer the public the opportunity to make a complaint about poor or unfair treatment, which can then be investigated impartially by a complaints agency.

There are two main procedures for investigating and monitoring the public services, through:

- inspectorates
- local organisations.

Inspectorates and HM Inspectorates (HMI)

Inspectorates and HMIs are set up by the government on a national basis to ensure the smooth running of specified public services.

The Defence Vetting Agency (DVA)

The DVA exists to carry out national security checks. This kind of check might be applied to anyone who wishes to join the armed services, civilians who work for the Ministry of Defence, civilian contractors who might build on MOD land or supply MOD services and other background checks on individuals in other government departments. The DVA conducts around 140,000 checks on individuals each year, which makes it the largest government vetting agency.

Independent Police Complaints Commission (IPCC)

The IPCC was created in 2004 to replace the Police Complaints Authority, although it gains its regulatory powers from the Police Reform Act 2002. It is funded by the Home Office, but remains entirely independent of it. This ensures that any decisions it makes are free of any government influence. The IPCC can investigate in several different ways, it can choose to supervise a case being investigated by a Police Service internally or it can carry out an independent investigation if the complaint is about a serious matter. Serious complaints might include:

- incidents involving death or injury
- police corruption
- police racism
- perverting the course of justice.

The IPCC has teams of investigators allocated to certain regions so that it can deal with complaints quickly and efficiently. In 2008–9 a total of 31,259 complaints were received, a 15 per cent increase on the previous year. The most common causes of complaints were as follows:

- Neglect or Failure in Duty (24%)
- Incivility, Impoliteness and Intolerance (21%)
- Assault (13%)
- Oppressive Conduct or Harassment (7%)
- Unlawful/Unnecessary Arrest or Detention (5%)

Quality Care Commission (QCC)

The Quality Care Commission is the independent regulator for healthcare and social care for adults in England. The role of the QCC is to ensure that all healthcare provision, including private healthcare, meets quality standards and that patients receive the standard of care they should expect. It conducts reviews and inspections of healthcare facilities such as midwifery, surgery, mental healthcare and GPs. The QCC publishes the information it collects about these services to allow the public to make an informed choice about where they go for treatment or social care.

Case study: The G20 protests

In April 2009 leaders from the worlds richest and most influential nations met in London to coordinate global action on pressing financial and economic problems such as the recession and banking crisis. The G20 Summit attracted many protesters who are unhappy at the way the global economy is run and the financial inequalities that they see as causing so much poverty in the developing world.

There were numerous complaints about police tactics made to the IPCC in the days after the event, many alleging that assaults were made by the police on protesters and people who were trying to make their way home after work. The controversial tactic of 'kettling' also came under scrutiny. Kettling is the penning in of protesters to a confined area and not allowing them to leave for significant periods of time. Some protesters and passers-by in London accused the Metropolitan Police of keeping them 'kettled' for up to eight hours without access to food, water or toilet facilities, this included parents with children and the elderly. Liberal Democrat MP Martin Horwood, who was an eyewitness, has said he saw the police use dogs on the protesters.

Even more controversial was the death of Ian Tomlinson who was a newsagent trying to make his way home on the day of the protests. He died after an alleged assault on him by a Metropolitan police officer. At the time of publication, this matter is still under investigation by the IPCC.

1   Research the police response to the G20 protests using sources such as Youtube, broadsheet newspapers and the Metropolitan Police statements. Do you think the response to the protesters was appropriate? Explain your answer.

2   Why are independent commissions like the IPCC necessary?

3   What might happen to the public if there was no way to complain about unfair treatment?

4   Many of the protesters had camera phones and were able to record police actions on the day. Is this a good thing or might it lead to a 'trial by media' once the clips are shown?

PLTS

By answering the research-based questions on this case study you may be contributing to the independent enquirer and reflective thinker aspects of your PLTS course.

Functional skills

By conducting internet-based research you will be practising your ICT functional skill.

HMI of Probation for England and Wales

This inspectorate was originally established in 1936, and although it receives funding from the Home Office and reports directly to the Home Secretary, it is independent of the government. The inspectorate exists to assess the performance of the National Probation Service and Youth Offending Teams in reducing re-offending and protecting the public. It also works very closely with the Inspectorate of Prisons to assess the effectiveness of offender management.

HMI of Prisons for England and Wales

Like the inspectorates we have already examined, HMI Prisons is also funded by and reports directly to the government while maintaining its independence. Although inspecting prison establishments is its main priority it also has a responsibility to inspect immigration holding centres and it has been invited to inspect the military prison at Colchester. In terms of its main responsibilities, it must inspect every prison in England and Wales at least once every five years. However there are a variety of different types of inspection, some of which the prison will know about in advance and some that they will not. A prison cannot refuse entry to the inspectorate.

The purpose of the inspections is to ensure that the prison is fulfilling its aims. A 'good' prison should be safe for the inmates and be an environment where they are treated with respect and dignity. The prison should provide activity and education that may lead to the rehabilitation of the offender and prepare them for release in to the community.

HMI of Constabulary for England, Wales and Northern Ireland (HMIC)

The HMIC is one of the oldest inspectorates in England and dates back to the County and Borough Police Act of 1856. Like the other inspectorates it is funded by and reports to the Home Office, but is independent of it. The role of the HMIC is to formally inspect and assess the 43 police services in England and Wales and support the Chief Inspector of Criminal Justice in Northern Ireland, but it also has other inspection roles with the:

- Central Police Training and Development Agency
- Civil Nuclear Constabulary
- British Transport Police
- Ministry of Defence Police
- Serious Organised Crime Agency.

HMIC is able to conduct several different types of inspections. Some of the types are described below:

- **Thematic Inspections.** Here a particular aspect of performance is measured across several different police constabularies. For example, dealing with child protection or the training of police officers.
- **Best Value Inspections.** This type of inspection centres round ensuring that the police authority is allocating and spending money in a manner which could be considered best value.
- **Command Unit Inspections.** This type of inspection focuses on leadership and management.
- **Baseline Assessment.** This type of inspection seeks to monitor the improvement or deterioration in performance against a pre-established baseline.

Local organisations

Local organisations are also responsible for ensuring the quality and performance of the public services. Table 1.7 shows the key organisations involved at a local level.

Table 1.7: The key local organisations investigating and monitoring the public services.

Organisation	Description
The Police Authority	There are 43 Police Authorities in England and Wales, one for every police constabulary. They aim to make sure that the police service in that area is as efficient and effective as it can be. A Police Authority can vary in the number of representatives it has, but most have around 17 members who are made up of local councillors, local magistrates and lay people from the community. The Police Authority sets the strategic direction of the force and holds the Chief Constable accountable for the performance of his or her organisation. Another important function of the Police Authority is deciding how much council tax needs to be raised to pay for the police service.
Strategic Health Authorities (SHA)	There are currently 10 SHAs in England and Wales (this matches the Regional Assembly areas in Figure 1.2, except for the addition of a South Central region between the South West and the South East). The SHAs were created in 2006 from the merging of smaller health authorities. The role of each SHA includes: • strategic oversight and leadership of the healthcare system in a particular region • ensuring better value for money for taxpayers • leading service improvements • accountability to the Department for Health for providing high quality healthcare • reducing health inequalities.
Fire and Rescue Authorities (FRA)	FRAs are like Police Authorities in that they are made up of local representatives from the council. Most FRAs have somewhere between 12 and 30 members depending on the size of the area they manage. Their primary responsibility is to be accountable to the public in the area for providing an efficient and effective fire and rescue service. The authority must ensure that the fire service has all the firefighters, equipment, premises and vehicles it needs in order to fulfil its duties to the public. It also has a responsibility for ensuring equality and diversity as a key role in brigade recruitment and training policies.

2. The democratic election process for each level of government in the UK

There are several types of election in the UK but the most common types are general elections and local elections. A general election occurs when all the **seats** in the House of Commons are open for re-election. The maximum term that a parliament can sit without a general election is five years and three weeks, so this type of election tends to happen between every three to five years depending on when the party in power think they might have the best chance of winning the most seats. It is the Prime Minister who makes the decision. Local elections follow a four-year cycle, but not all councils elect at the same time.

Key term

Seats are places in an elected parliament (especially in the House of Commons).

2.1 Who can stand for election?

This depends on the type of election. For a Parliamentary election, whether a general election where all 646 UK constituencies are open for re-election, or a by-election for just one constituency, you must be over 21 years of age and a British, Commonwealth or Republic of Ireland Citizen. You must be nominated by at least 10 of the registered electors in the constituency and if you want to stand for a particular party you must receive authorisation from that party. If you don't have authorisation from a party you are classed as independent. In addition, you must pay a £500 deposit when you register as a candidate, and you only get this money back if you receive over 5 per cent of the votes cast. You may not stand for election if you are a prisoner serving a sentence of over 12 months.

For a local election (that is an election to a local council) you must satisfy similar criteria, but an individual who is a citizen of a nation in the European Union may also stand. You are not eligible to stand for local election if you are employed by the local authority, are subject to bankruptcy restrictions or have been sentenced to a prison term of three months or more.

Candidate selection processes

If you are standing as an independent representative there are no candidate selection procedures, as long as you are eligible you may stand for office. However the political parties often have more potential candidates than they need to fill the seats they are hoping to win. A selection procedure becomes necessary to ensure that the best candidate, or the candidate most likely to win the seat, is selected.

There are many selection methods. For instance

- the party can draw up a list of centrally approved candidates from which the local branch can choose. The list is drawn up in a very rigorous way and in many ways mirrors the public services selection procedure. There will have been a paper sift of the candidates' CVs and application forms, a background check will have been run and they may have been subjected to a weekend full of aptitude tests. Existing MPs who want to stand for election again are normally automatically approved.

- the local branch of the party can interview the potential candidates to find the one they want to serve their area. A party may draw up a shortlist containing only women or only candidates from ethnic minorities so as to increase the diversity of MPs in the party, but this can be a controversial tactic and not everyone agrees with it.

Did you know?

By September 2008 Barack Obama had managed to raise $454 million to fund his presidential campaign. This was money used for publicity and electioneering activities. How difficult do you think this would make it for new or independent candidates to become the US president?

Influence of political parties

Political parties have a tremendous amount of influence on the election process. Firstly and most importantly, the political party in power is the one that chooses when to have a general election. This means they can call a general election at any time within the five-year period that suits them and makes it more likely for them to win. The party in power also has opportunities to make popular moves such as reducing taxes just before an election. The party in power and the main opposition party are likely to have the funds to support their candidates and the resources for publicity to help them win the seat. This puts smaller parties and independent candidates at a distinct disadvantage.

Period between elections

Periods of election in the UK can range from 1-5 years depending on the post the candidate is elected to. Mayors typically serve for one year, councillors for up to four and MPs for up to five before they must stand down or be re-elected.

Some people feel that negative campaigning is a good thing and brings to light what voters need to know.

Publicity and electioneering activities

It is important that a candidate becomes well known in the area they are hoping to represent and to this end they will often undertake a great deal of publicity work, such as leafleting houses, displaying posters, and canvassing door-to-door for votes. Publicity costs money and so the more wealthy parties will have an advantage. In addition, during a general election you will often see party political broadcasts for the main parties outlining their policies. This is because they can afford publicity campaigns that include film-making.

Did you know?

During election campaigns the main parties often have publicity campaigns that concentrate on telling you why you shouldn't vote for the rival parties, rather than good reasons why you should vote for their party. This is called negative campaigning.

Case study: Negative campaigning

LABOUR'S HIGHWAY ROBBERY

72p in every £1 of petrol is tax.

Is this what you voted for?

Sign the Anti-Petrol Tax petition

Look at the election slogan in the poster. It is trying to get a message across to the public, but the message focuses on the negative qualities of a rival party rather than positive qualities of their own party.

1 What message is the political poster trying to get across?

2 What is your opinion of negative campaigning?

3 Why do political parties often focus on the faults of others rather than the benefits of themselves? Find some other slogans used in negative campaigning in support of your answer.

4 What are other slogans that have been used in negative campaigning?

2.2 The voting processes

As technology has evolved there have become more ways to cast a vote than ever before. Most people are familiar with the traditional way of going to a polling office (usually a church, school or community centre that has changed purposes for the day) to go into a voting booth and place a cross on a ballot slip next to the name of the candidate you wish to vote for. However, it is also possible to vote by post or electronically through the internet. There is also a facility where you can name someone to cast your vote for you. This is called voting by proxy.

Activity: Election day

Working as a group

Election day is busy for candidates, political parties and the media. Conduct some research and find out what kind of activities happen on election day in general and local elections. Put your findings into a poster.

Voting systems

There are many methods used in both the UK and worldwide to decide who gets to be part of the government and these include:

- first past the post
- the single transferable vote
- the alternative vote
- proportional representation.

First past the post (FPTP)

The British electoral system is based on the FPTP system. This system is very clear-cut and well-defined, the candidate with the highest number of votes in a constituency wins. In order to vote in a FPTP system you simply mark a cross (X) next to the name of the candidate you are choosing. If your candidate polls more votes than the others they win, regardless of whether he or she has more than 50 per cent support. For example, the results of a by-election are as follows:

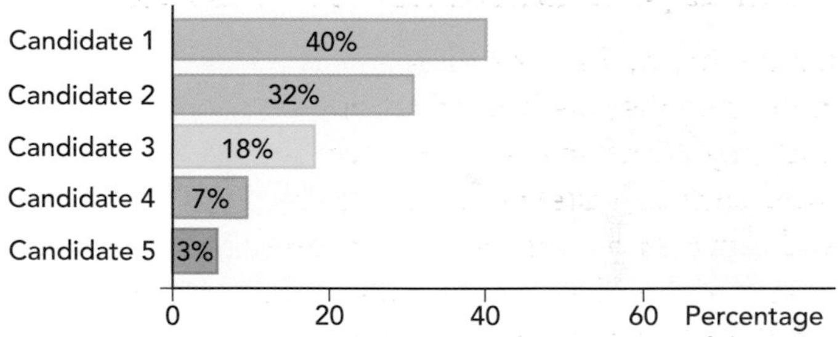

Figure 1.7: Results of a by-election.

Table 1.8: Advantages and disadvantages of the FPTP system.

Advantages	Disadvantages
• Cheap and simple way to hold an election • Counting of ballot papers is fast and accurate • Ballot papers are easy to understand • Allows a new or incumbent government to either take over the reins or continue as usual, swiftly and with the minimum of upheaval • FPTP gives a clear mandate to the party in power • Provides a stable and legitimate political system with usually just two parties dominating. It means a party can pass legislation and tackle the country's problems without having to rely on other parties for support • Provides a close and direct link between the MP and the constituency	• More people in a constituency can vote against a candidate than vote for them and the individual is still elected. The example described above had the winning candidate poll 40% of the vote. This means that 60% of the constituents voted against them. Is this truly democratic? • Individuals may cast negative votes, i.e., voting against a candidate they dislike rather than voting for one they like. • There is a lack of choice of representatives, usually only 3 or 4 will stand for election, so if you don't like them there is no alternative choice. • The government as a whole may not represent the will of the people. For example in 1997 the Labour Party gained just over 40% of the vote nationally but received over 60% of the seats in the House of Commons. • The government can change constituency boundaries to affect the results of elections; this is called 'gerrymandering'. • Voters in strong party constituencies may feel their vote is wasted. If you know the other candidate will win why bother to vote? This badly affects smaller parties such as the Liberal Democrats.

This means that Candidate 1 is empowered to act as a representative for the constituency despite the fact that only 4 out of every 10 constituents voted for them.

When members have been elected in this fashion the party with the most elected representatives is invited by the Queen to form the government. The FPTP system is used in both Parliamentary (House of Commons) elections and local elections.

The alternative vote (AV)

Voters must rank the candidates on the ballot paper in order of preference. If a candidate receives 50 per cent or more of first preferences then they are elected. If not, then the candidate with the lowest number of first choices is eliminated and their second choices are redistributed to the other candidates. This process continues until one candidate has an absolute majority.

Table 1.9: Advantages and disadvantages of the AV system.

Advantages	Disadvantages
Ensures the winner has a majority	Does not give parties the proportion of seats that their votes have earned
Strong bond between representatives and constituents is maintained	Does not help change the status of those who have been traditionally under represented in political processes
Removes issues of wasted votes	
Extreme left or right wing parties would be unlikely to get enough support to be elected	Time-consuming and more complex than FPTP

Single transferable vote (STV)

This system involves multi-member constituencies in which parties can field as many candidates as there are seats. Voters then rank the candidates on a ballot paper in order of preference. If a voter's first-choice candidate doesn't need their vote because they have already accrued enough votes to be elected then the vote is transferred to the second choice and so on.

Table 1.10: Advantages and disadvantages of the STV system.

Advantages	Disadvantages
Power is in the hands of the voters	Link between representative and constituency is gone
Wide choice of candidates	Leads to weak coalition governments
Reflects the views of voters	Voters have no say in which individuals are chosen
No wasted votes	
Voters can rank in preference based on things other than party allegiance, such as gender or ethnicity	Favours big parties
It is a relatively simple procedure	Power is in the hands of the party leadership
Small parties will benefit	

Proportional representation

This is a voting system which tries to match the proportion of votes cast with the proportion of seats a party receives. For example, under proportional representation if you received 35 per cent of the votes you should get 35 per cent of the seats in Parliament.

Table 1.11: Advantages and disadvantages of the proportional representation system.

Advantages	Disadvantages
Represents the wishes of the voters as a whole	Can be difficult to make decisions if no party has a clear majority
Minority parties end up with a fairer share of the seats	Requires good voter turnout and knowledge
Increases the opportunities for independent candidates	Can lead to unstable **coalition governments**
Reduces the possibility of one party dominating	

Key term

Coalition government is a government where no single party has a majority and so they have to team up to form an alliance in order to ensure decisions can be made and legislation is passed. However, because different parties are involved they often disagree on how best to do things and this can lead to instability.

Assessment activity 1.3 (P3) (M2) BTEC

You have applied for a job working for the local council's electoral department during your summer break. As part of the interview process you need to take part in a group discussion with the other candidates to demonstrate your knowledge about elections. In the group discussion you must address the following:

1 Explain the electoral processes used in UK elections **P3**

2 Compare the electoral processes used at different levels of government in the UK **M2**

Grading tips

You have a lot of freedom with a discussion so it is important to make sure you keep focused on the subject and answer the tasks. For **P3** make sure you explain the election process used at local and national level and for **M2** make sure you can draw clear comparisons, this means identifying the similarities and differences between local and national processes.

3. The impact of UK government policies on the public services

The policies created by the UK government can have significant effects on the public services. Some policicies can be targeted at the public services and others can affect the whole population. The government can create:

- policies that affect all the services
- policies that affect the armed services
- policies that affect the emergency services.

3.1 Policies that affect all the services

Human rights

The public services have a tremendous amount of power over our lives. They can take away our freedom, investigate our private lives, monitor our actions and use the information they find out against us if required. These powers must be carefully regulated to avoid abuses by the state and its public services against individual members of the public. In a democracy there must always be checks and balances on power to ensure that no one agency or service has power over the public that cannot be challenged. Generally speaking, the public services operate with the consent and cooperation of the public and are respected and respectful. However, even in a country like the UK with highly trained and knowledgeable officers, a breach of human rights can still occur. This is why laws and policies as the Human Rights Act 1998 exist. The Act makes it clear that certain rights are given to all UK citizens and if these rights are broken by the public services then an individual has the right to take the service to court and challenge its actions.

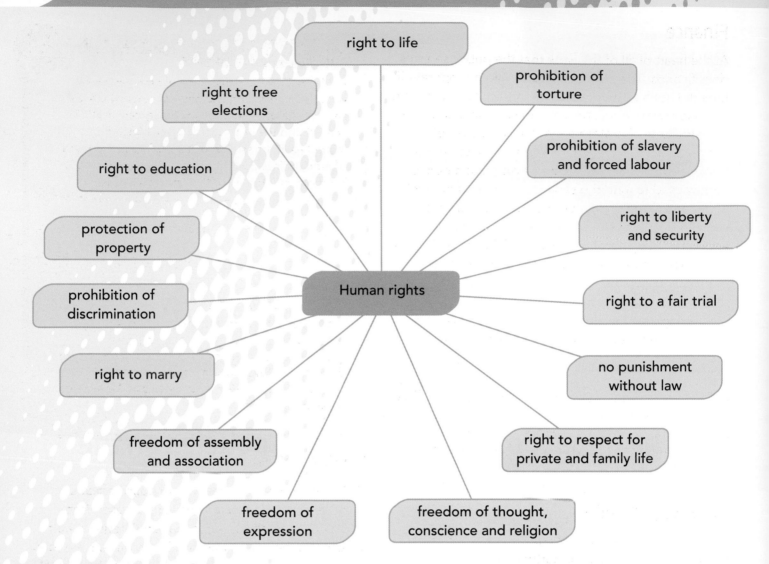

Figure 1.8: The human rights of an individual are shown here. Can you discover any more about the rights of the individual?

Case study: The right to protest

In 2006 coaches full of anti-war demonstrators were detained by the police for more than 2½ hours and prevented from joining a peaceful demonstration against the war in Iraq at RAF Fairford in Gloucestershire. The police argued that by preventing the demonstrators from attending the protest they were protecting the demonstrators right to life since the American forces at the base had reserved the right to use 'deadly force' if the base were breached. The protesters argued that the detainment violated their right to freedom of speech and assembly, and freedom from arbitrary detention. The House of Lords agreed with the protesters and found the police in breach of the Human Rights Act 1998.

Helen Wickham, a coach passenger, said: *I think it is deeply worrying that Gloucestershire police,* *confronted with the possibility of US troops shooting unarmed protestors, chose to defend the US use of lethal force over our right to protest.*

1 Do you think the police made a sound case for wanting to protect the lives of the protesters?

2 Why do you think the protesters felt the need to take the case to court?

3 What impact might this case have had on the police?

4 Examine the quote from the coach passenger: where should the responsibilities of the UK public services be, with the UK public or with our US defence partner?

5 In your opinion, did the House of Lords make the right decision?

Finance

At the heart of all of the work that the public services do is finance. The public services could not operate if they did not have the resources to pay their personnel, buy and maintain equipment and support a complex infrastructure. Therefore the financial policies of the government have a tremendous impact on the public services. It goes without saying that if public money used to fund the services is reduced then this will have a direct impact on the work the services can afford to do. For instance, fewer officers may be appointed, they may have less specialised training and equipment and so respond less effectively to social or military problems. If public spending is increased then the reverse may be true. However, there are many competing uses for public money and some argue that the public services are inefficient and could manage with less money.

Did you know?

The Centre for Economics and Business Research (CEBR) puts the total cost of the UK public sector at £58.4 billion per year.

Equal opportunities

The public services place a great deal of emphasis on the importance of equal opportunities and this has impacted on procedures in a number of ways. Firstly, the services are bound to reflect the communities which they serve and so the presence of ethnic minority groups and women in the public services is encouraged. This enriches the service and makes it more representative of the people it serves. To this end many public services are actively recruiting women or individuals from ethnic minority backgrounds, although there is still some way to go on this. Equal opportunities policies and legislation can have an impact on uniform requirements, for example Muslim police women may wear a dark blue head covering under their police hats, Sikh male police officers may wear a dark blue police turban with the badge of the force clearly displayed upon it. In the armed services ration packs with kosher and halal provisions are available for Jews and Muslims. Equal opportunities legislation such as the Equal Pay Act, the Sex Discrimination Act and the Race Relations Act have fundamentally changed the way the services interact with their officers and the public.

Did you know?

In March 2009 the percentage of ethnic minority police officers in England and Wales was 4.4%, the percentage of ethnic minority firefighters in 2008 was 3% and the RAF recorded just 1.8% ethnic minorities in the service in 2007–8. The percentage of ethnic minorities in the population as a whole is 7.9 per cent (from the 2001 National Census).

Activity: Women in the service

In the armed services there are some job roles that are not open to women, such as serving in the infantry or as a submariner. This does not promote equal opportunities. Can you think why they might make decision such as this? Discuss the issue with your colleagues and make a list of possible answers.

Civilianisation

Civilianisation is a process where police officers (or other public service officers) are released from doing non-operational tasks that don't require their specialist expertise or training. These officers are then free to work in an operational role. This makes use of these staff much more efficient since they are doing

Key term

Civilianisation is the process of freeing up public service personnel by employing civilians to do non-operational work.

Activity: Equal opportunities

Working in pairs

Why is it important that the public services are representative of the rest of society? What benefits could this bring? Consider these questions and make a list of your answers ready to feed back to the rest of your group.

the job they were trained to do rather than routine administrative work. The routine or non-specialist support then comes from civilians employed by the service. It is cheaper to employ a civilian on non-operational duties than to use a public services officer.

Environment

The environment is an important issue affecting all parts of public life. The government is bound to tackle the environmental problems that face us as a society and so the public services have become more aware of the need to recycle resources and move towards procedures that limit damage to the environment. For example, some MOD areas of land have been set aside to protect species that may not have a chance to thrive elsewhere. The Fire Service needs to dispose safely of dangerous chemicals after attending chemical fires.

Activity: The Sanctuary Awards

The MOD holds an annual awards ceremony for outstanding efforts in conservation, wildlife, archaeology and environmental improvement. Research the Sanctuary Awards and find out which projects achieved an award last year. What does this tell you about how the MOD views environmental issues?

3.2 Policies affecting the armed services

Military operations

As you will appreciate the start of war will have a large and immediate impact on the military services. They will begin to be deployed almost immediately to a particular battle zone, along with their resources and equipment. They will be fighting for an aim or set of aims specified by the government.

The armed services exist as servants of the government and can only go into military action when ordered to do so by the government. They cannot pick and choose where they serve or when they serve. The implications of this on the services are far reaching as there is the ever present risk to the lives of serving soldiers who are in combat or in an area of global instability. They may be killed or seriously injured by the enemy, by civilians who resent the military presence or even by friendly fire. There is also an impact on the families of military personnel who may experience extreme stress and anxiety about the welfare of their loved one. Going to war is also a tremendously expensive prospect and a war can quickly use up a variety of resources, including fighting vehicles, ammunition and protective equipment.

Reserve forces

Until the late 1990s military **reserve forces** were barely ever used on active duty. In 2006 reserve forces numbered 36,000 with the largest proportion of these coming from the Territorial Army plus around 52,000 regular reserves (former full-time army personnel who can be called up to serve). As the commitments of the armed services have grown over the last 10 years with operations in Afghanistan and Iraq, reserve forces have had to be used as an essential component of the UK fighting force. The National Audit Office report on reserve forces in 2006 notes that over 12,000 reservists have been deployed in Iraq since 2003 and they contribute approximately 12 per cent of the fighting force.

Reservist medical personnel have been even more important as they have staffed up to 50 per cent of the field hospitals in the conflict. There are advantages and disadvantages of using reserve forces. Commanding officers have noted that reservists may be less physically fit to cope with the demands of conflict and often they had not received adequate training or had the chance to be deployed with a regular unit. On the plus side, they bring a wealth of experience from their civilian lives which can enhance the service greatly. The government is committed to maintaining reserve forces although they are considering policy changes on how they are trained and deployed to try to bring them in line with their regular counterparts.

Key term

Reserve forces are volunteer troops who may be called up in time of conflict, but have a normal civilian life and do their military training in their spare time.

Use of technology

The armed services have always been at the forefront in the use of technology. They have provided the impetus for the development of many areas of technology with war and conflict driving technological changes as each side seeks an advantage over the other. One example is the war against terrorism where advanced technology and surveillance equipment have been used by both military and civilian counter-terrorist specialists to protect the public.

Links with international services

As a result of the coordinated policy of the North Atlantic Treaty Organisation (NATO), of which the UK is a founder member, we are required to maintain collective defence capabilities. This means that NATO forces must be able to integrate into operations seamlessly where possible. To this end UK troops often exercise with NATO troops from allied nations in combat simulations. This ensures they can be more 'combat-effective' should a situation arise where they have to collaborate. Our own three armed services , the Royal Navy, the Royal Air Force and the Army, also regularly train and **exercise** together since they are reliant on each other for a variety of roles.

Key term

Exercise is another word for a real-life simulation, it's a chance for the public services to practise their skills and knowledge in a simulated battle or emergency situation.

3.3 Policies that affect the emergency services

Fire station closures

The Fire and Rescue Service have had success in their campaigns to prevent fire accidents and the figures for the annual number of fires have been falling. This has resulted in a spate of fire station closures, particularly in smaller more rural areas as an efficiency measure. This is despite concerns from local residents that if local stations are closed it could take longer for a fire crew to reach the area in times of emergency.

Target setting

Central government sets targets for all of the public services. Public services also set their own targets on a range of tasks such as 999 response times, ethnic minority recruitment, female recruitment, budget expenditure, reductions in crime or fires, patient survival rates and many more. This can lead to a tremendous amount of pressure on all levels of the public services as they work to meet the targets and avoid the possible consequences if they are not met. For instance, another reason for closing the Ringinglow fire station (see Case study below) was that the brigade was not meeting 999 response times in certain other areas of South Yorkshire and so it needed to move the under-utilised resources to a place where they would have a better impact on targets. In this case, the corporate plan put forward by the South Yorkshire fire authority included a new Dearne Valley fire station which would help to meet the target set for response times in that area. This shows how government and local targets have a real influence on the operation of the services.

Case study: Fire station closure

Every fire authority in the UK has to create a three-year corporate plan that demonstrates improvement to the services and shows the taxpayer that the services are offering value for money. The 2006–2009 corporate plan for South Yorkshire Fire Authority included the closure of Ringinglow fire station despite enormous local opposition in the area.

As the area in question is rural the local people were extremely concerned that response times in the case of an emergency would be increased, potentially putting lives and property at risk. However, the rationale for closing it presented by the South Yorkshire Fire Authority was that it was a station with consistently low call-out rates and the firefighters and equipment could be better deployed elsewhere without compromising the safety of people in the area.

1   Should public services have to produce a corporate plan like a business?

2   What are the potential problems with closing fire stations in rural areas?

3   What is the likely impact on the community of such a closure?

4   In your opinion were the South Yorkshire Fire and Rescue Authority correct in closing the station and redeploying the resources elsewhere?

Assessment activity 1.4

(P4) (M3) (D2) :BTEC

Working individually

When examining the relationship between the government and the public services it is important to realise the impact government policies have on the services. This assessment task will help you make the connections between them. Produce two fact sheets which could be given to new members of the public services to explain the impact of government policies, your fact-sheets should address the following tasks:

1 Describe, with examples, the impact of government policies on different public services (P4)

2 Explain the impact of different government policies on a range of public services (M3)

3 Evaluate the impact of government policies on public services and the communities they serve (D2)

Grading tips

The assessment guidance for this requires you to examine two different policies and two different services, so you need to make sure that you follow this guidance. For (P4) and (M3) choose two different government policies and explain how they have impacted on two services. For (D2) make sure you evaluate these policies by examining the positive and negative aspects of the policies.

PLTS

Completing this assessment will help you develop your independent enquirer skills.

3.4 How society is affected by social responses to UK government policies on the public services

Although many aspects of government policy are open to public consultation there will be decisions made that some of the public do not agree with and feel so strongly about that they are prepared to have their say. There are several ways a society or an individual can make a response to a policy. These can take the form of support, opposition or changes in behaviour and are summarised in Table 1.12.

Assessment activity 1.5 (P5) :BTEC

Working individually

Government policies don't just affect the uniformed services, they also affect the general public. Understanding how the public can respond to the policies is very important as some of their responses may require a public service presence. Write a report that addresses the following task.

1 Identify how society is affected by government policies (P5)

Grading tips

This is a very straightforward task, if you identify and give a brief explanation of the issues identified in the table above, perhaps with some examples, you should achieve the criterion.

Table 1.12: Responses to a policy.

Response	Explanation and example
Civil disobedience	Civil disobedience is a deliberate and planned breach of policy or law by an individual or group of people. It is usually done peacefully to highlight how inappropriate a law is and promote the need for a change in the law. This was a very common tool used in the Black civil rights movement in the USA in the 1960s where Black men and women would deliberately break the racial segregation laws to show how deeply unfair they were and how much the law needed to change. A good example of this is the case of Rosa Parks who in December 1955 refused to give up her seat on a bus to a White man when asked to do so. She was arrested and this arrest sparked a chain of events which led to the US Supreme Court deciding in 1956 that racial segregation on transportation was illegal.
	Civil disobedience, even when peaceful, often requires a coordinated public service response to try to ensure no one is hurt or injured. Sometimes the police arrest protestors who are breaking the law but sometimes decide that it is in the interests of keeping the peace not to.
Demonstrations and meetings	Meetings to discuss problems with policy and decisions are very common and are a way for like-minded individuals to air their concerns in a supportive environment.
	Sometimes these meetings are held outdoors and include a march or demonstration to show the government or local authority the depth of public feeling against a decision. An example of this might be the 2009 G20 protests in London which required a police and paramedic presence as so many individuals were involved.
Picketing	Picketing is a very common way of employees showing that they are unhappy with a policy decision made at national or local level on issues that usually have an impact on pay, redundancies, or working conditions. The Royal Mail Strikes in 2009 are an example of this. The public services themselves rarely strike (in fact many are forbidden from doing so by law) but the fire service has a history of national strikes, the last being in 2002.
Sit-ins	Sit-ins are a peaceful way of demonstrating against an issue by causing great inconvenience and delay to the people trying to implement the decision. For example, it is a tool often used by environmental protesters who want to oppose the building of new roads. They build camps underground, in trees and generally make it impossible for work to begin safely. The Newbury bypass which opened in 1998 had a total of 29 camps set up at one point including tree houses and a tunnel network. Although the protesters didn't stop Newbury it led to a change in government thinking on the building of new roads, which led to the Salisbury bypass being stopped on the basis of the environmental impact.
Speech/writing	The most common form of opposition to a government policy is writing or talking about why you oppose it. Examples are debates and motions in Parliament, letters to newspapers, starting a political campaign or pressure group, political pamphlets, newspaper columns, books and blogging, and petitions.
Terrorism	Terrorism is an extreme response to public policy. It involves using violence or the threat of violence against civilian and military targets in order to force the government to change its policy on a specific issue.
	Governments do not respond well to terrorism, and many have a policy of not negotiating with hostage takers under any circumstances. For example, in Northern Ireland in the second half of the twentieth century Loyalist and Republican terrorist groups were active in Northern Ireland and on the British mainland with great cost to civilian and military life and property. One of the worst atrocities was the bombing of a shopping centre in Omagh (1998) which killed 29 people. The UK government did not agree to the terrorists' demands. Negotiation may be considered as rewarding violence and may make future violence more likely while others feel it is justified if terrorists can be persuaded to abandon violence.

4. The process of developing government policies

Government policy can be generated by a number of factors such as a need identified by the public or organisations, a reaction to an issue in the media or a new issue such as terrorism. All of these can change the way the government runs the country. The creation of law and policy can be a complex procedure and there are many parts to it. This section of the unit discusses the policy-making procedure in the UK so you can have a better understanding of how our laws and policies are generated.

4.1 Development processes

Initially policies begin life as ideas on how to change or manage a situation. These ideas can come from a variety of sources, such as:

- the public
- the media
- the public services
- politicians
- subject experts.

If the policy is needed and the idea has merit it is subject to a great deal of discussion in governmental meetings such as **cabinet meetings** and **parliamentary committees and subcommittees**. If after these discussions the idea is still considered to be worthwhile then the procedure becomes more formal and the proposed policy takes the form of a Green Paper.

Key terms

Cabinet meeting is a meeting of the senior government ministers that happens once a week. During the meeting they may discuss the creation of new policies and laws.

Parliamentary Committee/Subcommittee is a smaller more focused group of politicians and civil servants who meet to discuss potential new policies. They may have more time and more knowledge of the issue than the Cabinet, if they think the policy is needed they may move to the next stage of policy creation which is called a Green Paper.

Draft is a term used when a policy is not yet in its final form and might be subject to change after further discussion and debate.

Green Paper

This is a document about a proposed change in the law that is distributed to interested parties to gather their views on the change and open up a period of consultation and debate. This debate might take the form of public meetings, specialist consultation meeting or open enquiries from outside government. Sometimes the discussions around a Green Paper make it clear that the policy or law would not be welcome or is not needed and the policy stops there. However, sometimes the discussions show that there is a need for the law and it moves ahead to the next stage. The next stage is a White Paper.

White Paper

This is much more formal than a Green Paper and contains a set of formal proposals on the new law or policy. White Papers are the **drafts** of what will become known as bills in later stages of development.

There are other ways in which views on new policy can be heard. Letters to MPs, seeing an MP in their surgery and taking into account the views of the opposition are all ways that new public policy can be influenced from outside the government.

4.2 The legal processes used to create legislation

All potential laws and legislation begins life as a 'bill'. A bill is a proposal for a piece of legislation. There are three kinds of bills:

A public bill. This is usually a proposal for a large piece of legislation that will affect the whole country. Public bills are created by the government currently in power, examples include: the Crime and Disorder Act 1998, Police and Criminal Evidence Act 1984 and the Theft Act 1968.

A private bill. This is usually proposed by a local authority or large corporation and generally will only affect the group of people who proposed it, for instance if the building of a new motorway requires a local authority to compulsory purchase land. An example of a private bill is the Henry Johnson, Sons and Co Limited Act 1996 which was an act that allowed the company of Henry Johnson, Sons and Co to transfer to the republic of France.

A Private Members Bill. This is usually prepared by a Member of Parliament who has to enter a ballot in order to be guaranteed the time to introduce the Bill in Parliament. This allocated time is very important because it allows the bill to be debated in Parliament and the reason Private Members Bills often fail is due to a lack of time for debate. Sometimes Private Members Bills are introduced as a way of drawing attention to a particular public concern, examples include the Abortion Act 1967 and the Activity Centres (Young Persons Safety) Act 1995.

The process of a policy

What is the procedure for these bills to become Statutes or Acts of Parliament? There are seven stages that a bill must proceed through before it can become law. These are listed in Table 1.13 and shown in Figure 1.9.

Implementation and guidance

A new law or policy is rarely implemented immediately. It is important to have a period where the public services can become familiar with the new law, undertake relevant training if necessary and be ready for when the bill becomes law. For this reason laws are rarely implemented on being signed, but have an implementation date. For example, the Human Rights Act 1998 didn't come into force until 2000. Also, before new laws come into force the government issues guidance and directives to the public services that are affected, identifying the changes and the areas the public service will be responsible or accountable for.

It is also important that the general public have an opportunity to become familiar with a new law. If a new law was implemented immediately the public would have difficulty conforming to it. One way in which changes to policy and the law are promoted and introduced to the public is through the use of the media.

Case study: The use of mobile phones while driving

On 27 February 2007 new legislation came into force that increased the penalties that drivers receive if they use a hand-held mobile phone while driving. The new policy means a punishment of a £60 fine and 3 penalty points on the driving licence. The penalties can be much worse if the case goes to court and worse still if the offence was committed by a bus driver, or the driver of a heavy goods vehicle.

A national multimedia campaign began on 22 January 2007, which involved radio, television and internet. The government also targeted key employers and industries with leaflets and posters. Road safety officers and police were heavily involved in promoting the changes in the law to the public.

1 Why did the media campaign begin a month earlier than the actual change in the law?

2 Why did the government decide on a multimedia campaign?

3 Which form of advertising do you think would be most effective and why?

4 Do you think the government have been successful in promoting the change to the law?

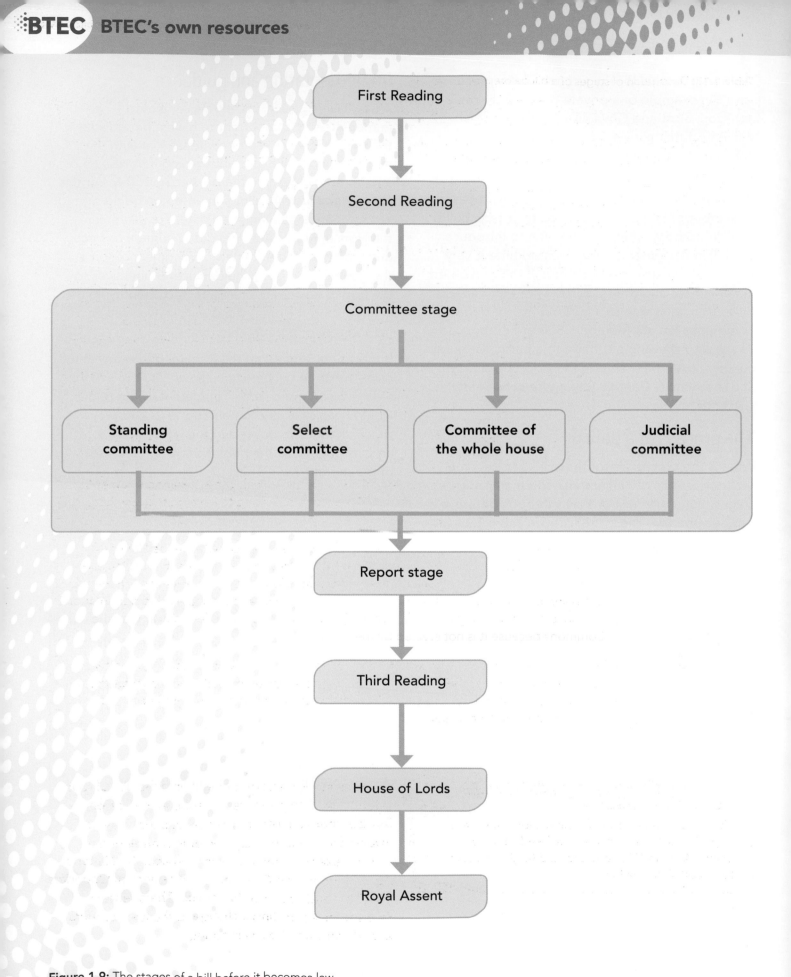

Figure 1.9: The stages of a bill before it becomes law.

Table 1.13: Description of stages of a bill before it becomes law.

Stages of a bill	
First Reading	This is the notification to the house that a proposal is made. The title of the bill is read out and copies of it are made available. There is little or no debate at this stage.
Second Reading	This is a crucial stage for the bill as it is the main debate on the proposals contained within it. The house must then decide whether to send it forward for then next stage. In practice a government with a clear majority will almost always get its bill through this stage.
Committee stage	As you can see in Figure 1.9 this can be a complex part of the procedure. In short this is where the bill is examined in detail and the committee considers the changes it would recommend to the house. Most bills are dealt with in standing committees of about twenty M.P's and this is the usual practice, however if a bill is introduced late in the parliamentary session is may be sent to a select committee which can hear evidence from outside individuals or agencies. The members of the committees are chosen for their qualifications and personal or professional interests. If a bill is controversial or very important this stage is examined in a committee of the whole house. For private bills only the committee stage might be judicial, this is where anyone whose business or property may be affected can lodge a petition to amend a bill in order to protect their interests.
Report stage	The committee reports back to the house with suggested amendments, which are then debated and voted on by the house at large.
Third Reading	The bill is re-presented to the House of Commons and a final vote is taken on whether to accept the proposed legislation. If the bill is accepted it is said to have 'passed the house' and is then sent on to the next stage.
House of Lords	The bill goes through a similar procedure in the House of Lords to that in the House of Commons and it must pass all of these stages in one session of parliament. The House of Lords cannot reject most legislation passed from the House of Commons although they do retain some powers such as the ability to reject a bill which attempts to extend the duration of a government for longer than five years. The House of Lords has less power than the Commons because it is not elected by the public.
Royal Assent	When a bill has successfully passed through both houses it must go to the monarch for approval and consent. It will then become law on a specified date. It is not usual for the monarch to give consent in person, it is normally done by a committee of three peers including the Lord Chancellor.

Did you know?

The Royal Assent stage of a bill is a formality these days. The last time a monarch refused a bill was Queen Anne in 1707 who declined to give consent to a Scottish Militia Bill.

The case study on page 31 highlights the use of road safety officers to promote a change in road safety law, but there are other organisations that may be involved in promoting change or implementing a law. For example, the Probation Service, the National Association for the Care and Resettlement of Offenders (NACRO) and of course the police. The agencies involved in supporting a change to the law depends entirely on what the law is about.

Assessment activity 1.6

Working in groups

You have been asked by a local school to explain to their Y10 learners how policy is decided and made by government. The students have not studied government before so rather than provide them with written materials their teacher has asked if you and your colleagues would be willing to do a role-play explanation instead to make the subject more interesting and interactive. For this activity develop your own government role-play where you address the following tasks:

1 Demonstrate how government policies are developed **P6**

2 Analyse how government policies are developed **M4**

Grading tip

Role-plays can be tricky to do. The key is good preparation and a good script, so spend some time on developing this and make sure everyone has a role to play. Choose a policy to develop and talk through all the stages it must go through in order to become law. Then translate this into an interesting and interactive role-play which would be informative and interesting for your audience.

PLTS

Completing this assessment will help you develop your self manager skills.

Linda McLoughlin
Local Councillor

I work as a local councillor in the town where I live. My job is to make sure that local money is spent on the right things and to make sure that the people of my community are represented and their views get heard by the council. I also have to work closely with lots of other agencies to make sure that the people of my town get all the high quality services they are entitled to and sometimes I represent the people of my town at national or regional events.

A typical day

I wish I could say what a typical day for a councillor might be but the tasks are so varied there's no such thing. It's not a full time job so I juggle my responsibilities with working full time and raising my family. Usually I will be required to attend meetings and respond to council business and the correspondence of my constituents.

Most councillors spend around 15 hours a week on their role unless they have extra responsibilities in the council.

The best thing about the job

This is when I get to see my constituents and help them with their problems. They elected me to serve them and represent their interests so helping them when they are in difficulties is a really big part of my job. It might involve matters of housing or refuse collection or even lobbying for community facilities such as a bike track or footpath to be created. All of this goes to making my community a better place to live for everyone.

Think about it!

What topics have you covered in this unit that might give you the background to work in local or national government?

What knowledge and skills do you think you need to develop further if you want to be involved in policy creation in the future?

Just checking

1 Name the parts of parliament.
2 What are the three branches of government?
3 How many MPs are there?
4 What is gerrymandering?
5 What does the Ministry of Justice do?
6 What is the role of the Independent Police Complaints Commission (IPCC)?
7 Who can stand for election?
8 What is the 'first past the post system'?
9 Name three policies which affect all uniformed services.
10 What responses can the public make to policies they disagree with?

edexcel

Assignment tips

• In a unit like this that focuses on how the government works and how this affects the services, one of the best things you can do to help improve your grade and your knowledge is to make sure you keep up to date with current events by reading a reputable news source on a daily basis. This means using your lunch hour or an hour after school/college to read the BBC News website or picking up a broadsheet newspaper such as *The Times*, *Telegraph* or *Guardian* (all of these have websites where you can read the news if you can't get hold of the paper see: www.timesonline.co.uk, www.telegraph.co.uk and www.guardian.co.uk). Not only will you become more informed about government policies and the public services, but you will also pick up lots of information which can be used across all of your national diploma units.

• This may sound very basic, but make sure you have read your assignment thoroughly and you understand exactly what you are being asked to do. Once you are clear about this then you can move on to your research. Doing your research well and using good sources of evidence is essential. Lots of students rely too much on the internet and not enough on other sources of information such as books, newspapers and journals. The internet is not always a good source of information, it is very easy to use information from American or Australian government websites without noticing – but your tutor will notice. Always double check the information you find, don't just accept it at face value. Good research and preparation is the key to getting those higher grades.

2 Leadership and teamwork in the public services

The public services could not operate efficiently and effectively without leaders and without teams – they are essential if an organisation is to meet its goals. This unit provides you with an understanding of effective team leadership skills and an overview of how teams operate and how you can be a good team member.

This unit looks at the key principles in effective team leadership skills in a public services context. You will identify and investigate the different styles of leadership and how and when they may be used. You will gain a clear understanding of team aims and goals and explore the benefits of working in teams. You will look at effective communication, both verbal and non-verbal, and understand its importance within a group setting, especially when giving instructions and feedback. Throughout the unit you will develop your interpersonal skills, helping you to interact and deal effectively with team members, through feedback, group encouragement and individual support. You should take every opportunity to reflect on your performance and identify the skills needed to develop and become a more effective leader.

You will also identify a range of barriers to effective teamwork and look at solutions and techniques in overcoming them. Finally, you will use your skills to carry out planning sessions and demonstrate your ability to conduct group and individual evaluations. This unit is designed to help you identify and understand a range of qualities which are required for successful leadership in a variety of public services, such as the armed forces and emergency services. You will have the opportunity to develop and practise your own leadership skills and review your progress. In addition, you will explore both the practical and theoretical aspects of leadership in order to understand that what makes an effective leader can vary from situation to situation.

Learning outcomes

After completing this unit you should:

1. understand the styles of leadership and the role of a team leader
2. be able to communicate effectively to brief and debrief teams
3. be able to use appropriate skills and qualities to lead a team
4. be able to participate in teamwork activities within the public services
5. understand team development.

Assessment and grading criteria

This table shows you what you must do in order to achieve a **pass**, **merit** or **distinction** grade, and where you can find activities in this book to help you.

To achieve a **pass** grade the evidence must show that the learner is able to:	To achieve a **merit** grade the evidence must show that, in addition to the pass criteria, the learner is able to:	To achieve a **distinction** grade the evidence must show that, in addition to the pass and merit criteria, the learner is able to:
P1 describe the different leadership styles used in the public services **See Assessment activity 2.1 page 47**	**M1** compare the different leadership styles used in the public services **See Assessment activity 2.1 page 47**	**D1** evaluate the effectiveness of different leadership styles used in the public services **See Assessment activity 2.1 page 47**
P2 identify the role of the team leader in the public services **See Assessment activity 2.2 page 49**		
P3 brief and debrief a team for a given task **See Assessment activity 2.3 page 57**	**M2** brief and debrief a team for a given task using effective communication **See Assessment activity 2.3 page 57**	**D2** evaluate own ability to lead a team effectively **See Assessment activity 2.4 page 61**
P4 carry out a team task using the appropriate skills and qualities **See Assessment activity 2.4 page 61**	**M3** effectively lead a team using the appropriate skills and qualities **See Assessment activity 2.4 page 61**	
P5 describe the different types of teams that operate within a selected public service **See Assessment activity 2.5 page 65**	**M4** appraise own performance in team activities **See Assessment activity 2.6 page 71**	**D3** evaluate team members' performance in team activities **See Assessment activity 2.6 page 71**
P6 participate in team activities **See Assessment activity 2.6 page 71**		
P7 explain how teambuilding leads to team cohesion in the public services with reference to relevant theorists **See Assessment activity 2.7 page 72**	**M5** analyse the impact of good and poor team cohesion on a public service, with reference to relevant theorists **See Assessment activity 2.7 page 72**	

How you will be assessed

This unit will be assessed by an internal assignment that will be devised and marked by the staff at your centre. The assignment is designed to allow you to show your understanding of the learning outcomes for leadership and teamwork. These relate to what you should be able to do after completing this unit.

Assessments can be quite varied and can take the form of:

- reports
- leaflets
- presentations
- posters
- practical tasks
- case studies

- simulations
- team activities
- personal evaluations
- peer assessments
- tutor observations.

Claire experiences teamwork

I really enjoyed this unit and I learned a lot from it. I am quite outspoken so people often look to me for leadership when we are doing group tasks, but just because I can speak my mind doesn't mean I'm a good leader – or even a good team member. In fact, I've been in groups where speaking my mind has actually made things worse for the team.

This unit helped me to understand the skills I already have in terms of leadership and teamwork and also the skills I need to develop. A leader is a bit like a chameleon, they have to adapt their style to differing circumstances and I've struggled with that a bit, but I have got better as I have had more experience.

Having the chance to be a leader has also helped me develop my teamwork skills. I tend to think before I speak now as I need to be careful not to undermine the leader or contradict what they have said. If I have something to say, I think about how I can make it constructive rather than critical. I've found this helps the team far more than me just saying what I think and not offering any suggestions for improvement.

This unit has also improved my confidence not just at college, but also in my personal life.

Over to you!

- What areas of leadership and teamwork might you find interesting?
- Have you ever been involved in leadership before?
- How well do you work in a team?
- What preparation could you do to get ready for your assessments?

1. The styles of leadership and the role of a team leader

Thinking about leadership and teamwork
- Make a list of your leadership strengths and weaknesses. What actions can you take to improve your weak areas?
- Think about a recent experience you have had being part of a team, did it go well, could you have been a better team member? What can you do to improve your teamwork skills?
- Feedback to the rest of your group and make an action plan for improvement with your tutor.

This unit is essential in providing you with an understanding of how leadership and teamwork influence those working in the services every day of their working lives. It is important that you have a clear grasp of your own leadership and teamwork skills and a clear idea how to develop your strengths and overcome your weaknesses.

Effective leadership is essential in the uniformed public services as employees often work in teams and rely on each other as they carry out their individual roles, and also rely on a leader to direct them. Leadership is particularly significant for the uniformed public services due to the rigidity of the hierarchical structures, the necessity for obedience and the following of lawful orders, and the dangerous nature of the roles they perform. Without an effective leader the chances of a team achieving its goal is greatly reduced.

1.1 Leadership styles

A leadership style is the manner and approach of providing direction for a team, implementing plans and motivating people to complete a task. There are several different leadership styles, each with advantages and disadvantages. The public services are constantly changing in response to changes in public expectations, the law and the current political environment and so the styles of leadership they use change and evolve too.

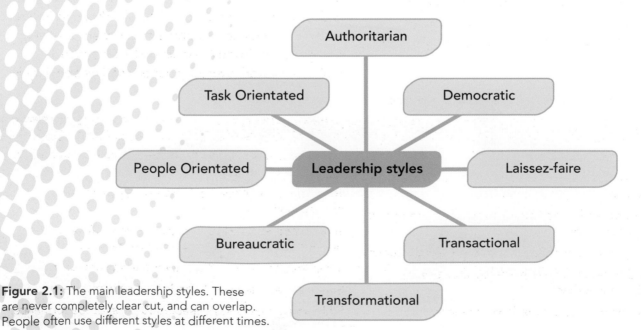

Figure 2.1: The main leadership styles. These are never completely clear cut, and can overlap. People often use different styles at different times.

Authoritarian

Key term

Authoritarian leadership is a very direct leadership style where the leader tells the team members what they must do.

Sometimes this style is also described as autocratic. It is often considered a classic leadership style and is used when a leader wishes to retain as much power as possible and maintain control over the decision-making process. It involves the leader telling the team members what they must do without any form of consultation or negotiation. Team members are expected to obey orders without receiving any explanation. Appropriate conditions when you might use this leadership style are when:

- you have all the information to solve the problem
- you are working to a tight deadline
- the team is well motivated and used to working for an authoritarian leader.

Generally, this approach is not considered to be the most appropriate way to get the best response from a team in ordinary working life, but it has distinct advantages in situations where there is great urgency and pressure to achieve, such as the armed forces. Autocratic leaders may rely on threats or intimidation to ensure that followers conform to what the leader requires. In addition, this approach could devalue team members by ignoring their expertise and input and discouraging demonstrations of initiative.

Activity: Responding to the authoritarian style

After examining the autocratic style of leadership described above consider how well you would respond to this particular style. How would you feel if you were working under it?

Democratic

Key term

Democratic leadership is a style of leadership where the leader maintains control of the group, but team members' opinions and views are encouraged and the leader informs the team about issues which may affect them.

In this approach the leader encourages the followers to become a part of the decision-making process. The leader still maintains control of the group and ownership of the final decision, but input from team members is encouraged and the leader informs team members about factors that may have an impact on them, the team and the project.

This encourages a sense of responsibility in team members who feel that they have a vested interest in the success of the project or operation. It allows a leader to draw upon the expertise and experience of a team in order to achieve the best results for all and it also helps to develop the skills of individuals in the team. The democratic approach is viewed positively as it gains employees' respect and it can produce high-quality work over long periods of time from highly

Table 2.1: Pros and cons of authoritarian style of leadership.

Advantages	Disadvantages
It maintains order and discipline.	Team members rely on the leader for instruction and do not develop initiative.
It allows public services to be deployed quickly and efficiently.	Team members have less responsibility for their own actions.
It allows young and inexperienced recruits to know what to do and when to do it.	Team members may feel angry and resentful at being ordered to perform tasks without explanation.
It allows large-scale coordination with other shifts or units.	It can lead to high staff turnover and absenteeism.
It ensures that decisions are made by those best equipped to make them.	Staff may feel devalued and fearful of punishment.
It enables decisions to be made very quickly.	Staff morale may decline leading to poor job performance.

motivated teams. Employees and team members also feel in control of their own destiny, such as gaining promotion and progressing up the ladder. However, its application in the field of public service work is slightly more problematic and the drawbacks are seen as follows:

- Democratic discussion takes time. A public service may have to respond very quickly, so gathering the views of all team members may not be a viable option.

- A participative approach may not be the most cost effective way of organising a service. The time of service officers is expensive and in terms of public perceptions and government funding it is best if the public services, especially the uniformed services, are doing the job and not talking about how to do it.

- A time-consuming approach is not appropriate if the safety of team members is paramount. Safety is not open for negotiation; a public service must endeavour to protect its members from harm wherever operationally possible. Equally, when members must risk their personal safety in the defence of others, it is not open to discussion.

Case study: Taking a democratic approach

Simon is a Senior Community Police Officer involved in an initiative to reduce the amount of youth crime occurring in the centre of a large city. He has called a meeting to discuss what the current problems are, how effective current preventative action is and to create a plan to move forward in achieving the local authority's goals.

Many organisations are involved in this initiative such as Social Services, youth action groups, the Probation Service, Victim Support and local business owners. All of them have sent senior representatives to this important meeting. After reviewing his preparation notes for the meeting, Simon decides to take a democratic approach to the meeting rather than using another style.

1 Why do you think Simon chose to employ a democratic style for the meeting?

2 What are the advantages to Simon in using this style?

3 What are the disadvantages to Simon in using this style?

4 What are the advantages to the project as a whole in using this style?

Laissez-faire

Key term

Laissez-faire leadership is a hands-off approach to leadership, where the group are trusted to complete the task by the leader.

The laissez-faire approach can also be called the 'hands-off', 'free-reign' or 'delegative' approach. This style differs from the others in that the leader exercises very little control over the group and leaves them to establish their own roles and responsibilities. Followers are given very little direction but a great deal of power and freedom. They must use this power to establish goals, make decisions and resolve difficulties should they arise. This style is difficult to master as many leaders have great difficulty delegating power and authority to others and allowing them the freedom to work free from interference. It is also a difficult approach to use with all teams as some people experience great difficulty working without a leader's direction and projects or goals may fall behind schedule or be poorly organised.

In general, a laissez-faire approach is most effective when a group of followers are highly motivated, experienced and well trained. It is important that the leader can have trust in their followers to complete tasks without supervision and this is more likely to happen with a highly qualified team or individual.

However, there are situations where a laissez-faire style may not be the most effective style. An example of this would be when a leader lacks the knowledge and the skills to do the job and employs this style so that the work of the followers or employees covers the leader's weaknesses. This is not the same as a leader who brings in outside expertise, such as a scenes of crime officer, to complete a task they are not qualified to do. In addition, it would be inappropriate to use this style with new or inexperienced staff who may feel uncomfortable if the direction of a leader weren't readily available. For instance, a commanding officer would not approach the training of new recruits in a laissez-faire manner, but as an individual progresses through a rank structure they will become more skilled, experienced and trustworthy and they may encounter this style more often.

Transactional leaders use conventional rewards and punishments to gain the support of their team. They create clear structures whereby it is obvious what is required of the team and what incentives they will receive if they follow orders (salary, benefits, promotion or praise). Team members who perform adequately or accomplish goals will be rewarded in some way that benefits their own self-interest. Those who don't perform or meet the standard required will be punished by the leader through the 'management by exception principle', whereby, rather than rewarding work, they will take corrective action against those who don't work to the required standards.

Transactional

Key term

Transactional leadership is a very direct style of leadership and uses rewards and punishments to motivate the team.

This is similar to autocratic but not as extreme, even though transactional leaders, like autocratic leaders, are direct and dominating and spend a great deal of time telling others what is expected of them. Transactional leaders are very common in businesses where people receive rewards such as bonuses, training or time off if they demonstrate good performance.

Transformational

Key term

Transformational leadership style is a form of leadership style that focuses on team performance as a whole by encouraging team members to think of the group rather than themselves. It is about moving forward as a team rather than individuals who just happen to be on the same project.

Transformational leaders aim to make team members better people by encouraging their self-awareness and helping them to see the bigger picture of what they do. They want team members

Table 2.2: The advantages and disadvantages of transactional leadership.

Advantages	Disadvantages
• The leader actively monitors the work and each individual's performance. • People are motivated by being rewarded for exceeding expectations. • There is a clear chain of command. • Formal systems of discipline are in place. • The team is fully accountable for its actions and will be sanctioned for failure. • It ensures that routine work is done reliably.	• Leaders tend to be action oriented and focus on short-term tasks. • Team members may not get job satisfaction because of the reward and punishment ethos. • It has serious limitations for knowledge-based or creative work but remains a common style in many organisations. • Team members do exactly what the manager tells them to do and have no authority. • The team might not have the resources or capability to carry out a task. • The style assumes that people are motivated by money and not by emotional and social factors. • The leader could manipulate others to engage in unethical or immoral practices and control others for their own personal gain. • It creates an environment of power versus perks.

Table 2.3: The advantages and disadvantages of transformational leadership.

Advantages	Disadvantages
• People will follow transformational leaders because of their passion, energy, commitment and enthusiasm for the team and their vision. • They add value to the organisation through their vision and enthusiasm. • They care about their team and work hard to motivate them – this reduces stress levels and increases well-being. • They have belief in others and themselves. • They spend time teaching and coaching the team.	• The team may not share the same vision if they are not convinced by it. • If the team do not believe that they can succeed, then they will lack effort and ultimately give up. • Followers need to have a strong sense of purpose if they are to be motivated to act. • Leaders believe their vision is right, when sometimes it isn't. • Large amounts of relentless enthusiasm can wear out the team. • Leaders see the big picture but not the details. • Leaders can become frustrated if transformation is not taking place.

to overcome self-interest and move towards achieving the common goals and purposes that are shared with the group.

Transformational leaders are often charismatic with a clear vision. They spend a lot of time communicating and gaining the support of the team through their enthusiasm. This vision may be developed by the leader or the team, or may emerge from discussions. Leaders will want to be role models that others will follow and will look to explore the various routes to achieve their vision. They look at long-term goals rather than short-term goals. They are always visible and will be accountable for their actions rather than hiding behind their team. They act as mentors and demonstrate how the team should behave and work together through their own good practice. They listen to the team and often delegate responsibility – they trust their team enough to leave them to grow and solve the problems through their own decisions.

Activity: Transformational leadership

Consider how you could transform a team you are leading into a highly motivated, inspired team who think of others rather than themselves when the job they have to do is routine, low paid and uninspiring? What difficulties would you encounter? How could you overcome them?

Bureaucratic

Key term

Bureaucratic leadership is a style of leadership that focuses on rules and procedures to manage teams and projects.

A bureaucratic form of leadership is one in which authority is diffused among a number of departments or individuals and there is strict adherence to a set of operational rules. This is also considered to be a classic leadership style and is often used in organisations that do not encourage innovation and change, and by leaders who may be insecure and uncertain of their role. It involves following the rules of an organisation rigidly. People who favour using this style of leadership are often very familiar with the many policies, guidelines and working practices that an organisation may have.

If a particular situation arises that is not covered by known rules and guidelines then a bureaucratic leader may feel uncomfortable as they like to 'do things by the book'. They may feel out of their depth and will have little hesitation in referring difficulties to a leader higher up in the chain of command.

This approach is commonly found in many uniformed and non-uniformed public services. Often the public services are very large and bureaucratic themselves and, although it may seem unlikely, there are several situations where the bureaucratic leadership style may be useful, for example, when:

- a job is routine and doesn't change over a long period of time
- a job requires a definite set of safety rules or working guidelines in order to comply with the law.

However, if the bureaucratic style is used inappropriately it can have negative consequences, leading to a lack of flexibility, an uninspired working environment and workers who do what is required of them but no more.

People-orientated

Key term

People-orientated leadership style focuses on participation of all team members, clear communication and supporting and developing the individual in order to improve skills.

The people-orientated leader is focused on organising, supporting and developing the team. They are competent in their role and inspire others by unlocking their potential. They allocate roles based on a person's strength and individual skills.

This style of leadership is participative and encourages good teamwork, loyalty and creative collaboration and helps to avoid work-based problems such as low morale, poor communication and distrust. The style has a human element and good relationships are crucial to its success. The key to this style is people power – the organisation is made successful by utilising the knowledge, skills, abilities, life experiences and talents of the individuals and groups. A people-orientated style also looks to develop a person's skills and help them acquire new ones through continuous and regular training. A disadvantage of this style is that it can focus so much on the well-being of the team that the job they do is neglected.

Task-orientated

Key term

Task-orientated leadership style is about getting the job done. The completion of the task rather than the needs of the team is the key goal.

Task-orientated leaders focus mainly on getting the task done, whether it is structured or unstructured.

They will define the work and the roles required, put structures in place, plan, organise and monitor with little thought for the well-being or needs of their teams. This approach can have many flaws, such as difficulties in motivating and retaining the team.

This style of leadership is the opposite of people-orientated leadership. In practice, most leaders use both task-orientated and people-orientated styles of leadership. As an example, a police inspector organising crowd control at a football match may use a task-centred approach, but back at the station, when dealing with junior police officers, she might employ a people-centred approach.

Activity: Which leadership style?

List possible situations when the public services will use a task-orientated approach and situations in which they would use a people-orientated approach to lead teams.

Remember!

Choosing the right leadership style depends very much on the situation but to help you select the most appropriate style you need to consider the following:

- The authoritarian approach tells others what to do and how to do it.
- The bureaucratic approach has clearly outlined procedures that must be followed if you are to know what to do and how to do it.
- The democratic approach discusses with others what to do and how to do it.
- The laissez-faire approach lets followers decide for themselves what to do and how to do it.
- The transformational approach encourages individuals to share the goals of the organisation and work towards its success.
- The transactional approach rewards people for good performance and punishes those who don't perform well.
- The people-orientated approach focuses on the needs, problems and skills of team members and identifies the support individuals will need.
- The task-orientated approach focuses on getting the task done and the leader considers what needs to be done to achieve this.

Case study: Winston Churchill 1874–1965

"It was the nation that had the lion's heart. I had the luck to be called upon to give the roar."

Winston Churchill (1954)

Winston Churchill was born into a well-recognised military and political family in 1874. After serving as a military officer in three campaigns and also as a war correspondent he developed skills that set him on the road to greatness. Many of the qualities that would help save Britain from Nazi invasion 40 years later were already emerging. These qualities included intense patriotism, an unshakeable belief in the greatness of Britain and her empire, inexhaustible energy, a strong physical constitution, a willingness to speak out on issues despite the fact that to do so would prove unpopular, meticulous organisational skills and the ability to inspire and motivate others.

When the First World War broke out in 1914, Churchill was Lord of the Admiralty and had a crucial role to play in the events of 1914–18. His experiences during the First World War educated him about political office and large-scale battle tactics, and it helped him come to terms with his leadership failings.

Not all of Churchill's military campaigns in the First World War were successful. In 1915 he was instrumental in sending a naval and army force to Gallipoli in the Mediterranean. Gallipoli was a disaster and cost thousands of allied solders and sailors their lives. Admitting responsibility, Churchill resigned from both political and military office; he would not regain his pre-war political status for over 25 years. Failures by leaders last much longer in the minds of the public than successes.

It seemed that his troubled political years helped to develop his leadership skills and mental faculties to such an extent that in the hour of Britain's crisis at the beginning of the Second World War, his skills and abilities matched the requirements of the situation better than those of his political contemporaries. During the 1930s Churchill spoke out vigorously on the rise of totalitarian regimes such as the Nazi party. This ensured that when confrontation between Britain and Germany inevitably arose, Churchill stood out as a statesman who had fought against the threat of Nazism for many years while other politicians had tried to appease Adolf Hitler.

The nation felt they had found a politician who understood the situation and whom it could trust. Churchill was reappointed to head up the Admiralty office on the same day that war officially broke out: 3 September 1939.

Norway fell to the Germans in April 1940 and this was quickly followed by the fall of Belgium and the Netherlands in May. Neville Chamberlain, the Prime Minister of the time, lost the confidence of Parliament and resigned. It was clear at that point that Churchill had the skills and spirit to unite and lead the nation. He was appointed Prime Minister to a coalition government headed by a war cabinet. After the fall of France, Britain stood without substantial allies and faced most of 1940 under German air bombardment and the constant threat of Nazi invasion. Churchill used his personal skills and patriotism to motivate and inspire the British public to endure the hardships they faced with good humour, strength and resourcefulness. Churchill also used his extensive diplomacy and communication skills to forge alliances between nations with differing political and social philosophies, such as the communist Soviet Union and the capitalist United States.

Churchill's leadership qualities were present from the early days of his military and political career but it is fair to say that some of the decisions he made in his early career did not show him as an effective leader in all circumstances. His obituary written upon his death in January 1965 notes the following:

His career was divided by the year 1940. If he had died a little before that he would've been remembered as an eloquent, formidable, erratic statesman. An outstanding personage, but one who was not to be put in the class of such contemporaries as Lloyd George or even Arthur Balfour. Yet all the qualities with which he was to fascinate the world were already formed and matured. They awaited their hour for use.

Despite his many and varied leadership skills it is unlikely that he would have risen to greatness without the Second World War. It was the circumstances that Churchill found himself in that allowed his best abilities to dominate in a way they might not otherwise have done.

1 **What were Winston Churchill's key leadership strengths?**

2 **How did his leadership style suit the situation in 1940?**

3 **Do you think great leaders are born or made?**

4 **Does it take the right situation to bring out the best in someone's leadership skills or can they be a good leader in all circumstances?**

1.2 Appropriate style for the situation

The public services receive their strategic plans either directly from a government ministry or they must draw up their own plans under the prevailing political will of the time. This means that even very senior officers often have no input into the goal setting of the organisation but are given authoritarian dictates that they have to impose on their employees. Despite this a public service leader must be ready to respond to the challenges and changes that may arise in society with a whole range of leadership techniques that can be deployed singly or all at once. Public service leaders must be highly adaptable and comfortable using all styles of leadership.

1.3 Team leader role

Team leaders can be appointed in many different ways, for example through:

Assessment activity 2.1   P1 M1 D1   BTEC

Understanding the different leadership styles the public services might use will be essential in your future career. In the form of a presentation slideshow address the following tasks:

1 Describe the different leadership styles used in the public services **P1**

2 Compare the different leadership styles used in the public services **M1**

3 Evaluate the effectiveness of different leadership styles used in the public services **D1**

Grading tips

Your slides should describe the leadership styles outlined in the information above, make sure you cover them all in order to pass **P1**. For **M1** your slides should also make comparisons about these leadership styles noting the differences and similarities and commenting on situations where one style might be more appropriate than another. For **D1** you should supply some supporting notes to your presentation that draw conclusions about how effective these styles are for leaders in the public services.

Activity: Examining great leaders

One of the ways you can find out more about leadership styles, skills and qualities is to examine great leaders who you admire. These can be leaders in any field from successful football managers, military leaders, political figures or someone you know and admire in your personal life. Consider what makes these people good leaders, how can they be a role model for you to develop your own skills and abilities?

- promotion
- nomination
- election
- delegation
- volunteering.

Some people make better leaders than others, however, as long as someone is interested and willing, with an idea of how to communicate well, understand the needs of others, offer support and be flexible, then they have the basics to develop their leadership skills.

Position and responsibilities

There are many functions of a team leader. These range from helping the team to decide how roles and responsibilities will be divided amongst its members to helping to coordinate the task and resolving interpersonal conflicts.

The team leader is the contact point for communication between the team members. He or she should:

- encourage and maintain open communication
- help the team to develop and keep to a good way of performing and focusing on the task
- be an active listener and show initiative when things become flat by building up rapport to help maximise performance
- look to delegate their authority when appropriate and follow up on any points after a task has been attempted or completed
- encourage the team members to reflect on the task
- coordinate multi-agency responses such as emergency service or military teams working together to achieve a common goal.

Did you know?

One example of a leadership position within a uniformed public service is that of a Commanding Officer (CO). The CO is the officer in command of a military unit, post, camp, base or station. He or she has authority over the unit and is given legal powers, within the bounds of military law, to discipline and punish certain behaviour.

A CO has a range of significant responsibilities with regard to the allocation of service personnel, finances and equipment. They are accountable to the higher ranks and have a legal duty of care to the team. COs are highly valued and progression within the service is awarded to the best officers who have worked their way up the ranks.

Table 2.4: Key qualities for leadership roles.

Leadership qualities	
Decisiveness	**Adaptability**
A leader within the uniformed services needs to demonstrate good judgement by making effective, timely and sound decisions in response to situations that arise. Decisions need to be made quickly and include consideration of the impact and implications of their decision. Many decisions need to be made proactively before a problem arises.	A leader within the uniformed services needs to be able to adjust any long-term plans when new information is available and constantly apply critical thinking to address any new demands and prioritise and reprioritise tasks in a changing environment to fit any new circumstances. This is particularly important in public services where the political climate or operational conditions can change with very little or no warning.
Courage	**Compassion**
A leader within the uniformed services needs courage to accomplish tasks, especially when he or she is faced with tough decisions and has to take action in difficult circumstances. Leaders need to use courage to manage dangerous situations whilst appearing calm to the rest of the team at all times, even when under stress.	Compassion is an awareness and sympathy for what other people are experiencing. A good team leader needs to understand how the team might be feeling and be able to help, particularly considering some of the heartrending situations the public services have to deal with such as child abuse, murder and combat which can take a significant emotional toll on team members.
Leadership skills	
Communication	**Organisation and multi-tasking**
A team leader needs to be able to tell the team what they are going to be doing and be certain they have understood. This is where effective communication becomes important. If a military combat team is in doubt about their target or strategy then their safety and the safety of others might be at risk. Clear communication helps a team achieve its goals.	A team leader will have many jobs to do at once, including, dealing with the actual task they are trying to achieve, monitoring their personnel, securing equipment, monitoring finance, reporting to the public or senior officers and dealing with on the ground changes as they happen. In order to do this their organisational and multi-tasking skills must be well developed.
Planning	**Motivating**
Team leaders must be able to plan effectively, not just so they can deal with the task at hand but also so that they can deal with anything unexpected that crops up. For example a senior police officer must plan effectively to manage the policing of a football match, but they must also have contingency plans for pitch invasions, hooliganism and public safety situations. Good leaders share their plans with others when appropriate so that all other officers know what they are expected to do in a given situation.	Another key skill a leader must have is the ability to motivate their team. Motivation is the drive to successfully reach a goal or aim, a leader must help their team be motivated to complete the task they have been set. If a leader cannot motivate their team then it is les likely the team will be successful. For example in a mountain rescue scenario the physical conditions may be very difficult to deal with, severe cold and poor weather might sap the team's energy and they may become demotivated. The job of the team leader is to find strategies to keep them motivated and committed until the missing person is located.

Leadership qualities and skills

An effective leader will have a range of personal and professional qualities and skills that they bring to their role. Table 2.4 highlights some of the key qualities and skills you will need to be aware of when developing your own leadership abilities.

Activity: Your leadership skills

Consider your own leadership skills and qualities. Would you make a good leader, if so why? What are your main areas for development?

Draw up an action plan that helps you maintain your strengths and overcome your weaknesses.

Assessment activity 2.2

P2 **BTEC**

Understanding what a team leader does and the skills and qualities they are expected to have is an essential part of your course. Produce a public services job description for a leader, manager or senior officer that addresses the following task.

1 Identify the role of the team leader in the public services **P2**

Grading tips

Make sure your job description is detailed and interesting and could be used to guide people who might want to be a team leader in the future. Make sure you include what the role of a team leader is and the skills and qualities an effective team leader should have.

2. Communicating effectively to brief and debrief teams

It is important that a leader possesses good communication skills. Effective communication is crucial for the uniformed public services, particularly as a major part of their work involves **briefing** and **debriefing** teams.

Key terms

Brief is a verbal process of getting information to people quickly and efficiently, very similar to a meeting but with less open discussion.

Debrief is the process of gathering information about the success of a task or activity after it has been completed. This helps improve the planning process for next time.

Briefings and debriefings can be done on a team or individual basis.

2.1 Communication

Communication is an integral part of all our lives and is a critical factor in most areas of employment. This is particularly so when the job involves substantial contact with the public and teamwork situations with colleagues, both of which occur almost all the time in public service work. Communication is the mechanism by which we give and receive messages and articulate ideas in order to interpret the situation and environment around us and act accordingly.

When we communicate studies suggest that the actual literal content and the words we say are far less important than how we say it, the tone of our voice, our facial expression and body language. Our senses are involved in giving and receiving communication all the time and it is a major part of how we present ourselves to others. The manner in which we communicate determines the way in which people respond.

Verbal communication

Effective communication means that other people take you seriously and only occurs if the receiver understands the exact information or idea that the sender intended to transmit. To ensure this happens while speaking in groups, communication should be clear and concise and as simple as possible so that it is understood. Communication should be relevant to the task and clarification should be sought from the recipient, even if it is just a nod of the head. Straightforward questions should be asked to ensure the communication has been understood.

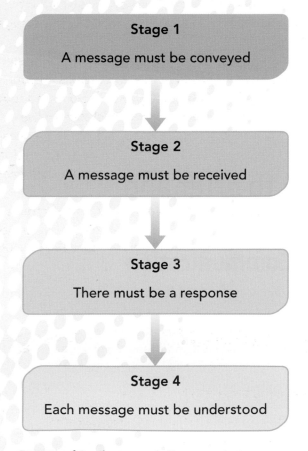

Figure 2.2: The four elements of effective verbal communication.

The content of the message can be affected by the tone, pitch, quality and speed of your voice. You should ensure your voice complements the message that you

convey to avoid misinterpretations. The cornerstones to effective speaking are:

- clarity
- simplicity
- preparedness
- conciseness.

Did you know?

The best way to improve your communication and ensure that communication is active in your teams is to:

- Ensure you know the names of all members of the team as this will help the group to be responsive and supportive.
- Try to be confident in situations where you don't always feel comfortable.
- Be open and responsive to problems when they occur and be prepared to talk about them as a group.
- Respect and seek the opinions, thoughts and feelings of all members of the group or communication will break down as people feel alienated.
- Exhibit emotions such as concern, empathy, sympathy and remorse when they are needed as these put people at ease.
- Ensure that you use the right tone of voice when speaking to avoid unnecessarily upsetting or offending anyone.

Non-verbal communication

Non-verbal communication refers to all the actions that accompany communication. Many of these have a recognised meaning and can give an indication to someone's state of mind. For example, a nervous person is likely to fidget, pinch or tug their flesh and a defensive person might cross their arms or legs and avoid eye contact. These can be valuable signs for any public service employee to look out for when doing their job as it may alert them to signs of danger or help them understand how a situation is affecting others. In briefing and debriefing situations it can help the leader know that information is being received and understood.

Activity: Body signals

How would you convey the following through body signals? Demonstrate and see if a friend can guess what they are:

- upset
- angry
- happy
- bored
- shocked
- amazed.

Table 2.5 shows some examples of non-verbal communication you may come across and shows what each one might mean. Looking for these non-verbal forms of communication in briefing and debriefing situations can help you understand how other people feel, what they are likely to do next and whether they have understood your message.

Activity: Interpreting signs

- Imagine someone has told you a lie in the past. How would you know it was a lie? Was it because of the things they said or was it the way they acted?
- How do you let someone know that you like them if you are too shy to speak to him or her?
- How do you know that a team leader is showing you approval and recognition for your achievements without using words?

Listening skills

Studies have found that listening accounts for between 42–53 per cent of the time that an average individual spends communicating. Listening is not simply hearing and understanding the spoken word, it involves listening to the tone of the communication and the sentiment behind it. Understanding the tone of communication is crucial in most societies, but especially so in the UK where **sarcasm** and **irony** are natural forms of humour.

Key terms

Sarcasm is the use of irony to mock someone or something.

Irony is a statement that, when taken in context, may actually mean the opposite of what is written or said.

You must hear what is being said, pay attention to the speaker, understand the content of the message and be able to remember it. This process is very important on several levels. Firstly, if you don't listen, you are placing yourself at risk and increasing your vulnerability. For example, if you are told not to touch a piece of electrical equipment which carries live electricity, and you do not listen, the consequences could be fatal. Secondly, in a public service situation it is of vital importance that you listen to the commands of your senior officers. If you do not, you may compromise the safety of yourself, your colleagues and the general public. Thirdly, listening and paying attention are also a crucial factor in the achievement of team goals.

Table 2.5: Some common forms of body language.

Non-verbal communication	What it might indicate
Making direct eye contact	Friendly, sincere, self-confident, assertive
Shaking head	Disagreeing, shocked, disbelieving
Smiling	Contented, understanding, encouraging, happy
Biting the lip	Nervous, fearful, anxious
Folding arms	Angry, disapproving, disagreeing, defensive, aggressive
Leaning forward	Attentive, interested
Shifting in seat	Restless, bored, nervous, apprehensive
Having erect posture	Self-confident, assertive

Listening can be divided into two main categories:

- active
- passive.

Active listening. This can be summarised as listening with a purpose. It involves paying attention to what is being said and questioning the speaker to ensure real understanding has been achieved. Active listening requires as much energy as speaking and it is a skill that requires practice and development if it is to be perfected.

Did you know?

Active listeners generally possess the following skills:

- They do not finish other people's sentences.
- They do not daydream or 'wander' while others speak.
- They do not talk more than they listen.
- They may make notes to help them remain focused.
- They ask questions for clarification.

Activity: Active listening

You are a public service employee and a complaint has been made against you by a member of the public. You are anxious to defend yourself and go to see your line manager at the earliest opportunity. Your line manager hears what you say but her eyes continually wander and she stifles a couple of yawns.

Explain how this makes you feel and why it is important that she actively listens.

Passive listening. This type of listening simply involves hearing what has been said without needing to respond or check understanding. This type of listening occurs when you are watching TV or listening to music.

Activity: Your listening skills

Are you generally an active or passive listener? How might being an active listener help you develop your team of staff? How could being a passive listener detract from the potential your team has to succeed?

Listening is more than just hearing. Hearing is the act of perceiving different sounds. Listening, however, is the art of consciously taking the sounds and concentrating on processing and understanding what the sounds mean. As with any skill, listening takes practice and it will develop the more you use it. You will spend a lot of time using this skill, especially in group situations. It is worth considering that your ability and capacity to listen is four times greater than your ability to speak.

Activity: Repeating and understanding

Try this exercise with a friend. Start talking about any topic related to the public services for about 30 seconds. When you stop talking, ask your friend to repeat back to you the main points that you said. Then, reverse the roles and repeat the exercise. You could also increase the time or talk about a topic your friend knows little about to really test their listening skills.

Did you know?

Listening is difficult – a typical speaker says about 125 words per minute and an active listener can receive 400–600 words per minute. Ensure that you listen to the full message and don't jump to any conclusions about the remainder of the message.

Communication in teams is very important in building confidence and morale; positive feedback given at the right moment can lift a team's performance. Equally, negative feedback can demoralise a team and harm their performance. Even if you need to be firm with a team about their behaviour or performance, it is still possible to do this with tact, sincerity and with concern for the feelings of the team members.

Effective communication is also used in the services for:

- **Articulation of ideas.** The communication of an idea about how to tackle a problem or issue which can then be examined for merit.
- **Self presentation.** Effective communication can say al lot about the kind of leader and team member you are. If you present yourself well you have more chance of being listened and responded to.

- **Questioning.** Communication is also essential for questioning. If you have not understood an aspect of a team brief you must get clarification on it, effective questioning is the way to do this.
- **Defusing and resolving conflict.** Good communication skills can prevent conflict and help diffuse it if it develops.

2.2 Briefing teams

Team briefings are similar to meetings and are a verbal process of getting information to people quickly and efficiently. A briefing should be an open but structured two-way communication process and not just about informing the team about what they are required to do. Often there will be no written records of team briefings as they are applied to one-off situations, which are often practical in nature.

Successful team briefings will avoid misunderstandings and conflict. Teams who are involved in the briefing process are more likely to perform, progress and achieve the desired results as they will have clear direction and awareness of the main issues and won't need to rely on constant guidance from the team leader.

There is no single recognised model for briefing teams but a successful team briefing should follow a reasonably consistent format so that everyone knows what to expect. However, it could include some of the features outlined below.

Remember!

Tips for a successful briefing include being:

clear – avoid unfamiliar technicalities and acronyms and keep communications adult to adult – never patronise or talk down

brief – be precise and only repeat yourself to make sure the main points have been understood

in control – be prepared and lead, keep in control by ensuring you can focus on all members of the team so that you can read their body language

positive – be confident and don't appear nervous. Monitor your body language (avoid negative signs such as crossing arms or no eye contact). If things start to go wrong, or not to plan, don't panic and persevere with the task.

Ground orientation

- Commonly used in the military.
- Involves the use of objects and models to help explain the location and surrounding area.
- Can be adapted to suit more conventional team briefings by ensuring the team is aware of the environment it is working in (including issues such as facilities and resources at their disposal).

Safety points

- A risk assessment of any location/task needs to be carried out in order to highlight safety points and identify hazards and risks.
- Identify the precautions that should be taken to minimise the risk and decrease the likelihood of harm (for example, avoiding certain behaviour, wearing special equipment). Uniformed services often rely on dynamic risk assessment when working in teams. This is a process of identifying hazards and risks on a situation by situation basis and taking appropriate steps to eliminate or reduce them. This means as new risks occur, or as the circumstances change, the uniformed services will adapt the risk assessment and inform the team of any changes to the safety points.
- An example of this would be firefighters dealing with a factory fire and discovering that the factory has some highly explosive and very toxic chemicals stored in the basement. On learning this, they will adapt the risk assessment and take new measures and precautions to protect their colleagues and the public.

Summary of situation

- When briefing a team, a clear summary of the situation should be offered – this could take the form of a brief and concise statement that presents the main points.
- It should include the things a team must and should know about the situation.
- From this, the **primary aim** or aims should be established (these are the most important and immediate concerns).

Key term

Primary aim is the key objective of the team, the task or goal that must be achieved.

- An example of this is at a road traffic incident where the primary aim of the public services will be to coordinate and work together to ensure the preservation of life and safety of the people involved or affected directly by the incident. This may mean closing the road and diverting traffic to preserve the scene for later investigation and removing the vehicles involved.

Method to achieve aim

- Briefings should not just be a one-way communication from the leader but should involve the team being able to suggest possible ways of achieving the primary aims and goals.

- After all the possible solutions have been presented, discussion should take place on the pros and cons of each suggestion along with the likelihood of their success.

- It may ultimately be down to the team leader to select the method used to achieve the aim, based on the solutions offered by the group.

Designated roles

- The team leader is not expected to achieve the goals and aims unaided. A team briefing will allow the team leader to delegate and designate roles based on people's strengths and abilities.

- One way this could be done is by using team roles defined by Meredith Belbin in 1981 after an extensive study on the interaction between team members. A summary of the nine major roles she identified is shown in Table 2.6.

- Although organisations won't have these designated roles named, in any team there will be people who match up to one of more of these roles. It is important that public service workers know what their role in any situation is and what is expected of them if the team is to succeed.

Timings

- It is likely that briefing will have to take place quickly and often under situations of extreme pressure and stress. (Think about how the combined uniformed services would have to respond to a terrorist attack within an urban area.)

Table 2.6: Belbin's definitions of team roles.

Team role	Summary of role
Coordinator	Clarifies group objectives, sets the agenda, establishes priorities, selects problems, sums up and is decisive, but does not dominate discussions.
Shaper	Gives shape to the team effort, looks for patterns in discussions and practical considerations regarding the feasibility of the project. Can steamroller the team but gets results.
Plant	The source of original ideas, suggestions and proposals that are usually original and radical.
Monitor-evaluator	Contributes a measured and dispassionate analysis and, through objectivity, stops the team committing itself to a misguided task.
Implementer	Turns decisions and strategies into defined and manageable tasks, sorting out objectives and pursuing them logically.
Resource investigator	Goes outside the team to bring in ideas, information and developments – they are the team's salesperson, diplomat, liaison officer and explorer.
Team worker	Operates against division and disruption in the team, like cement, particularly in times of stress and pressure.
Finisher	Maintains a permanent sense of urgency with relentless follow-through.

- This means that resources, equipment and safety issues will need to be identified immediately and the team will need to quickly establish the situation and primary aims, along with how they will tackle the problem.

- In the example of a terrorist attack, the uniformed services will coordinate and designate roles based on their service's strengths. For example, the fire service will focus on search and rescue, the paramedics will deal with casualties at the scene and the police will manage the scene to bring the situation under control and ensure general safety.

Equipment

- When offering solutions to problems, the team can be aided or restricted by the equipment they have available.

- This means that you should consider the equipment you have and ensure the team are informed of, or can see it.
- Possible solutions to problems made by team members will be no good if the equipment isn't there to support them.

Team motivation

A successful team is a team that is well motivated and eager to work together to implement the identified aims. There are many ways that a team can be motivated to perform.

- **Clear focus** – if the team has a clear aim and understands how to achieve that aim it is more likely to work towards its completion in a positive manner.
- **Challenge** – a team will be motivated if the task is a sufficient challenge to them but is less likely to be motivated if the task is too simple or too difficult.
- **Camaraderie** – a sense of comradeship and loyalty will help a team to work together as the members will have a genuine respect for each other and will work hard to develop and maintain this relationship.
- **Rewards** – this could be money or benefits that the team will receive upon completion of the task.
- **Responsibility and authority** – having a sense of ownership of the task and a clear role is likely to help motivate the team.
- **Growth** – if the team feels they are moving forward, learning new skills and stretching their minds then they are likely to have a high level of motivation as personal growth enhances an individual's self-esteem and self-worth.
- **Treating people fairly** – it is important that all members of the team are treated equally and are all involved in the task; this will ensure that each member is motivated and that they work as a team.

Check understanding

- During the briefing you should check understanding.
- This could be done by generally observing a person's body language and facial expressions or by asking questions for clarification.
- The team should also be encouraged to ask questions and make comments to gauge their understanding of the task.

Remember!

The standard military SMEAC briefing system is a good open but structured model.

Situation: what's happening/happened?

Mission: the role of the group

Execution: the specifics of accomplishing the mission

Any questions: questions from the group

Confirm understanding: ask the group questions, to check they have understood the briefing.

Activity: Team briefing

Think of a team activity you would like to lead and develop a team brief that you can give to your team members. Remember to include:

- assessing your surroundings and consider potential risks and likelihood of harm
- summarising the task
- identifying the main aim and possible ways of achieving success
- assigning roles and responsibilities
- identifying how long you have to complete the task and the equipment you have available
- asking questions to clarify that people understand what they are doing or are expected to do.

2.3 Debriefing teams

Debriefings are used extensively by the Armed Forces (and other services) and involve troops or personnel giving feedback about their mission/task. The information generated is then assessed and troops or personnel are instructed on what they can talk about and what information is strictly confidential. The information given is also used to assess the troops or personnel's mental condition and to determine when they can return to duty.

Debriefings with teams can be seen as reviewing what has been learned from a task. It is a process that helps a leader and a team to reflect on the completed task in order to aid personal and professional development.

Successful reviewing will help the leader and the team to improve their interpersonal skills and work more effectively. Reviewing a task involves more than just reflecting on the task, it involves open communication between the team that leads to analysing and evaluating the task to ensure learning takes place.

Reasons why you should debrief after completing a task include:

• It keeps you in touch with the team and helps maintain motivation and enthusiasm for future tasks.

• It adds value to the experience and shows that you care for and are interested in the team.

• The team benefits from discussing, reviewing and evaluating the task which will in turn increase confidence and allow the team to become more independent and more capable of self-development.

• It increases the amount of strategies and ideas that may be used in future tasks as people will be imaginative and express themselves.

• It develops your skills (such as communication, perception and observation).

• Everyone learns from the task as they will share understanding and knowledge and gain an appreciation of their own strengths and weaknesses.

Case study: Debriefing after the Hatfield rail disaster

On 17 October 2000, a GNER train travelling from London to Leeds was derailed one mile outside Hatfield train station in Hertfordshire. The incident killed four people and injured many others. All of the subsequent debriefings conducted by the services were synthesised and pulled together by Hertfordshire Emergency Services Major Incidents Committee (HESMIC) into one debriefing report. This could then be widely circulated and have its recommendations acted upon. Some of the issues and concerns raised in the debrief are described below:

• There was confusion in communication between the emergency services and Railtrack over the safety of power lines which was not resolved for over an hour into the incident.

• There were many people milling around in the inner and outer cordons who had no role to perform. They were not challenged on their reason for being present.

• A helicopter was used but the noise of its rotors meant that safety instructions could not be easily heard by emergency services on the ground.

• The identification of silver/tactical commanders was difficult as many individuals were wearing similar high visibility tabards.

• Some survivors of the derailment had to complete their onward journey by train.

• Although the clergy were put on standby to help survivors in the reception centres, they were not deployed.

• The Queen Elizabeth II Hospital was put on standby but it was never given the signal to activate its major incident response. The hospital made the decision to activate the plan itself when the casualties began to arrive.

These are just some of the issues raised by the debriefs on the Hatfield incident. It is clear that there is no such thing as a perfect incident response – there are always lessons to be learned in an ongoing cycle of development.

1   Why was it inappropriate for a major incident survivor to continue their onward journey on the same form of transport that was involved in the incident?

2   How would this debrief help improve a response for next time?

3   What is the benefit of detailed debriefs for all the uniformed services?

4   What might be the consequences if the uniformed services did not monitor and evaluate their performance in relation to significant incidents?

- It helps to reinforce the objectives of the task and can be used to clarify and measure the amount of achievement that has taken place.

- The team is likely to work better and be successful in future tasks as they feel engaged and integrated into the process and can see the bigger picture.

- It helps people to acknowledge and enjoy success.

Feedback

One of the key aspects of any team debriefing is giving feedback. There are three common types of feedback including:

- **Negative feedback** – this should be avoided when debriefing teams as it is likely to cause conflict and a decrease in future participation by the whole group or certain members of the group.

- **Positive feedback** – this is obviously a great way of maintaining good group cohesion and output. However, it could be detrimental when there are obvious flaws in the team that go unmentioned as this could cause long-term problems.

- **Constructive feedback** – the best approach when giving feedback is to do so in a constructive way. Reassuring the team that supportive comments will be given, even if they fail, will encourage people to take risks. Also both failure and successful experiences will be analysed so that the team can develop further and move forward.

The key aspects of a debrief are to acknowledge the successes of the team, identify the strengths and weaknesses of their performance and put into place an action plan for future development. If the situation arises again the team will then be better prepared for it and therefore more effective.

Assessment activity 2.3 (P3) (M2) BTEC

It is important that you are able to practise your briefing and debriefing skills if you are going to become an effective communicator in the public services. Choose a team-based activity that you are going to lead and then address the following tasks:

1 Brief and debrief the team for a given task (P3)

2 Brief and debrief the team for a given task using effective communication (M2)

Grading tips

Consider all the things you have learned about brief and debrief and incorporate it into a plan to communicate with your team about the activity you have chosen. To gain (M2) make sure you are clear and concise and that you check people have understood what you want them to do.

3. Skills and qualities to lead a team

This is a practical outcome and you will need to demonstrate most of the content in leadership and teamwork situations that your tutor should help you develop. When considering the content below you should have in your mind how the knowledge could be practically applied to show that you can use the appropriate skills and qualities to lead a team.

3.1 Skills and qualities

There are many skills associated with leadership and the skills demonstrated may vary from situation to situation. For example, the skills needed by a commanding officer in a conflict situation may vary from the skills needed by a station officer in charge of the day-to-day running of a fire station. However there is a general set of skills which are useful for any leader to have, such as:

- time management
- commitment
- motivation
- delegation.

Time management

A successful team is one that manages its time, as time is the most valuable (and undervalued) resource you have. It can be managed effectively by determining which task or element of a task is most important. This will help you use your time in the most effective way you can. A well-managed team will also look to control the distractions that waste time and break the flow of work.

Did you know?

The 80:20 Rule (or Pareto's Principle) states that typically 80 per cent of unfocused effort generates only 20 per cent of results. The remaining 80 per cent of results are achieved with only 20 per cent of the effort.

Is your time management a strength or a weakness? What can you do to develop your skills in this area?

Commitment

A leader within the uniformed services needs commitment. This is demonstrated by the time and energy they put into the job and leading from the front. They put effort into the task until a level of success has been achieved.

Motivational skills

To create a motivated team you need ground rules. However, these should not be too complex or rigid in order to avoid confusion. Any counter-productive behaviour should be addressed and communication should be clear and consistent. Also team members should be given team roles that suit their personalities and complement their strengths.

Morale has a profound effect on a team. When it is high, a team will be enthusiastic about its work and function better by being more productive as its members will be committed and confident of success. Good morale makes communication easier, clearer and more energetic. When a team is happy, all the members will feel a sense of pride in being a member of that team. Good morale gives your team a good mindset and good team spirit. This often means team members become friends. Morale can be observed directly through people's behaviour and the productivity of the group.

Key term

Morale is also known in the services as 'esprit de corps' and it refers to the spirit and enthusiasm of a team and their belief and confidence in their purpose and success.

Delegation skills

Delegation is not about the leader handing over authority. It's about giving the team clear roles and responsibilities and leaving it to the team member to manage and control their task.

The key to delegation is to delegate as much as possible so that team members feel empowered and to delegate equally amongst the team so that everyone has a role or responsibility. Apart from giving a person responsibility for the completion of the task, you should also give them ownership of how they complete it.

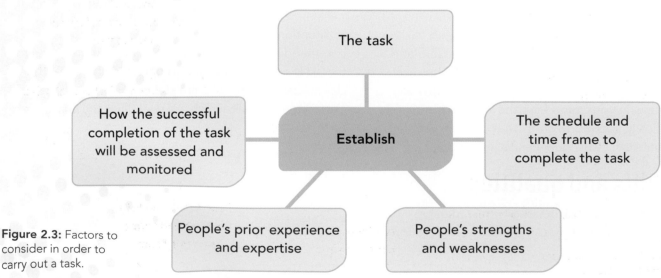

Figure 2.3: Factors to consider in order to carry out a task.

Activity: Delegation in leadership

Delegation is not an easy skill to master. Look back at the styles of leadership and the skills and qualities of effective leaders you have covered (page 40). Consider which styles use delegation and the reasons they value delegation so much.

3.2 Implementing a plan

Planning is the process by which you and the team will determine the most effective way to attempt and complete a task. The time you spend planning will often make the difference between success and failure.

By planning effectively you can:

- **Avoid wasting effort** – it is far too easy to spend large amounts of time trying to complete a task with ideas and methods that are completely irrelevant.

- **Take into account and consider all possible solutions** – this ensures that you are aware of all the methods available to complete the task and that you are prepared for a variety of different eventualities. This will help your team work effectively with minimum effort

- **Be aware of all possible changes and alternative solutions** – if you have a number of possible solutions to the task, then you can assess in advance the likelihood of being able to change the way you tackle the problem throughout the duration of the task.

- **Identify the resources needed** – by planning the task you will be able to evaluate the worth of the resources you have available and how they are to be used to complete the task and, in some cases, be able to work out if additional resources are needed.

Key factors in implementing a plan and choosing a course of action include:

- identifying primary aim(s)
- considering factors which may crop up unexpectedly
- the available resources you have
- team member capabilities.

3.3 Leading the team

The key information you need in order to be able to develop the skills and knowledge to lead a team effectively is summarised in Figure 2.4.

Link

Leading the team is covered in more detail on page 40.

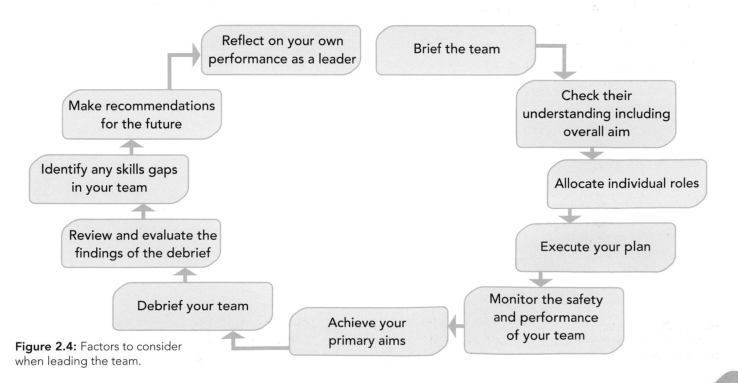

Figure 2.4: Factors to consider when leading the team.

3.4 Personal organisation

There are many aspects to personal organisation that are likely to make you a better team member. These are shown in Figure 2.5.

Personal organisation is very important to leadership and teamwork in the uniformed services. If you are not personally prepared to do your part, you are letting the team down as their leader and harming the overall team performance.

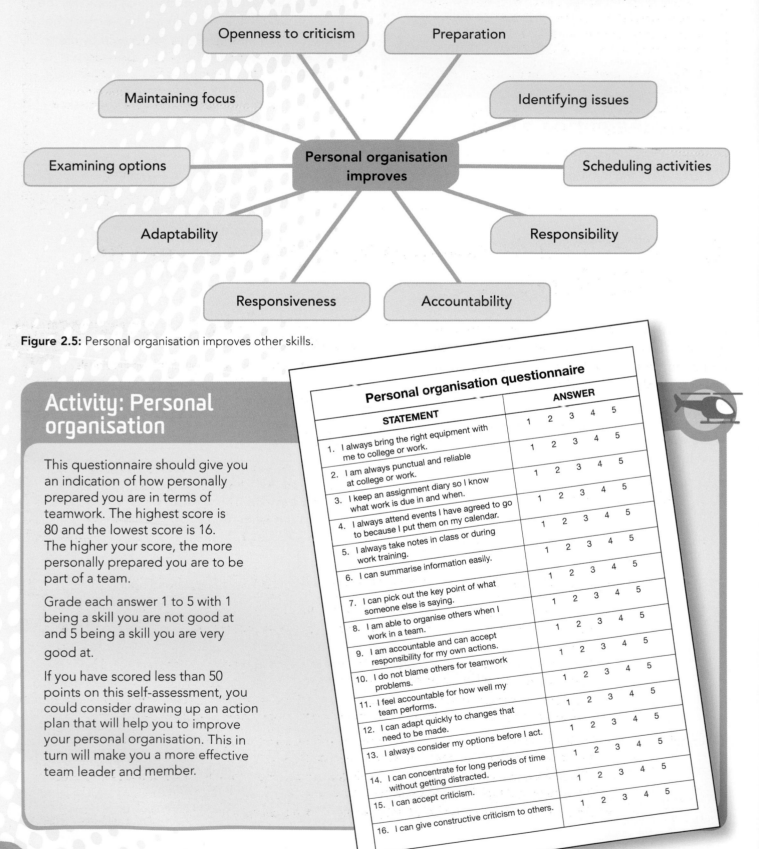

Figure 2.5: Personal organisation improves other skills.

Activity: Personal organisation

This questionnaire should give you an indication of how personally prepared you are in terms of teamwork. The highest score is 80 and the lowest score is 16. The higher your score, the more personally prepared you are to be part of a team.

Grade each answer 1 to 5 with 1 being a skill you are not good at and 5 being a skill you are very good at.

If you have scored less than 50 points on this self-assessment, you could consider drawing up an action plan that will help you to improve your personal organisation. This in turn will make you a more effective team leader and member.

Personal organisation questionnaire

STATEMENT	ANSWER				
	1	2	3	4	5
1. I always bring the right equipment with me to college or work.	1	2	3	4	5
2. I am always punctual and reliable at college or work.	1	2	3	4	5
3. I keep an assignment diary so I know what work is due in and when.	1	2	3	4	5
4. I always attend events I have agreed to go to because I put them on my calendar.	1	2	3	4	5
5. I always take notes in class or during work training.	1	2	3	4	5
6. I can summarise information easily.	1	2	3	4	5
7. I can pick out the key point of what someone else is saying.	1	2	3	4	5
8. I am able to organise others when I work in a team.	1	2	3	4	5
9. I am accountable and can accept responsibility for my own actions.	1	2	3	4	5
10. I do not blame others for teamwork problems.	1	2	3	4	5
11. I feel accountable for how well my team performs.	1	2	3	4	5
12. I can adapt quickly to changes that need to be made.	1	2	3	4	5
13. I always consider my options before I act.	1	2	3	4	5
14. I can concentrate for long periods of time without getting distracted.	1	2	3	4	5
15. I can accept criticism.	1	2	3	4	5
16. I can give constructive criticism to others.					

Assessment activity 2.4

(P4) (M3) (D2) BTEC

For this assessment you need to come up with a team-based activity that you can lead (speak to your tutor for guidance on this) and then demonstrate the following abilities.

1 Carry out a team task using the appropriate skills and qualities (P4)

2 Effectively lead a team task using the appropriate skills and qualities (M3)

3 Evaluate own ability to lead a team effectively (D2)

Grading tips

(P4) and (M3) require you to lead a team in an activity and it is likely this will be assessed via observation from your tutor. For (D2) you should be prepared to discuss your successes and failures with your tutor in order to evaluate your own ability.

4. Participate in teamwork activities within the public services

In this unit so far we have focused on team leaders and the qualities and skills needed to implement a plan and brief and debrief teams. We are now going to look at some of the different types of teams that can be formed within the public services and that you might encounter in your working life.

4.1 Types of team

Table 2.7: Different types of team that you may come across in the public services.

Remember!

The size of teams can vary greatly from two individuals working on a task to thousands working towards achieving the same goal. Increased human resources doesn't mean the job will get done any quicker or better – two people working on a small task may work much more efficiently than two thousand people on a large task.

The size of the task largely dictates the size of the team. For example, securing a border against terrorism would need a great many uniformed public service officers while responding to a non-emergency call would take only one or two.

Type of team	Description and example
Formal	• Formal teams have a clear membership and a defined structure. They have clear goals and objectives and there are monitoring systems in place to ensure that goals are reached in a timely fashion. • Formal teams have the backing of senior management and may have been created by management to solve a particular problem. • An example of this would be a multi-agency safer city partnership team who work together across a variety of organisations to combat antisocial behaviour on behalf of the government.
Informal	• An informal team may have more elastic membership allowing individuals to move in and out of the team with some flexibility as their particular skills are needed. • The goals and structure may be less well defined but the informal nature of the team allows for innovative and new ideas to be considered. • An example of this could be a best practice working group.

Table 2.7 (cont): Different types of team that you may come across in the public services.

Type of team	Description and example
Temporary	• Temporary teams come together for a short space of time to solve a particular problem and then disband once the objective has been achieved. • It can be difficult for temporary teams to work well as they do not know each other's strengths and weaknesses in the same way as permanent teams do. However, they can be efficient at troubleshooting as they sometimes see things differently from established teams. • An example of a temporary team in the public services might be operational, tactical and strategic command teams at the site of a major incident. These groups come together for the duration of the incident only and then disband once the situation is resolved.
Project	• Project teams are very like temporary teams – they come together to achieve a specific task based project and they may disband as soon as the project is finished or they may then move on to another task. • Project teams are usually made up of specialists and a project manager who runs the schedule and ensures objectives are met. • A project in the Fire Service might be to ensure all primary schools in a region have a visit from a fire safety team to warn about the dangers of fires and hoax calls.
Permanent	• Permanent teams are very common in the public services; many shifts, watches and regiments can have predominantly the same members for years at a time. • They are considered strong teams who know each other's strengths and weaknesses and can use that knowledge to best effect in achieving aims and goals. On the downside they can become set in their ways and it can be difficult to change how a permanent team works.

4.2 Benefits of teams

Working as part of a team is common in the public services and many other organisations. There are many benefits at both an operational and an individual level. It is also important to note that some organisational objectives simply cannot be met by one individual alone – a team is required to achieve them.

Contribution or productivity and effectiveness

Teams are a vital part of making an organisation flexible and responsive to new challenges and customer needs. The public services have around 60 million customers in the UK alone and each man, woman and child has the right to expect the services to be ready to respond to their needs.

Reduction of alienation

Key term

Alienation This is a feeling of being withdrawn or isolated from those around you

Psychologists would argue that humans are social animals by nature – we like to be part of a social group, to belong to a team. This includes all manner of things such as sports clubs, churches, pressure groups and hobby groups. Teams allow individuals to feel as if they belong and are more than a payroll number. Effective teams can allow individuals to express their ideas, educate themselves about the organisation they work in and become part of it on a wider scale by having a say in policy-making procedures.

Fostering innovation

Innovation is about new ideas and new approaches to both old and new problems. Teams can be very good places to foster innovation as they allow for idea sharing activities between individuals in a critical yet supportive environment. All team members can throw ideas into the pot and have them examined and evaluated by others to see if they would work in practice. This can lead to new approaches to issues that have traditionally been hard to solve.

Sharing expertise

All team members, whether young or old, experienced or inexperienced, will have a unique area of expertise that they can share with others in the team. An effective team will allow each person to share their expertise and specialist knowledge. This has two benefits: firstly, it educates other team members in areas where their knowledge might not be as up-to-date or extensive as others and, secondly, it allows experts to have their say on how certain goals and objectives can be achieved.

Implementing change

The role of the uniformed public services, and indeed any large organisation that serves the public, is dynamic and ever changing. The services are subject to the changes made by successive governments, funding plans, target setting, social changes and global needs. They move on and the roles they fulfil change. A fundamental role of teams is to move change forward and this is driven by leaders with the vision and knowledge to understand why the changes must take place. They will also have the communication and interpersonal skills to help others understand why the change needs to take place.

Identification and development of talent

Team performance is based on the skills and talents of its members. It is therefore very important to identify

team members who have talent in a particular area and ensure that they attend the right training events to develop it. For example, a senior officer might spot that a new police recruit manages difficult situations very well and may ensure he or she receives training and opportunities in their career that helps to develop those skills still further.

Case study: The Apollo Syndrome

The researcher Meredith Belbin noticed an occurrence in teams that was subsequently termed the Apollo Syndrome. The Apollo Syndrome is a trend whereby teams of extremely talented and clever individuals under-perform against teams of 'ordinary' individuals. When this phenomenon was looked at in more detail, it was discovered that Apollo team members often undermined each other's strategies while trying to achieve their own solutions to a group problem. They were essentially working as individuals in competition rather that as a united team pulling together. Experiments such as this made it clear that the intelligence, talent and understanding of the team were not the only factors in its success.

1 Why do you think that groups of talented individuals perform less well against those who are less talented?

2 Why did individual Apollo team members believe their own goal was the right one to pursue?

3 Why did Apollo team members undermine each other?

4 What would you do to improve teamwork if you were in charge of an Apollo type team?

Link

Meredith Belbin's pioneering work is introduced on page 54.

This US poster from the First World War reminds us that teamwork is effective work.

4.4 Types of teamwork activities

There are many types of teamwork activities that the public services use to train teams. These are generally divided into three categories: the practical or activity-based ones, the ones using pen and paper and the ones carried out at work (see Table 2.8).

Table 2.8: Training activities used in building teams.

Paper-based	
Disaster	There are two main kinds of paper-based disaster teamwork scenario.
	Seminar: This is a discussion-based exercise that is designed to outline to all the agencies involved exactly what their roles and responsibilities are and what the procedures would be in dealing with a particular major incident. This can be done as part of a large team or services attending can break down into smaller groups to discuss one particular aspect of the emergency response or focus on the responsibilities of one particular service.
	Table top: This is similar in nature to a seminar exercise but it generally involves smaller teams. The public services and any other agencies talk through their responses to a specified major incident in the order in which they would occur if the incident were real. They generally conduct these exercises around a conference table, hence the name of the exercise. Table top exercises are effective for testing major incident plans as they highlight any weaknesses in a safe environment where lives are not at risk.
Logistics	This is the process of managing and tracking the raw materials and components needed for a project. For the Armed Forces this might be the movement of troops and equipment to a battle zone along with all the support services such as medical, housing, catering and chaplaincy support. This can involve the movement of thousands of troops and millions of pounds worth of equipment in a situation which is time critical and in which mistakes may compromise the safety and security of service personnel. The best way to ensure the move goes as planned is to have a team of logistics experts plan it out prior to the actual move. Although it is called a paper-based activity it is much more likely to be done via computer software these days.
Activity-based	
Physical training	Physical training is an excellent way of promoting effective teamwork. Competitive sports such as football, basketball and rugby encourage team members to work together to achieve the goal of winning a match. Team sports can also foster a sense of camaraderie and encourage less physically able members of the team to strive to improve and encourage more physically able members of the team to assist them.
Teambuilding	Teambuilding exercises can be any activity that is used to bring a team together and make it work more efficiently. This could include activities such as outward-bound training courses or bringing in consultants who will help the team find better ways of working together.
Military / emergency exercises	Live exercises can test a small part of a major incident or military response plan (such as an evacuation) or they can test a full scale response. The exercise is carried out as realistically as possible including fake casualties and a simulated media response. This provides all the service teams involved with an opportunity to get to grips with the problems arising from a major disaster or military incident and attempt to solve them in real time, just as they would need to do in a real incident.
Work-related	
Achieving objectives	A major goal of teams in the workplace is to achieve the objectives set by the organisation. These objectives could range from reducing patient waiting times, to reducing the instances of self-harm in prison, to securing a building against terrorist activity.
Planning and achieving a project	Projects and initiatives that require planning and implementation are common in the workplace. Teams are largely responsible for developing a strategy to achieve a project and for monitoring its success. They are also accountable if the project is unsuccessful.

4.5 Types of team in the public services

Each public service has its own way of structuring and deploying teams in order to help it achieve the organisational objectives set for it by the government. The types of team in the service you wish to join will be very different from the types of team in another service. Some of the most common teams are shown in Figure 2.6.

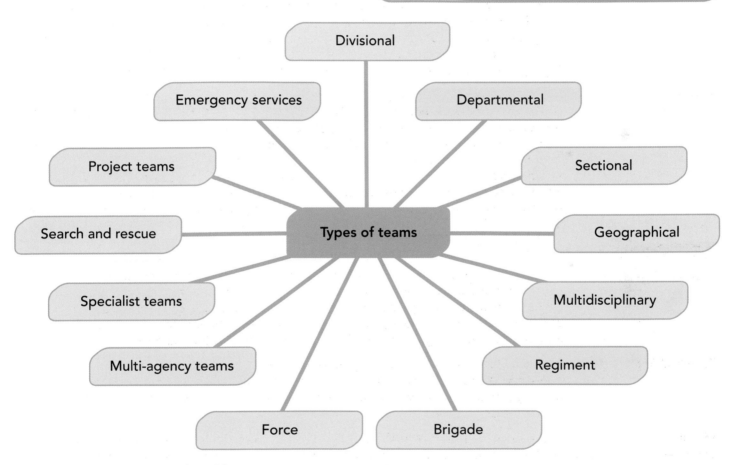

Figure 2.6: Common teams in the public services.

5. Understanding team development

5.1 Roles in teams

Different kinds of teams require different kinds of members. For example, a committee might need a chairperson, a football team might need a captain and a government needs a Prime Minister or President. Each person in a team usually has a specific role to play, such as leader, expert, researcher or team player, and each role is equally important. There have been several well-known and detailed research studies on team roles, such as those carried out by Bruce Tuckman, Peter Honey and Meredith Belbin.

Link

A brief description of Belbin's research is covered on page 54 and Tuckman's research is discussed on page 67.

Activity: Theories of team development

Research the theories of Tuckman, Belbin and Honey in detail. Produce a summary of each approach and then compare them to identify any similarities or differences. Which theory do you think has most merit and why?

5.2 Teambuilding

Everyone who works in a team needs to know what the various growth stages of a developing team are and they should know how best to move the team through these stages. Knowing that it is normal for a team to go through a roller coaster ride to achieve their goal will help you understand and anticipate the team-building process, and take action to be more productive when working in groups in the future.

Building an effective team is not easy. It involves enlisting the right people with the right skills in the right place within the team. Some key factors in teambuilding are described below.

Recruitment

Recruitment of the right individuals is a key aspect of building and maintaining a successful team. The right person is not always the best qualified or the most confident but the one who has the right mix of abilities and social skills to be able to join and improve an existing team. Recruiting a new team member can be fraught with difficulties. There are usually two options available: firstly, you can appoint a brand new member of staff from outside the organisation or, secondly, you can search within an organisation to find an existing member of staff with the right skills and qualities. Unless you are in a position to try these new members out on a trial basis, there can often be no way of knowing if they will be the right choice until after they are already in post.

Induction

Induction is the process by which new employees become familiar with their new workplace. It is a vital part of ensuring a new employee knows the full range of tasks they are required to do and how to do them. This includes finding out about canteen arrangements, learning about company policy and procedures, and where to go for help if with your job role. Induction is important in the public services and they often have probationary periods or terms of basic training for new staff to learn how things are done.

Motivation

The motivation of a team is essential. Motivation has been covered on several occasions throughout this unit already.

Link

For information on motivation see page 48.

Training/Coaching

Training and coaching are a key aspect of any role in the public services. Many of the tasks employees are expected to do are highly specialised and require extensive training and knowledge in order to do perform them well. This might involve the use of complex and technical equipment, legal knowledge or tactical knowledge. In the public services, training is an aspect of the job that never stops – an employee is never fully trained. New laws, new equipment and new theatres of battle all mean that training and coaching may be ongoing for an entire public service career.

Mentoring

Some organisations offer mentoring whereby an experienced colleague is on hand for an employee to turn to for advice. A good mentor will never be a person's line manager as there may be a conflict of interests. The mentor offers advice on how to deal with difficult work-based interpersonal situations or how to achieve an objective to best effect. Some organisations do not have mentors at all.

Team knowledge

Team knowledge is about understanding the strengths and weaknesses of your team and using this knowledge to get the best performance out of them. Only by knowing what members of your team do well can you allocate tasks and responsibilities efficiently. The team development process is an interesting one – teams do not develop overnight. Simply assembling a group of individuals and assigning them to a task will not make them an effective team; they must go through a team development process that establishes relationships and provides them with the team knowledge they need to work effectively. One of the better known models of team development is the model developed by Bruce Tuckman described below

Did you know?

Tuckman's theory of Team Development

Bruce Tuckman first published this model of team development in 1965. It is effectively a theory of how teams develop from the very start of a project to the end. It describes four main stages, although he added a fifth stage (adjourning) later in his career. The stages are described below:

Stage 1 – Forming. In this stage the team may be meeting for the first time. They will have a high level of dependency on the leader and roles and responsibilities will not be particularly clear. The processes that the team should follow will not be known and the majority of information and guidance comes from the leader as they explain why the team exists and what it is intended to do.

Stage 2 – Storming. As the name suggests this can be a very turbulent stage in a team's development. During this stage, individuals might be struggling for position and power with other team members and there may be some challenges to the authority of the leader. Personal relationships are starting to form, both good and bad, and the team needs to be very goal focused otherwise it may become distracted by these internal difficulties.

Stage 3 – Norming. This is a much calmer stage. There is usually clear consensus and agreement and the leader is not challenged so much. Aims and objectives are

clear and team roles and responsibilities are established. Commitment to the team is strong and there is a sense of bonding and unity between team members.

Stage 4 – Performing. This is a crucial stage of team development as it is where the team really begins to work like a well-oiled machine. The team is able to work positively towards its goals and resolve conflict in a positive and constructive way. Team members support each other and look for new and innovative ways to develop.

The fifth stage that Tuckman added is often not seen as part of the main theory but organisational change happens quickly in the public services and teams can be broken up routinely once they have achieved their objectives. Hence, it is important to examine it.

Stage 5 – Adjourning. This is the stage when the team breaks up to move on to new projects. The original team goal has hopefully been achieved and the team is no longer needed. This can cause tremendous insecurity in team members, particularly if they like the team they work in and have formed strong bonds with their colleagues. It is a stage which needs to be dealt with sensitively to ensure that all team members can move on to pastures new with no ill feelings. It allows for team members to be promoted as recognition of their achievement, with some going on to potentially lead teams of their own.

| Forming | → | Storming | → | Norming | → | Performing | → | Adjourning |

Weaknesses

There are many possible barriers to a team's successful performance of a given task. Some of these problems are relatively easy to rectify while some can cause long-term resistance and continual poor performance.

Common barriers include:

- Team members simply don't understand their role or all have similar roles, which leads to disorganisation, conflict and a disjointed team structure.

- Teams can also be affected by being unclear about the exact aims of the task or by a lack of support from the team leader. This could lead to the team lacking focus and wasting valuable time.

- If the team or individual members don't have the appropriate skills or abilities to complete the task, they may refuse to cooperate with the rest of the team. This lack of skills or abilities could be simply down to the fact that they lack prior knowledge or are poorly prepared.

- Poor relationships between certain team members or with the team leader can create barriers to performance and lead to a breakdown in communication along with a non-conducive working environment, especially if the team leader tries to control the group through a dictatorship style approach.

- Little or no recognition can make a team member lose enthusiasm and commitment for future tasks as they may not feel valued. This can lower their self-esteem, especially if others do receive recognition or reward for their participation.

- Barriers can also be created when the team question the credibility of the team leader as this will lead to them having little confidence in the team leader and competition may arise for the team's leadership.

- Further barriers can also be created if certain team members have hidden agendas or individual interests that go against the group ethos.

- Teams that have low standards and little expectation of success, along with no accountability for the team's performance, will create a blame culture. This can lead to conflict or ultimately the group will completely break down.

- Teams that receive and give little or no encouragement to their members, especially when things are tough, can lead to a drop in motivation. Team members will become fragmented and discouraged from performing the task.

- Inconsistent teams can also be problematic as in one task they will work well together and in the next task they will not perform. This could be due to the nature of the task – the team may perform well in a task that involves a mental challenge but, due to a lack of overall fitness, they may perform poorly or choose not to take part in a physical challenge.

Finally there are some factors that can affect the team's performance that are purely out of their control. These include:

- A lack of adequate resources to complete the task (which may be down to financial constraints) leading to having no resources at all, poorly qualified staff or substandard equipment.

- The environment and facilities can also affect team performance, especially when attempting outdoor tasks, as bad weather or poor conditions can make the task more challenging and test the group's resolve.

When building a team it is important to take into account the sensitivities of the people involved, perhaps consider what might offend them or upset them and be aware that if you are building a team your role as leader is to support all team members.

Activity: Teambuilding in your service

Conduct some independent research on the service you would like to join. What kinds of teambuilding activities do they use?

5.4 Team performance

Team performance hinges around measuring how well a team meets its aims and objectives. This can be measured in different ways.

Performance indicators

These are a set of figures designed to measure the extent to which performance objectives and agreed targets are being met on an ongoing basis.

Performance indicators in the public services can be things such as:

- customer satisfaction ratings
- emergency response times
- crime statistics
- measurement against the performance of other similar services.

Performance indicators for teams are usually set around a specific theme. For example, for a police team it might be the reduction of incidents of antisocial behaviour by 10 per cent in a six-month period or for a healthcare team it might be to reduce incidences of infection in patients by 35 per cent in a three month period. Although the performance indicators will vary from service to service, what they have in common is that the indicators will follow a SMART target setting process. SMART targets are:

Specific – clear and direct, they say exactly what a team is going to achieve

Measurable – so that the team knows when they have been achieved

Achievable – they can be reached in a realistic timescale

Realistic – they are genuinely in the team's control and they can actually take action on them

Time-related – there are clear deadlines for completion.

Activity: Achieving targets

Do you use SMART targets yourself? Do you think they might help you plan your college work and time? Set yourself some SMART targets to achieve your qualification goals.

Target setting

The process of target setting is very important if teams are going to achieve their goals. If you don't know what a target is, how can you plan your time and resources to make sure you achieve it? Sometimes public service targets are set independently of the service, for example at central government level and sometimes services can set their own targets. Performance is then measured against the achievement of these set targets.

Monitoring

Team performance in the public services is monitored in exactly the same way as described above with the use of performance indicators and target setting. Services will also use benchmarks, which are national performance indicators that inform the public and other services how well a similar service is performing. For example, there are 43 police constabularies in England and Wales, each of which will be able to compare itself against the performance of the other 42 to indicate how well or poorly it is performing compared to the national average. In reality, these statistics do not take into account the particular circumstances of a constabulary, for example, the Metropolitan Police Service may deal with far more violent crime than a predominantly rural police service such as Devon and Cornwall. This doesn't mean that the rural police service is better because they have less crime, it just means that they are policing in very different circumstances.

Review

Reviewing your team's performance is an important part of team development and is particularly valuable if you are going to work again as a team. A review is a considered analysis of the team's performance against the set targets and an assessment of the reasons for success or failure from which lessons can be learned for next time.

5.5 Evaluation of team performance in the services and the support and development of team members

Often when a task is being attempted, everyone will make observations about what is going well and how things could be better, but most of the time they will not reflect and discuss these issues together as a team.

It is important to **evaluate** as it helps the team to remember the goals initially set and determine whether they have been achieved. It also helps the team to praise each other and celebrate success, along with identifying any problems or weaknesses that could be rectified in future tasks.

Evaluating is an effective way of gathering information as a team, which can then be used to set group boundaries, devise improvement strategies and identify individual development issues. Individuals can acknowledge the benefits of teamwork, reflect on their own performance, plan for future development and make adjustments to how they work and interact within a future group situation. It also helps team leaders support and develop the skills and abilities of team members.

Key term

Evaluation A process used to gather information to determine whether or not the team has been successful and achievement of its aims has occurred.

Case study: Evaluating individual performance

The use of appraisal is widespread among the public services. It is an organisational version of a personal action plan that is usually conducted by your immediate line manager. In general it follows the following structure:

Identify strengths and weaknesses

Ensure that the role you fulfil makes use of your identified strengths

Identify how your weaknesses could be overcome by training

Kerry is a new recruit to the Fire Service. In the 12 months she has served so far she doesn't feel she

has made a major impact on the role and feels that male recruits who started at the same time as her have adapted better to their role. She is concerned that her team leader thinks very little of her and this is causing Kerry to lose confidence in her abilities and make mistakes while on duty. The ongoing training and physical demands of the job are causing Kerry a great deal of distress and she believes she is falling further and further behind the other new recruits. Kerry is due to have an appraisal shortly and she wants to make the most of it to improve her performance and rebuild her confidence.

1 How should Kerry prepare for her appraisal?

2 What questions should she ask during her appraisal?

3 What support should she ask for?

4 What type of feedback is she likely to encounter with regard to aspects of her job performance?

5 What could she do to help improve her performance after the appraisal?

Group evaluation in the public services

Group evaluations can be more complex as they involve multiple individuals and different teams from different agencies. They usually try to evaluate a project or an incident to see what can be learnt for next time from the experience the team has just had. For example, in the aftermath of a major incident, many questions are likely to be asked about what the causes were and how such events could be avoided in the future.

The public services go through a similar procedure, questioning and evaluating their own performance and the effectiveness of their major incident plan. This procedure is called a debrief, which has already been discussed in detail on page 49, and it provides all of the organisations and agencies involved with an opportunity to discuss and comment on various aspects of the combined response and the overall operation. Debriefings do not just happen as a result of major incidents – the services use them routinely to evaluate group performance at any level.

Assessment activity 2.6

P6 M4 D3 BTEC

This is another practical activity designed to help you improve your teamwork skills and improve upon them if necessary. Your tutor will organise a series of team activities for you which will enable you to address the following tasks:

1 Participate in team activities P6

2 Appraise own performance in team activities M4

3 Evaluate team members' performance in team activities D3

Grading tips

Participating in and being confident in your team activities is likely to gain you P6 and M4. In order to achieve D3 be ready to discuss with your tutor the strengths and weaknesses in your own performance and draw up and consider an action plan to address the weaknesses.

5.6 Team cohesion

Team cohesion is the process of team bonding. It is what makes a team stick together and achieve their goals even when everyone is tired, under pressure or experiencing difficulties and challenges. There are many aspects to promoting a strong team bond and some of these are outlined in Table 2.9.

PLTS

Completing this assessment will help you develop your teamworking skills.

Team cohesion has several key factors to it.

- defining team goals
- resolving conflict
- group turnover
- opportunities for career progression
- recognition of contributions.

Table 2.9: The features that encourage team cohesion.

Feature	Description
Clear vision and team understanding	The team needs a clear idea of why it exists, what it is there for and how it is intended to work together. Without this knowledge the team is aimless and will find it harder to bond.
Clear goals	The team must have SMART targets which it can strive to achieve in unity but each team member should have individual targets too. This ensures all team members pull their weight and contribute equally to team performance.
Role satisfaction	In order to promote team cohesion, team members must have satisfaction in their role and feel valued and needed within the team. Roles should be clear or this can harm team bonding.
Positive work environment	The work environment should be positive and happy. Working in teams can require a keen sense of humour and there should be opportunities for socialising and laughter. Some teams also respond well to having a unique identity within a larger organisation. Again this can help the team to bond.
Positive and cooperative relationships	Team members need to trust and rely on each other. Personal respect and trust can promote team cohesion more than anything else. If the members of a team genuinely like each other, they will perform better as there is likely to be less conflict.

Definition of team goals

As has already been discussed a team must have clear goals if it is to succeed. The Apollo Syndrome case study on page 63 indicates what can happen if a team do not work with each other in a cohesive way.

Group conflict (actual/potential)

Conflict is unavoidable in any team. This might be conflict about choosing goals, achieving aims or other work related issues. Some conflicts are inter-personal and are based on a clash of personalities. The important thing to remember is that conflict is not necessarily a bad thing. Conflict can be a tremendous help to a group as it can challenge old ideas and bring forward new and innovative ones. Conflict is not necessarily a challenge to a leader's authority or group cohesion - resolving conflict well can often lead to a stronger more unified team. And it is always better to resolve conflict where you can rather than leaving it to simmer under the surface and harm team and individual performance. Resolving conflict positively can have several benefits for teams including:

- *An increased understanding of other team members* – resolving the conflict through constructive discussion can help to improve an individual's awareness of the points of view and needs of other team members. It can help an individual to know how to achieve their own goal without undermining the goals of others or harming overall team performance.
- *Improved team cohesion* – if conflict is resolved constructively and successfully it can strengthen the team. Individuals can develop more respect for other team members and have more faith in the team's ability to work together as a whole.
- *Increased self-awareness* – conflict can be very challenging and, at times, upsetting. However, it can also make people explore their own motivation and help them to understand why they behave in certain ways that might create a poor impression.

Group turnover

People can and do move in and out of teams and groups. Low group turnover can be good for team cohesion as members have time to get to know each others capabilities and ways of operating, however new members can bring in fresh ideas an perspectives that established team members may not have considered.

Opportunities for career progression and recognising contributions

Team cohesion can also be helped if there are opportunities for career progression involved. People often work well together when there is a potential or actual reward such as a promotion on offer in the future. However team cohesion can also be aided by something as simple as the team leader recognising and appreciating the individual contributions of the team members. No one likes to think their hard work goes unnoticed and by using praise and appreciation a team leader can often motivate and improve a teams performance.

Assessment activity 2.7

Understanding how teambuilding works and how team cohesion can be maintained will make you a better leader when you join the service of your choice. In a written report address the following tasks:

1 Explain how teambuilding leads to team cohesion in the public services with reference to relevant theorists **P7**

2 Analyse the impact of good and poor team cohesion on a public service, with reference to relevant theorists **M5**

Grading tips

Using the theories of Honey, Belbin and Tuckman consider how teambuilding promotes an effective and cohesive team and then assess the impact that good and bad team cohesion might have on the performance of a service or team within a service.

I always wanted to be a police officer. I think it was the idea of giving something back to the community and helping to make people lives better by helping to get rid of crime.

It sounds idealistic now, but the truth is that's still why I do the job of a police officer after 10 years in the service.

A typical day

My current role as Police Sergeant means that each day is so different and I don't ever have a typical day. Generally I will be involved in supervising a safer neighbourhood team who respond to the concerns of citizens in the area where I am posted. This could be anything from antisocial behaviour to serial burglaries to nuisance neighbours.

I often have to meet with local councillors and other public service agencies to try and come up with solutions to the problems the area has. I also go out on patrol with the team to see first hand what the issues are.

The best thing about the job

The best thing about the job for me is seeing the difference my team makes on the lives of people in the community by reducing crime and the fear of crime. As a Sergeant you also get a different perspective from the average Police Constable as you get to see a wider picture and have some say in how issues can be tackled.

Think about it!

What topics have you covered in this unit that might give you the background to work in a team or as a leader?

What knowledge and skills do you think you need to develop further if you want to be involved in teamwork and leadership in the future?

Just checking

1 Identify four different leadership styles.
2 When might a bureaucratic leadership style be used in the public services?
3 Why is non-verbal communication important?
4 Define the terms brief and debrief.
5 Why is time management important to a team leader?
6 Why is personal organisation important in the public services?
7 List the types of teams you might encounter in the uniformed public services.
8 What are the benefits of teams?
9 Briefly describe Belbin's team roles.
10 Briefly describe Tuckman's five stages of team development.

edexcel

Assignment tips

- This unit had a large practical element and involves lots of teamwork and leadership activities. Don't be worried about this, even if your teamwork and leadership is not very strong the whole point of doing the unit is to improve your abilities. One of the best things you can do is make sure you take part in some regular teamwork or leadership activities such as a team sport or join the cadets of a particular service. This will enable you to constantly practise your teamwork and leadership skills.

- This may sound very basic, but make sure you have read your assignment thoroughly and you understand exactly what you are being asked to do. Once you are clear about this then you can move on to your research. Doing your research well and using good sources of evidence is essential. Lots of students rely too much on the internet and not enough on other sources of information such as books, newspapers and journals. Always double check the information you find, don't just accept it at face value. Good research and preparation is the key to getting those higher grades.

Credit value: 10

3 Citizenship, diversity and the public services

Citizenship and diversity have become important concepts in the public services over the last 20 years. This unit aims to examine these issues in detail so that you are better informed when you begin your public service career.

It is important that you are fully aware of the rights that citizenship gives to an individual and the impact that these rights might have on the public services called upon to protect them, but who may also potentially breach these rights in the course of their duties. In this unit, you will examine what a 'good' citizen is, the personal qualities they might have and the activities they might undertake. You will look at the benefits of good citizenship to the public services and to society as a whole.

This unit will also focus on concepts of diversity and will promote respect for equality throughout. This will be done by examining legislation in place to prevent discrimination and promote human rights, and by exploring strategies used in the public services to combat discrimination. You will define the key terms in the field of diversity and understand how the public services enforce equal opportunities legislation.

One of the most important aspects of this unit is assessing how the media and current affairs can affect the work of the public services. This includes how the media portray the services, and the impact of national and international events such as terrorism and natural disasters on the public services.

Learning outcomes

After completing this unit you should:

1. understand the meanings and benefits of citizenship and diversity
2. know the legal and human rights that protect citizens and promote diversity
3. understand the role of public services in enforcing diversity and providing equality of service
4. be able to investigate current affairs, media and support.

Assessment and grading criteria

This table shows you what you must do in order to achieve a **pass**, **merit** or **distinction** grade, and where you can find activities in this book to help you.

To achieve a **pass** grade the evidence must show that the learner is able to:	To achieve a **merit** grade the evidence must show that, in addition to the pass criteria, the learner is able to:	To achieve a **distinction** grade the evidence must show that, in addition to the pass and merit criteria, the learner is able to:
P1 explain the range of meanings attached to citizenship, diversity and the associated terminology **See Assessment activity 3.1 page 88**		
P2 discuss the key concepts associated with diversity **See Assessment activity 3.2 page 91**	**M1** analyse the importance to public services of good citizens in respecting equality and supporting them by respecting the key concepts associated with diversity **See Assessment activity 3.3 page 93**	**D1** evaluate the role of good citizens in supporting the public services in dealing with issues of equality and diversity **See Assessment activity 3.3 page 93**
P3 assess the benefits of good citizens to public services and society in respecting equality **See Assessment activity 3.3 page 93**		
P4 describe the legal and human rights that protect citizens in the UK **See Assessment activity 3.4 page 98**	**M2** analyse the effectiveness of legal and humanitarian measures to protect citizens in the UK **See Assessment activity 3.4 page 98**	
P5 review the methods used by public services to ensure they have a diverse workforce **See Assessment activity 3.5 page 100**	**M3** analyse the effectiveness of the methods used by public services to promote equality and diversity in society and within the service **See Assessment activity 3.5 page 100**	**D2** evaluate the effectiveness of the methods used by public services to promote equality and diversity in society and within the service **See Assessment activity 3.5 page 100**
P6 explain the duty of the public services to provide equality of service to all citizens **See Assessment activity 3.6 page 101**		
P7 report on three examples of current affairs that affect public services and citizens **See Assessment activity 3.7 page 107**	**M4** analyse the effects on citizens and public services of the way that three current affairs examples have been reported by the media **See Assessment activity 3.7 page 107**	**D3** evaluate the impact that media reporting has on citizens and on the level of support from public services in relation to examples of current affairs **See Assessment activity 3.7 page 107**
P8 present information on how the media reports current affairs involving public services **See Assessment activity 3.7 page 107**		
P9 demonstrate how support is provided to citizens by statutory and non-statutory public services **See Assessment activity 3.8 page 108**	**M5** justify the involvement of statutory and non-statutory public services in providing support to citizens **See Assessment activity 3.8 page 108**	

How you will be assessed

This unit will be assessed by an internal assignment that will be designed and marked by the staff at your centre. The assignment is designed to allow you to show your understanding of the learning outcomes for citizenship, diversity and the public services. These relate to what you should be able to do after completing this unit.

Assessments can be quite varied and can take the form of:

- reports
- leaflets
- presentations
- posters
- practical tasks
- case studies
- discussions.

Laura examines her own prejudices

This was a really big unit, and I was a bit worried at first that I wouldn't be able to understand all the different parts of citizenship and diversity that we had to cover. It actually turned out to be really interesting and when I'm interested in something I tend to get better grades in it.

The most interesting part for me was learning all the different terms that can be used about the issue of diversity. I think it can be really difficult to know what terms to use and in what situation, but I feel far better informed now. I also really liked learning about the different pieces of legislation that exist to protect people's rights in society and how the public services address this legislation.

One of the most difficult things for me was examining my own prejudices. I hadn't realised how much my views on equality and diversity were picked up from people around me and sometimes from what I had seen on the telly. It's quite hard to admit you have prejudices, but this unit helped me examine them and realise that some of my views weren't actually based on any evidence other than personal opinion, and judging people on that basis is really wrong.

I feel much better equipped to deal with a public service recruitment procedure now, and as a result of this unit I feel I am more open minded and appreciative of the differences between people.

Over to you!

- What areas of citizenship and diversity might you find interesting?
- Have you ever been involved with discrimination and rights issues before?
- Do you have strong opinions on current affairs?
- What preparation could you do to get ready for your assessments?

1. The meaning and benefits of citizenship and diversity

Thinking about citizenship and diversity

- The public services are dynamic and changing organisations. New government initiatives, national and international issues, and pressure groups can all affect the way they are allowed to operate and conduct their operational role. When you go for a public services interview they will expect you to be aware of the current issues of importance not only to them, but to society as a whole. Understanding the issues and problems they face will help you start your career.

- Therefore, it is important to keep up to date with national and international current affairs and issues of diversity if you are to be successful in a public service interview. One of the best ways of doing this is to read a broadsheet newspaper such as *The Times* or *Guardian* at least once a week and more often if you can. Try to make a point of doing this throughout your study of this unit – you will be surprised at how many other units you are studying will benefit from your reading as well.

Citizenship and diversity are concerned with many issues that are important to the public services and society today. They involve questioning rather than accepting your role in society and trying to understand complex topics such as:

- your role as a citizen
- your influence on society and how much power you have to change things
- what is going on in society and how it will affect you personally and in your professional life
- what makes a good citizen and how citizenship benefits society
- why equality is important
- how we can make sure all people have equal access to opportunities.

Citizenship and diversity is concerned with debates, discussions, evaluation of evidence and examining your own views and opinions. It will make you more socially and politically aware, a vital quality in any potential public service recruit and one you should be actively seeking to develop.

1.1 Citizenship

There are lots of different ways of defining what a citizen is; generally speaking a citizen is someone who is a member of a political community or state such as a country like the UK. There are several key aspects that might make you a citizen depending on the country or state you live in, such as:

- your place of birth
- your family background
- where you live
- whether you are a taxpayer
- whether you are eligible to vote in elections
- whether you work
- whether you are a student
- what community activities you take part in
- what organisations you are a member of.

Not everyone who lives in a country can be a legal citizen of that country and not even everyone who is born in a country can be a citizen of it since their parents may not be from that country.

There is not a great deal of debate about legal requirements in this context because they are created by parliament and are relatively fixed and static, but the moral and political definitions of citizenship are constantly changing and developing as our society evolves and changes.

Definition of citizen and citizenship

Government initiatives to define moral and political citizenship have focused around three main elements, described as follows.

Social and moral responsibility. This is the development of behaviour that is respectful towards others including peers and those in authority. It also includes the understanding of the concept of civic duty – this is the fact that you have a responsibility towards the people in your community and they have a responsibility towards you, to ensure that all community members can live safe and productive lives, helping and supporting each other. It could include acts such as checking on the welfare of elderly neighbours, or reporting a crime that you witnessed against a community member's property. It is about treating others as you would wish to be treated by them.

A citizenship ceremony. What are some of the requirements for legal UK citizenship?

Did you know?

Some children of armed service personnel are born abroad while their parents are posted overseas. If they were born at a British Army base in Germany they would not automatically become German; they would take their nationality from their British parents and become British citizens.

There are two ways of looking at the term 'citizen'. The most common way is being a 'legal citizen' – this is when you have all the requirements to claim nationality in a particular country and have the right to live there. For example, one of the ways to become a British citizen is if one of your parents is a British citizen. Another example is if a person has lived in Britain for the first 10 years of their life. Not just anyone can become a British citizen – there are clear rules about who can live permanently in the UK and who cannot.

Another way of looking at what the term 'citizen' means is being a 'moral and political citizen'. This is about how a person should behave in their communities and society in general. In this definition being a citizen refers to behaviour that is respectful and helpful to the community; this could include things such as checking in on elderly neighbours, picking up litter, volunteering for charity work or becoming involved in local politics.

Social and moral responsibility

Citizenship

Political literacy

Community

Figure 3.1: The three main elements of citizenship.

Community involvement. This is about taking an active interest in your community, and becoming involved with the life and concerns of your neighbourhood through giving service to it. This could mean things like volunteering in your area, taking part in community initiatives like Neighbourhood Watch or becoming involved in environmental issues that may have an impact on your community.

Political literacy. This means understanding the political life of society locally, regionally and nationally. It involves knowing about the way local and national governments work, and being clear on the role you can play in democracy in terms of participation in political issues and encouraging social change that might benefit your community. This may involve speaking to your local MP or councillors about a variety of issues or it may involve you becoming politically active yourself; at the very least it involves understanding how your vote in an election works and why it is important to use it.

Moral and political definitions of citizen and citizenship centre around the responsibility you feel towards other people and your community as a whole. This is about becoming involved in public affairs and taking part in the life of your community with the hope of improving it for everyone. It is also about knowing your rights as a citizen and making sure you live up to your responsibilities.

Although citizenship in a strictly legal sense for this unit applies only to the UK, it should be apparent that social and moral citizenship is not restricted by geographical borders. With the increase in sophistication in communications technology such as the media, the internet, social networking and online gaming, it is possible to be a citizen of a much broader social world than ever before. Increasingly, we are seeing concepts such as global or environmental citizenship develop, which place a duty on the individual to behave in a way that benefits others right across the globe. This could include recycling, reducing energy usage or campaigning against human rights violations in other parts of the world.

Legal view of citizenship

The UK Border Agency has clear guidelines on how you can become a British citizen; most countries have their own very strict set of rules about who can and who cannot become a citizen. British citizens have the right to live in the UK permanently and can leave the country and re-enter at anytime. The six types of British citizenship are described in Table 3.1.

Table 3.1: Types of British citizenship.

Type	Details
British citizen	People who gained British nationality because they are connected with the UK, i.e. • being born in the UK • their parents were British citizens • they have registered to be a British citizen • they have applied to become a British citizen This is the only group of people who have the right to live permanently in the UK and enjoy freedom of movement throughout the EU. This is called the *Right of Abode*
British Dependent Territories citizens (BDTC)	People who live in dependent British colonies, e.g. • Gibraltar • British Virgin Islands These are territories that the UK still has responsibility for
British Overseas citizens (BOC)	These are groups of people who have a connection with the UK because they lived in a former British colony that is now independent
British Nationals (Overseas) (BNO)	People from Hong Kong were given the chance to acquire this status as many were unhappy at the thought of losing British nationality when Hong Kong was returned to China in 1997
British Protected Persons (BPP)	Individuals who had a connection with a former British Protectorate. This is an overseas territory that Britain used to protect, such as the country of Brunei
British Subjects	Individuals who were British subjects under the 1948 British Nationality Act were allowed to keep their status under the 1981 act. Applies mainly to citizens of Eire and India which had very strong links to the UK

Case study: Gurkhas' right to live in the UK

The Gurkhas are Nepalese soldiers who are recruited into the British Army from their home country of Nepal. They have fought with the British Army for almost 200 years and are considered to be an elite fighting force, having shown bravery, heroism and dedication to the UK in every conflict we have engaged in since Victorian times. They make up about 3 per cent of the army's total strength and 8 per cent of its infantry.

Gurkhas who retired before 1 July 1997 were not allowed to settle in the UK even if they had been wounded or disabled in battle. They had to resettle in Nepal regardless of how many years' service they had given to the UK.

This was widely considered to be unfair and, after a public campaign backed by several newspapers and celebrities, the Home Secretary agreed to change the rules in May 2009 to allow retired Gurkhas and their families the right to live and settle in the UK as long as they had given at least four years' service.

1 Why do you think the public considered it unfair that Gurkhas were not allowed to live in the UK after they retired?

2 Do you think Gurkhas show the qualities of a good citizen?

3 Do you think it is beneficial for the UK to have former Gurkhas living and working here? Explain your answer.

Did you know?

That people who are successful in becoming British citizens have to take part in a citizenship ceremony. They are required to take an oath or an affirmation of allegiance and make a pledge of loyalty to the United Kingdom.

Oath of allegiance

I (name) swear by Almighty God that on becoming a British citizen, I will be faithful and bear true allegiance to Her Majesty Queen Elizabeth the Second, her Heirs and Successors, according to law.

Affirmation of allegiance (used when people do not want to swear by God)

I (name) do solemnly, sincerely and truly declare and affirm that on becoming a British citizen, I will be faithful and bear true allegiance to Her Majesty Queen Elizabeth the Second, her Heirs and Successors, according to law.

Pledge

I will give my loyalty to the United Kingdom and respect its rights and freedoms. I will uphold its democratic values. I will observe its laws faithfully and fulfil my duties and obligations as a British citizen.

If you do not fall into one of the categories above – for example you may have settled here because of work or as an asylum seeker – you can still apply for British citizenship. There are two main ways to do this: registration and naturalisation.

Registration. This is a way of becoming a British citizen if you already have some connection with the UK, such as being a British Overseas citizen or a British Protected Person. You can also register if you have previously given up British citizenship and want to have it back.

Naturalisation. Individuals who have no connection with the UK, including people from Ireland and the Commonwealth nations, must apply for a certificate of naturalisation. In order to qualify for a certificate, you must have lived legally in the United Kingdom for five years and

- be 18 or over
- be of sound mind
- be of good character
- have sufficient knowledge of English, Welsh or Scottish Gaelic
- stay closely connected with the United Kingdom.

Also, you can apply for naturalisation if you are married to a British citizen and have lived in the UK for three years.

Activity: Naturalisation

Why do you think there is a three-year wait for naturalisation if you are married to a British citizen? What do you think might be the implications if you automatically became a British citizen when you married one?

Activity: Armed service views of citizenship

Contact your local armed services information and recruitment office. They often have a presentation team who will come to your school or college to discuss what citizenship means to them. They may also have leaflets, posters and other information that will help you establish how the armed services see citizenship.

Public service view of citizenship

The public services define moral and political citizenship in much the same way as everyone else does but different aspects of citizenship are important to specific public services, such as diplomacy to the BTP. Usually, these definitions revolve around:

- community involvement
- taking responsibility for the safety of others
- taking responsibility for the safety of the environment
- a commitment to continually develop life skills
- a positive attitude that welcomes challenges

- respect for equality and diversity
- an interest in wider society
- a commitment to making society a better place for all citizens.

Although the armed services and emergency services perform different tasks in society, their definitions of citizenship are very similar. All of them require active citizens to fulfil the above criteria; it is important that

Case study: British Transport Police (BTP)

The BTP has responsibility for policing Britain's railway infrastructure. They deal with well over 100,000 offences each year, including all major crimes, such as murder and rape, and minor crimes such as graffiti and theft. The BTP also deals with specific railway issues such as trains being obstructed, the transport of sports fans and issues of managing safety on tracks and at stations. The force has over 2800 officers and almost 1500 support staff in seven operational areas. The key citizenship qualities they look for in potential recruits are:

- diplomacy
- respect for diversity
- decisiveness
- flexibility
- versatility
- determination
- personal responsibility and discretion
- good communication skills
- excellent interpersonal skills
- teamwork
- good sense and balanced judgement
- personal responsibility.

1 How do you think the BTP would describe citizenship based on the information given above?

2 How could you improve your citizenship skills if you wanted a career in the BTP?

3 How would the skills listed above make you an asset to your community and to a service?

4 Are good citizenship skills the same as having good interpersonal and leadership skills? Explain your answer.

the services set a good example of citizenship to civilians due to the power and influence they have. Many young people aspire to join a uniformed service and competition for a career can be fierce, so you must remember that you will have a much better chance of being recruited if you are an active citizen.

Members of public services often have to deal with situations that are challenging, dangerous and emotionally draining, and although they receive training to help them deal with difficult situations they must be able to demonstrate many key citizenship qualities in order to be considered suitable for entry in the first place. These key qualities underpin the training they receive, making it more effective. So what citizenship qualities do the public services look for?

Case study: Citizenship in the Fire and Rescue Service

The Fire and Rescue Service has a wide remit, including emergency response to fires, responding to other emergency situations that threaten life or property, inspection/safety matters and fire prevention education. For the varied and demanding role of a firefighter, good citizenship skills are naturally very important. They look for qualities in potential recruits such as:

- teamwork
- communication skills
- community involvement
- reliability
- flexibility
- ability to act quickly.

Firefighters go to work every day with the knowledge that they may be required to compromise their own safety to ensure the safety of others. The mark of a good/active citizen is that they are prepared to compromise their own needs for the greater good of the society or community they live in; firefighters do this on every shift they work.

1 Why are good citizenship qualities important to the role of firefighter?

2 How do you think the Fire Service would describe citizenship based on the roles they fulfil?

3 Do you think you have the necessary citizenship skills to become a firefighter? Justify your answer.

4 How do the qualities of a good firefighter differ from those of a good citizen?

Activity: Citizenship, the BTP and the F&RS

Now you have completed the case studies, consider why the BTP focuses on diplomacy and respect for diversity more than the F&RS. Are there any other differences between the requirements for these two services?

Qualities of good citizens

A good citizen will have many qualities that are desired by the public services in their new recruits. Some of the most common ones are described in Table 3.2.

Table 3.2: Qualities of good citizens.

Qualities	Explanation
Responsibility	A good citizen takes personal responsibility to improve the community in which they live. They don't complain about litter or how poor their local council might be; they get up and go and move the litter themselves or organise a group of people to work with them to achieve the task. Good citizens see themselves as responsible for changing things for the better; they do not wait for someone else to do it for them
Dedication	Good citizens don't give up on tasks; they persevere until change is achieved. They are dedicated to the task at hand and set themselves on a course of action that they are prepared to see through
Positive attitudes to other people	Good citizens have a positive attitude to others in their community. They are helpful, respectful, considerate and non-judgemental. They are not racist or homophobic; they welcome diversity as enriching a society and don't judge people by their colour, age or religion
Participation in community activities	A good citizen participates fully in community activities such as Neighbourhood Watch, community fund raising and environmental campaigns
Awareness of the needs of others	Good citizens have an awareness that we are not all the same and that some people need more support than others in contributing to a community because of issues such as poverty, language or disability. They are aware of and sensitive to these issues to help provide a supportive, inclusive community which values all its members

1.2 Diversity

In general terms, diversity describes the range of visible and non-visible differences that exist between people. These differences include gender, skin colour, hair type, sexuality, religion and disability. The human race is very diverse – we are all different from each other. The key to understanding diversity is to value these differences rather than discriminate against them.

The public services value diversity, as a diverse workforce brings with it additional skills and strengths that can help when dealing with local and national communities, and even overseas conflict situations, such as:

- additional languages
- cultural knowledge
- religious knowledge.

So for the services diversity is more than just identifying the differences between officers, who are recruits of the community. It is about valuing those differences as a way to make the service more efficient, effective and responsive to the needs of the diverse public they serve.

Activity: Derbyshire Police Force

Consider the following section of the Derbyshire Constabulary diversity statement:

Diversity Statement

The force aims to be an open, attractive and diverse employer. It seeks to recognise, value and embrace the differences of all its employees; through these differences, we become a more pro-active organisation, recognising issues before they become problems and reflecting the wide and varied experience of different communities and individuals in our decision-making.

1 Why do the public services value diversity?
2 How does the Derbyshire Constabulary benefit from valuing diversity?

Composition of local and national communities

The UK of the twenty-first century is a modern dynamic environment in which the public services must be equipped to deal with a variety of faiths, beliefs, religions and cultures, not only in their official capacity in dealing with the public but also as employers who must comply with the law and should have the best interests of their employees at heart.

It is vitally important that the religious, ethnic, gender and age diversity in the UK is understood and appreciated by the public services as it can have a tremendous impact on their day-to-day operation. An understanding of diversity in all its forms will help the public services address cultural issues which may cause conflict and misunderstanding in society at large and damage the relationship between the services and the public.

National statistics are gathered from the whole country once every 10 years in the National Census. The last National Census was conducted in 2001 and the next is due in March 2011. It shows the statistical breakdown of the nation as a whole on the basis of factors such as ethnic group, religion, gender, age and a whole host of other issues.

As you can see, in 2001 the overall population of the UK was just short of 60 million, and the overall population from an ethnic minority was 4.6 million. This means that only 7.9 per cent of the UK population was from an ethnic minority in 2001, leaving the UK 92.1 per cent White.

Of the ethnic groups that make up the 7.9 per cent, four main ones are represented strongly. Those who described themselves of mixed ethnicity made up 14.6 per cent of all ethnic minorities, the Asian population made up 50.3 per cent, Black citizens made up 24.8 per cent and the Chinese population made up just over 5 per cent.

There is sometimes a view held by the media and some political parties that the UK takes in too many people from ethnic minorities and that the White UK population is in danger of being swamped by immigrants. The actual data shows that in 2001 the UK was over 92 per cent White.

Ethnicity

Table 3.3: The UK population by ethnic group, 2001.

United Kingdom	Total population		Non-White population (Percentages)
	(Numbers)	(Percentages)	
White	**54,153,898**	**92.1**	–
Mixed	**677,117**	**1.2**	**14.6**
Indian	1,053,411	1.8	22.7
Pakistani	747,285	1.3	16.1
Bangladeshi	283,063	0.5	6.1
Other Asian	247,664	0.4	5.3
All Asian or Asian British	**2,331,423**	**4.0**	**50.3**
Black Caribbean	565,876	1.0	12.2
Black African	485,277	0.8	10.5
Black Other	97,585	0.2	2.1
All Black or Black British	**1,148,738**	**2.0**	**24.8**
Chinese	**247,403**	**0.4**	**5.3**
Other ethnic groups	**230,615**	**0.4**	**5.0**
All minority ethnic population	**4,635,296**	**7.9**	**100.0**
All population	**58,789,194**	**100.0**	

Religion

The 2001 National Census data indicated that there were 37.3 million people in England and Wales stating they are Christian, making Christianity by far the most popular religion in the country, with well over 50 per cent of the population. The statistics for other religions are as follows:

Muslim	3.1%
Hindu	1.1%
Sikh	0.7%
Jewish	0.5%
Buddhist	0.3%
No religion	14.6%

Did you know?

The 2001 census gave the option of choosing 'other religion': 390,000 chose 'Jedi' from the Star Wars films as a religion, which is almost 0.8 per cent of the population. This makes the number of people saying they were Jedi followers more numerous than every other religion, apart from Christianity, Islam and Hinduism.

Age and gender

According to the Census results, the total population of England and Wales in 2001 was just over 52 million, split into 49% male and 51% female. The age breakdown was as follows:

0–15	20%
16–17	3%
18–24	8%
25–59	48%
60–64	5%
65–74	8%
75+	8%

However, as you will read later in the unit (see page 103), the average age of the UK population is getting older and this could have serious implications for the public services.

Activity: Your community

Using the Office of National Statistics website or the website of your local authority, find out the range of diversity in your local community. Gather statistics on:

- gender
- ethnicity
- age
- religion.

What does your research tell you about your local area? How can the public services benefit from the diversity in your community and how can they ensure they meet the needs of all members of the community?

What was the population of the UK at the beginning of the twentieth century?

Terminology

In order to understand issues of diversity, it is important to be aware of the key terminology you may come across while researching the issues. Table 3.4 provides a brief description of some of the terms.

Table 3.4: Key terminology for diversity issues.

Term	Meaning
Racism / Racist	Race is the separation of the human population into groups based on their inherited visible characteristics such as skin colour, hair texture and facial features. Racism is the belief that one of these groups of people with different characteristics is better than or superior to another group. A racist is someone who allows their belief that one racial group is superior to another to negatively influence the way they behave and act towards the other racial groupings
Institutional racism	Institutional racism happens in organisations and businesses such as the public services, universities, charities or privately owned companies. It occurs when the organisation fails to deliver a high quality and professional service to a person or group of people based on their colour, culture, religion or ethnic origin. Institutional racism can be built into the structure of an organisation, for instance if the organisation only places recruitment advertisements in newspapers that are rarely read by ethnic minorities. This term has had a large impact on UK public services since the release of the Macpherson Report in 1999 which dealt with the Metropolitan Police's investigation into the murder of Stephen Lawrence. The report accused the Met of institutional racism in the service they provided to Stephen's family
Multiculturalism	Multiculturalism is the presence and acceptance of a variety of different ethnic or religious cultures withiin a community or society. The idea of multiculturalism is that all cultures are equal in a society and no one culture should be promoted as the central or primary culture
Ethnocentricity	This is a belief that your own ethnic or cultural group is central to society and all other groups are judged in relation to yours. It is a very inward way of looking, which focuses on a person's own culture at the expense of others
Sexism	Sexism is a form of discrimination based on gender. It can mean that women may be treated less favourably in the job market, politically or socially because they are female. It is important to understand that the term does not exclusive apply to females only; sexism can also affect men and individuals who are transgender, if they are discriminated against based on their gender
Heterosexist	You may not have heard this term before. It means to believe that heterosexual relationships (i.e. relationships between members of the opposite sexes) are superior to homosexual relationships, or it can even be the assumption you make when you meet people that they are heterosexual
Homophobia	Homophobia is the fear of or feeling of hatred towards individuals who are homosexual (i.e. have relationships with members of the same sex) such as gay men or lesbians. Homophobia can be linked to violent attacks and abuse of lesbians and gay men
Equal opportunities	Equal opportunities can be difficult to define, but generally speaking it is the principle that everyone has the right to live their lives free of discrimination. This usually means two things: firstly that people have equality of opportunity, so all are presented with the same options in a workplace, social setting or educational environment, regardless of gender, ethnic background, religion, sexual orientation, disability, age, marital status, social position, nationality, politics, etc.; and secondly that success in these settings is not influenced by any such factors. The key indicator of success for anyone should be how hard they work, what they know and their personal abilities, not the colour of their skin or their sexuality
Equality	Equality when simply defined means people having the same value as each other; no one human being or group of human beings are more important than any other group. When you start to value one group over and above another group it creates inequality
Prejudice	Prejudice means to hold a strong negative or positive belief about an issue or person based on stereotyping. It can be a way of dehumanising others who are different from ourselves, and it can happen in two ways. Intentional prejudice is where a person deliberately engages in discriminatory and prejudicial activities and behaviour. An example is using racist language or attacking a member of an ethnic minority, or deliberately choosing not to employ them based on the colour of their skin
Unintentional prejudice occurs when the individual does not even realise that they are being prejudiced, and may sincerely deny it if challenged.
Prejudice can also be overt (open) or covert (hidden). Openly making statements that members of a particular group all have some bad quality is overt prejudice. Secretly rejecting all job applications that come from people with names typical of ethnic minorities while claiming that they are being rejected because of lack of qualifications, is covert prejudice.
Covert prejudice is more widespread than overt prejudice, and unintentional prejudice is more widespread than intentional prejudice – and has much more subtle effects

Table 3.4 (cont.): Key terminology for diversity issues.

Term	Meaning
Harassment	Harassment is unwelcome attention which you receive from another person or group of people. It can range from inappropriate comments to touching to physical violence. The unwelcome behaviour can be linked to a person's gender, sexuality, ethnic origin, religion or disability. An example could be sexual harassment at work, where a female employee is subjected to inappropriate sexual comments, derogatory comments about her performance based on gender, or unwanted physical contact
Victimisation	This is another word that can mean different things in different contexts. In the context of equality and diversity it means that a person has been exploited or treated unfairly based on personal characteristics, or more commonly because a person has complained about their discriminatory treatment
Disability	Disability can mean very different things to different people. The definition provided by the Disability Discrimination Act is anyone with 'a physical or mental impairment which has a substantial and long term adverse effect upon his ability to carry out normal day-to-day activities'. This could include a whole range of issues such as a speech impediment, learning difficulty or mental health problem, as well as a physical or sensory impairment such as mobility problems or deafness. The problematic aspect of defining disability is that many people with a recognised disability under the DDA would not call themselves disabled, and equally there are people who would not count as disabled under the DDA but consider themselves to be so
Direct and indirect discrimination	Discrimination is the unfair treatment of an individual or group based on their gender, ethnicity, disability or any other characteristics that the individual or groups may have. Direct discrimination is overt and happens when someone is treated less favourably than someone else and the reason for this is their personal characteristics; e.g. if someone refused to serve a member of an ethnic minority in a shop. Indirect discrimination is often more subtle and can be much harder to spot. It can involve issues such as failing to provide appropriate services for a particular group of people, such as prayer facilities or helping with dietary needs

Assessment activity 3.1 (P1) BTEC

Knowing the key terms used in the subjects of citizenship and diversity is essential if you are going to understand the larger concepts we will be discussing shortly, and if you are going to apply to the service of your choice. Produce a glossary fact sheet that addresses the following task:

1 Explain the range of meanings attached to citizenship and diversity, and the associated terminology (P1)

Grading tip

You should look at the terms used in citizenship and diversity, including those in Table 3.4, and provide a clear explanation for those terms, including how they might relate to the public services.

PLTS

By conducting some individual research into the definitions of these terms you will be practising your skills as an independent enquirer.

Functional skills

You will contribute to your functional skills in English by producing a glossary of definitions.

Key terms

Apartheid was the policy of racial segregation in South Africa that ended in 1990. It was used to keep the black and white populations separate. The South African black majority were forced into racially segregated living areas, education and healthcare, all of which was significantly inferior to the facilities provided by the government for the white minority.

Segregation is the separation of people by race, culture or custom. Sometimes it happens in law such as in the US prior to the 1960s and in South Africa up to the 1990s, and sometimes it is based on custom, tradition or choice.

State is often described as a geographical area in which a government operates without outside interference.

Concepts

Britain has never been mono-cultural; there have always been differing religions, languages and identities, such as after the invasion of the Vikings or the Norman Conquest. The Welsh and Gaelic traditions in Britain date back thousands of years, so it should not come as a surprise to us that Britain in the twenty-first century comprises a variety of people from a variety of backgrounds.

Integration

In its simplest terms this is about the integration of a religious or cultural group into the wider community. This includes living in the same areas, attending the same schools and enjoying the same leisure opportunities. There have been many instances where ethnic or religious groups have been denied integration and kept segregated from the rest of the population, such as under **apartheid** in South Africa and the rigid racial **segregation** rules that existed in the US before the 1960s civil rights movement.

Tolerance

Tolerance in an equal opportunities context is the willingness of individuals to recognise and respect the beliefs and cultural values and practices of others. In the UK, we have a history of tolerance in that people can worship where they like, dress how they see fit and practise any legal cultural customs they please.

People who can't accept differences can often be the focal point for trouble or nuisance in a community, making the lives of those around them miserable. As potential public service recruits, dealing with these people both inside a service and out in the wider community is likely to be part of your job.

Multiculturalism

Some countries have very clearly defined national identities and some do not. It has been argued that Britain does not have a clear sense of its identity and that no one can really define what 'Britishness' actually means. A survey of British Social Attitudes in 2007 found that only 44% of the population would describe themselves as British; the rest prefer to use Scottish, Welsh, Irish or English instead.

The UK also has a background in accepting immigrants. Over the last thousand years we have seen immigration from Ireland, the Huguenots in the sixteenth and seventeenth centuries and the Ashkenazi Jews of the late nineteenth century, to name just a few. In the twentieth century we have had immigration from Commonwealth nations such as the West Indies, India and Pakistan. Each cultural group brought its own traditions, professions, food and religion, and each group enriched British culture by its presence.

Rights and responsibilities of individuals

The interrelationship between the **state** and the individual is very complex; however, if an individual has a set of legally defined rights that are balanced by a series of responsibilities and obligations then that individual is said to be a citizen of the state. A state acts on behalf of its citizens and expects them to participate in activities that will benefit the state and keep it safe.

For example, a citizen may expect the right to live in freedom and safety within the borders of a country, but they then have the responsibility to the state to fight for the country if those borders are under threat from an enemy. Equally, in the UK you have the right to a free education and healthcare, but in return you must pay your taxes. Each right you have has a responsibility that goes along with it.

Here in the UK we do not have a modern written document that sets out all of the rights that a citizen is entitled to. (The Magna Carta of 1215 and Bill of Rights of 1689 have been overtaken by changes in the law.) A document that does set out such rights is called a constitution or a bill of rights; the US constitution is an example of this. The rights of citizens in the UK come from a variety of sources such as:

- acts of Parliament
- common law and judicial precedent
- customs and tradition.

The government can change the rights of any and all citizens simply by passing an act of Parliament however, there is an unwritten constitution under which certain basic rights are guaranteed.

Responsibilities you must uphold to the state

You → Citizenship → State

Rights given to you by the state

Figure 3.2: The rights and responsibilities of the individual.

Table 3.5: Rights and responsibilities of the individual. Responsibilities covers legal responsibilities, which by law, you must fulfil, and moral responsibilities that you should fulfil in order to be a good citizen.

Moral and legal responsibilities	Explanation
Rights and responsibilities	As a citizen of the UK you are allowed certain rights and freedoms, such as the right to privacy or the right to free health care and the right to an education. With these rights come responsibilities; these are things you must be prepared to do in order to enjoy the rights you are given. Responsibilities can include things such as not breaking the law, paying your taxes and being prepared to fight for your country if necessary.
Responsibility to others	A citizen has a responsibility to do the best that they can for others. Society can only exist when we reach agreements and co-operate with each other. We have a responsibility to judge people fairly rather than discriminate and to treat others with consideration and respect.
Public life and affairs	A citizen should try and live their life as a role model for others, they should be honest and trustworthy in their public life, this is particularly true of the public services.
Behaviour and actions	Your behaviour and actions can indicate what kind of citizen you are and demonstrate whether you care about your community. Do you drop litter in the street or do you care about your environment? Do you check on elderly neighbours or do you ignore them? Citizens can be judged on their behaviour and actions.

Equal opportunities and positive action on inclusion

Equal opportunities are important for both society and the public services. Equality and equal opportunities are based around the ideas of fairness and respect. Everyone ought to be able to take part in the political, social and cultural life of a society, regardless of their personal traits and characteristics, such as:

- gender
- religion
- sexuality
- race
- disability
- class.

Positive action is the encouragement of under-represented groups of the community to join a service and the supporting of these groups during the recruitment and selection process. If a service or any other organisation can show that particular groups are under-represented then they may choose to use positive action initiatives. Positive action does not mean any change in standards – all candidates are appointed on merit and all must undergo exactly the same recruitment and selection procedure.

Case study: Positive action in a fire service

Women and Black and other ethnic minority firefighters are under-represented in the Humberside Fire and Rescue Service. This means the service can legally undertake positive action under the Sex Discrimination Act 1975 and the Race Relations Act 1976. Some of the measure they have put into place to encourage applications include:

- the appointment of an equality and diversity officer who goes into the community to discuss career opportunities with women and ethnic minority groups
- evening and weekend awareness courses so people from under-represented groups can find out more about the service
- the opportunity for members of the community to ask questions of currently serving ethnic minority and female firefighters.

1　What are your views on positive action?

2　Can you think of anything else the fire service could do to encourage under-represented groups to apply?

3　Why are some groups under-represented in the first place? What might deter them from applying?

Corporate social responsibility

Corporate social responsibility is about how organisations, including the public services, manage their actions to produce a positive impact on society. It is about how the services can behave in an ethical manner and improve the lives of their workforce and the local and national community. This might include issues such as reducing their impact on the environment by introducing environmentally friendly policies, helping employees have a better work/life balance by introducing flexible working patterns or by allowing employees time off to work in the community.

Assessment activity 3.2   P2   BTEC

Once you have understood the key terms as assessed for P1, it is important that you can build upon this knowledge with a clear and detailed understanding of the key concepts associated with diversity, such as those described above. Produce an A3 poster that addresses the following task:

1 Discuss key concepts associated with diversity P2

Grading tip

Your poster should contain all the key concepts highlighted in the content above, and you could use images and pictures to support your ideas.

PLTS

By discussing the key concepts in diversity and producing a poster, you are practising your skills as a creative thinker.

1.3 Benefits of a good citizen

A good citizen has many benefits for communities and society as a whole (see Table 3:5). One way in which people can show good citizenship is by volunteering.

Volunteers in the public services

There are many opportunities to volunteer in the public services in a variety of roles, such as:

- Special Police Constable
- Retained Firefighter
- Territorial Army
- St John's Ambulance
- Lifeboat Volunteers
- Mountain/Cave Rescue.

Although some of these involve paid work, such as the Territorial Army, most are unpaid and are done entirely in the spare time of the volunteer or when they are called upon to attend an emergency incident. Volunteers provide essential support to the regular services and often serve alongside them doing exactly the same role. It can be very difficult for ordinary members of the community to volunteer as they may be juggling a family and a full-time job already. They should be well respected because they volunteer to make society a better place; they don't do it for the money.

Remember

The Special Police Constabulary (SPC) is a part-time volunteer police force. The 'specials' support regular officers by patrolling alone or with another special or regular police officer, either on foot or in a car. They are issued with the same kit (baton, handcuffs, CS spray) as a regular police officer.

The Territorial Army (TA) is made up of over 30,000 volunteers. They meet regularly and commit to a minimum of 40 days training a year as well as taking an active role in supporting the cadet organisations.

Most of the personnel in the Royal National Lifeboat Institute (RNLI) are volunteers who give their time to rescue others, often putting themselves in danger. This life-saving service operates all day and every day throughout the UK and Republic of Ireland. The RNLI works closely with the emergency public services and the Maritime Coastguard Agency (MCA) who coordinate rescues on the coast and at sea.

Mountain Rescue (MR) and Cave Rescue (CR) teams consist of highly trained volunteers who work with a range of public services and other voluntary organisations to rescue people injured or stranded on mountains and in caves within the British Isles.

Case study: Lance Corporal Kelly Stevens, 38 Signal Regiment Territorial Army volunteer

I left school at 16 and went straight into working in a factory. I didn't really have any idea what I wanted to do so I suppose I followed the crowd and did what my friends did. After working for a few years I found myself in a real rut – I was unfit, unhealthy and going nowhere, I knew I needed a change but I had no idea what to do about it. I saw one of the TA adverts on the telly and it just caught my eye – I liked the idea of being part of a team and learning new skills and challenging myself in a totally different environment. It took a lot of courage to go to the TA centre and get myself signed up and I was really worried about the fitness, but it was the best thing I ever did. That was eight years ago and since then I have travelled all over Europe taking part in Army competitions and overseas training exercises. My fitness is now excellent and I have a lot more confidence and self assurance than I did before. The best thing about the TA is the people – you work together as a team, and because we are all volunteers and are there because we want to be, not because we have to be, it makes for a good working environment. We have the opportunity to serve on tours of duty alongside the regulars and many TA volunteers have served in Iraq and other conflicts. The TA play a vital role in supporting the regular services and I'm proud to be part of that.

1   Why are public service volunteers so important to the regular services?

2   Are there any occasions you can think of when a volunteer service would be used before a regular service?

3   What are the benefits of working as a public service volunteer to the individual?

4   Have you considered becoming a public service volunteer during your studies? Explain your answer.

Table 3.5: Summary of the benefits of good citizenship to society.

Benefits	Explanation
Improves society and makes a positive difference	Good citizens make our society a better place by improving the social environment we live in. They provide a sense of community to an area and a sense of pride in their surroundings. They may do this by very simple things such as ensuring their property is well maintained and presentable or they may act as role models for younger people
Protects the environment	Good citizens are conscious of the importance of the environment on several levels. At a local level they may ensure they clean up litter and that their dogs don't foul the pavement, which means the area is cleaner and safer; they may engage in local projects such as recycling initiatives or cleaning up waste land, and encourage their friends and neighbours to do the same. On a larger scale they may support renewable energy initiatives or environmental charities and pressure groups such as Greenpeace and Friends of the Earth
Challenges injustice and enables fairness	Good citizens should aim to challenge injustice and the origins of injustice. This might mean challenging people who use racist or homophobic language; or acting as an advocate for someone who may have difficulty speaking for themselves, such as elderly neighbours. A good citizen supports the principle of fairness and equality and encourages others to do the same; this makes for a fairer, more inclusive society in the long term. They should be involved in reporting crimes and cooperating with the police, being willing to challenge anti-social behaviour and appear as a witness in court, and taking part in jury service

Activity: Volunteering in the community

Volunteering will help you become more employable to the public services and will also help your interpersonal skills such as communication and teamwork develop. Consider undertaking some volunteering activity such as the Duke of Edinburgh Award Scheme. This is a programme for people aged 14–25 who want to develop their confidence and knowledge in a variety of areas, such as:

- service (volunteering to help people in the community)
- skills (a hobby or personal interest)
- physical recreation (sport and fitness)
- expeditions.

The scheme fits in extremely well with the BTEC Level 3 National in Public Services and it is worth exploring whether you can combine the two.

Volunteers in the community

There are thousands of people who give up their time to volunteer in their local communities on a range of issues including youth work, environmental activities and charity work. There are also organisations that promote voluntary work in the community such as The Duke of Edinburgh Award Scheme and BTCV. Volunteering is seen as a very worthwhile way to contribute to society and help you achieve valuable skills that you may be able to transfer into your paid employment.

Adding value and supporting society

Volunteers enrich the lives of the communities and individuals they serve and in doing this add a tremendous amount of value to society.

Assessment activity 3.3

The public services are very keen to recruit good citizens as they bring many benefits to the services and to society as a whole. Produce a PowerPoint presentation that addresses the following tasks:

1. Assess the benefits of good citizens to public services and society in respecting equality **P3**

2. Analyse the importance to public services of good citizens in respecting equality and supporting them by respecting the key concepts associated with diversity **M1**

3. Evaluate the role of good citizens in supporting the public services in dealing with issues of equality and diversity **D1**

Grading tips

P3 is very straightforward, and your slides should show the key benefits of good citizens to the public services and community. For **M1**, your slides and verbal delivery should include more detail on the importance of good citizenship. For **D1**, you should supply some supporting notes to accompany your slides which consider the positive and negative aspects of good citizens in supporting the services as they deal with issues of equality and diversity.

2. The legal and human rights that protect citizens and promote diversity

People's rights can be compromised for a variety of reasons from ethnic origin to their beliefs and values, including their religion and sexuality. It is important to remember that often human rights abuses are committed against those with the least amount of power in society, either because they are a minority ethnic group or because their beliefs and values marginalise them from the government and the wider community. Many societies have laws and guidance that are used to protect the rights of others such as the United Nations Universal Declaration of Human Rights (UDHR). Although one of the most important, the UDHR is not the only legal protection individuals have to ensure they are treated fairly; this section of the unit covers both human rights and legal rights.

2.1 Human rights

Rights are certain things that an individual is entitled to have or do based on principles of fairness and justice. Many rights are written down in the constitution of a country, which lists the basic rights a citizen can expect, but some countries such as Britain do not have a constitution and in those countries it is assumed that people have the right to do anything unless the law expressly forbids it. These are called legal rights, but they are not the whole story. People also claim rights based on general ideas of fairness and equality. These are called moral or human rights and they may or may not be supported by the law of the land. It is important in any examination of citizenship and diversity to consider the issue of human rights.

Universal Declaration of Human Rights

One of the most fundamental documents in the field of human rights was developed by the UN. It is called the Universal Declaration of Human Rights (UDHR) and it remains the standard of acceptable conduct across the globe.

Figure 3.3: The roles and functions of the UN.

The UDHR was a post Second World War initiative and it is easy to see why; there had been two global conflicts fought in less than 30 years, and terrible atrocities had been committed against the European Jewish population, prisoners of war in the Far East and the populations of Hiroshima and Nagasaki in Japan amongst many others. These atrocities had shocked the world and it was felt that a better way must exist for dealing with international problems and treating people in times of both peace and conflict. The newly formed UN organised a commission to draw up a declaration that would state the importance of civil, political, economic and social rights to all people, regardless of colour, religion, nationality, gender or sexuality.

The declaration was agreed in December 1948 and consists of 30 rights or articles, although some of these are broken down into sub-sections.

Activity: The UDHR

Go to www.un.org/en/documents/udhr/ and print out then read the full list of 30 rights.

1 Which rights do you understand immediately and which require more research?

2 Are there any rights that strike you as being more important than any others?

3 Are there any rights on this declaration that you disagree with?

4 Are there any rights that you would add?

5 What are the key rights the public services might be involved in directly upholding?

Asylum seekers

Human rights exist to protect individual and group beliefs, and to protect those people who might otherwise be under threat because their values may be different from the majority of the people in the society where they live. The structure of a society can have a great impact on the issue of human rights, as it is often the most vulnerable people in society who have their rights infringed the most. Vulnerable people may include **asylum seekers** or foreign nationals who are sometimes excluded by our social structure.

Case study: The imprisonment of asylum seekers

A *Guardian* newspaper report highlighted that government figures released in August 2009 showed the UK was holding 470 asylum seeker children with their families in detention centres that they are not permitted to leave until their case is decided. The vast majority of the children were under five years old and were from countries in conflict situations such as Sudan and Zimbabwe. Often the welfare needs of these children are not taken into account and many developed symptoms of post-traumatic stress disorder such as bed wetting, self-harm, weight loss and depression as a result of their imprisonment.

1 Why does the UK routinely imprison most asylum seekers and their children?

2 What other strategies could be used to deal with asylum seekers until their application for asylum is heard?

3 What could be the long-term impact on children who are imprisoned?

Key term

Asylum seeker is an individual who has fled their own country due to conflict or persecution and has applied to stay in another country (such as the UK) until their own country is safe to return to. If an asylum seeker is successful in their application they become a refugee. If they are unsuccessful they are deported to their country of origin.

2.2 Legal rights

The rights that an individual has depend on the society that they live in. Although the UDHR provides an idealised list of rights, it is not law and many nations do not adhere to them. However, in the UK we have a number of pieces of legislation which set out to codify the rights we as citizens are entitled to, and these include:

- Human Rights Act 1998
- Police and Criminal Evidence Act 1984
- Data Protection Act 1998
- Freedom of Information Act 2000
- Equal Pay Act 1970 and 1983
- Sex Discrimination Act 1975
- Race Relations Act 1976
- Disability Discrimination Act 1995
- Employment Equality Regulations 2003 and 2006.

The acts above are given with their original dates, but as with all legislation many have been amended and changed over the years as the laws have developed or new forms of legal protection became necessary. Looking at the original legislation is an excellent start, but don't forget to check whether any amendments or changes have been added since it was created.

Human Rights Act. Although passed through Parliament in 1998 this piece of legislation was not incorporated into UK law until 1 October 2000. It was intended to make the European Convention on Human Rights law in this country, and it outlines and protects a variety of rights such as freedom of religion, right to family life and privacy. More importantly, this act makes clear that an individual is entitled to these rights regardless of sex, race, colour, language, religion, national or social origin, political affiliation or any other status. The act is therefore a crucial piece of equal opportunities legislation outlawing recruitment discrimination on the grounds of sexual orientation, religious belief and family circumstances – all charges that have been levelled at UK public services recruitment in the past.

Police and Criminal Evidence (PACE) Act. PACE is a key piece of legislation that both provides the police with powers and creates safeguards against the misuse of these powers. This means that the public are protected against over-zealous police officers who may decide to stop and search on the basis of ethnic group or age rather than genuine suspicion of wrong doing.

Data Protection Act. This is the main piece of legislation that governs the protection of personal information and data in the UK. In essence, it is a way by which personal information about you such as your address, blood group, medical problems or financial records can be controlled. This helps provide a measure of privacy to individuals as organisations cannot share information about you unless you allow them to do so. The public services have some exemptions from this; otherwise police force areas could not share information about criminals without the criminals' consent.

Freedom of Information Act. This act made the public services and public sector in general more open with the information they have and collect. It made it possible for members of the public to request access to information held by the services. However, these requests can be

denied if the information might affect the rights of others to privacy or might affect issues of security. An organisation can also charge an administration fee for the information.

Equal Pay Act. Originally this legislation was created and implemented in order to eliminate discrimination in pay between men and women who did the same work. In 1983 it was improved to include work of equal value as well as the same work. It is an important piece of legislation as it recognises the equal contribution of women in the workplace and in the public services.

Sex Discrimination Act. This act makes it unlawful to discriminate on the grounds of sex or marital status in recruitment, promotion and training. It includes both direct discrimination (where a person is treated less favourably than another person of the opposite sex would've been in the same circumstances) and indirect discrimination (where a condition is applied equally to both sexes but the proportion of one sex meeting the condition is considerably higher than the proportion of the other sex). This has certainly been an issue in the fire service fitness recruitment tests.

Race Relations Act 1976 and amendment 2000. This act performs a similar function to the Sex Discrimination Act. It outlaws discrimination on the grounds of race, colour, nationality or ethnic origin, and like the Sex Discrimination Act it covers important issues to the public services such as recruitment, promotion and training, and deals with both direct and indirect discrimination. Racism in the public services is an ongoing problem, and the Macpherson report on the Stephen Lawrence enquiry is likely to highlight only the tip of the iceberg in its assessment of institutional racism within our public services.

Disability Discrimination Act. This is a particular issue for the public services. Currently they can exclude people with disabilities on the grounds of operational effectiveness, but it is difficult to see how they will be able to maintain this stance as increasing technological advances mean that a great deal of public service work can be done from a computer or be office based. As public services rely increasingly on technology rather than 'able-bodied' manpower to perform efficiently and effectively, they may need to be more progressive and less traditional in their recruitment practices. The act itself became incorporated into UK law on

2 December 1996 and operates much as the sex discrimination and race relations acts do. In addition, it places a duty on employers to make reasonable adjustments to premises or working practices, which would facilitate the employment of a person with a disability.

Employment Equality Regulations. The 2003 regulations ban employers from discriminating against employees based on their sexual orientation or their religious beliefs. The 2006 regulations ban employers from discriminating against employees based on their age.

Documentary records

All citizens are required to have a set of documents which provides evidence of their citizenship (see Table 3.6). Citizens do not have to have all of the documents, but they are part of everyday life and they can be asked for by a variety of official government agencies and private businesses, such as the police, schools and employers.

> ## Activity: Amendments to legislation
>
> Having read the summaries of the important pieces of rights legislation above, conduct some research on each one and produce a list of the main amendments to the acts (if there are any) and what the amendments changed or added. Produce a leaflet to show your findings.

Table 3.6: Documents of citizenship.

Document	Description
Passport	In the UK a passport is an official government document that is issued to a citizen which allows them to travel outside of the UK and return when they see fit. It confirms the identity of the holder and acts as proof of their nationality. It also reassures other governments that the person who holds the passport is a UK citizen and is unlikely to end up permanently resident in their country as an illegal immigrant
Birth certificate	In the UK a birth certificate is an official copy of the information registered when a person is born, including who the parents are, and the date and place of birth. It is a legal requirement in the UK to register a new birth within 42 days. If the parents are married then either parent can register; if the parents are unmarried then the mother must register the birth. Birth certificates are commonly used as a way of proving an individual's identity and age
National insurance	National insurance is a system in the UK that allows you to pay money out of your wages in order to be entitled to certain benefits at a later date, such as the state pension or unemployment benefit. In order for your contributions to be identified and not given to someone else, each person who is resident in the UK should have a unique national insurance number; this is usually issued to individuals just before their sixteenth birthday and it makes sure that all the money you give to the government is properly recorded on your account. It acts as a reference number for the whole social security system and is also a way of identifying you to employers and the government
Work permit/ Visa	A work permit is fairly self-explanatory – it provides someone who is not a UK citizen with the right to work in the UK for a specified amount of time. Most EU citizens can work in the UK without one, so it mainly applies to individuals from outside the EU who might choose to work in the UK for a period of time. A visa is a document which individuals from some countries need in order to enter the UK. It contains a variety of information such as why you are coming to the UK and how long you intend to stay. Individuals who are not part of the EU and don't have a UK passport might be refused entry if they don't have a UK visa

Assessment activity 3.4

P4 M2 **BTEC**

As a public service employee you will be expected to uphold the rights of citizens so it is essential you understand the legal and human rights that all UK citizens are entitled to. Working in small groups, take part in a discussion that addresses the following tasks:

1 Describe the legal and human rights that protect citizens in the UK **P4**

2 Analyse the effectiveness of legal and humanitarian measures to protect citizens in the UK **M2**

Grading tips

Your discussion will be observed by your tutor so it is important to remain focused and on topic. For **P4**, consider the entire range of legal and human rights legislation we have covered so far, and ensure you provide an accurate description of each one. For **M2**, make some considered comments and conclusions on how effective these legal and humanitarian measures are at protecting the rights of UK citizens.

3. The role of public services in enforcing diversity and providing equality of service

3.1 Policies and procedures within services

All public service organisations have to have a range of policies that they follow to ensure they are upholding the highest standards in respecting equality and diversity. These policies include:

- equal opportunities policies
- grievance procedures
- bullying and harassment at work policies
- anti-discriminatory policies
- recording and monitoring of equal opportunities data and complaints
- complaints procedures for service users

and are explained in Table 3.7.

Diversity issues

The public services have to deal with a multitude of diversity issues, but the key aspect for them is how to build and maintain a diverse workforce which represents the communities they serve.

Public service employment and development of a diverse workforce through recruitment and staff selection procedures

The public services often struggle with building a diverse and representative workforce. The recruitment of women and ethnic minorities in particular can be an issue. The Home Office put the proportion of female police officers at 25.1 per cent in March 2009. This means three quarters of police officers are male. Estimates in 2008 put female firefighters at just 3 per cent. In March 2009, the proportion of ethnic minority police officers in England and Wales was 4.4 per cent, firefighters in 2008 were at 3 per cent, and the RAF recorded just 1.8 per cent ethnic minorities in 2007–8. The percentage of ethnic minorities in the UK is 7.9.

Although attitudes in the public services are changing, more needs to be done in terms of encouraging females, ethnic minorities and other under-represented groups to apply, and ensuring the opportunities they have are free from discrimination.

Link

One possible strategy a service can use to improve diversity in their workforce is positive action (see page 90).

Table 3.7: Policies and procedures on equality and diversity.

Policy/Procedure	Explanation
Equal opportunities and Anti-discrimination policies	These are policies that set out how employees should be treated in terms of recruitment, selection, training or promotion. The policies are often based on codes of good practice issued by the Equality and Human Rights Commission (please look back at Table 3.4 Terminology, for more details)
Grievance procedures	A standardised set of procedures and steps should be taken when an employee has an issue or a problem which cannot be solved on an informal basis, e.g. unfair treatment, bullying or a change in job role
Bullying and harassment at work policies	These are policies that are designed to prevent behaviour that could be considered as bullying or harassment and state what should be done about it if it happens
	Bullying and harassment can cause workplace stress, cause valued employees to leave and reduce the effectiveness of the service offered by the organisation. Usually these policies place a great deal of weight on each individual taking responsibility for their own behaviour and treating others with dignity and respect
Recording and monitoring of equal opportunities data and complaints	The public services are funded with public money; this means they are accountable to the public for their performance on equal opportunities as well as a whole host of other factors. The government demands that they maintain records in areas such as recruitment and selection, and monitor the amount of complaints they receive and how they were resolved
Complaints procedures for service users	Each service should have a complaints procedure that can be used by the general public or other organisations to report poor service or any other issues of concern. For example, the police have the Independent Police Complaints Commission which deals with complaints against police officers or the behaviour and conduct of multiple officers during incidents

Catering for employee needs through support mechanisms (staff unions, associations and federations)

There are a variety of support organisations that represent the interests of public service personnel. These offer services to employees such as:

- legal advice and representation
- counselling and personal support
- negotiations on pay and conditions
- lobbying government on issues important to a particular service
- monitoring health and safety and issuing guidance
- advice to anyone suffering from discrimination or harassment
- training events
- media liaison.

Unions and associations provide invaluable support to service personnel who have to do a very physically and emotionally demanding role. Some of the associations you might come across are:

- Police Federation
- Prison Officers Association
- Fire Brigades Union
- British Paramedic Association
- Royal Air Forces Association
- Soldiers, Sailors, Airmen & Families Association
- Royal British Legion
- Army Welfare Service.

Activity: Support mechanisms

Choose one of the professional associations listed above and research the benefits it brings to its members. How does it support the public service employee in the course of their job?

Case study: Religious beliefs in the army

Article 2 of the Equal Opportunities Policy for the Army (2000) states:

Equality of opportunity is a critical factor in delivering the human element of fighting power and is, therefore, directly linked to operational effectiveness. All commanders have a duty not only to comply with the law, but also to foster an environment, both on and off duty, which attracts high quality recruits from the broadest possible societal base, and to maximise the potential and teamwork of all soldiers serving under them.

However, there are some aspects of religious belief that can come into conflict with the operational needs of the services, such as the need for regular prayer, the observance of holy days, religious dress codes and dietary requirements. The British Army and public services in general have made very significant adjustments to ensure that individuals from all religious backgrounds can join the service without detriment to their religion. These include measures such as:

- the provision of specialist food such as kosher and halal ration packs
- allowing religious clothing to be worn as long as it does not compromise safety of operational effectiveness, such as a turban for Sikh males
- regular liaison with a variety of faiths to take advice on best practice
- support for all religions via the chaplaincy service
- celebration of holy days where practical
- daily prayer arrangements where safe and practical.

1 Do the services do enough to help people observe their religious beliefs?

2 Can you think of anything else the services could put in place to help balance the need for a diverse workforce with religious observance?

3 Can you describe the aspects of public service work which might impact on an individual's beliefs?

Assessment activity 3.5

P5 M3 D2 **BTEC**

It is extremely important that the public services support and encourage the development of a diverse workforce if they are going to serve their communities effectively. Produce a written report which addresses the following tasks:

1 Review the methods used by public services to ensure they have a diverse workforce **P5**

2 Analyse and evaluate the effectiveness of the methods used by the public services to promote equality and diversity in society and within the service **M3 D2**

Grading tips

You need to examine the recruiting policies and other policies which are designed to combat the under-representation of some groups in the services, and also consider how equality and diversity are promoted. To gain **M3** and **D2** you will need to consider how well and why these policies and methods work (or don't work) both in society and the public services.

PLTS

By conducting some individual research into the methods used by the service to develop a diverse workforce, you are practising your skills as an independent enquirer.

Functional skills

Since you are producing a written report, your functional skills in English are being used.

Equality of service

The public services have a duty to ensure that all members of the community can access their services, and that they provide equal services to all community groups and individuals. With a diverse population of 60 million in the UK, this poses significant difficulties for the services as they must recognise the needs of citizens as individuals and groups.

Link

You have already seen that there is a whole range of equality and rights legislation that the services are bound by, and these provide the statutory requirements that must be followed in terms of equality (pages 95–97).

The services have put many support mechanisms in place to ensure that diverse groups and individuals have equal access, such as:

- leaflets and website availability in different languages
- information in audio and Braille format
- ensuring buildings are accessible
- developing a diverse workforce to represent the community as a whole
- specialist training on issues of religion, culture and disability
- specialist measures for reporting homophobic and hate crime
- use of minicom and text phone for individuals with hearing difficulties
- use of interpreters
- specialist equality and diversity officers.

Activity: Service accessibility

Consider the service you want to join. What is done to ensure it provides an equal service to all its users and all potential users have equal access to it?

Assessment activity 3.6

The public services need to provide an equal and effective service to all citizens. Produce a leaflet that addresses the following task:

1 Explain the duty of all public services to provide equality of service to all citizens **P6**

Grading tip

For **P6**, you need to consider the methods used by the public services to ensure all members of society can access their services and receive protection from discrimination within society.

PLTS

By discussing equality of service and producing a colourful and engaging leaflet, you are practising your skills as a creative thinker.

Functional skills

If you produce your leaflet on a computer you can practise your ICT functional skills.

4. Investigate current affairs, media and support

In order to truly understand the implications of citizenship and diversity for the work of the public services, it is important to examine the context in which they operate. This includes examining current affairs that may affect the public services, how they are represented by the media and the support they offer to citizens.

4.1 National issues affecting public services and citizens

There are many national issues that affect the operation and priorities of the public services such as:

- immigration issues
- discrimination in society and in the public services
- asylum seekers
- housing issues
- demographic changes
- poverty
- reductions in army regiments
- increased police civilianisation

Asylum seekers and illegal immigrants

The issue of immigration is a local, regional, national and international subject, which is often misunderstood by both the general public and the public services alike. Asylum seekers are individuals and families who have to flee from their homes in the face of persecution, war, religious intolerance, racial hatred or any number of other factors, which may harm them or their children. Being an asylum seeker means that your life may be under threat in your home country – it is not about individuals who want to gain entry into more economically affluent nations. It is also important to understand that most asylum seekers are kept in detention centres, which operate along the lines of prisons, and those that are not kept in such centres have a very restricted standard of living; there are arguments about whether this breaches their fundamental right to freedom.

Illegal immigrants are those people that go to another nation to have a better standard of life, but do not go through the legal channels in terms of applying for a visa. This is because the majority of illegal immigrants would not qualify for a visa so the only way into the country is to stay there illegally. Economic migrants may have entered a country legally or illegally in order to seek a better standard of life. While there is nothing wrong with being an economic migrant, after all most of us will move around the UK to get a better job or a better standard of living, they should not be confused with genuine asylum seekers whose situations are much more complex and desperate.

Did you know?

There exists a myth that the UK is being swamped by people claiming asylum, a myth that is often supported by both politicians and the media. The belief is that asylum seekers are pouring into our small country and that they are using up resources such as jobs, education and medical services, leaving our own citizens without the vital public services they need. In actual fact, we have very strict rules on who can and cannot claim asylum. In 2008 there were 25,670 asylum applications which is a fall of almost 50% over the last five years.

In actual fact the UK takes far fewer asylum seekers than many other nations. About 80% of the world's refugees are living in developing countries, usually across the Middle East, Africa and Asia. The whole of Europe looks after just 14% of the world's refugees. In 2008 the UK was ranked by the United Nations as 17th in the league table of industrialised countries for the number of asylum applications we accept.

Discrimination in society and in public services

As you will remember from earlier in this unit (see Table 3.4), discrimination is the unfair treatment of an individual or group based on their gender, ethnicity, disability or any other number of characteristics that the individual or group may have. This is important to society because if you exclude certain groups based on one or more of the above characteristics you lose the contribution they can make to society. For example, it used to be frowned upon for married women to work. This was changed by the needs of industry in the First and Second World Wars when women had to take over the bulk of jobs as the men were away fighting. If women today were excluded from the jobs market 50 per cent of the talent and skill in the country would be going to waste. This clearly does not benefit society, which needs a skilled and diverse workforce to compete against other countries in a global economy.

Attitudes to equality have changed greatly in the public services over the last 30 years. It used to be the case that the uniformed services as a whole were mainly made up of white males, but this is changing. The services now realise that they must reflect the communities they serve and must welcome more diversity in the form of more women or more ethnic minorities.

Activity: Housing

Inadequate or substandard housing has been linked with poverty and crime. Conduct some research into this area. How do you think the issue of housing might affect the following services?
- the police
- the fire service
- social services.

Demographic changes

These are changes to the make up of a population over time. In the UK, the Office for National Statistics (ONS) monitors these changes through population surveys such as the **National Census**.

Key term

National Census is a count of people and households that provides statistical data on the population of the UK. This happens every 10 years. The next one is due on 27 March 2011 and will involve around 25 million households.

Statistics released by the ONS highlight that pensioners are now outnumbering children. They predict that by 2031 there will be 15 million pensioners and 13 million children, and that the average age of the population will increase from the current 39 years to 42 years old – this is what is known as an aging population. This has very serious implications for the public services as the number of people paying taxes to support them will fall with the declining birth rate,

while the need for public services, such as care homes and health care, in an increasingly elderly population, will grow.

Currently in the UK there are four working adults paying taxes to support each pensioner. By 2035 this number is predicted to have fallen to just 2.5, making sustaining public services and pensions at their current level very difficult indeed. There are several things that might be done to help the public services overcome issues of demographic change:

- increase the retirement age so that people become pensioners later and work for longer
- enforce pension arrangements so that everyone who works must contribute a proportion of their income for their retirement rather than simply relying on a state pension
- increase immigration of overseas workers to increase the labour market and pay taxes – this is a controversial option as generally in the UK people favour reducing immigration not increasing it.

Poverty

A general definition of poverty is that people do not have sufficient food or money to supply their everyday needs. However, there are various levels of poverty, which need to be examined if you are to understand the impact of this issue.

Absolute poverty. This is a lack of the basic necessities needed in order to support human life such as food, water, shelter and heat. Primary absolute poverty is when an individual has no basic necessities at all. An example of this would be the famine and drought in Ethiopia during the 1980s in which people starved to death by the millions. Secondary absolute poverty is when an individual has some basic necessities but they are not sufficient to sustain them, such as refugees in Afghanistan where people tried to create shelters and feed their families with almost no basic necessities at all.

Relative poverty. This is a level of poverty which leaves an individual unable to participate in the cultural and social life of a community. A survey reported in the Sunday Times showed that 50 per cent of people thought that a family was in poverty if they could not afford a phone, TV or washing machine. Clearly these people are not starving and they have access to healthcare and education but they are poor relative to others in their society.

Subjective poverty. This is also a perceived sense of poverty where you are poor because you think you are. For instance, if you compare your current position with a previous position you were in or you consider yourself poor because the rest of your family is wealthy.

Poverty is a major contemporary social issue across the globe, although there are distinct differences in the types of poverty that each nation suffers. Poverty can have a substantial impact on the UK public services in the following ways:

- possible increase in crime and violence leading to greater strain on the budgets and skills of the emergency services
- aid and humanitarian missions for the armed services.

This homeless man carries all his possessions on his back.

Reduction of regiments in the army

The armed services have been undergoing a series of structural changes since the publication of the 2003 government white paper 'Delivering Security in a Changing World'. The paper set out the changes that

Did you know?

The full white paper 'Delivering Security in a Changing World' can be found on the Ministry of Defence (MOD) website under corporate publications, along with supporting fact sheets which summarise the need for change, or on the Office of Public Sector Information website.

needed to be made across all three armed services if they were going to become efficient and effective in delivering national and international security.

Some of the changes outlined in the 2003 proposals have led to the reduction of regiments in the army, with some regiments amalgamating with others. For example, the Yorkshire Regiment is one of the largest infantry regiments in the country; it was created in 2006, as a result of the white paper, from three regular battalions and one territorial battalion:

- Prince of Wales Own Regiment of Yorkshire
- Green Howards
- Duke of Wellington's Regiment
- TA units from across the region.

Some of these amalgamations were viewed very negatively at the time, since many of these regiments had long and distinguished histories and a proud tradition of battle, but the armed services have continually changed to meet operational needs throughout history, and this was just the latest stage in this evolution.

Increased use of civilian roles in the public services

Civilianisation is a process whereby police officers (or other public service officers) are released from completing non-operational tasks that don't require their specialist expertise or training. They are then able to be deployed in an operational role, which makes the use of these staff much more efficient, since they are doing the job they were trained to do rather than routine administrative work. The routine administration or non-specialist support then comes from civilians employed by the service. In effect, it is cheaper to employ a civilian on non-operational duties than to use a public services officer. It also puts the officer back where they ought to be – policing the streets. However, there are concerns that civilianisation may result in a less flexible service, since it's not feasible to send a civilian worker to front-line duties as is possible with police officers, soldiers or firefighters.

Activity: Current affairs

The list above only describes some of the possible current affairs that affect the services. Look on a reputable news website such as BBC News and see how many of the current affairs stories discussed there would have an impact on the public services.

4.2 Media representation of uniformed public services

The public services are portrayed in a variety of ways by the media, depending on the situation they find themselves in and the type of media doing the reporting. There are many types of media, such as:

- newspapers (tabloid and broadsheet)
- magazines
- television
- radio
- internet
- books
- journal articles
- service magazines.

The coverage can be either factual, in that it highlights real members of the public services performing the actual job that they are employed to do, or it can be a fictional portrayal, which may not be based on the real experience of most public service officers and may actually differ a great deal from the job they do.

All of the public services are portrayed by the media, but the police and the portrayal of crime dominate real and fictional representations of the public services. Newburn (2007) notes the following:

- roughly 25 per cent of all TV programmes are crime related
- 20 per cent of films are crime based and even when they are not directly crime based about 50 per cent have a significant crime content
- between one quarter and one third of all paperback book titles are crime-based thrillers.

A study by Ericson and co-workers (1987) in Canada found around 45 per cent of stories in the written media were crime or deviance related. In the UK, Williams and Dickinson (1993) found that **tabloids** portray more crime than **broadsheets**. The *Sun* newspaper contained 30.4 per cent crime news, compared to 5.1 per cent in the *Guardian*. What this highlights is that a substantial proportion of media time and energy goes into the portrayal of public services and the police role in solving crime in particular.

Key terms

Tabloid newspaper is one that has smaller sized pages compared to broadsheets. Tabloids tend to report news that is sensational rather than serious. This means they often focus on entertainment, celebrity scandals or crime. Examples include the *Sun*, *Daily Mirror* and *Daily Star*.

Broadsheet newspaper traditionally has larger pages which cover more serious news content. Examples include *The Times*, *Guardian* and *Telegraph*. Nowadays some broadsheet newspapers are tabloid-sized.

Portrayals of the public services take up a great deal of air time. But how accurately are the services actually represented? A US-based National Television Violence study found that over a four-year period every reality-based police show contained acts of visual violence, including shoot outs, dangerous car chases and assaults. They also included portrayals of murder, sexual assault and robbery at a much higher rate than actually happens in real life. The study found that police shows depicted 33 per cent of police officers using or threatening physical aggression compared with only 10 per cent of criminals. This clearly highlights the media portrayal of police officers as aggressive or brutal at times.

Case study: **The media and compensation**

The issue of compensation for police officers who are injured in the line of duty is one that the media feel very strongly on.

Officers who attended the Hillsborough football stadium disaster were able to claim hundreds of thousands of pounds after they developed post-traumatic stress disorder (PTSD) in response to the events they witnessed at Hillsborough. The media had a great deal to say on this and were scathing at times in their coverage, noting that the families of the victims received 100 times less than one of the officers who claimed PTSD. The media in this instance opened the debate as to whether public service workers should be entitled to any compensation at all since the activities which are likely to cause PTSD are an integral part of the job that they sign on to do.

The issue of PTSD is not the only police compensation issue to appear in the papers. There have also been headlines surrounding pension fraud and malingering in order to claim sick pay. *Police* magazine had the following to say about compensation in the media: ... *according to our friends in the media, bobbies no longer look for criminals, but cracks in the pavement to fall over or polished station floors to slip on.*

The media have often portrayed the issue of public service compensation very negatively, but the fact of the matter is that officers, just like any other employees up and down the country, are entitled to compensation for workplace injuries. In fact, due to the hazardous nature of public service work it could be said to be even more important that they are able to claim compensation.

1 Do you think all public service workers ought to be able to claim compensation for workplace injuries?

2 Should all public service workers be able to claim for PTSD?

3 How would an officer claiming compensation be seen by the public or by the victim of a crime?

Positive images of the public services

The public tend to hear only about the negative aspects of the public services. The outstanding contribution of the vast majority of the public services to social order, stability and personal safety on a day-to-day basis is not something you often read about or see on the news. The public services operate 24 hours a day, 7 days a week, 365 days a year, performing acts of tremendous courage, bravery and

self sacrifice – for example, firefighter Rob Miller from Leicester Fire and Rescue service who died in 2002 while searching a burning factory to see if anyone was trapped; Fleur Lombard, a firefighter in Avon who died in a supermarket blaze in 1998; PC Andrew Jones of South Wales Police who was fatally injured by a car while chasing a burglar in 2003; or the five British servicemen killed while mentoring

Afghan police officers in Nad Ali District, Afghanistan, in 2009.

The list of public service officers who have given their lives for the protection and safety of others is long and distinguished. Although the press doesn't often comment on the excellent day to day performance of the public services, they do pay respect to remarkable acts of bravery such as those described above which helps create admiration and respect among the public for the services.

While the mainstream media often report news stories about the public services which may be scandalous or highlight poor practice, the services have their own method of representation in the form of service magazines. These are special interest magazines which focus almost entirely on the concerns, changes and issues of interest in one particular public service. A couple of good examples of this are *Police Review* and *Soldier*. If you are interested in reading them your school or college library may already have them in stock or be able to order them for you. They give an insider's view of the service and can be extremely useful in providing a balanced account of service life and helping you become ready for a public service interview.

Assessment activity 3.7

P7 P8 M4 D3 BTEC

An understanding of current affairs, how the media report them and the issues that directly and indirectly affect the public services is essential in any public service line of work. Produce a slideshow presentation to address the following tasks:

1 Report on three examples of current affairs which affect public services and citizens P7

2 Present information on how the media reports current affairs involving public services P8

3 Analyse the effects on citizens and public services of the way that three current affairs examples have been reported by the media M4

4 Evaluate the impact that media reporting has on citizens and on the level of support from public services in relation to examples of current affairs D3

Grading tips

P7 is very straightforward and just requires the selection and discussion of three current affairs that have an impact on the services and on citizens. P8 is linked to P7 and can be researched at the same time. As you are researching your three chosen current issues, make notes to discuss how the media reported the events: did the coverage differ in different newspapers, were some reports favourable to the services and some unfavourable? M4 and D3 require more depth and detail, and you should examine how media reporting impacts on the services and the public in terms of public confidence and service morale.

PLTS

By reporting on examples of current affairs that affect public services and citizens, you are practising your skills as a reflective learner.

Functional skills

By producing a slideshow presentation you are practising your ICT functional skills.

4.3 Services – statutory and non-statutory

In general, public services can be divided into two categories: statutory and non-statutory. One group are created and maintained by law whereas the others are not:

- statutory – the Police, Fire Service, armed services
- non-statutory – Citizens Advice Bureau, Victim Support, Salvation Army, and so on.

All statutory public services are government funded in one way or another, but non-statutory services rely on charitable donations or seek alternative methods of funding, such as bidding for government or European funds and lottery money. All public services, whether uniformed or non-uniformed, perform a crucial role for the public. The roles and responsibilities of the statutory public services are outlined in Unit 1, so they will not be repeated here, but it is crucial to remember that the term 'service' is of vital importance. Public services should exist to serve the citizen, and members of the public services should always remember that they have a duty towards the public, which should be conducted with fairness, respect and impartiality.

Assessment activity 3.8   P9   M5   BTEC

The public services provide a great deal of support to citizens. In order to establish what they do and how they do it, produce a fact sheet which addresses the following tasks:

1 Demonstrate how support is provided to citizens by statutory and non-statutory public services **P9**

2 Justify the involvement of statutory and non-statutory public services in providing support to citizens **M5**

Grading tip

Using the information in this unit, you will need to consider examples of statutory and non-statutory services and the work they do to support citizens. For **M5**, you need to justify why statutory and non-statutory services are needed to deal with current issues in society.

Anish Singh

Equality and Diversity Officer

I work for a local authority in an inner city area where there is a high level of racial and cultural integration. I'm very lucky that the area I work in has excellent community relations, and a reputation for a diverse and thriving community.

It's my job to advise and help the local authority and other agencies in maintaining those good relationships and making sure we meet our legal obligations in relation to equality and diversity legislation.

A typical day

I spend a lot of my day office based or in meetings where we develop policy and action plans to support the equality and diversity agenda. I also spend a lot of time with managers, helping them develop equality impact assessments.

When I can, I like to meet with our partner agencies and get out and about in the local community to see how the changes we implement actually affect the quality of people's lives on the ground.

The best thing about the job

The best thing about the job for me is seeing the changes we can make to the service and to citizens by implementing equality and diversity policies. It makes the services the local authority provides open and available to anyone, which enables people from all walks of life to participate in their community.

Think about it!

What topics have you covered in this unit that might give you the background to work in a team or as a leader?

What knowledge and skills do you think you need to develop further if you want to be involved in citizenship and diversity in the future?

109

Just checking

1 What is a citizen?

2 What is diversity?

3 What are the qualities of a good citizen?

4 What are human rights?

5 What are the key pieces of equality legislation in the UK?

6 What is a grievance procedure?

7 What is positive action?

8 How will demographic changes affect the public services?

9 List three fictional and three factual portrayals of the public services.

10 What is the difference between a statutory and a non-statutory public service?

edexcel

Assignment tips

- In a unit like this which focuses on citizenship, diversity and current affairs. one of the best things you can do to help improve your grade and your knowledge is to make sure you keep up to date with current events by reading a reputable news source on a daily basis. This means using your lunch hour or an hour after school/college to read the BBC news website or picking up a broadsheet newspaper such as *The Times*, *Guardian* and *Telegraph* (these have websites where you can read the news if you can't get hold of the paper). Not only will you become more informed about government policies and the public services, but you will also pick up lots of information which can be used across all of your BTEC National units.

- This may sound very basic, but make sure you have read your assignment thoroughly and you understand exactly what you are being asked to do. Once you are clear about this then you can move on to your research. Doing your research well and using good sources of evidence is essential. Lots of students rely too much on the internet and not enough on other sources of information such as books, newspapers and journals. The internet is not always a good source of information. It is very easy to use information from American or Australian government websites without noticing – but your tutor will notice. Always double check the information you find, don't just accept it at face value. Good research and preparation is the key to getting those higher grades.

4 Understanding discipline in the uniformed public services

The efficiency and effectiveness of the uniformed public services, as with many other organisations, depends on discipline and the self-discipline of its members. If you intend to have a career in the uniformed public services it is very important that you have a comprehensive understanding of the concept of discipline.

Through this unit, you will explore the various forms of discipline in detail, beginning with the need for discipline and its role within the uniformed public services. You will then look at self-discipline before being given the opportunity to demonstrate it to a high standard.

Next, you will be presented with some interesting psychological studies on conformity and obedience, as well as taking part in some conformity simulations. Finally, you will examine the complex nature of authority and its relation to the uniformed public services.

Learning outcomes

After completing this unit you should:

1 understand the need for discipline in the uniformed public services
2 be able to demonstrate self-discipline as required in the uniformed public services
3 know what conformity and obedience mean, highlighting their place in the uniformed public services
4 know the complex nature of authority in the uniformed public services.

Assessment and grading criteria

This table shows you what you must do in order to achieve a pass, merit or distinction grade, and where you can find activities in this book to help you.

To achieve a **pass** grade the evidence must show that you are able to:	To achieve a **merit** grade the evidence must show that, in addition to the pass criteria, you are able to:	To achieve a **distinction** grade the evidence must show that, in addition to the pass and merit criteria, you are able to:
P1 explain the need for and role of discipline in the uniformed public services **Assessment activity 4.1 page 125**	**M1** justify the need for and role of discipline in the uniformed public services **Assessment activity 4.1 page 125**	**D1** evaluate the impact of discipline on the uniformed public services **Assessment activity 4.1 page 125**
P2 demonstrate self-discipline through relevant activities **Assessment activity 4.2 page 129**	**M2** perform relevant activities with a high standard of self-discipline **Assessment activity 4.2 page 129**	**D2** evaluate personal levels of self-discipline for entry to the uniformed public services **Assessment activity 4.2 page 129**
P3 outline what is meant by the terms conformity and obedience with reference to the public services **Assessment activity 4.3 page 140**	**M3** explain why conformity and obedience are important in the public services, with reference to research studies **Assessment activity 4.3 page 140**	
P4 participate in conformity simulations **Assessment activity 4.3 page 140**		
P5 describe 'authority' as it relates to the uniformed public services **Assessment activity 4.4 page 150**		

How you will be assessed

This unit will be assessed by an internal assignment that will be designed and marked by the staff at your centre. The assignment is designed to allow you to show your understanding of the learning outcomes for understanding discipline in the uniformed public services. These relate to what you should be able to do after completing this unit. Your assessments might include some of the following:

- portfolios of evidence
- wall displays
- learning journals
- video diaries
- role-play
- presentations
- leaflets
- reports.

James experiences army cadet training

I'd been looking forward to this unit, and it was even better than I thought it'd be. I thought I knew all about discipline because I've been in the Army Cadet Force for a couple of years and my brother's in the army, which is what I want to do; but I didn't realise there was so much to it. I mean, I know all about drill and different ranks, and even why squaddies get beasted, but there's a lot more to it than that.

I really enjoyed the section on self-discipline, especially the practical sessions with the drill, and it made me aware of things that had never occurred to me before. And those studies we did on conformity and obedience were very interesting, and the role plays we did were quite funny. It was hard to keep a straight face when you looked at the confusion on some of the faces of those students who joined us from the other year, who couldn't understand what was happening. You know, we did Asch's conformity experiment in class – we were the stooges and some volunteers from the first year were the naïve participants – and we deliberately gave the wrong answer to the line test, same as in the original experiment. And when it got to the turn of the naïve participants they looked amazed and confused at why we gave the wrong answer but, surprisingly, most of them gave the same answer as we did.

In a way, the part about blind obedience got me thinking and I still keep thinking about possible examples where I wouldn't want to obey orders because they could lead to atrocities, like the ones we studied.

Overall, I thought this unit was one of the best we'd done.

Over to you!

- What areas of understanding discipline might you find interesting?
- What do you think would be the consequences of a lack of discipline in the uniformed services?
- Do you have good self-discipline?
- What are your opinions on blind obedience?
- What preparations could you do to get ready for your assessments?

1. The need for discipline in the uniformed public services

Thinking about discipline

What, exactly, is discipline?

What is self-discipline?

Do people respond better to being asked politely to do something, or is it better to shout at them?

Would you dare to disobey an order from someone in authority, regardless of what that order was?

Would you knowingly do something that was not right just so you did not lose face with your friends?

What is the difference between conformity and obedience?

1.1 The uniformed services

Emergency services

- The emergency services are made up of the Police, Fire and Ambulance Services. They are known as the emergency services because they are the services that always respond to emergency situations.
- Like all other uniformed public services, the emergency services have a **hierarchical** structure, with each rank having clearly defined roles and responsibilities within that service.
- Table 4.1 shows you the hierarchical structure of the emergency services, with the most senior ranks at the top. The rank structure for the Police Services differs between territorial (or county) services and the Metropolitan Police Service. You should note that there are more ranks in the Metropolitan Police Service.

Key term

Hierarchy is a system in which grades or classes of authority are ranked one above the other.

The Police Service

All police officers, regardless of rank, are constables. Constable is used to mean a person who is authorized to enforce the law as well as being the lowest rank in the Police Force. They all have the same purpose and responsibility: the protection of life and property, the maintenance of the Queen's peace, the prevention and detection of crime, and the prosecution of offenders against the peace.

A **Police Constable** has many duties to perform and these include: routine patrol, attending road traffic accidents, taking witness statements, investigating crime and dealing with sudden deaths.

A **Police Sergeant's** role is a supervisory one, often supervising a small team of constables, and although a sergeant is senior in rank in the hierarchical structure, they both have the same powers in executing their duty to the public.

Inspectors and **Chief Inspectors** are classed as middle managers and they are responsible for managing sergeants and constables in performing their duties. While most of their time is likely to be spent in a police station, where they organise and plan the work of their colleagues, they often go out on patrol in the company of sergeants and constables.

Table 4.1: The hierarchical structure of the emergency services (please note that ranks across each row are not a comparable level).

Police	Fire	Ambulance
Commissioner (Metropolitan Police only)		Chief Executive
Deputy Commissioner (Metropolitan Police only)		Director
Chief Constable (Assistant Commissioner in Metropolitan Police)		Assistant Director
Deputy Chief Constable (Deputy Assistant Commissioner in Metropolitan Police)		Locality Manager
Assistant Chief Constable (Commander in Metropolitan Police)	Brigade Manager	Customer Relations Manager (ensures enough human resources)
Chief Superintendent	Area Manager	Paramedic Practitioner
Superintendent	Group Manager	Clinical Team Leader
Chief Inspector	Station Manager	Paramedic
Inspector	Watch Manager	Emergency Medical Technician
Sergeant	Crew Manager	Emergency Medical Dispatcher
Police Constable	Firefighter	Ambulance Healthcare Assistant

Police officers above the rank of Chief Inspector are regarded as senior management, with overall responsibility for policing a division (or district), or with responsibility for a certain area. For example, the criminal investigation or road traffic department will be commanded by a **chief superintendent** who, in turn, would be accountable to an **assistant chief constable**.

The Fire Service

It is the duty of all Fire Service personnel, regardless of rank, to protect life and property from fire or other hazards by carrying out rescues and preventing the escalation of hazards. They are also responsible for conducting risk assessments and advising on matters relating to public safety, as well as enforcing safety legislation.

A **firefighter** works as part of a crew consisting of five or six firefighters. Their duties include attending emergencies and dealing with fires, flooding, terrorist incidents, road and rail crashes, bomb alerts, dangerous spillages, as well as testing hydrants and checking emergency water supplies.

A **crew manager** is still a firefighter but has the extra responsibility of supervising or managing the crew.

A **watch manager** is responsible for a 'watch', which is a number of crews that work on the same shift.

A **station manager** is in charge of all the watches (there could be four or five) that operate from a fire station. The station manager could be the fire officer in charge of an incident, unless it is a very large or serious incident where the fire officer in charge could be the **brigade manager**. The fire officer in charge of an incident is responsible for assessing the situation and deciding upon the best plan of action, directing the crews as necessary and completing a report of the incident.

The Ambulance Service

The Ambulance Service is accountable to the National Health Service and is responsible for providing accident and emergency cover by responding to emergency 999 calls and major incidents. They are also responsible for transporting non-emergency patients to and from their hospital appointments.

All the ranks shown in Table 4.1, apart from the three highest – namely, Assistant Director, Director and Chief Executive – are operational ranks, each with different roles and responsibilities.

An **ambulance healthcare assistant** is responsible for patient transport services and hospital transfers in a non-emergency situation, while an **emergency medical dispatcher** is responsible for handling and grading calls, and dispatching the appropriate response.

An **emergency medical technician** responds to general emergency incidents and can administer a limited amount of medical care. They usually accompany a **paramedic** who is more qualified to administer drugs and a greater amount of medical attention at the scene.

A **clinical team leader** is responsible for ensuring that there are enough human resources to cover each shift, and they may accompany any of the emergency responders to the scene of an incident.

A **paramedic practitioner** is the most highly medically qualified of the ambulance team. They often work alone, responding to emergency incidents, including really serious ones.

A **customer relations manager** ensures there are enough medical and human resources throughout the division, and that the appropriate resources are directed efficiently, while the **locality manager** is in charge of the Division or District. In the event of a major incident, the locality manager would take charge or oversee the work of the ambulance staff at operational (or bronze) command.

Did you know?

St John Ambulance is a voluntary service and it does not have a rank structure.

Table 4.2: The hierarchical structure of the armed forces.

Army	Royal Navy	Royal Marines	Royal Air Force
Field Marshall (in war time only)	Admiral of the Fleet		Marshall of the RAF
General	Admiral	General	Air Chief Marshall
Lieutenant General	Vice Admiral	Lieutenant General	Air Marshall
Major General	Rear Admiral	Major General	Air Vice-Marshall
Brigadier	Commodore	Brigadier	Air Commodore
Colonel	Captain	Colonel	Group Captain
Lieutenant Colonel	Commander	Lieutenant Colonel	Wing Commander
Major	Lieutenant Commander	Major	Squadron Leader
Captain	Lieutenant	Captain	Flight Lieutenant
Lieutenant	Sub-Lieutenant	Lieutenant	Flying Officer
2nd Lieutenant	Midshipman (junior to the ranks in the other services)	2nd Lieutenant	Warrant Officer
Warrant Officer Class 1	Warrant Officer Class 1	Warrant Officer Class 1	Flight Sergeant
Warrant Officer Class 2	Warrant Officer Class 2	Warrant Officer Class 2	Sergeant
Colour Sergeant	Chief Petty Officer	Colour Sergeant	Corporal
Sergeant	Petty Officer	Sergeant	Senior Technician
Corporal	Leading Rate	Corporal	Junior Technician
Lance Corporal	–	–	Senior Aircraftman/woman
Private	Able Rate	Marine	Leading Aircraftman/woman

Armed forces

The British Army, Royal Navy (including the Royal Marines) and Royal Air Force are known collectively as the British Armed Forces and they are responsible for protecting the UK and its overseas territories by land, sea and air. They are also responsible for promoting the UK's security interests, as well as supporting international peacekeeping. Table 4.2 shows their hierarchical structures.

> ### Link
>
> Rank in the armed forces is discussed more fully in Unit 13, pages 288–92.

HM Prison Service

The role and responsibilities of HM Prison Service are explicit in their mission statement:

> Her Majesty's Prison Service serves the public by keeping in custody those committed by the courts. Our duty is to look after them with humanity and help them lead law-abiding and useful lives in custody and after release.

The Prison Service needs to be a disciplined organisation because of the difficult and demanding nature of the work. Like any of the uniformed public services, prison officers have a duty to behave in a professional manner, and the way in which they behave can have an impact on the people for whom they are responsible.

The role of a prison officer includes:

* supervising prisoners and maintaining order
* promoting anti-bullying procedures
* assessing and advising prisoners
* writing fair and accurate reports on prisoners.

Just as important as carrying out their tasks efficiently, prison officers should set an example for prisoners, who may never have had a role model to aspire to before. Therefore, it is essential that discipline, respect and integrity are maintained at all times, and a hierarchy is required to ensure this (see Table 4.3).

Activity: Role of prison officer

The list opposite is only a sample of the responsibilities of prison officers. For a more comprehensive list, visit the website at: www. hmprisonservice.gov.uk/careersandjobs/typeswork/ prisonofficer/ Compile a list from the website and compare this with the duties listed opposite.

Do you have what it takes to be a prison officer? Could you be a role model? Can you write accurate and fair reports?

Draw up a list of your skills and qualities and rate them from 1 to 5, where 1 is very good and 5 is poor. Include all the qualities that you believe a prison officer requires and score yourself truthfully. You should then think of ways in which you could improve your skills where you have not scored so well.

HM Coastguard

HM Coastguard is an emergency organisation that is always on call and is responsible for performing search and rescue missions at sea, as well as assisting people at risk of injury or death on cliffs or the shoreline of the UK. HM Coastguard is responsible for coordinating and organising the necessary resources for dealing with emergency situations within the waters or shores of the UK. See Table 4.3 for the hierarchical structure of HM Coastguard.

Table 4.3: The hierarchical structures of HM Prison Service and HM Coastguard.

HM Prison Service	HM Coastguard (full-time)
Chief Officer Grade 1	Regional Operational Manager
Chief Officer Grade 2	Area Operations Manager
Assistant Chief Officer	District Operations Manager
Principal Prison Officer	Watch Manager/Sector Manager
Senior Prison Officer	Watch Officer
Prison Officer	Watch Assistant
	HM Coastguard (volunteers)
	Station Officer
	Deputy Station Officer
	Team Leader
	Auxiliary Coastguard

HM Revenue and Customs

HM Revenue and Customs is responsible for the administration and collection of all taxes and duties in the UK including: income tax, national insurance, VAT and excise duties (for example, tax on alcohol and tobacco). The organisation is also responsible for maintaining the security of the UK's frontiers in terms of preventing smuggling, as well as import and export prohibitions.

Table 4.4 shows the ranks of HM Revenue and Customs alongside the equivalent police rank.

Table 4.4: The ranks of HM Revenue and Customs.

Police rank	HM Revenue and Customs title
Superintendent	Anti-Smuggling Manager Cargo Operational Manager Investigation Team Leader Passenger Services Division Operations Manager
Inspector/ Chief Inspector	Anti-Smuggling Team Leader Cargo Team Leader Excise Fraud Investigation Team Leader Excise Verification Unit Team Leader Passenger Services Division Team Manager Road Fuel Control Officer
Sergeant	Anti-Smuggling Officer Cargo Team Member Drug Dog Unit Team Leader Excise Fraud Investigation Team Member Excise Verification Officer Local Value Added Tax Office Investigation Team Officer Passenger Services Division Team Member Road Fuel Testing Officer Specialist Investigator

Private security services

Private security services may have ranks, depending on the size of the firm and the nature of the security work.

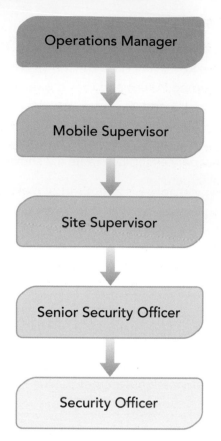

Figure 4.1: A typical rank structure in a security firm.

1.2 The need for discipline

'Obedience to authority' is one brief definition of discipline, but discipline can be used in many different contexts. For example, it may be used as an order, a deterrent, a threat, or to control or train, and it may or may not have the authority of a written law to reinforce it.

Rules and regulations

For any organisation to operate efficiently there must be a system of **rules** and **regulations**, which are strictly followed, particularly if an organisation serves the public. Rules are standards or principles to which an action is required to conform and they apply to many organisations, as well as individuals. Rules may be written laws or they could be customs or codes of conduct that have been adopted by a particular society or culture.

All of the public services are regulated, or controlled, by rules to ensure that:

- procedures are standardised and consistent
- lawful orders are followed

- there is no abuse of authority
- people are treated with respect and without favour
- the service is not brought into disrepute.

To ensure that rules are followed correctly, organisations may instigate disciplinary proceedings against those who break them. This could take several forms, including verbal reprimand, loss of privileges, suspension or dismissal.

In this sense, discipline is a method of making people conform to rules and regulations. It is important to note that discipline does not mean the same as punishment; discipline is a way of producing efficiency, uniformity and order, and is applicable to all personnel in the uniformed services, irrespective of rank.

Did you know?

Up until 1998 mutiny (the open revolt against military authority) was punishable by death.

Activity: The need for rules

- What sort of rules do you have at home?
- What sort of rules do you have at school or college?
- What happens if you break those rules?

Why orders need to be followed

During the course of normal duty for any of the public services, decisions have to be made about many complex and potentially dangerous situations. Delegation of tasks, clear instructions and the ability to follow orders are all key to ensuring that unnecessary risks are avoided and that efficiency and public confidence are maintained.

Failure or refusal to carry out a lawful order not only undermines that authority but it also means the service is less efficient, resulting in disorganisation and confusion. To avoid this happening, the uniformed public services have codes of discipline to ensure that lawful orders are obeyed.

Discipline ensures that colleagues and the public are not put at unnecessary risk.

In the event of a house fire, while firefighters concentrate on extinguishing the fire and rescuing anyone trapped inside, the watch manager considers the broader picture and assesses the risk of the fire spreading to adjacent premises. If they decide the risk is high, then they could give an order to the lower ranks for the evacuation of neighbouring premises.

Discipline in this context, then, is needed to bind personnel to the authority of lawful orders and to ensure that colleagues are supported in the lawful execution of their duty.

Maintenance of order

We have already seen how discipline may be used to ensure that rules and regulations are followed, as well as orders. Where order is required, such as when something needs to be done in a systematic or orderly fashion, discipline can be used to achieve it. There may be written rules and regulations that govern orderly conduct (for example, there may be certain rules regarding making a noise after a certain time in barracks).

Activity: Consequence of breaking a rule

When you have taken part in a fire drill, either at school, college or work, you will have been told not to run or panic. If you did run or panic, which rule would you be breaking?

Would it be a written rule you were breaking or would you be going against unwritten good advice?

Activity: Discipline and logistics

Considering the large number of personnel and the huge amount of supplies required, what would be the logistical challenges of transporting them safely?

How would discipline ensure these challenges were overcome effectively?

In the public services, it is not unusual for large numbers of personnel to be transported to a particular area – an area that is foreign to the personnel and even to those in charge of them. For example, in 2003, the UK government sent 45,000 armed forces personnel to fight in the Gulf War. Since that time, arrangements have had to be made for their return, as well as the deployment of thousands of military personnel to Afghanistan, with further plans to despatch another thousand troops in the future.

Transporting supplies and equipment requires meticulous planning and the maintenance of order.

Rewards

A reward is generally regarded as some kind of positive reinforcement for performing a good deed; it is a token of appreciation of someone's efforts. In the armed forces, for example, personnel may be granted extended leave after a tour of duty abroad. This is a way of saying thank you for the personal sacrifices they have made by being away from their friends and families for long periods. When a member of the uniformed public services performs a task of a heroic nature, something that is beyond the call of duty, then their reward could be in the form of a celebrated medal.

It is not only those individuals who have performed especially good deeds who can expect to be rewarded. By merely performing their duty according to their contract and behaving appropriately, members of the uniformed public services can expect recognition. This could be in the form of good conduct medals and long-service medals, as well as medals to reflect their contribution during a particular conflict, for instance in Afghanistan.

In this context, discipline can be seen as a positive reinforcer; a way of training members of the uniformed public services to behave correctly by rewarding their good behaviour.

Punishment

If a reward is the positive reinforcement for good deeds and proper behaviour, then punishment is the negative reinforcement for wrongful acts, such as neglect of duty or inappropriate behaviour. In each

Case study: Hero marine leads bayonet charge

In December 2009, Corporal Malone of 45 Commando Royal Marines received the Conspicuous Gallantry Cross for exceptional courage. The corporal and his fellow Royal Marines were ambushed by insurgents in a notoriously dangerous area of Afghanistan. With remarkable calm, the corporal ordered his men to fix bayonets before leading them in a courageous, close-combat counter-attack, which caused the attackers to run for their lives.

In a previous incident, whilst on his six-month deployment in Afghanistan, Corporal Malone rescued his troop sergeant, who had been isolated after being pinned down by enemy fire. The corporal left the safety of his trench and went to the aid of his sergeant, and together they managed to fight their way back to their unit.

In yet another incident, where his section commander had been killed, the young corporal took charge and fought for an hour, firing 900 rounds of ammunition to keep the Taleban at bay, while a casualty was safely evacuated.

1 Most people would say that to receive recognition for an act of bravery is one of the best rewards that anyone could receive. Have you ever received any form of recognition for good work you have done? How did it make you feel?

2 Do you have the ability to remain calm under extreme pressure?

3 Do you easily lose your temper? If so, what steps are you taking to remedy this?

4 Are you the type of person who would help others less fortunate than yourself?

5 Have you ever displayed courage (this could be doing something you feared but overcame, e.g. abseiling)?

6 Are you prepared to take the initiative and do what needs to be done without being told, or would you tend to sit back and let someone else do it all?

You should do an honest appraisal of yourself, because you might need to work on the skills and qualities that are needed to be an effective member of the uniformed public services.

service, a system of rules and regulations ensures that *all* members behave correctly and professionally. Failure to comply with these rules and regulations could result in punishment.

Activity: Effect of punishment

Imagine that you are a new recruit in the army, undergoing your initial training. You are looking forward to your first weekend leave and spending some time with your friends and family. However, on three occasions you have failed to observe the lights-out rule and as a punishment your Commanding Officer has cancelled your weekend leave. All your friends are going home because they have conformed to the rules and regulations.

- How would this make you feel?
- Would it make you obey rules in future?

Discipline through punishment can take several forms, which may include confinement to quarters, cancellation of leave, reduction in pay, reduction in rank, reprimand or dishonourable discharge. The purpose of punishment is, through negative reinforcement, to show the person who has committed a wrongful act the error of their ways.

Consequences of a lack of discipline in the public services

Part of the effectiveness of the uniformed public services is that all members comply with rules and regulations. Without discipline, there would be no means of bringing to account those members of the services who did not abide by them. The same could be said of those who do not follow orders – it would be impossible to impose punishment. The rank structure would be pointless and promotion to the higher ranks would be worthless, because the higher ranks would have no authority over the lower ranks to ensure that they complied with the rules of the organisation.

Activity: Treatment of prisoners in Iraq

In 2004, during the conflict with Iraq, several US soldiers humiliated some Iraqi prisoners by abusing them and publishing photographs. Look for information about this event on the internet. Consider what these actions did for the reputation of the US forces and discuss your thoughts with your friends.

Our uniformed public services are part of the public sector and are, therefore, ultimately responsible to the public. Discipline, hierarchy and structure, rules and regulations all play their part in maintaining accountability and public trust.

Effect on social order and anarchy

Social order is maintained in the UK because of the efficiency and dedication of our uniformed public services in enforcing the laws of the land. Social disorder can easily lead to **anarchy**.

Key term

Anarchy literally means 'without rule' and is used to describe a state of political or social disorder.

Lack of discipline in the uniformed public services could lead to civil disturbance or anarchy.

Activity: Discipline and social order

Give five key points that summarise the uses of discipline.

In pairs, think about the following questions and discuss.

- How is social order maintained in an orderly society?
- Why could lack of discipline in the uniformed public services lead to social disorder and anarchy?
- What would society with no social order be like?
- If we lived in a society without rules, then how would we protect our families, our home and our property?
- If anarchy prevailed, how could we bring wrongdoers to account?
- Anarchists believe that we would be better off without a government. Can you think of ways in which this might work?

1.3 The role of discipline

Team spirit

Many young people aspire to join the uniformed public services because of what the services have to offer in terms of security, promotion prospects, adventure, job satisfaction and a sense of belonging. However, the demanding nature of the work means that gaining entry and acceptance is not easy. It requires certain attributes such as courage, physical fitness, reliability, determination, integrity and confidence.

Once you have been accepted and earned your uniform, you will have a sense of pride knowing that not everyone is fortunate enough to be accepted, and you will have a feeling of camaraderie with other colleagues which is built on mutual trust, respect, loyalty, pride and the interests of the service for which you have been selected.

This is known as *esprit de corps* or **team spirit** – and should be preserved by introducing rules and regulations. For example, the Police Discipline Regulations ensure that officers have a duty to act in a manner that will not bring the reputation of the police service into disrepute. They must not discredit the police service, or any of its members, whether on or off duty.

Sense of duty and honour

If you choose to join the public services, you do so because a particular service appeals to you. For example, you might like the prospect of a career that is challenging and varied, with good promotion prospects and security. Whatever your reasons, you must not lose sight of the fact that there is a job to do. You must acknowledge that there is a sense of duty and that life within the public services is not one big adventure with no mundane tasks involved.

As a uniformed public service employee, the manner in which you carry out your duties can affect many people, sometimes with serious consequences. Whatever your role within a uniformed public service, you have a duty to your colleagues, the service and the public. While life in the uniformed public services may appear to be glamorous and adventurous some of the

time, there are other times when it may seem tedious and unrewarding – but you must still perform your duty to the best of your ability.

Serving the public

Each of the uniformed public services has evolved to serve the public. You have only to look at the mission statements of the services to see that the public is the focus of the services' aims and objectives. For example, the role of the police and fire services includes protecting life and property, while the armed forces are there to defend the UK, its overseas territories, its people and interests.

By committing yourself to work within a service you undertake to serve the public by protecting them and looking after their interests in a courteous manner, without prejudice or reward. This is to say that you are expected to treat everyone as equal, regardless of race, colour or creed, and without seeking financial or personal gain. For example, you would not expect a firefighter to give preference to someone trapped

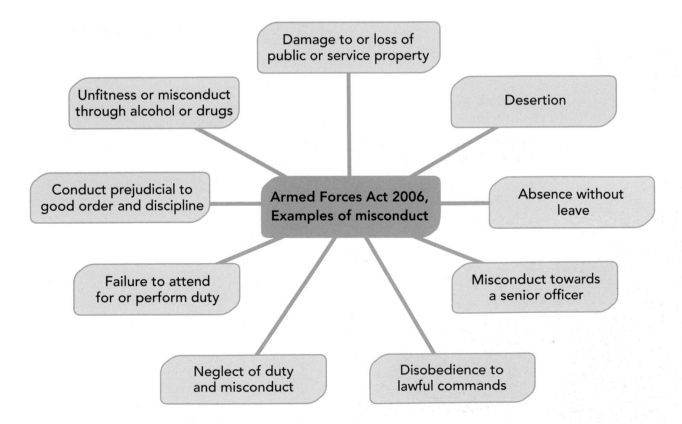

Figure 4.2: The conduct of personnel serving in the armed forces (British Army, Royal Air Force and Royal Navy) is covered under Section 1 of the Armed Forces Act 2006, and there are a total of 49 disciplinary rules to ensure the correct conduct of serving personnel.

in a burning building because they had promised some kind of reward. In this context, discipline has the role of ensuring that the public is served in a fair and courteous manner.

Rules, procedures, policies and legislation

We have already seen that without rules, regulations and legislation there can be no enforcement of social order. Similarly, if rules and regulations do not govern the conduct of members of the uniformed public services, then discipline cannot be encouraged or enforced.

The rules of conduct for the armed forces and police service make it clear that, amongst other things, members are encouraged to remain professional, loyal to each other, their service and the public, and not to bring their service into disrepute.

Case study: The Code of Professional Standards for police officers

The police service has a Code of Professional Standards for police officers, drawn up in 2006 by a working party of the Police Advisory Board. The new code sets out 10 principles that govern the conduct of serving police officers. These are listed below.

Code of Professional Standards

1. Police officers are personally responsible and accountable for their actions or omissions.
2. Police officers are honest, act with integrity and do not compromise or abuse their position.
3. Police officers obey lawful orders and refrain from carrying out any orders that they know, or ought to know, are unlawful.
4. When police officers use force it is only to the extent that is necessary and reasonable to obtain a legitimate objective.
5. Police officers do not abuse their powers or authority and respect the rights of all individuals. Police officers act with self-control and tolerance, treating members of the public and colleagues with respect and courtesy.
6. Police officers act with fairness and impartiality. They do not discriminate unlawfully on the grounds of sex, race, colour, language, religion or belief, political or other opinion, national or social origin, association with a national minority, disability, age, sexual orientation, property, birth or other status.
7. Police officers treat information with respect and access or disclose it only for a legitimate police purpose.

8. Police officers when on duty or presenting themselves for duty are fit to carry out their responsibilities.
9. Police officers on duty act in a professional way. Police officers do not behave in a manner which brings, or is likely to bring, discredit on the police service or that undermines or is likely to undermine public confidence in the police, whether on or off duty.
10. Police officers challenge and, when appropriate, take action or report breaches of this code and the improper conduct of colleagues.

1 A police officer is struggling to arrest a man who has just assaulted a shopkeeper. You see the police officer kneeling on the detainee's back in order to handcuff him. The man is shouting and complaining that the officer is hurting him, but the officer continues to kneel on his back while wrestling to overcome him. Discuss whether the officer has contravened the fourth principle.

2 You are having a drink in a café when you overhear two off-duty police officers talking about a woman they have just arrested for shoplifting. You happen to know the woman they are talking about. Which principle will the officers have breached?

3 Give three examples of when a police officer would be in breach of principle 8 with relevant explanations for each.

Assessment activity 4.1

Discipline is fundamental to any of the uniformed public services, and if you are contemplating a career in any of them you need to have a firm understanding of why and how discipline is applied. If you do not understand the notion of discipline, in all its contexts, then you would not be an effective member of the services, which could mean the organisation would not be as efficient as it should be.

Address the following tasks in the form of a leaflet:

1   Explain the need for and role of discipline in the uniformed public services **P1**

2   Justify the need for and role of discipline in the uniformed public services **M1**

3   Evaluate the impact of discipline on the uniformed public services **D1**

Grading tips

P1 requires you to explain why discipline is need in the uniformed public services, as well as the role it plays. You should include the content covered in this section.

M1 is an extension of P1 and you could show the justification by giving examples of the uses of discipline in different situations.

D1 requires you to examine the effects of discipline in the uniformed public services, saying what is positive and what is negative about the effects, and drawing a balanced conclusion from what you have said.

2.   Self-discipline as required in the uniformed public services

2.1 Self-discipline

Self-discipline is another form of discipline, and an essential quality for a member of any service. Self-discipline can be defined as the ability to apply yourself in the correct manner, including controlling yourself and your feelings. To appreciate the qualities needed for self-discipline fully, you need to understand the following areas.

Personal grooming and presentation

If you can't be bothered to take a pride in your own appearance, what message does that convey to others? Would you like to eat in a restaurant if the waitress had dirty fingernails? In the uniformed public services, where members of the public may be looking to you for help or guidance, it is particularly important that you are of smart appearance. People form impressions and opinions about us from the way we appear to them, so if you want to create the right impression it is important that you are correctly presented.

When you wear the uniform of a public service you are representing your organisation and people will judge the organisation by your appearance.

Punctuality

In order to run efficiently and effectively, organisations have to keep to tight schedules and this means being governed by time. In the public services punctuality is vital so that, at any time, someone can say where, when and how many people are on duty. At the beginning of a shift, public service personnel are briefed about any major issues that may have arisen; for example, police officers would be kept updated about a missing child. If you are late for a shift and miss the briefing, then you are preventing that organisation from operating at its full efficiency. What would happen if everyone was late for their shift?

Reliability

An organisation is only as reliable as its members. Uniformed public service employees must be reliable, so that an employee can be depended upon. Forgetfulness or dishonesty can bring disrepute to the entire service, thus destroying public trust and confidence.

Composure is one of several essential qualities of self-discipline.

Composure

Can you keep your head in a crisis? As a member of the public services, you will be the person to whom people turn for help, information and attention. You can only give help and bring about order by remaining calm and thinking clearly.

Attitude

Can you show sympathy and understanding, even when you feel frustrated and annoyed? Police officers have to be fair, unbiased and courteous and must not allow their personal problems to interfere with their professional responsibilities. People in distress often turn to the police because they see them as figureheads – someone they believe they can trust to advise and help sort out their problems.

What would happen if people were reluctant to seek help and advice from the police because they were made to feel that they were being a burden or a nuisance? They might seek help elsewhere if they felt that going through the normal channels was of no use.

If you are sulky or off hand with your colleagues, then this could affect morale, which could have an effect on the efficiency with which you execute your duties.

This is not to say that you should always try to be happy and enthusiastic to the extent that you are overpowering. You should be able to alter your attitude to suit the mood of the moment.

Performance

You might be happy with just doing enough, but members of the public or your colleagues might not be. In the public services, you not only have yourself to think about; you have a duty to perform to the best of your ability at all times. If your performance is perceived as relaxed or care free in the wrong situation, this may affect the morale of your colleagues. Remember, you have a duty to show team spirit – you should be proud and have a high regard for your chosen service.

The performance of public service employees is always monitored in some form by members of the public. Good performance instils confidence in the public, knowing that, if needed, the services can be relied upon to perform to the best of their ability.

Personality

When we talk about 'personality' in the uniformed public services, we mean the distinctive, attractive qualities that make us stand out from others. Just because everyone wears a uniform and has a service number, it doesn't mean that public service employees don't have personality.

You might think that we can't alter our personalities, but this isn't necessarily so. As with many other qualities, we have to work at improving things by practising and then reflecting on what we did right or wrong. Your personality can make a huge difference to your role within the public services: it can make you a popular colleague to work with and it can ease relations with the public both at home and abroad.

Activity: How is your self-discipline?

Look at the seven qualities required for self-discipline, listed above, and grade yourself honestly for each one. You could grade yourself as poor, average or good. Now ask one of your peers to grade you and compare the grades.

Are you as good as you thought?

Is there room for improvement? If so, how can you improve?

Consequences of a lack of self-discipline

If you lack any of the qualities that make up self-discipline, then you cannot meet the expectations of your job. For example, poor attendance could mean that you are not fully informed of important issues at briefings, which will mean that your team cannot rely on you to respond correctly to situations. This could make you feel as though you are not accepted by the group. What would this do for team morale?

Teams in the uniformed public services are only effective if the public have confidence in them. It only takes one member to lack self-discipline and the entire team, or possibly the entire organisation, could suffer. Disciplinary action could be taken to punish an individual for breaking rules and regulations but it cannot replace the public's trust in that organisation. Trust and a good reputation are built up over years of hard work and devotion to duty, yet one selfish act can ruin all that effort.

2.2 Activities requiring self-discipline

Drill

Regimental drill is a highly disciplined, military exercise that demands self discipline of the highest standard. Whilst the police and fire services use a little drill in their initial training, it is the serving members of the armed forces who are expert in the art of regimental drill, and to see a military parade performing drill as it is meant to be performed is a fantastic spectacle.

When taking part in drill, you must move only on the command of the drill instructor and once you have been brought to the attention position you must remain in that position and stay perfectly still. This means you cannot move your head, hands or any visible part of your body, even if you develop an incontrollable urge to scratch your chin, or giggle at someone who cannot march as well as you can. One move at the wrong time will ruin the meticulous appearance of the parade and draw the wrath of the drill instructor, who is likely to punish the entire parade. Hence, for the good of the parade, it is important to use self-discipline.

Activity: Forms of drill

What other forms of drill, military or otherwise, can you think of?

Uniform maintenance

Smartness is a sign of good self-discipline and pride. It takes an effort to press your trousers, shirt and tunic, as well as polishing your boots (or shoes), buttons and buckles to a high standard. It would be so easy not to bother, especially if you have been busy working in conditions that caused them to get dirty. But what does it say about you if you don't look smart? How would the public regard you and your service?

When you take a pride in your appearance you are reflecting your belief in a sense of duty and honour to your service, your colleagues and yourself. Uniforms should be worn with pride as they represent responsibility, integrity and many other attributes, especially self-discipline, that the wearer of that uniform possesses.

Adhering to a team code

To belong to a team, especially an elite team, is a privilege and even a great honour, where there is mutual respect among members because they all share the same values. When the morale of the team is high then the team spirit is also high, leading to efficiency and success, which is why morale should be maintained. Any attempt to bring the team into disrepute through neglect or thoughtlessness will disrupt morale and affect the productivity of the team. When morale is low, there will be no *esprit-de-corps* and the team will suffer.

Teams, large or small, often have mottos which tend to reflect the spirit or tradition of the team.

Time management

In the uniformed public services you have to manage your time by prioritising your workload and ensuring that important reports and documents are produced on time, even if this means rearranging your work schedule or social time. For example, the emergency services are often involved in dealing with serious accidents or major incidents, which are very time consuming. Certain reports have to be completed, statements must be taken and enquiries followed up. If there are fatalities, then HM Coroner needs to be informed, as well as relatives and friends.

The complex demands of such incidents mean that any other plans you might have must take second place because the matter that you are dealing with has taken priority.

Attendance

There may be times when we have to do something we are not looking forward to – perhaps a presentation in front of class or an important examination. It would be easy to make excuses and convince ourselves that we are not well enough to perform the task in hand and just not bother to turn up.

In the public services you are part of a team and non-attendance, without good reason, lets yourself and the team down. Previous hard work – e.g. painstaking enquiries and observations – may be in vain if you don't attend on the day an arrest is to be made. Plans cannot be made for a whole team when one member has a poor record of attendance.

Activity: Mottos

Which team (large or small) has each of the following mottos?

- Who Dares Wins
- Per Ardua ad Astra (and what does this mean?)
- Ubique.

What is meant by *esprit-de-corps*?

Assessment activity 4.2 (P2) (M2) (D2) BTEC

If you are to be a member of the uniformed public services, it is not good enough to say you have good self-discipline; you need to demonstrate that you have it. You will have the opportunity to demonstrate your level of self-discipline by taking part in several activities, such as drill, time management and uniform inspections.

Address the following tasks in the form of relevant activities:

1 Demonstrate self-discipline through relevant activities (P2)

2 Perform relevant activities with a high standard of self-discipline (M2)

3 Evaluate personal levels of self-discipline for entry to the uniformed public services (D2)

Grading tips

(P2) requires you to show your self-discipline over a period of time. You can show this by taking part in drill activities, taking part in a uniform inspection, keeping to a dress code and maintaining standards of punctuality and time management. Your tutor will give you further guidance.

(M2) requires you to perform the activities to a high standard.

(D2) requires you to evaluate your personal levels of self-discipline by giving an honest summary of the positive and negative aspects of your self-discipline, and a balanced conclusion.

3. What conformity and obedience mean, and their place in the uniformed public services

3.1 Conformity

What exactly do we mean when we say that someone is conforming? Since the 1930s, psychologists have been interested in the nature of conformity and obedience, and one psychologist, Crutchfield (1955), attempted to formulate a definition of **conformity** as: *yielding to group pressure* (that is giving in to the demands of a group). Much later, Zimbardo and Leippe (1991) proposed a definition as: *A change in belief or behaviour in response to real or imagined group pressure when there is no direct request to comply with the group nor any reason to justify the behaviour change.*

See Figures 4.3 and 4.4.

Key term

Conformity is to act or behave in accordance with established practice.

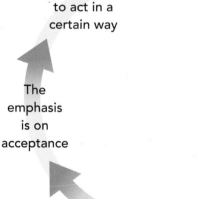

It is normally peers or equals who influence us

No direct requirement to act in a certain way

Behaviour adopted is similar to that of peers

The emphasis is on acceptance

Conformity regulates the behaviour among those of equal status

Figure 4.3: The key points of conformity.

Low self-esteem, worried about personal relationships **+** Need for social approval, afraid of ridicule **=** Conformity

Figure 4.4: Influences on conformity.

Activity: To conform or not

Have you ever been in situations that require conformity? Have you conformed and why?

Compliance with common practices

Key term

Compliance is to act in accordance with a wish or command.

When we comply with something we act in accordance with a request or command to perform a task; such a request or command could be spoken or unspoken. When you have completed the task requested or ordered, you have performed an act of **compliance**.

Members of the uniformed public services comply with common practices every day, possibly without even realising it. For example, lower ranks salute their officers as a mark of respect and the officers return the salute – it is a common practice. Sometimes these common practices are just customs and sometimes there is a rule demanding that you do them, but people usually obey the rule without being asked.

However, when you comply with certain practices (which could be practices that you are bound to follow by law or simply practices that have evolved through tradition) you may be said to be conforming because you are acting in accordance with an established practice.

The key thing to remember is that with conformity there is no explicit request.

Activity: Examples of conformity and compliance

Look at the following examples and decide whether they refer to conformity or compliance (or both).

- Jamie was smoking a cigarette at the bus stop but his friends started coughing and grimacing with disgust so he put it out.
- Sally was new to the area and wanted to make friends. She noticed that many of the girls in the neighbourhood had had their tongues pierced and she believed that by having her tongue pierced she would be accepted as a friend.
- Scott was a new recruit in the Royal Marines and although his hair was short he noticed his friends had had their heads shaved. The next day he went to the barbers and had his head shaved.

Social norms

It is a well-known fact that humans are social creatures, who like to share beliefs and attitudes and live in societies. When we are integrated into society we feel that we belong – we have a sense of purpose – and this gives us a sense of being in control of our lives, which makes us happy and confident.

However, for those who are unable to socially integrate, feelings such as loneliness, failure, vulnerability and deficiency may result, or it might simply be the case that a person is not comfortable with a particular culture and so chooses another one. Some psychologists (Hewitt, 1998) believe that:

Social integration allows us to develop our interactive skills, to communicate, to evaluate and to compromise.

Every culture contains a set of ideas and beliefs about the nature of human beings, what motivates them to act, the way they perceive the world, how their minds work, and the emotions that are natural to them.

What is it that influences us into adopting social norms? According to psychologists Deutsch and Gerard (1955), there are two main types of social influence that affect conformity – **informational social influence** (ISI) and **normative social influence** (NSI).

ISI is the theory that we have a basic need to weigh up information and opinions, but when we are in a strange environment we are susceptible because we don't have the information that makes us feel comfortable and in control. Instead, we have to pick up on the thoughts and behaviour of others as a measure of the behaviour that is expected of us. In other words, we turn to others for direction and tend to behave according to the majority.

For example, suppose you were waiting to cross the road with a crowd of people at a pedestrian crossing and you couldn't see the lights because someone was obstructing your view. When the crowd begins to cross the road, you join them without even checking to see if the lights are in your favour. You look to others for guidance on how to behave and you tend to conform to the behaviour of others. If you are familiar with an environment then you are less likely to rely on the behaviour of the majority and, hence, you are less likely to conform.

The **NSI** theory claims that we conform because we have a fundamental need to be accepted by others, and we may only be accepted by making a good impression; usually, this will be by saying what the majority want to hear or behaving in a manner that meets their approval. It's difficult to imagine succeeding in a job interview by saying 'no' and frowning, when you ought to be saying 'yes' and smiling.

Closely related to ISI and NSI is the theory of **internalisation** – when a private belief or opinion is consistent with public belief and opinion. However, in Asch-type experiments (see pages 136–137), the naïve participants faced conflicts and complied publicly with the stooges, but what they said publicly was not necessarily what they believed privately.

Abrams and others (1990) argue for a social influence known as **referential social influence (RSI)**. Social influence occurs when we see ourselves as belonging to a group that possesses the same beliefs and characteristics, and uncertainty arises when we find ourselves in disagreement with group members. In other words, it is more likely that we will take notice of and be influenced by a group with which we have an affinity than one with which we don't. When we categorise ourselves in groups in this way, we are concerned, above anything else, with upholding the norms of the group.

The role of self-esteem

Do you have a good opinion of yourself? Are you confident? If you can answer 'yes' to both of these questions then, according to the dictionary definition, you have high self-esteem; that is, you consider yourself to be worthy of respect.

Self-esteem comes from the way we are seen to conform to, or comply with, norms. Our behaviour is guided by comments such as: 'Well done, that was a really good effort' or 'Perhaps it would be better if you did it this way'. By receiving positive feedback, our self-esteem rises and we gain confidence in our own ability.

If you lack self-confidence or self-respect, you may be tempted to act out of character in order to gain the respect of others. For example, impressionable teenagers might decide to take up smoking or drinking alcohol because that is what the members of their group do. While this will harm them physically, it will show the group that they are conforming, which may persuade the group to accept them as a member.

This is not to say that all people who conform are suffering from low self-esteem or some kind of anxiety. On the contrary, it is believed by many psychologists that conformity to socially accepted demands is perfectly normal and is one of the main ways in which we develop our character and recognise our role in society.

Low self-esteem has been described as an illness in which people have negative perceptions of themselves and are more likely to feel frustrated and not in control of their lives. This may result in people losing confidence or having reduced self-awareness.

Case study: Colin's story, overcoming low self-esteem

'When I was nine years old my father died in a car accident and I can remember my mum crying and telling me that I was now the man of the house, and I shouldn't cry because brave men didn't cry. Mum told to be strong to look after my younger sister while she went out to work to support us.

When I was 12, I got a job delivering milk before school so I could save some money to take my mum and sister on holiday. I had to go to bed very early which meant I never had the social life that other kids my age had; I didn't watch much television or listen to music but I did like reading when I got the chance. I never had any close friends and some of the kids at school used to make fun of me for not knowing about television shows and they used to call me a geek.

It was about a year or so later that Mum's boyfriend moved in with us and he was okay with my mum and sister, but he used to shout at me saying I was useless and should forget about reading and think about a proper job. I never told my mum because I'd promised her I'd be brave, and even if I were useless I could still be brave.

I became so upset with my home and school life that I used to play truant from school, and I started knocking around with a gang of youths who were a bit older than me but they never made fun of me and they made me feel welcome. I started smoking and we used to get cans and bottles of booze and just go and get drunk. I know it was wrong but it made me feel good and I felt, for the first time in years, that I belonged. We used to go shoplifting and stealing from cars to get money for booze and then some older ones in the gang started giving us drugs. They never said I had to take them but I didn't want to lose their friendship.

By the time I was sentenced to a Young Offenders Institution at 17 years of age, I'd been a heroin addict for 18 months. I never realised how much I'd broken my mother's heart until she first came to see me when I was inside.

That was 10 years ago, and after rehabilitation and counselling I now have a career as a Youth Worker – I advise and offer help and support to young people who lack confidence and direction.'

1 What led Colin to feel that he had little self-value?

2 What was it that attracted Colin to the gang?

3 With regard to his home circumstances, what do you think might have prevented Colin from seeking companionship in the gang?

4 Is this an example of conformity? Explain.

5 Could Colin have done anything differently?

6 What would you have done if you were Colin?

The purpose of uniforms

It is generally considered that uniforms are a symbol of unity, pride and authority, especially those worn by public service employees. They are instantly recognisable and members of the public can relate to the personnel who wear them. But some uniforms can convey power (for example, the army helmet) while other uniforms are used to identify professional authority, such as a doctor's white coat. Powerful institutions such as the Ministry of Defence and the police invest officers with authority, and this is symbolised by their uniform which indicates the hierarchy of authority to the members of that institution.

Uniforms also offer protection and security to the officers who wear them. For example, firefighters require special protective equipment as part of their

Uniforms are worn with pride and honour.

uniform because of the nature of their work, as do the police when dealing with riots and members of the armed forces when serving on active duty.

Activity: What uniforms symbolise

Think of four types of uniform, outside of the public services, that may be worn by members of a profession or voluntary organisation.

- What do those uniforms symbolise?
- How do you think members of the public would view those who wear uniform?
- Does wearing a uniform mean conformity?

The relevance of conformity in the public services

We have seen that conformity, from a psychological perspective, means to be accepted. In a general sense, it also means to comply with or be in accordance with something. In the uniformed public services, both senses of conformity are relevant.

Every member of the uniformed public services wants to feel accepted and that they belong to a team of professionals, otherwise they would not have wanted to join that particular service. Teamwork is an essential quality in any of the services and is vital in achieving effective outcomes. We have already mentioned team spirit, together with the need for discipline to ensure that it continues. If one member of the team does not conform to the norms of the team, it is likely to disrupt the dynamics of the team, making it inefficient or perhaps bringing the team, or even the service, into disrepute. It is in the best interests of the other members, therefore, to deal with the member who is not conforming and remind them that if they wish to continue to be accepted then they must conform to the ethos of the team.

3.2 Obedience

In the uniformed public services you are expected to obey orders and commands from those in authority. In some respects, **obedience** is similar to conformity in that it is a form of compliance. Unlike conformity, obedience means that you must comply with orders and commands; you have no choice. If you do not obey a command from a higher authority, then you are likely to face disciplinary procedures for disobedience, otherwise known as insubordination.

Key term

Obedience means carrying out the command of some authority, doing what you are told to do.

Remember!

With conformity there is no requirement to behave in a specific way. With obedience you are ordered to do something by someone in higher authority, whereas with conformity the influence comes from your peers or equals. Obedience involves social power and status, whereas conformity is generally seen as a psychological need to be accepted by others.

Obedience as an act

Obedience is the act of obeying orders given by someone in authority and if you are obedient then you are carrying out, or willing to carry out, those orders. For example, if a private in the army stood to attention on parade, on the orders of the sergeant, then the private would be said to be performing an act of obedience.

Obedience as a practice or quality

Obedience in the uniformed public services is an essential practice as it makes the service efficient and disciplined and able to respond quickly to any situation. It allows mutual trust and respect because all those involved in the organisation know that they can depend on each other to achieve their objectives effectively by playing their part. Without the practice of obedience the uniformed public services would be in chaos and the hierarchical structure within the service would have no authority.

If you are thinking of joining one of the services, you should ask yourself if you possess the quality of obedience because without it you would find a career in the services very difficult. You may have to work at this quality, especially if you are the type of person who has personality clashes or you dislike being told what to do. Obedience does not mean you are weak willed or cannot make decisions for yourself. It means that you know where you fit into the service and that you trust those in authority, who have the experience to make the correct decisions for you to carry out for the good of the service. After all, it is the rank of the person in authority that you must respect, not necessarily the person who holds the rank.

Following orders

Orders are commands given by someone in authority. Following orders is an essential part of the uniformed public services. You should remember that orders are given by those in authority with the intention of reaching an objective efficiently and effectively. The objective may be simple and uncomplicated; for instance, the refuelling of a fire engine at the end of a shift to make sure it is ready for the next watch. On the other hand, the objective could be something as complex as, say, responding to an incident like the London bombings. Each order is given for a reason and no matter how simple or how complex an order is it must be followed to prevent serious consequences to your colleagues, the service and members of the public.

Verbal commands are not the only type of orders. In the uniformed public services, the written rules and regulations concerning the conduct of personnel and the manner in which procedures are carried out are called 'standing orders.' All uniformed public service personnel should be aware of and follow standing orders. Failure to do so would be a disciplinary offence.

Conscious and unconscious obedience

When you are awake and aware of what you are doing you are said to be conscious; you are consciously aware of your actions. If you were to try and remember your actions a short time later, then you would probably

remember what you did very clearly. However, if you were to perform a task so often that it became routine – a habit – then you might not remember so clearly. For example, if you had to pack eggs into boxes for eight hours a day, you would probably not recollect packing, say, the eighty-third box because the task had become so mundane that you were performing the task out of habit. Therefore, instead of you being conscious of packing the eggs into boxes, you were unconscious of doing so.

Obedience in the uniformed public services can be conscious or unconscious, depending on whether the obedience is routine or not. For example, if you were in the Royal Marines and you had followed orders to search a series of caves in Afghanistan, then that would be conscious obedience because you wouldn't normally search caves as part of your job. But when you were at the training camp doing your initial training you would have reacted to so many orders that they just became routine and you would have followed them unconsciously.

Compliance

Remember: compliance means to act in accordance with a wish or command. When we looked earlier at 'compliance with common practices' we saw that it was the same as conformity in that it was an act in accordance with a practice; that is, there was no specific request. However, compliance is also the same as obedience because as a member of the public services you have to act – or comply – in accordance with orders from a higher authority. By demonstrating compliance you are showing that you are obedient and following orders as instructed.

Status as a factor in obedience

Within the uniformed public services, obedience status depends on your rank within the hierarchy of authority. You have to obey those of senior rank, while those of a lower rank have to obey you. The higher the rank, the more responsibility you have for making decisions and ensuring your orders are carried out.

Status in the uniformed public services is a factor in ensuring obedience, because if you have ambition and want promotion you have to show that you can obey orders, just as all those of the higher ranks have done.

You cannot reach a position of authority and expect the lower ranks to obey your commands if you cannot demonstrate obedience.

It is not only the lower ranks of the public services who have a role of obedience to play within the hierarchy of authority – society also gives its members a certain status. For example, as children we are taught to respect our elders and obey authority. We are also conditioned, from an early age, to be obedient and comply with requests from those we perceive to be in authority. For example, children will wait at the side of the road until the school crossing patrol warden waves them across.

Activity: Obedience to authority

Think of six occasions when you have obeyed the instruction or request of someone you have perceived to be in authority.

Linton (1945) identified five different social groupings (see Figure 4.5). With the groupings, unlike the public services, there is no law that binds a member of the group to an act of obedience. Rather, the obedience status has been derived from tradition or culture.

Influences on obedience

Fear

Fear is a strong influence in ensuring obedience within the uniformed public services, both physically and psychologically. Disobedience could lead to a reduction in rank or pay, loss of privileges, dishonourable discharge, suspension from duty or even imprisonment.

Apart from the fear of punishment, there is the fear that failing to obey orders could stand in the way of your career development. Furthermore, you may fear that you will be letting down your team by failing to obey orders, thus weakening the strength of the team and bringing about a feeling that you are no longer part of it.

Reward

Unlike the private sector, the uniformed public services do not receive financial rewards beyond their pay for performing their duty. For example, you would not expect a firefighter to receive a bonus for the amount of fires they have fought in a week; they do their job regardless. However, as mentioned earlier, members are positively reinforced with medals for good or heroic conduct, or extended leave after a tour of duty abroad. Members don't join the services to be rewarded for doing their job; they are rewarded by the personal satisfaction they receive from doing their job well.

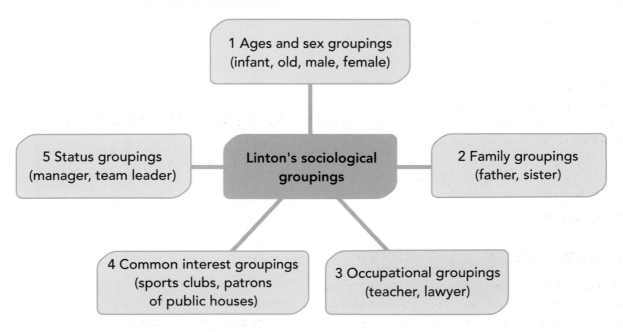

Figure 4.5: Linton's groupings which all have different status and expectations.

Love

While many people are obedient as a mark of love for the people they are obeying, this is not usually the case in the uniformed public services. A different kind of love influences obedience in the services – it is a love for their service and the camaraderie within it that influences obedience. This affection for the team and the service has developed as a result of obedience to duty.

Respect

If you respect someone you value them or admire them for what they have achieved. In the uniformed public services promotion is gained through merit; that is, loyalty to the service, hard work, experience and displaying the kind of qualities needed for leadership. As a member of the uniformed public services you must respect the rank of seniority and what it stands for, even though you might not personally know the officer carrying the higher rank. Some people say that 'you can't respect someone until they've earned it' but in the uniformed public services respect goes with the rank because it has certainly been earned. Respect in the uniformed public services is therefore an influence on obedience.

Relevance of obedience in the uniformed public services

Just as conformity is relevant in its own way to the uniformed public services, so is obedience. When you obey an order you may be doing something that can affect a large number of people in a positive or negative way, depending on the order. For example, you may be ordered to destroy enemy buildings, which would have a negative effect on the enemy but a positive effect on your colleagues and your service. You must always remember that when obeying orders you are doing so for the good of yourself, your colleagues, the service and the public. By disobeying orders you are not only being selfish and risking disciplinary proceedings, you are letting your colleagues, service and the public down. Nor should you forget that you joined a uniformed public service for the good of the service and the public, not just because it offered you a promising career.

Without obedience in the uniformed public services there would be no teamwork, team spirit, trust, respect or authority; all the things that make the uniformed

public services what they are. However conformity and obedience can also have bad effects as well as good. The next section discusses psychological experiments which demonstrated that sometimes a desire to conform can lead people to act irrationally or irresponsibly. In Section 4, concepts such as legitimate authority and obedience to lawful orders are discussed – these are ways to give obedience a moral framework.

3.3 Research on conformity and obedience

Psychologists have conducted many conformity and obedience experiments, the results of which are quite remarkable. Four well-known studies are presented below.

Asch's paradigm

Asch (1951) wanted to show that people's behaviour is a response to group pressure, either real or imagined. The test was a line judgement task, which involved participants being presented with two cards: one card – a standard card (A) – contained a single vertical line and the other card – comparison card (B) – contained three vertical lines of varying length. The participants simply had to decide which line on the comparison card matched that on the standard card.

Asch arranged for some of the participants to act as stooges (people who played a specific role but pretended that they were not involved in the

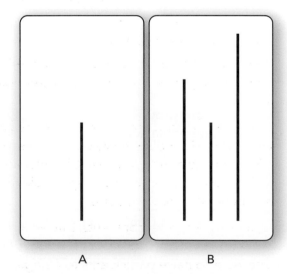

Figure 4.6: Asch's test. Are any black rules the same?

experiment). They were told that the group would contain one participant who was unaware that they were stooges.

Asch ran several trials, some of which were critical (where the results were monitored) while others were not. All the stooges knew when the trials were critical because Asch would indicate this with a secret signal; the other participants (naïve participants) didn't know which were critical and which were neutral.

During the critical trials, of which there were 12, the stooges were required to unanimously say aloud the incorrect answer and the experiment was rigged so that the naïve participant was always last, or last but one, to give their answer.

The results from the experiments were not overwhelmingly in favour of conformity being a matter of group pressure, though they were quite convincing. Asch showed that in 11 out of 12 critical trials one person out of 50 conformed totally (i.e. gave the wrong answer each time) and 37 out of 50 conformed at least once. Many similar experiments have subsequently been conducted and the participants, when asked to explain their behaviour, said that they:

- wanted to act in accordance with the experimenter's wishes and not give an unfavourable impression of themselves, which they might have done had they disagreed with the majority
- doubted the validity of their own judgement because of eye strain or because they could not see the task material properly
- didn't realise they had given the wrong answers and used the stooges as guide posts
- didn't want to appear different
- didn't want to be made to look foolish or inferior, even though they knew the answer they were giving was wrong.

Interestingly, Asch noticed that when the stooges gave their answers verbally and the naïve participants wrote theirs down, conformity was considerably reduced. He concluded that group pressure was responsible for conformity, rather than anything else.

In subsequent Asch-type experiments, but where there were more naïve participants than stooges (in some there were 16 naïve participants to a single stooge), when the stooge gave a wrong answer, the participants reacted with laughter and sarcasm, thus giving credence to the theory that people conform because of group or peer pressure.

Milgram's electric shock experiment

Milgram (1974) researched obedience because he was concerned about the serious social problems that it had caused in the past. Milgram wanted to find out if high-ranking officials and accomplices in the Nazi Party were just following orders: *From 1933 to 1945 millions of innocent persons were systematically slaughtered on command. Gas chambers were built, death camps were guarded, daily quotas of corpses were produced with the same efficiency as the manufacture of appliances. These human policies may have originated in the mind of a single person, but they could only be carried out on a massive scale if a very large number of persons obeyed orders.*

(from Gross and McIlveen, 1988)

Milgram used volunteers from all walks of life to participate in the experiments, which involved three people at a time: the experimenter, the

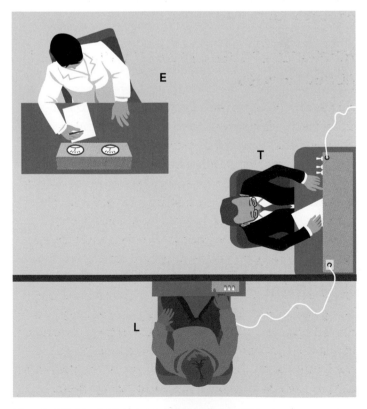

Figure 4.7: The Milgram experiment where E is the experimenter, T the teacher and L the learner.

learner and the teacher. The experimenter and learner, who were stooges, acted out a carefully pre-prepared script, whereas the teacher (who was always a naïve participant) only knew that the experiment was concerned with the effects of punishment on learning.

Prior to the commencement of the experiment, all three people went into a room where the teacher witnessed the learner being strapped into a chair with his arms attached to electrodes that would, apparently, deliver an electric shock. The teacher was then led into an adjacent room where he was shown a generator, which contained a number of switches, clearly marked with a range of volts from 15 to 450. This equipment was to be used by the teacher to supposedly administer an electric shock to the learner if the learner didn't remember a word correctly or refused to respond with an answer. Every time the learner made a mistake, the shocks increased by increments of 15 volts. The learner would respond as if he was really receiving the shocks.

During the experiments, the teachers showed reluctance to deliver the shocks but after being prompted by the experimenter with phrases such as, 'please continue', 'please go on', 'the experimenter requires that you continue' and finally, 'you have no other choice, you must go on', the teachers continued.

Milgram was astonished by the result of his experiments: every teacher administered at least 300 volts and 65 per cent administered 450 volts (a possibly lethal amount). He concluded: *[T]he most fundamental lesson of our study is that ordinary people, simply doing their jobs, and without any particular hostility on their part, can become agents in a terrible destructive process.*

(from Gross and McIlveen, 1988)

Zimbardo's prison simulation experiment

In 1971 Zimbardo investigated human response to captivity. He advertised for student volunteers to take part in a simulated prison experiment. After being judged to be emotionally stable and physically fit, 25 male volunteers were told that they would be randomly selected to be either a prisoner or a guard, although all of them had stated a preference to be a prisoner.

In Philip Zimbardo's Stanford Prison Experiment simulation the basement of the University had been adapted to resemble a prison.

One Sunday morning, the 'prisoners' were unexpectedly arrested and handcuffed by the local police and taken to a police station where they were searched, fingerprinted, charged, and taken to prison blindfolded.

Upon arrival at the prison cells, the detainees were stripped, skin-searched, and issued with bedding, uniform and an identification number. They were chained and wore nylon stockings to simulate shaven heads. They were referred to only by their identification numbers and were kept in a cell shared by two others, only to be allowed out for meals, exercise, toilet and work.

The guards wore khaki uniforms and silver reflector sunglasses to prevent eye contact. They carried clubs, whistles, handcuffs and keys to the main gate, and had complete control over the prisoners. The prisoners assumed a passive nature as the guards became aggressive towards them, with roll calls in the middle of the night, for instance, to disrupt the prisoners' sleep.

As the prisoners seemed to lose control of their lives, the guards appeared to enjoy their role. One guard was quoted as saying, 'Power can be a great pleasure'. However, because of severe depression, fits of rage and uncontrollable crying, one prisoner was released after just 36 hours, with three others leaving shortly after with the same symptoms.

Although the experiment had been scheduled for two weeks it was terminated after only six days because of the emotional deterioration of the prisoners, who had initially been selected because of their emotional stability. (from Gross and McIlveen, 1988)

Hofling's nurses

In 1966 Hofling and his team conducted an experiment to see if nurses would deliberately cause harm to a patient if ordered to do so by a doctor. Hofling spoke to 22 nurses and told them about reports of a new drug, Astroten, which indicated that it was very toxic. In fact, the drug Astroten was made up by the research team; it didn't really exist. After speaking to the nurses, Hofling asked for a doctor who was familiar to the nurses to telephone each of them in turn while they were working on the wards. The doctor was told to instruct the nurses to administer 20 mg of Astroten to a patient on the ward; 21 out of the 22 nurses did administer the drug (which was nothing more than a glucose substitute) in spite of the following factors:

- the nurses had been told that the maximum dose of the drug was 10 mg
- hospital policy stated that drugs shouldn't be prescribed over the phone
- the drug was not on the ward stock list.

So, how do these studies apply to the uniformed public services? With reference to the studies of Asch, Milgram and Hofling, we could conclude that most people will obey, without question, those who appear to be in authority. It seems to be the case that people have been conditioned to obey authority. Certainly, nurses (as in Hofling's study) would find nothing odd in carrying out the orders of a doctor, when that is what they are accustomed to. Personnel in other uniformed public services are also used to obeying authority without question and perhaps they feel secure in the knowledge that, if anything were to go wrong, they can say that they were only following orders.

Two of the studies tended to show **obedience** – the subjects were specifically asked to perform a task, which they did, and this is applicable to all the uniformed public services.

Charles Hofling conducted a field experiment on obedience in the nurse-physician relationship.

Activity: Conformity and obedience studies

In order to see if any or all of these studies apply to the uniformed public services, you will need to show that similar traits are demonstrated by personnel in the services. If you look at the following websites you will find some strikingly similar traits of members of the uniformed public services that suggest the studies do, indeed, apply:

http://news.bbc.co.uk/1/hi/uk/257693.stm
http://news.bbc.co.uk/1/hi/uk/2372983.stm

In relation to the experiments:

1 What was each one designed to prove?
2 What were the similarities between the experiments?
3 Which did you find convincing and why?
4 What are the conclusions from the experiments?
5 How do they apply to the uniformed public services today?

The other two tasks tended to highlight **conformity** – the subjects acted of their own volition, as opposed to being asked to perform a specific act of obedience. While Asch's experiment showed that individuals did not want to feel left out of the group, Zimbardo's showed a certain bonding of like-minded individuals who tended to abuse their power by bullying those in their charge. It is worth remembering that while there was no evidence to suggest it, some of the guards

might have joined in the bullying because of fear of ridicule from the group. In other words, it is possible that they were conforming to the behaviour of others.

You should remember that the experiments were precisely that, experiments; it could be argued that the subjects were not behaving as they might under normal circumstances because they knew they were taking part in an experiment.

Assessment activity 4.3

 P3 P4 M3 BTEC

Understanding human behaviour, in terms of conformity and obedience, will be of benefit to you in the uniformed public services because it will give you a broader outlook on life. It will raise your awareness of how and why some groups and gangs are formed, making you a more informed officer.

Address the following tasks in the form of a presentation:

1 Outline what is meant by the terms conformity and obedience with reference to the public services
P3

2 Explain why conformity and obedience are important in the public services, with reference to research studies M3

Address the following task in the form of a role-play:

1 Participate in conformity simulations P4

Grading tips

P3 requires you to prepare and deliver a presentation that will outline conformity and obedience, with reference to the content covered in this unit. You should relate your presentation to the public services.

M3 is an extension of P3 but you need to explain, as opposed to outline; and you should relate at least three research studies to the public services.

P4 requires you to take part in at least two different conformity simulations, which you should plan with your group. It would be a good idea to invite some innocent participants from different classes or courses so that they are unaware of any pre-planned motive.

PLTS

Completing this assessment will help you develop your effective participator and teamworking skills.

4. The complex nature of authority in the uniformed public services

4.1 Authority

We have already mentioned rules, regulations and obedience to authority. Now we will consider what authority is, the nature and types of authority, and various legislation that gives authority its force.

Authority, as with discipline, can have different meanings, and the meaning of 'authority' is dependent upon the context in which it is used. For example:

- the power or right to enforce obedience
- delegated power
- a person whose opinion is accepted because of expertise.

Activity: The meaning of 'authority'

Consider the following statements and try to decide on the meaning of 'authority'.

- When Private Johnson told his friend Private Williams to get a haircut, he ignored him because he had no authority. However, he didn't ignore the sergeant, who quoted the act and section.
- Blue watch responded to the authority of Crew Manager Bryant because they knew the station manager was in a meeting.
- The jury didn't believe Mrs Chambers' evidence that the deceased died of poisoning but they listened to the authority of the pathologist.

The Independent Police Complaints Commission (IPCC)

The IPCC was formed in 2004 as a result of the Police Reform Act 2002. It replaced the Police Complaints Authority as the independent body to oversee complaints against the police in the 43 police services in England and Wales. It currently comprises 15 commissioners, who are appointed by the Home Secretary for a period of five years, and a team of independent investigators.

Each team of investigators is headed by a regional director in each of its four regions, covering England and Wales. The IPCC carries out investigations into serious allegations of misconduct by serving police personnel. These include allegations:

- of serious or organised corruption
- against senior officers
- involving racism
- of perverting the course of justice.

You can find out more about the IPCC by visiting their website: www.ipcc.gov.uk.

HM Chief Inspector of Prisons

Her Majesty's Chief Inspector of Prisons is another independent body which reports to the Secretary of State for the Ministry of Justice on the condition and treatment of prisoners in England and Wales. Its authority is given under section 5A of the Prison Act 1952 and by section 57 of the Criminal Justice Act 1982.

The inspectorate is appointed by the Home Secretary for a period of five years and its authority extends to Northern Ireland, the Channel Islands, Isle of Man and some Commonwealth-dependent territories. It reports to the Home Secretary on whether the objectives for prisons are being achieved in terms of accommodation, treatment of prisoners, conditions in prisons, and the progress made by prisons in reducing re-offending through appropriate programmes and preparing offenders for release.

HM Chief Inspector of Fire and Rescue

The former position of HM Chief Inspector of Fire and Rescue was replaced in 2007 by the **Chief Fire and Rescue Advisory Unit**.

While the former inspectorate was responsible for inspecting fire and rescue services and reporting to the Government, the new unit, established by the Department for Communities and Local Government, is responsible for providing ministers and civil servants with independent professional advice on matters concerning the structure, organisation, performance and future development of fire and rescue services. Furthermore, the new unit, led by a Chief Fire and Rescue Adviser, will advise on training and preparing for a range of major emergency issues, and provide recommendations to local authorities and other interested parties.

Extent of authority

The extent of authority relates to the limit of control held by an individual or organisation. The limit of control is governed by the job description of the role, as well as the jurisdiction, with authority coming either from statute or company policy. For example, Her Majesty's Chief Inspector of Prisons has the authority under the Ministry of Justice to inspect and report to the Government on the treatment and conditions of all prisoners in England and Wales. The inspectorate also has a statutory responsibility to inspect all holding facilities on behalf of the Immigration and Nationality Directorate, as well as the Military Corrective Training Centre in Colchester. The authority of the inspectorate extends to Northern Ireland, the Channel Islands, the Isle of Man and some dependent territories of Commonwealth countries.

Power or right to enforce obedience

The power or right to enforce obedience means the authority of an individual or organisation to enforce obedience. It is similar to the extent of authority in that the right is granted by statute or policy and the person or organisation enforcing obedience does so within an accepted legal framework. For example, a senior police officer has the right to ensure that colleagues remain honest because such a principle is included in the Police Code of Conduct. Similarly, any officer in the uniformed public services has the power or right to enforce obedience from any officer of a lower rank provided that such an act of obedience does not contravene the rules and regulations of that particular uniformed public service. Any request to perform an

illegal act is not a lawful order and the person making the request has no power or right to enforce it.

4.2 Nature of authority

Power

Power, like discipline, has several applications and, again like discipline, it depends upon the context in which it is used. It can refer to the strength or might of something or someone (for example, military strength) or it can mean the ability to persuade someone to act in accordance with a demand because the person doing the persuading has some sort of power.

Power is used as a tool of persuasion where there is a conflict of interests or an unwillingness to respond to a request. If there was no unwillingness to respond, there would be no need for power to be used as a tool of persuasion. The power may come from a lawful or unlawful source. For example, a person may be reluctant to hand over their wallet to a stranger but might do so if the stranger produces a gun to reinforce the demand.

Power, in the context of authority, means the right to ensure an individual or organisation complies with reasonable and lawful requests, even though there may be unwillingness on the part of the individual or organisation. For example, a serving soldier may be ordered to perform a fatigue (a non-military, mundane task), such as sweeping the barrack room floor, and they may be unwilling to do this. The soldier would not perform this act were it not for the power of the senior officer. Hence, for power to be exerted there must be a conflict of interests before the task is completed. Without a conflict of interests there would be no need for power in order to make a person carry out a task.

The difference between the two examples above is that the power of the senior officer came from a legitimate authority, whereas the power of the gunman came from an unlawful source.

Raven (1965) identified six bases of power:

- **reward power** – we do what we are asked because we desire rewards or benefits, such as praise, a wage increase or promotion

- **coercive power** – we do what we are asked because we fear sanctions, such as being made to perform mundane tasks, lack of privileges or even fear of dismissal
- **informational power** – we do what we are asked because we are persuaded by the content of a communication (verbal or written) and *not* by any influencing figure
- **expert power** – we do what we are asked because we believe that the power figure has generally greater expertise and knowledge than us
- **legitimate power** – we do what we are asked because we believe that the power figure is authorised by a recognised power structure to command and make decisions
- **referent power** – we do what we are asked because we can identify with the source of influence; we may be attracted to them or respect them.

Position

When we talk about someone being in a position of authority, we usually mean that they hold a certain rank or status within society or within an organisation such as the public services. There are several ways in which a person could find themselves in a position of authority. For example, a priest has the authority of the church while a mother or father has parental authority over children. In the uniformed public services, positions of authority come with promotion. An officer may be promoted because of certain achievements and special attributes, such as experience in the service, good character, knowledge of the job, dedication, self-discipline and the respect of one's colleagues.

If you join the uniformed public services and are placed in a position of authority, you may lawfully command team members, who recognise your authority and their duty to obey those legitimate commands. When authority is legitimate, there is no need to influence or use power. Indeed, if a senior officer were unable to gain the respect of a team member by command alone, then there would be no recognisable authority.

Status

Status relating to authority is akin to that of obedience. Many of the reasons why people obey can be applied to why we accept authority. For example, we respect the authority of:

- experts who are supposed to know more – those who may have answers we want or need
- people with higher status
- people with titles
- people who wear uniforms or who are of smart appearance
- people with power
- people whom we believe can punish us.

In the uniformed public services, each officer knows their status and the status of their colleagues, and where they fit into the hierarchy of authority.

Influence

Influence is different from power because power is often used to apply pressure where there is a conflict of interests, whereas influence can make a person carry out a task or alter their ways simply by reason or evaluation. The status of a person can have an influence on someone who aspires to be like that person. On the other hand, a person can be influenced by someone without any particular status, but who holds their respect and trust.

Corruption

Corruption is where a person lacks moral fibre and may be willing to undertake acts of dishonesty. Examples could be altering documents or evidence, taking bribes, and theft. Dishonesty in any of the uniformed public services is seen as an abuse of authority. Members of some of the uniformed public

Key term

Corrupt means to be without morals; to be influenced by bribery or fraudulent activity. Corruption is usually motivated by greed.

services have the authority to seize property, e.g. the proceeds of crime, and they are entrusted to follow correct procedures to ensure the property is returned to the rightful owner. Furthermore, they have access to confidential information that should not be used for personal gain.

Disobedience

Disobedience within the uniformed public services can be an extremely serious charge, depending on the degree. Serious cases of disobedience in the uniformed public services can lead to dishonourable discharge.

Blind obedience

Blind obedience means to follow orders unquestioningly – to carry out whatever is asked without question or thinking of the consequences. Early in their training, members of the uniformed public services are encouraged to obey orders immediately. This is so they become accustomed to obeying orders when they are in, for example, a conflict situation. If you thought about all the different consequences before carrying out orders, the result might not be what was intended by those giving the orders. There are many occasions on which lives have been saved and

Case study: The Holocaust

The Holocaust was the systematic persecution and slaughter of approximately six million Jews, and other people, by the Nazi regime between 1933 and 1945. The Jews were deemed to be inferior by the Nazis, who regarded them as a threat to the so-called 'racially superior' Germans.

Between 1941 and 1944, millions of Jews were deported from Germany and its occupied territories and brought to concentration camps and specially developed extermination camps, where they were gassed to death in what the Jews were led to believe were shower blocks. At first, piles of dead bodies were bulldozed into mass graves until special crematoria were constructed to burn the bodies.

Towards the end of the Second World War, the Nazis partially destroyed the gas chambers and crematoria before forcing the inmates to march

to their death, as a way of preventing the Allied Forces liberating large numbers of Jewish prisoners. The marches continued until 7 May 1945, when Germany surrendered unconditionally to the Allies.

Adolph Eichmann was a high-ranking Nazi officer and played a leading role in the deportation and massacre of millions of Jews. After the war he escaped to Argentina but was kidnapped by the Israeli Intelligence Agency and brought to trial in Israel in 1961, charged with crimes against humanity. He said that his conscience was clear because he was only following orders and he never did anything without seeking instructions from a higher authority. Eichmann was hanged on 31 May 1962.

1 What are your views on Eichmann's defence that he was only following orders?

2 Do you think Eichmann thought about the consequences of his actions?

3 Can you think of other examples of appalling consequences resulting from blind obedience?

4 What would be the psychological effects of carrying out an order that you disagree with, yet feel duty-bound to comply with?

5 Can you think of some examples where this might be the case?

6 You might also think about the consequences of a service in which everyone questioned orders. What would that mean for the concept of discipline within that service?

Sometimes it is essential to carry out orders without thinking.

dangerous situations defused because members of the uniformed public services have obeyed orders immediately.

However, the problem with obedience is knowing *when* to speak out. At which point do you stop obeying and ask yourself if you are doing the right thing by carrying out an order? The question may be answered by balancing the consequences of disobedience with the consequences brought about by ignoring an order.

There are other occasions when blind obedience does not leave us with happy memories and feelings of gratitude. We know that during the Second World War, Nazis behaved atrociously, but when questioned they insisted that they were merely following orders.

Moral dilemmas and responsibility for decisions taken

A moral dilemma is a problem to which there is no obvious 'right' solution. For example, suppose you

Activity: Following orders and blind obedience

What are the positive effects of blind obedience?

What are the negative effects of blind obedience?

were walking alongside a fast-flowing river and you saw two young boys apparently drowning. They were both shouting to you to save them and you could see they needed rescuing immediately. With no support and no time to make a call for assistance you wade into the river but you only have time to save one of the boys. Assuming the boys are the same age and neither of them can swim, how do you decide which one to save? This is a moral dilemma.

Sometimes you can work out the answer to a problem by weighing up the consequences. That is to say, you can try to decide if one action would bring about greater happiness to a greater number than another course of action would. So, if the course of action A brought about greater happiness than that of action B, then action A would be the morally right course to take. However, to take account of all the consequences might not be as easy as it appears.

In the context of the uniformed public services, the responsibility for making decisions rests with the senior officer in charge, and a good leader would accept responsibility for their decisions and stand by them. However, sometimes junior officers may need to make difficult decisions.

Questioning of orders

The public services and armed forces are dependent upon orders being followed for their efficiency. For example, in a conflict situation, there could be serious consequences if orders were not followed immediately and without question. If orders are questioned then the authority of those giving them is undermined and the hierarchy of authority loses its effectiveness. Similarly, in a major incident situation, the success of the response and recovery stages by the emergency services is reliant upon teams of personnel following the orders of the coordinating officer without question.

As we have seen in the hierarchy of authority, certain ranks have a right to command lower ranks, and those lower ranks have a duty to carry out those orders. We should expect orders that come from a legitimate source to be carried out without question as they are issued by officers who have the experience to know what is required to bring about successful conclusions. But do the lower ranks have a right to question those orders?

Case study: A moral dilemma

A group of six people (two females, Lisa and Lorraine, and four males, Barry, Paul, Nick and Geoff) from a local club went caving one Sunday morning. While they all knew each other quite well, they were not particularly close friends, though they enjoyed each other's company and loved their outdoor pursuit.

Unknown to the group, as they descended the main entrance there was an unexpected, prolonged downpour of torrential rain which quickly began to fill parts of the cave, cutting off their exit route. The group, led by Barry, a very large muscular man, crawled in single file along a narrow channel until, at last, they came to a small opening, which was their exit.

Unfortunately, Barry was so eager to leave the cave that he tried to force himself out of the opening without realising that he was too large. He became immovably stuck at the waist, and the rest of the group were shouting frantically for him to move as the water was rising behind them and they were in imminent danger of drowning. As things stood, Barry would be the only one to survive because he could breathe the fresh air outside, whereas those behind him would certainly die by drowning. They had no breathing apparatus but they had a two-way radio and Paul had a stick of dynamite in his rucksack.

The emergency services and the Cave Rescue Organisation, having been alerted by a club member, had pre-empted the appearance of the group at the place where Barry became stuck, and were in attendance, along with the local press and radio.

The five members behind Barry are screaming down their radio that they are going to blow him up to free the opening by which they can all escape, and they want the senior officer to agree that this is what they should do. Barry is pleading with the officer not to agree with that course of action as he has four young children who need him and he does not want to be blown up.

1 What information would the senior officer need in order to ensure that the course of action decided upon was the one that brought about the least amount of suffering?

2 Bearing in mind there were only a few minutes to make a decision before the five people behind Barry would drown, would it be possible to get that information?

3 If you were the senior officer, what course of action would you take?

While it might not be acceptable, in most cases, to question authority, you have to take into account that while those giving the orders may have people's or even the nation's best interests at heart, they are still human and prone to error, especially in times of extreme stress or extraordinary situations, where their otherwise accurate powers of judgement might be temporarily impaired.

Activity: My Lai Massacre 1968

Carry out some research from the internet into the My Lai Massacre of 1968, and consider what you would have done if you had been a member of Second Lieutenant William Calley's platoon.

4.3 Types of authority

Authoritarian (autocratic)

This is a type of authority whereby a leader tells their team members what task to perform and how to perform it without consultation or advice from other parties. Used appropriately, an authoritarian style of leadership can be effective in bringing about the desired result, especially when time is limited. However, there are many occasions when this type of leadership would not motivate or command respect from those who are carrying out the task. This is because autocratic leadership does not encourage teamwork or initiative, since the leader knows the answers and does not need to consult anyone to achieve the desired result.

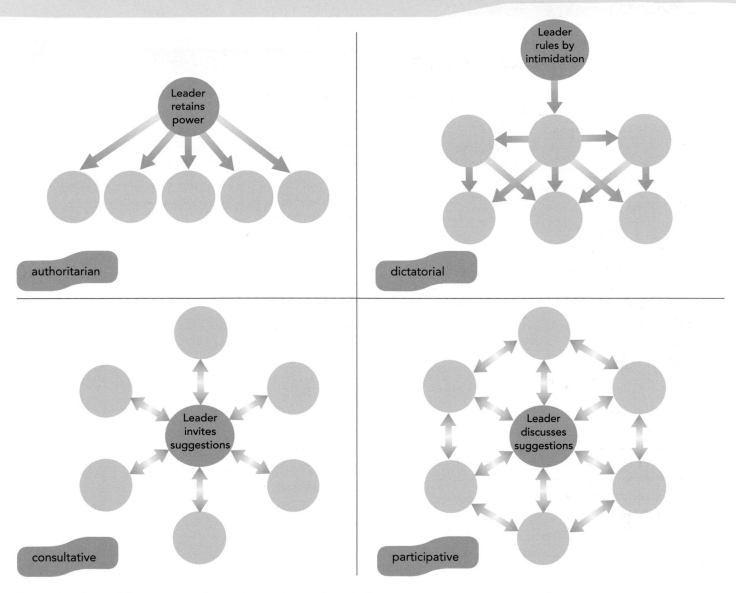

Figure 4.8: Some different types of authority and forms of leadership.

Dictatorial

Dictatorial authority is carried out without the consent of the people whom it affects. 'Dictatorial' is sometimes used to refer to someone who is domineering and arrogant in the manner in which they give orders. To remain in power, dictatorial regimes rule by intimidation and fear.

A dictator is a ruler with unrestricted authority over the state, as well as individuals, and who has complete power to render current laws invalid and create new laws without the prior consent of the very citizens who will be affected by them. Unlike democratically elected leaders, dictators can behave in any manner they see fit without fear of being defeated in elections, as the electorate are usually helpless in preventing a dictator from remaining in power.

Consultative

Consultative, also known as collective, authority is where a leader might share a problem with several members of a team, either individually or in a group, with a view to hearing ideas and suggestions. This form of authority is also used when a change in procedures or policy is being considered and members' views are sought on the changes. The leader will then make a decision, but not necessarily one that is influenced by suggestions and ideas from the group.

Participative (democratic)

With this type of authority, the leader allows one or more employees to be included in the decision-making process (determining what to do and how to do it).

Activity: Examples of the use of different types of authority

- A squad of new recruits in the British Army are about to have their first session of drill and they only have three months before their passing out parade. Which type of authority do you think would be applicable here, and why?

- Consider the huge exercise involved in the recovery operation following the London bombings in July 2005. The Commissioner of the Metropolitan Police Service at that time, Sir Ian Blair, was in charge of coordinating the operation – which style of authority do you think he would have used?

- The station manager has attended a multi-vehicle accident where people are trapped inside vehicles. There is a strong risk that leaking fuel could ignite, but there is an equal risk that people will die if they are left trapped in their vehicles without medical care. Which type of authority do you think would be applicable for the station manager to use, and why?

- Can you think of a situation where dictatorial authority is used in the uniformed public services? If not, explain why not.

However, the leader maintains the final decision-making authority. Using this style is not a sign of weakness; it is a sign of strength that employees will respect.

4.4 Legislation

Members of the uniformed public services are not only subject to the laws of the land, they also have to abide by codes of conduct and disciplinary rules and regulations relating to their particular service. These rules and regulations are written into acts of Parliament.

The rules and regulations are not solely for enforcing discipline. They also exist to protect the rights of serving officers who may have broken a rule, and to make sure procedures for dealing with disciplinary hearings are standardised. Furthermore, they exist to protect members of the public from such things as harassment and victimisation by clearly stating police powers of arrest and search.

Armed Forces Discipline Act 2000

This act provides the statutory framework for discipline procedures for our three armed forces. The basis for this statutory framework stems from the Army Act 1955, the Air Force Act 1955 and the Naval Discipline Act 1957, which are renewed by parliament every five years and are known collectively as the Service Discipline Acts (SDAs). Essentially, the armed forces have their own legal

system and it applies to personnel wherever they are based in the world, whether in peacetime or conflict. However, the act does not apply only to service personnel: it may apply to civil servants and their dependants, as well as the civilian dependants of service personnel.

The act deals with the processing and punishment of personnel who have been charged, or are likely to be charged, under disciplinary regulations. This legislation makes provision for:

- the right of the accused to apply for bail pending trial

- the trial judge to direct the accused's commanding officer to give orders for the accused's arrest

- the right to appeal against the summary award of the commanding officer

- appeals against a conviction by way of a fresh hearing

- appeals against sentence by way of a fresh hearing but only the evidence relevant to sentencing will be reheard

- the punishment from a summary appeal court having to be no more severe than that which was initially awarded by a commanding officer

- appeals having to be brought within 14 days beginning with the date on which the punishment was awarded or within such longer period as the court may allow

- the accused's right to elect trial by court martial

- where the accused elects trial, the court not being able to award any punishment which could not have been awarded by the commanding officer or appropriate superior authority had the election for trial not been made.

Police Act 1997, section 50

All Police Services within the UK are subject to a code of conduct as set out by the Police (Disciplinary) Regulations. Below are three examples of that code.

- Honesty and integrity – officers should not be inappropriately indebted to any person or institution and should be reliable in the discharge of their duties.

- Fairness and impartiality – police officers have a particular responsibility to act with fairness and impartiality in all their dealings with the public and their colleagues.

- Politeness and tolerance – officers should treat members of the public and colleagues with courtesy and respect, avoiding abusive or deriding attitudes or behaviour.

However, the National Crime Squad (NCS) is an organisation involved in tackling serious crime nationally, and does not, therefore, come under the jurisdiction of a single Police Service, although it does have its headquarters in London. The NCS consists of members who are seconded from different police areas and it is regulated by its own authority, the power of which is given to it by section 50 of the Police Act 1997. The act also makes provision for the secretary of state to issue and revise a code of conduct for the NCS, as well as setting targets and objectives.

Police and Criminal Evidence Act 1984, part IX

The purpose of this act was to standardise the rules that all police officers must follow in relation to persons whom they are searching, arresting or detaining. Part IX was introduced in 1985 to clarify the position regarding police complaints and disciplinary procedures.

The act sets out all the measures for investigating

It is important for the police to show honesty, fairness and politeness when doing their duty.

complaints against the police, including senior officers, from the initial stage until completion, as well as giving information on the manner of the investigation. It states when matters should be referred to the IPCC and also to the Director of Public Prosecutions.

Fire and Rescue Services Act 2004

This act, which applies in England and Wales, replaces the Fire Services Act of 1947. It sets out a variety of duties and powers by which fire and rescue authorities can promote fire safety, and respond to fires, road traffic accidents and emergencies, such as natural disasters and terrorist attacks.

The legislation empowers fire and rescue authorities to respond to the needs of the community and carry out risk assessments in preparation for emergencies. To meet the demands of our modern age, authorities have the right to combine with other authorities in order to promote fire safety and to deal with emergencies where one authority does not have adequate resources.

Case study: Working with the Fire and Rescue Services Act 2004

'I have been in the Fire and Rescue Services for over 18 years now. My role as Crew Manager involves using lots of communication skills, both verbal and written, on a day-to-day basis. On a broader level, I have to work with the community to organise school visits, fire safety talks and installing smoke detectors. I have to liaise with the Police Service and other agencies including the local council, especially in the event of any natural disasters or terrorist attacks. I am also the link between the firefighters and the Watch Manager.

When we go to a fire my first job is to assess the type of fire it is and how best to approach it. I then communicate this to the team. It is my responsibility to monitor the situation and to make decisions if the fire is getting worse. I keep an overall eye on health and safety issues to make sure the firefighters are safe at all times. I deal with members of the public to get witness statements and to make sure they are kept safe. Once we have finished an operation, it is my responsibility to write up a report on every incident.

In my job, I need excellent verbal as well as written communication skills. I also have to take a leadership role and a decision-making role. My job is really varied and very interesting'.

1 Why is there a need for discipline in the Fire and Rescue Services?

2 What new powers do you think the 2004 Act gives firefighters over the 1947 Act?

3 What impact do you think promoting fire safety has on the work of a firefighter?

Assessment activity 4.4

P5 **BTEC**

Just like discipline, authority is a very broad and complex topic, which as a member of the uniformed public services you must understand comprehensively. After all, authority is the foundation that makes discipline legal.

Address the following task in the form of a videoed documentary:

1 Describe 'authority' as it relates to the uniformed public services **P5**

Grading tip

P5 requires you to describe authority by acting out and describing different situations relating to authority and recording the scenarios on video. It would be a good idea for one of your group to assume the role of narrator, and introduce each scenario and tell the audience what they can expect to see.

PLTS

Completing this assessment will help you develop your independent enquirer skills.

Private Jack Marshall
(Yorkshire Regiment)

I signed up three years ago and so far I've travelled to five different countries. My parents weren't best pleased when I joined up, especially my mother, because she's thinking of all the trouble in Iraq and Afghanistan. I've already done a tour of Northern Ireland and, to be honest, I'm looking forward to going to Afghanistan but I haven't had my orders yet.

The training has been something else but I like the fitness and I've met some great lads. We always watch each other's backs and we'd do anything for each other. You learn to look out for one another and you don't let any outsiders put your mates down – that's what the training does for you.

I can handle the discipline and the initial training wasn't that bad. You get beasted for the first three months but it's brilliant training and you need it really, because it gets you used to jumping as soon as you get an order shouted at you. And you don't question it, you just get on with it or you pay the price.

A typical day

I can't think of any one day that's the same as another. I've done loads of courses and specialist training. I'm doing my sniper training at the moment and I love it. When you're on a course you normally start at eight thirty and finish at four thirty, but you have to do funny hours, you know, in the dark and all sorts of times so that you get used to being under pressure from lack of sleep. I know it's most squaddies' ambition but I really fancy the SAS and I'm going to go for it in a couple more years. I can just imagine earning my beret but that's a few years off yet.

The best thing about the job

Without a doubt it's the mates and sense of belonging. And you get well looked after.

Think about it!

What topics have you covered in this unit that will help you to become a member of the uniformed public services?

Can you handle discipline? Do you take it personally and do you resent authority? If so, then you have failed to grasp the concept of discipline and authority. Discipline is not a personal attack.

What do you think you need to improve about your personality in order to improve your chances of joining the uniformed public services?

Just checking

1 How does the rank structure of the Metropolitan Police Service differ from county or territorial police services?

2 What is the difference between a rule and a regulation?

3 What is meant by anarchy?

4 What is the role of discipline in the uniformed public services?

5 How does conformity differ from obedience?

6 What did Asch's experiment try to show?

7 What did Hofling's experiment try to show?

8 What did the studies of Zimbardo and Milgram have in common?

9 Give four reasons why self-discipline is needed in the uniformed public services.

10 What is the role of the IPCC (Independent Police Complaints Commission)?

11 What is meant by blind obedience?

12 What is a moral dilemma?

13 What legislation regulates the National Crime Squad?

edexcel

Assignment tips

- This unit gives you a good insight into the concept of discipline in its many forms, as well as an outline of conformity and obedience. You ought to apply what you have learnt to everyday scenarios you come across, either at home, work or school/college; this will reinforce what you have learned. For example, you could try to identify conformity, compliance and obedience. You could also apply what you have learnt when you read the news or watch television. It would be a god idea to carry out your own research into any of the public services that you have heard about on television or read about in the press, particularly with a discipline theme to them. When you carry out the research, see if you can apply the principles you have learned in this unit. Researching a topic for yourself gives you a greater insight into a subject, as well as giving you a better chance of achieving the higher grades in your assignment.

- Discipline, in one form or another, applies to any of the services outlined in this and other units on the course. They all require self-discipline and this is something you could practise every day, regardless of where you are; it will help you when you apply for the service of your choice. You should also remember that discipline is not a personal attack, and if you cannot accept discipline it is unlikely that you will be able to administer it. You should also practise critical thinking and making decisions based on reasoning so that you can justify them and stand by them. Again, you could practise this in many different situations, at home, work or school/college. It is important for you to keep assessing your skills and development against the skills and qualities that are needed for the uniformed public services.

5 Physical preparation, health and lifestyle for the public services

The uniformed public services are very active professions and there will be times when they need to respond physically to an incident or situation. This means in order to be a good public service officer you will need to be physically fit and healthy enough to do the job.

In this unit you will look at a variety of factors associated with health and fitness including: the major body systems and how they are affected by diet and exercise; the key components of nutrition and diet and the fitness tests you need to undertake and pass if you are going to be successful in being recruited to the uniformed public services.

The services will often support you in becoming fit and healthy and because the recruitment process in the services can be lengthy you will have plenty of time to improve your standard of fitness before they test you. However, the services do not want to recruit people who are not physically and mentally able to do the job, so it is really important that when you are preparing to apply to the service of your choice that you include fitness training as part of your preparation.

The fitness tests vary for each service and some are much harder than others, so you will have to adjust your preparation to match what standard you need to achieve, this unit also allows you to develop a personalised training plan and review how effective it has been in improving your fitness.

Learning outcomes

After completing this unit you should:

1. know the fitness requirements for entry into the public services
2. know the major human body systems
3. know the importance of lifestyle factors in the maintenance of health and well-being
4. be able to provide advice on lifestyle improvement
5. be able to plan a health-related physical activity programme in preparation for the public services.

Assessment and grading criteria

This table shows you what you must do in order to achieve a pass, merit or distinction grade, and where you can find activities in this book to help you.

To achieve a **pass** grade the evidence must show that you are able to:	To achieve a **merit** grade the evidence must show that, in addition to the pass criteria, you are able to:	To achieve a **distinction** grade the evidence must show that, in addition to the pass and merit criteria, you are able to:
P1 describe a fitness assessment for each of the major components of fitness **Assessment activity 5.1** **page 163**	**M1** explain the results of the fitness assessment and measure against relevant public service entrance test **Assessment activity 5.1** **page 163**	**D1** evaluate the results of the fitness assessment, analyse strengths and recommend improvements **Assessment activity 5.1** **page 163**
P2 describe the structure and functions of the muscular-skeletal, cardiovascular and respiratory systems **Assessment activity 5.2** **page 174**		
P3 undertake a fitness activity, record and identify the short-term effects of exercise on the major human body systems **Assessment activity 5.3** **page 175**	**M2** explain the short and long-term effects of exercise on the major human body systems **Assessment activity 5.3** **page 175**	
P4 describe the lifestyle factors that can affect health **Assessment activity 5.4** **page 179**	**M3** explain the effects of identified lifestyle factors on health and fitness, when applying for public service and long-term employment **Assessment activity 5.4** **page 179**	**D2** evaluate the effects of identified lifestyle factors on health and fitness, when applying for public service and long-term employment. **Assessment activity 5.4** **page 179**
P5 provide lifestyle improvement strategies that can have a positive effect on health **Assessment activity 5.5** **page 181**	**M4** explain lifestyle improvement strategies to justify their positive effect on health **Assessment activity 5.5** **page 181**	
P6 plan a six-week health-related physical activity programme based on personal results **Assessment activity 5.6** **page 184**		

How you will be assessed

This unit will be assessed by an internal assignment that will be designed and marked by the staff at your centre. The assignment is designed to allow you to show your understanding of the learning outcomes for physical preparation, health and lifestyle. These relate to what you should be able to do after completing this unit.

Assessments can be quite varied and can take the form of:

- reports
- fitness assessments
- leaflets
- presentations
- posters

- practical tasks
- case studies
- diaries
- fitness records
- action plans.

Danyl aims to improve his lifestyle

I'm really pleased I opted to do this unit. I used to play football on a regular basis and was reasonably fit so I didn't pay much attention to my lifestyle and eating habits. Then the time came when I couldn't devote as much time to training and playing football. I soon realised how easy it was to lose muscle tone and even put on weight.

One of the things I enjoyed most was looking at the fitness tests. I hadn't really appreciated that you could assess the fitness levels of different parts of the body and that some might be OK and others not. I decided to keep an exercise diary and look at my components of fitness, one by one, with the aim of making an overall improvement. Also, I've always assumed that my diet must be OK, but I could see that I needed to keep a count of the amount of fresh fruit and vegetables I was eating to be sure of getting my 5-a-day!

One of the good things about this unit is the amount of physical activity involved. I can spend time on my fitness targets and then get out and into some fresh air and kick a football around again. It's clear that a combination of good diet and plenty of exercise is a good lifestyle choice and will set me on the right path if I want to become a physical fitness instructor.

Over to you!

- What areas of health and fitness might you find interesting?
- Have you ever completed a public service fitness test?
- Do you have any fears or concerns about your level of fitness?
- Are you currently fit enough to pass the fitness tests for the service of your choice?
- What preparation could you do to get ready for your assessments?

1. The fitness requirements for entry into the public services

Thinking about physical fitness, health and lifestyle

Working individually

Consider the fitness requirements for the service of your choice. Will you have to make any lifestyle changes in order to pass the tests? Is your diet currently healthy and nutritious?

Write down an honest assessment of your health and fitness and consider what steps you can take to improve them.

Working as a class

Share your findings with the rest of your class. Did you come up with the same list of changes or was each learner's assessment different? Why do you think this is?

All of the uniformed public services have some kind of fitness assessment that you must pass in order to be considered for employment. Fitness is really important to the public services as the nature of their work is very physically active. This outcome looks at the components of fitness, fitness tests and the reasons testing is done.

1.1 Components of fitness

Being fit is not just about how fast you can run or for how long. It isn't about how much weight you can lift or how many times you can lift it. Fitness is actually all of these things, and more. To be truly fit and able to live healthily and deal with the rigours of an active life, you need to be fit in several areas. It is these different areas, or components, that make up the sum total of physical fitness.

Cardiovascular endurance

This is also known as aerobic endurance or stamina, which put simply is the ability to repeat an activity for a length of time without becoming tired. This is crucial to performance in many sports, whether it be a 90-minute football match or a 3-hour long distance run. Stamina depends on the efficiency of your cardiovascular system (heart, blood, blood vessels, lungs) in terms of

how well they provide the muscles with oxygen. The armed services often have rely on this because they may have to march for miles to reach a combat zone or safe area in battle.

This exercise is good for cardiovascular endurance.

Strength

Strength can be defined as the maximum muscular force we can apply against resistance. It can be demonstrated in three ways:

- **Static strength.** This involves resistance against a stationary load. For example, pushing as hard as you can against a wall or pulling against an equal force as in a 'tug of war'.
- **Dynamic strength.** This uses muscle contractions to move heavy loads, for example, in weight training or power lifting.
- **Explosive strength.** The use of fast and powerful muscular reactions. An example of this would be the static long jump.

There are many benefits to improving strength such as:

- Increased strength of tendons and ligaments, which may help prevent strains and sprains while taking part in physical activity. This increases strength in an individual's joints and this may also have the potential to help him or her become more flexible.
- Reduced body fat and increased lean muscle mass, which helps the body's metabolic system run more effectively and enables food to be utilised more efficiently.
- It may help to reduce blood pressure.
- It may help to reduce the amount of cholesterol in the body, offering some protection from the 'furring up' of arteries, which can lead to heart disease.

Muscular endurance

Muscular endurance (or stamina) is the ability to repeat an activity for a length of time (for example, press ups or sit ups) without becoming tired. Muscular endurance can be developed through resistance training or circuit training.

Flexibility

Suppleness and flexibility is defined as the range of movement possible at joints. Up until the age of 40, ligaments, tendons and muscles are relatively elastic but after this age, movement in muscles and joints that are not used frequently can be decreased and eventually lost. This can cause problems and injuries if the body is suddenly asked to do something it has not done for a while.

In terms of sports performance, suppleness and flexibility will help reduce the risk of injury, improve sports skills and reduce the likelihood of muscle soreness. Flexibility can be developed and maintained by stretching exercises or activities such as yoga and swimming. It is recommended that an individual should spend 5 to 10 minutes stretching prior to beginning any sport or physical activity, in order to prepare the muscles for what is to follow. Stretching should also be conducted after physical activity, since it helps the recovery process.

Speed

Speed is the ability to move a part of the body or the whole body quickly. Speed can be crucial in many sports where the activity is timed or you may be required to outpace an opponent. Speed is not just important for athletes, a quick physical reaction time might help you avoid injury in public service work or perhaps chase and run down criminal suspects.

Reaction time

This is how quickly messages are transmitted around the body. The brain receives information from a range of receptors in the body including: eyes, ears, skin and nose. The brain then reacts to this information. Putting a hand in a flame results in a pain signal being sent to the brain – this reacts by telling the hand to move away from the flame. How long the messages travel from the hand to the brain and back again is the reaction time.

Agility

This is the ability to move with quick fluid grace and it is critical for improving sports performance. It involves rapid changes in speed and direction while maintaining balance and skill. Like skill it can be developed with practice and is improved by developing strength, stamina and suppleness. The ability to change speed and direction rapidly could be of great benefit to the armed services in combat situations.

Coordination

Being coordinated involves using different parts of the body at the same time. Some actions require hand–eye coordination, for example catching a ball. Again, coordination is strongly linked to agility and can be practised with agility drills. This is an essential skill in the public services, which may require many body parts to be used simultaneously in activities such as firefighting.

Did you know?

Speed and strength together provide power. Power is an explosive movement, where the greatest force is moved as fast as possible. Various types of training can be used to develop power including resistance training (weights) or circuit training.

1.2 Health-related fitness

Body composition

This is a measure of the distribution of fat, bone and muscle in the human body. Muscle tissue takes up less space in our body than fat tissue, which means that our body composition, as well as our weight, can determine how lean we appear. Two people at the same height and same body weight may look completely different from each other because they have a different body composition.

Activity: Comparing body types

Can you think of two people you know who weigh around the same weight, but look very different in terms of body composition? Why is this?

Measurement of body fat is normally a key area of examining body composition since it has a direct relationship to health and fitness. Traditionally it was measured with skin fold callipers although many gyms now measure it electronically with a device very similar to weighing scales but which measures electrical resistance in the body. This is called bioelectrical impedance analysis. Callipers can pose a problem in that they can be difficult to use accurately. Measurements are normally taken in four places:

- biceps
- triceps
- subscapula (below shoulder blade)
- supraillia (just above the waist).

The measurements in mm are then calculated to give a body fat percentage. Generally a reading of 12–20.9 per cent in males would be acceptable and 17–27 per cent for women.

One of the key aspects of health-related fitness is the **body mass index** (BMI). The medical profession recommends a certain weight range for height, age and gender that is dependent on an individual's BMI. You can work out your BMI using the formula below if you know your weight and your height.

Key term

Body mass index is defined as the individual's body weight divided by the square of their height:

$$BMI = \frac{weight\ (kg)}{height^2\ (m^2)}$$

Testing methods

The methods the public services have for testing fitness and performance can range from service to service. Their purpose, however, is always the same – to see if you are physically fit enough to take on the role you are applying for. The main aim of public service performance assessments or fitness tests is to determine your stamina and strength. Table 5.1 shows some of the tests that might be encountered in the public services and how they relate to the components of fitness outlined above.

Table 5.1: Methods used for testing fitness.

Feature being tested	How
Cardiovascular and aerobic endurance	The **multi-stage fitness test** involves continuous running between two markers at 20 m apart and in time to a set of pre-recorded bleeps. (The MSFT is often called the **bleep test** for this reason.) The advantage of this test is that large numbers of people can be tested at the same time but the disadvantages are that you need to be highly motivated to run until you can't go any further. The armed services also use the combat fitness test (CFT which is an extended timed run completed with backpack and weapon. Other endurance tests include step tests and the maximal treadmill protocol.
Strength	The **grip test** measures the strength of an individual's grip by use of a grip strength dynamometer. The dynamometer is set at zero and the handle adjusted to fit the size of the palm. Then the dynamometer is simply squeezed as hard as possible. The reading on the gauge tells you how strong your grip is.
Muscular endurance	The **press up test** is an assessment of the muscular endurance of the chest, shoulders and arms. The total number of press ups completed in one minute is the score. The press ups for males and females differ as men should be in contact with the ground at their hands and toes while women should be in contact with the ground at their hands and knees or on a slightly raised bar. The resting position is up with elbows locked. The **sit ups test** is also an assessment of muscular endurance but this time the muscles involved are in the abdomen and hips. The test usually involves the number of sit ups completed in one minute.
Flexibility	The **sit and reach test** is a flexibility and suppleness assessment. The individual sits down with their legs straight out in front of them and the soles of their feet flat against a box with a measuring device such as a ruler or distance gauge on top of it. They then reach forward with the fingertips to see how far past their toes they can reach. The movement should be smooth and continuous rather than lunging. The test is very easy to administer but it only assesses hamstring flexibility rather than the flexibility of the whole body.
Speed	**60 m sprint** is a 60 metre course is laid out and candidates complete it as fast as possible.
Reaction time	One of the more common ways of testing reaction time is by rigging up a system where the performer pushes a button when a light comes on. Variations are available on the internet, where instead of pushing a button the individual clicks the mouse button when the background changes. The time taken to react will be monitored.
Agility	The **Illinois agility run** is a reasonably simple test to carry out, using only a flat, non-slip 10 x 5 m course, a series of cones and a stopwatch. The individuals start at the start line, lying on their front, hands by shoulders. When instructed they leap up and complete the course.
Balance	The **standing stork test** is a very simple test that only requires a non-slip, flat area and a stopwatch. The test is performed by lifting one leg and placing this foot on the other knee. The heel of the standing foot is raised and the hands are placed on the hips. The time that the position is held is recorded.
Coordination	The **alternate hand wall toss test** is used for hand-eye coordination. The individual stands at a set distance from a wall (for example, 3 m). A ball is thrown underarm at the wall and the aim is to catch the ball with the opposite hand. The test can be timed and the successful number of catches recorded.
Power	**Vertical and horizontal jumps** in fitness testing are designed to measure explosive power in the legs. • An example of a **vertical jump** is the 'sergeant jump' whereby an individual marks the full extent of their normal reach on a wall or vertical measuring board and then tries to touch a point as far beyond the initial mark as possible using the power of their legs. • An example of a **horizontal jump** is the 'standing long jump' where an individual stands at the edge of a horizontal measuring board and with both feet together jumps forward as far as they can.

Figure 5.1 Methods used for testing fitness include the sit and reach test for flexibility, the standing stork test for balance and press ups for muscular endurance.

There are many benefits to undertaking a series of fitness tests, for example:

- to establish the strengths and weaknesses of an individual in order to design an appropriate training programme
- to provide a baseline initial fitness level against which future progress can be measured
- to ascertain level of fitness loss after injury, illness or pregnancy
- to allow medical practitioners to recognise and assess some specific health problems such as coronary heart disease.

Did you know?

Fitness tests can be influenced and distorted by several factors such as the individual's health, their emotional state, the temperature, lack of sleep, the time of day and the time since the individual last ate or drank.

Key terms

Maximal treadmill protocol is a common test used to estimate maximal oxygen uptake in athletes. Oxygen uptake is linked to an athletes capacity to perform sustained activity.

Wingate test is a popular method of assessing anaerobic power.

1.3 Job-specific public service fitness tests

Most uniformed services have a fitness test as part of their selection process. It is used to ensure that:

- all new recruits start training at a minimum standard level of fitness
- applicants have the necessary motivation to perform in the services
- applicants understand that fitness is important to the job
- applicants will be able to physically do the job they are applying for.

The fitness tests are chosen to best represent the needs of each service and are often reviewed. The reviews can lead to changes so it is beneficial to keep up to date with the service you wish to join.

HM Prison Service

Individuals who want to be prison officers take a fitness assessment during an HM Prison Service assessment day. The fitness test comprises of:

- **Grip strength test.** Grip strength is measured using a dynamometer in both hands which is squeezed as hard as possible.
- **Multi-stage fitness test.** This is a shuttle run over a 15 m course.

- **Dynamic strength test.** This involves completing a set of upper body pulls and pushes to assess strength.
- **Speed agility run test.** This is concerned with moving as quickly as you can while negotiating obstacles and changing direction.
- **Shield test.** This involves holding a static position while holding a 6 kg shield during control and restraint tests.

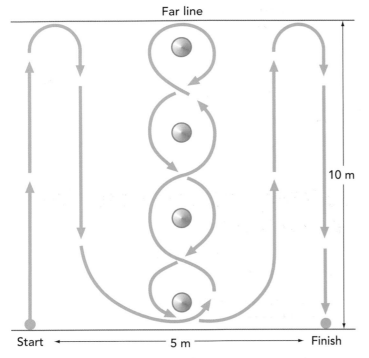
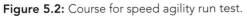

Figure 5.2: Course for speed agility run test.

The Royal Marines

The Royal Marines require very high standards of physical fitness and as well as completing the Potential Royal Marines Course (PRMC) there is also a pre-joining fitness test (PJFT) that must be passed. This was introduced because a significant number of candidates were failing the three-mile run on the PRMC. It was decided that a fitness test prior to attending the course would reduce the number of fails.

The PJFT consists of two 2.4 km runs conducted on a running machine inclined at 2 degrees. The first 2.4 km needs to be completed in under 12 mins 30 sec, after a one minute break the second run must be completed in under 10 mins 30 sec. If a candidate is successful they can progress to the PRMC.

The PRMC test is a non-stop three-day challenge including assault courses, fitness tests, shooting, interviews and drill. Like the Navy, the Marines are

experts in waterborne combat and so swimming tests are an essential component of the course. The fitness components are:

- **Three-mile run.** This consists of 1.5 miles out as a squad in under 12 mins 30 sec and 1.5 miles back individually timed in under 10 mins 30 sec.
- **Gym test 1.** This consists of:
  Bleep test (level 13 for maximum points)
  Press-ups (60 within 2 mins for maximum points)
  Sit-ups (80 in 2 mins for maximum points)
  Pull-ups (6 for a maximum score).
- **Swimming test.** This consists of swimming 2 lengths of breaststroke unaided after jumping off a diving board.
- **Assault course.** This involves completing the high obstacle course, assault course and determination test. Your teamwork, commitment and stamina will be a key aspect of this set of tests.
- **Gym test 2.** This consists of individual and team tasks to show teamwork and determination, each task lasting three minutes.

The PRMC is one of the most physically demanding selection courses, but is good preparation for the Commando Training Course (CTCRM). At all times during the PRMC recruits are being observed to see if they have the qualities required to be a Royal Marine Commando.

Activity: Testing for the Marines

Why does the physical selection test for the Marines have to be so demanding? What does a candidate's determination to complete the difficult three days show a Royal Marines recruiting officer?

The Fire Service

Like the Police Service, the Fire Service has been making an effort to rationalise recruitment and training. To that end, they too have recently introduced a new fitness test that represents common daily tasks. However, unlike the police test, this test requires more specialised equipment, is more time-consuming and is a much tougher physical challenge.

Potential Fire Service recruits must undertake the following tasks in order to be successful:

- **Enclosed space test.** Wearing full rescue equipment, including breathing apparatus (12 kg in weight) and with obscured vision, applicants must negotiate their way through crawl spaces and walkways.

- **Ladder climb.** Applicants must climb a ladder to a height of 9 m, this is two thirds of the height of a standard fire service ladder. Once there, they are to hook themselves securely on the ladder and look

down to read out a message or other similar task and then climb back down. Safety harnesses are used for this test.

- **Ladder lift test.** This is a simulated test for strength and skill. An apparatus loaded with 30 kg must be lifted to a required height of 182 cm and lowered again safely.

- **Casualty evacuation drag.** A 55 kg dummy casualty is dragged around a 30 m course safely and at walking speed in a timed exercise.

- **Equipment carry test.** Various items of firefighting paraphernalia are to be picked up and carried around a course measuring 25 m. The equipment includes hoses of assorted lengths and weights as well as a 35 kg barbell.

- **Equipment assembly test.** Using the instructions provided, applicants are required to assemble and then disassemble a piece of fire fighting equipment within a specified time frame.

The ladder climb test used in firefighter training.

Activity:
Fire Service tests

Not all of the Fire Service tests are completely fitness related. Identify those that aren't and explain what the tests show.

Reasons for inclusion of certain tests

As you can see from the physical fitness requirements outlined above, there is a wide variation in what is physically required in order to be a potential recruit to the services. It is important to remember that although we talk of the uniformed services as a whole, each of them performs a highly specialised role with its own set of physical fitness requirements. This is why the services show variation in their testing requirements.

Activity: Fitness tests

Conduct some individual research into the service of your choice and find out what the fitness requirements are. Are you physically fit enough to pass the test already? What could you do to prepare yourself in order to pass?

Reasons for repeated fitness tests

There are many reasons to undertake fitness tests, for example:

- to assess current levels of fitness
- to provide a baseline initial fitness level against which future progress can be monitored and measured
- to ascertain level of fitness loss after injury, illness or pregnancy
- to allow medical practitioners to recognise and assess some specific health problems such as heart disease.
- to motivate you to do better
- to allow you to see if a particular fitness programme is working
- to make sure you are as fit to do a job now as you were when you joined a service.

This is why some services have an annual fitness test.

Assessment activity 5.1   P1 M1 D1   BTEC

This is a practical activity that will be organised and observed by your tutor:

1   Describe a fitness assessment for each of the major components of fitness P1

2   After you have completed your tests write a brief report that explains your results and compares them against the public services entrance tests M1

3   Also in your written report evaluate your results by analysing your strengths and recommending areas where you can improve D1

Grading tips

It doesn't matter for this assessment whether you actually pass the tests or not as long as you can explain your results, compare them to the service requirements and honestly examine your strengths and weaknesses. This will help you develop an action plan to improve your performance if needed.

2.   The major human body systems

This part of the unit looks at how your body works and how it responds to the effects of exercise, diet and lifestyle. Although each individual is unique, the vast majority of people have an almost identical set of body systems. Each system is essential to health and well-being and has evolved specifically to perform a set of functions that no other body system can do. The major systems include:

- skeletal system
- muscular system
- respiratory system
- cardiovascular system.

Understanding your major body systems is essential in knowing how to improve your overall health, fitness and well-being.

Did you know?

There are many body systems in addition to the ones we will be looking at, such as the digestive system, the reproductive system and the nervous system.

2.1 The skeletal system – structure and function

The human adult skeleton consists of 206 bones, most of which are paired on the right and left part of the body. It is an internal skeleton (which means it sits inside the body, unlike some insects that have a skeleton on the outside of the body).

The skeleton can be divided into two parts:

- the axial skeleton, which consists of 80 bones concentrated in the upper central part of the body
- the appendicular skeleton, which consists of 126 bones concentrated at the extremities.

The structure of a human skeleton is shown in Figure 5.3.

The skeletal system is a network of bone, cartilage and joints. It provides several major functions and these are outlined in Table 5.2.

Table 5.2: Functions of the human skeleton.

Function	Detail
Support	The skeleton provides a shape for the body – a framework which takes the body's weight and supports body structures.
Protection	Bones help protect the body from injury, for example, the skull protects the brain and the sternum and ribs protect the heart.
Movement	Bones provide attachment points for muscles. The bones provide a structure for the muscles to work against. As muscles can only contract, the bones are used as levers against which one muscle contracts in order to extend another.
Storage	The bones serve as storage areas for minerals such as calcium and phosphorous which are used by your body.
Production of blood cells	Red blood cells, which carry oxygen around the body, and some white blood cells, which fight infection, are produced in the long bones.

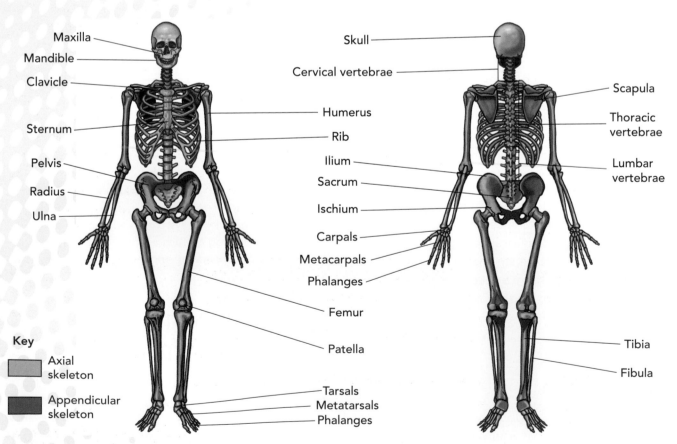

Key

Axial skeleton

Appendicular skeleton

Figure 5.3: Can you distinguish between the axial and appendicular parts of the human skeleton?

Bone

A living bone consists of about 35 per cent organic tissue, such as blood vessels, and 65 per cent minerals, such as calcium compounds.

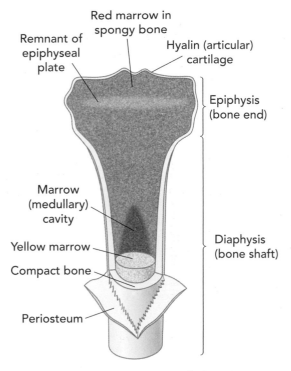

Figure 5.4: Diagram of a cross section of a long bone.

The bone illustrated in Figure 5.4 is called a long bone. It is covered by the **periosteum** which is like the skin of the bone. The periosteum contains the cells that make new bone. The bone itself is divided into two parts: the **epiphysis**, which is the two rounded end parts, and the **diaphysis**, which is the central, straight part of the bone. The end parts of the bone (epiphysis) are covered in a substance called **cartilage** which makes joints move together

easily and the inside of the end parts of the bone and the straight parts of the bone are filled with **bone marrow**.

The different types of bones are described in Table 5.3.

Joints

Joints occur at points in the body where bones come together. They are areas where flexible connective tissue holds bones together while still allowing freedom of movement. Since the skeleton is not naturally flexible, joints are essential for movement and are a key part of the skeletal system. There are three types of joint:

Fixed joints (also called fibrous or synarthroses)

These bones are held together by fibrous connective tissue that is rich in collagen fibres. Examples of this include the sutures in the skull and the connection between the teeth and the jaw. In adults these joints are not designed to be mobile. They serve their function best when held immovable and firm, for example in chewing food and protecting the brain.

Table 5.3: The different types of bones.

Type	Examples	Purpose
Long bones	Clavicle, humerus, radius, ulna, femur, tibia (collar bone, arm and leg bones)	Provide support and act as levers for muscles
Short bones	Carpals, tarsals (finger and toe bones)	Provide movement, elasticity, flexibility and shock absorption
Flat bones	Ribs, sternum, scapula (chest and shoulder blade bones)	Protection, attachment sites for muscles
Irregular	Skull, pelvis, vertebrae	Protection, support, movement
Sesamoid	Patella (kneecap)	Protection of tendons, makes the joint more effective and more powerful

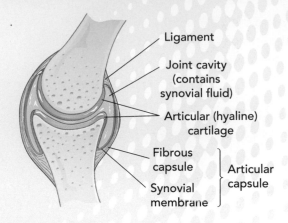

Ligament

Joint cavity
(contains
synovial fluid)

Articular (hyaline)
cartilage

Fibrous
capsule

Synovial
membrane

Articular
capsule

Figure 5.5: Can you name this type of joint?

Slightly moveable joints (also called cartilaginous or amphiarthroses)

These are joints that are connected by cartilage. Cartilage is a very important substance in the skeleton system. It is a type of gristly connective tissue that performs functions such as:

- preventing bones knocking together and becoming worn and damaged
- forming a cushion for bones in slightly moveable joints
- acting as a shock absorber
- helping freedom of movement by providing a slippery surface for bones to move against.

The cartilage and ligaments hold the joint together tightly and only permit small movements. Examples of this include the connection of the ribs to the sternum where the ribs move during respiration but are otherwise immovable, and the vertebrae where there is slight movement to help you bend but they are otherwise immobile.

Activity: Joints

Working in small groups

What problems would damaged joints pose for a member of the public services? How would their day-to-day activities have to change? Why are joints so important to the skeletal system and what would happen if we had no joints? Discuss these issues.

Freely moveable joints (also called synovial or diarthroses)

These joints have a cavity called the 'synovial cavity' between articulating bones. The cavity is filled with synovial fluid held in place by a synovial membrane. The fluid acts as a lubricant and reduces friction between the ends of the bones. When at rest the fluid is gel-like but as the joint moves it becomes more liquid. A warm-up before exercise stimulates the fluidity and production of synovial fluid and so acts as a benefit for the joints.

2.2 The muscular system – structure and function

Muscles are bundles of protein filaments that work together to produce motion in the body.

The main functions of muscles are shown in Table 5.4.

Table 5.4: Functions of muscles.

Function	Detail
Provide movement	The actions of muscles allow you to change position and move around.
Maintain posture	Believe it or not, standing upright is a very difficult thing for the body to do because gravity is always pulling you down. The reason you don't fall to the ground is due to the actions of your muscles.
Produce heat	The action of muscles produces heat and this is why you get hot when you are doing physical activity. If you are cold and inactive your muscles will start to rhythmically contract in an effort to keep you warm – this is called shivering.
Regulate blood flow	Your heart is a muscle which pumps blood around your body in accordance with your needs. If you need more oxygen to get to the muscles to enable them to work harder, your heart rate will increase.
Aid digestion and waste removal	The digestive system moves food through the body and eliminates waste due to muscle action. Equally, the bladder holds on to your urine until you relax the muscles that allow it to be eliminated.
Support the skeleton	Muscles act as a way to tie the skeleton together. There are muscle attachment points at all joints and this ensures the bones stay in position.

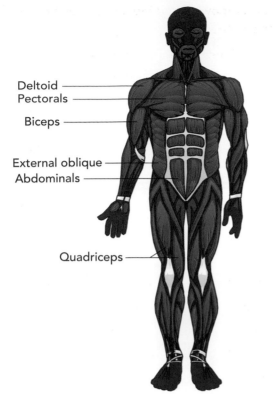

Figure 5.6: Muscle systems of the human body.

Muscle tissue typically composes 40–50 per cent of your body weight and the human body contains well over 600 muscles, which usually work in pairs. These pairs consist of the agonist, which is the prime mover, and the antagonist which works against it. For example, your arm moves by the bicep muscle (agonist) working against the triceps muscle (the antagonist).

Muscles can only pull, they cannot push. This is why they usually work in pairs. One muscle pulls a limb into the required position and the other muscle pulls it

back when required. Muscle action can be **voluntary** or **involuntary**.

Key terms

Involuntary muscle is a muscle automatically controlled by the brain, such as the heart, diaphragm and intestines. This means that they operate without you thinking about it.

Voluntary muscle is a muscle controlled by the individual themselves, such as the biceps and triceps in the arm. You can usually move these muscles whenever you like.

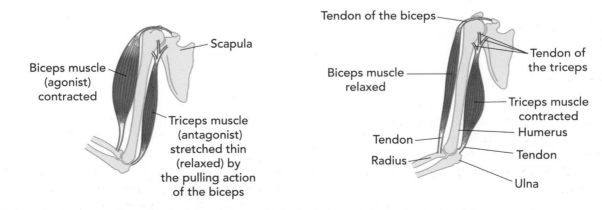

Figure 5.7: Muscle action usually occurs in pairs. Can you think of other pairs of muscles?

Types of muscle

The body must be equipped to deal with a variety of tasks and we have three types of muscle to carry out these tasks. These are described in Table 5.5.

Activity: Muscles

Why is it important to have cardiac muscle which resists fatigue? What would happen if your heart muscle got tired and didn't work efficiently?

Discuss these questions and write down your answers.

Types of muscle fibres

Muscle fibres can be classified into two different types: fast twitch and slow twitch.

- **Slow twitch** (also known as **type I**) – these muscle fibres are very efficient at using oxygen to create more fuel (**ATP**) for continuous physical activity over an extended period of time.

- **Fast twitch** (also known as **type II**) – these muscle fibres use anaerobic **metabolism** to create fuel to power themselves. They are better at generating short bursts of activity to give strength or speed but they tire easily.

Key terms

ATP (adenosine triphosphate) is a molecule that carries energy and is the only direct source of energy for all the processes in the body.

Metabolic rate is the rate that your body uses energy from food

Type 1 are muscle fibres that use oxygen to create more ATP for continuous activity over an extended period of time

Type II are muscle fibres that create power without oxygen but only for short bursts of activity

Activity: Fibres

Having looked at the types of muscle fibres explained above, do you think that each type of muscle fibre is suited to certain physical activities? For example, which type of muscle fibre would benefit a 100 m sprinter and which would benefit a marathon runner?

Muscle contraction and movement

Muscle contraction is powered by a chemical molecule called adenosine triphosphate (ATP). This is synthesised in the body from the food you

Table 5.5: The main types of muscle tissue.

Type of muscle	Explanation
Cardiac muscle	This is found only in the heart and makes up the walls of the heart or myocardium. It acts as a single sheet of muscle that operates on an involuntary basis and has its own blood supply. Unlike many muscles in the body the cardiac muscle is not attached to bone and resists fatigue.
Smooth muscle	Smooth muscle makes up a large part of our internal organs such as the bladder, veins and digestive tract. It is involuntary which means that it works without conscious thought on an automatic basis. Smooth muscle contracts very slowly and so it is able to resist fatigue. In addition, it can stay contracted for relatively long periods of time.
Skeletal muscle	This is the most common type of muscle found in the human body and can make up about 40 per cent of an adult male's body weight. It has stripe-like markings called striations and is composed of large cells bound together in bundles or sheets. The muscles are served by a system of nerves that connect them to the spinal cord and the brain which controls the activation of a muscle. Skeletal muscles are attached to bones by tendons and the majority of skeletal muscles are under your direct control and respond to what you want them to do.

eat and it provides energy for all cellular functions. Muscles need a constant supply of ATP in order to contract, however, supplies of ATP stored in the muscles are limited. During long periods of muscular contraction body fat becomes the main source of energy to power contractions.

There are three main methods of muscle contraction:

- **Isometric** (or **static**) **contraction.** This is when a muscle produces force without changing its length, i.e. without movement. Examples of static contraction include maintaining your posture standing upright or hanging from a chin up bar with your arms at a 90-degree angle. At its maximum level static contraction can only be maintained for about 10 seconds. This is because as force on the muscle increases blood flow to the muscle is proportionally reduced causing fatigue. However, low-level static contraction can be maintained for a long period of time.
- **Isotonic contraction.** This kind of muscle contraction is a controlled shortening of the muscle. For example, a bicep curl is a simple example of a contraction that shortens the bicep. Equally, bending at the knee produces an isotonic contraction in the hamstring.
- **Eccentric contraction.** This is when a muscle actively lengthens, such as the quadriceps (knee extensors) during walking.

Effects of exercise on the skeletal-muscular system

The skeleton is one of the few systems in the body that cannot be trained to improve directly. You cannot increase or reduce bone length and you cannot make a bone move faster, it is the muscles that are responsible for this. The use of regular load bearing exercise such as walking or weightlifting can help strengthen your bones. The exercise increases the activity of osteoblasts, which are the cells in your body that create new bone. This means that some naturally occurring bone degeneration or degeneration caused by diseases such as osteoporosis can be helped by regular activity.

Muscles determine whether you can perform your daily functions: the better your level of muscular fitness, the greater your ability to complete the tasks

in your life without fatigue or injury. Enhanced muscular fitness will boost athletic performance both in terms of capacity to perform a particular activity and also in terms of performing that activity for an extended period. This is useful in public service professions, which can be physical in nature such as the Armed and Emergency Services. Strong abdominal and lower back muscles can help prevent lower back pain, which can be a significant problem in many public service professions such as nursing, firefighting and the police. A good muscular system can help control your weight. The amount of lean muscle you have determines your resting **metabolic rate**, i.e. how quickly you can burn calories.

> **Link**
>
> For the short-term and long-term effects of exercise on the body systems, see page 174.

2.3 The respiratory system

Cells continually use oxygen (O_2) in their reactions and release carbon dioxide (CO_2) as a waste product. The body therefore needs a system that provides O_2 for the body and gets rid of CO_2 before it builds up and causes damage. This system is the respiratory

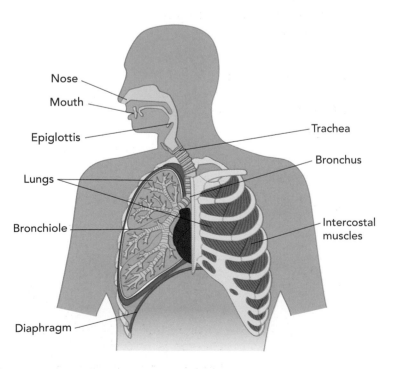

Figure 5.8: The respiratory system in humans. Can you name the two gases involved in respiration?

system. The exchange of O_2 and CO_2 is completed in three stages.

1 **Pulmonary ventilation** – this is the process of breathing in air (inspiration) and breathing out CO_2 (expiration).

2 **External respiration** – this is the exchange of O_2 and CO_2 between the air spaces in the lungs and the blood in the pulmonary capillaries. O_2 is picked up and CO_2 dropped off.

3 **Internal respiration** – this is the exchange of gases between the blood in the capillaries and the tissues in the body. O_2 is dropped and CO_2 picked up.

The respiratory system is sited within the rib cage. It comprises:

The nose
The mouth
The pharynx } leading to the lungs
The larynx
The trachea

The bronchi
The bronchioles } within the lungs
The alveoli

The main parts of the respiratory system

Nose. Air usually enters through the nostrils and proceeds to open spaces within the nose called the nasal passages and nasal cavity. The air is filtered by small hairs and mucus in the nostrils and warmed before it reaches the lungs. The mucus also helps moisten the air. This is why it is better to breathe through the nose rather than the mouth.

Did you know?

The impurities in the air which are filtered out by your nose hair and nose mucus become your bogies.

Pharynx and larynx. Moving on from the nose, air travels through the pharynx (throat) and the larynx (voice box). Air vibrates the vocal chords, which are on either side of the larynx, enabling us to make sounds.

Trachea. The larynx connects with the trachea (windpipe), which is a tube approximately 12 cm in length and 2.5 cm wide in adults. It is held open by

rings of cartilage and is covered with tiny hairs (cilia) and mucus which help filter the air and remove obstructions that have passed down the throat.

Bronchi. The trachea divides into two bronchi which lead into the lungs and further subdivide and spread like tree branches into bronchial tubes.

Bronchioles. The bronchial tubes further divide and spread becoming smaller and thinner tubes called bronchioles.

Alveoli. Each bronchiole ends in a tiny air chamber containing a cup-shaped cavity (alveolus). The tissue of an alveolus is very thin and this allows O_2 and CO_2 to be exchanged through its walls.

Key term

Intercostal muscles are the muscles between the ribs that also surround the lungs.

Inspiration and expiration happen because of changes in air pressure inside the lungs caused by the action of the diaphragm and **intercostal muscles**. Inspiration happens when the muscular action of the respiratory system expands the chest causing a decrease in air pressure, which makes air rush into the lungs. Expiration happens when the muscles return to their resting position causing an increase in air pressure which forces air out of the lungs.

Inspired air contains:

Nitrogen = 79%
O_2 = 21%
CO_2 = 0.04%
Trace other gases
Water vapour

Expired air contains:

Nitrogen = 79%
O_2 = 16%
CO_2 = 4.5%
Water trace

At rest a typical healthy adult will take 12 breaths per minute with each inspiration and expiration moving about half a litre of air. The function of the respiratory system is therefore to supply O_2 to the tissues and remove harmful waste products before they can build up and cause damage to the body. In order to do this effectively the respiratory system works in partnership with the body's transport mechanism, the circulatory system, in order that O_2 can reach tissues all over the body and CO_2 can be brought back to the lungs or expiration.

Activity: Healthy respiratory system

Working in groups

Why is a healthy respiratory system a requirement of many public services? Why might this be particularly important to the Fire and Rescue Service? Write a list of your answers and share them with your group.

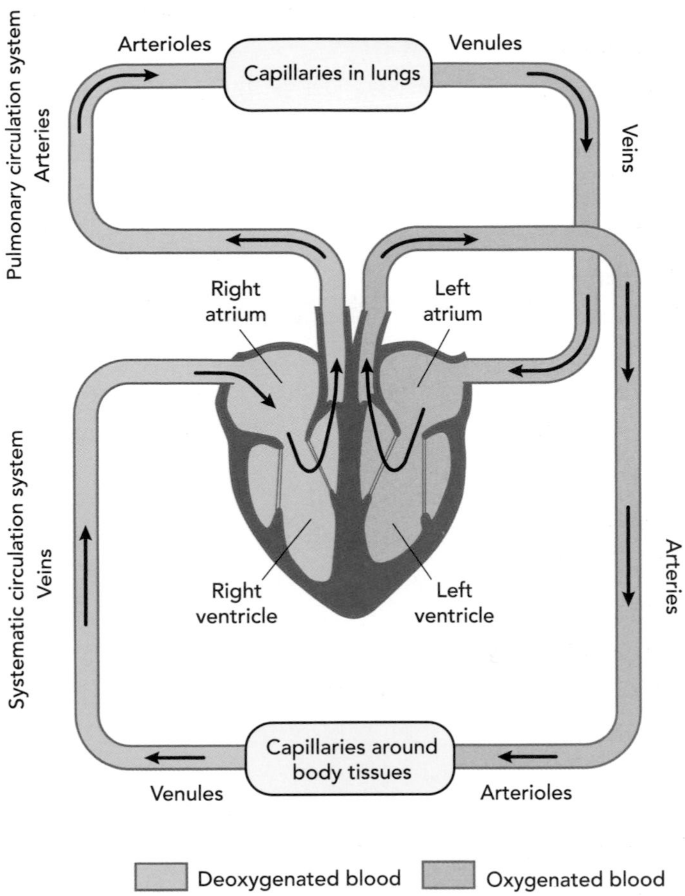

2.4 The cardiovascular system – structure and function

The cardiovascular system consists of the heart, blood vessels and blood. Oxygen and waste products are carried to and from the tissues and cells by blood. The heart is the mechanism that allows this by pumping blood around the body through tubes called veins and arteries.

The heart pumps continually throughout your life to the tune of around 30 million beats per year. While you are asleep it pumps approximately 10 litres of blood a minute through the 60,000 miles of blood vessels which make up the transport system of your body. The cardiovascular system is one of the most important of all the body systems.

The heart

The heart is about the size of a clenched fist and is located in the chest between the lungs with its apex (pointed end) slightly tilted to the left. It is made up of cardiac muscle (myocardium) and is surrounded by the pericardium, which is a fluid filled bag which reduces friction when the heart beats.

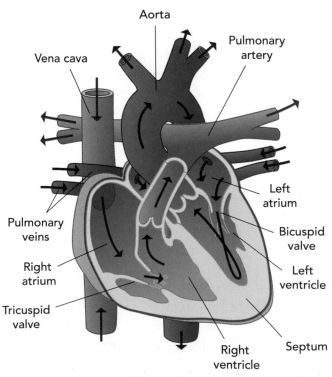

Figure 5.9: Can you name the main constituents of the cardiovascular system?

Figure 5.10: Can you identify the different regions of the heart?

The heart contains four chambers: the left and right atria, which are the upper chambers of the heart, and the left and right ventricles, which are the lower chambers. These form the basis for the two distinct transport circuits of the body, both of which begin and end at the heart.

The two blood transport circuits are:

- **The pulmonary circuit** – which carries blood to and from the surface of the lungs.
- **The systemic circuit** – which involves blood flow to the rest of the body.

Both of the blood flow circuits mentioned above rely not only on the heart but also on the blood and blood vessels.

The blood collects initially in the atria, which then pump it to the ventricles. The walls of the atria are relatively thin as they are only passing the blood to the lower chambers, but the ventricles have to have enough power to send the blood around the circuits and therefore the cardiac muscle in the ventricles is much thicker because more muscular power is needed. The right atrium receives deoxygenated blood from the rest of the body, which it then pumps into the right ventricle. The right ventricle pumps this deoxygenated blood to the lungs where it drops off any waste gases and picks up a fresh load of oxygen in a system of gaseous exchange. This newly oxygenated blood now returns to the heart where it is pumped into the left atrium, this has completed the pulmonary circuit.

The left atrium pumps the blood to the left ventricle which then pumps the oxygen rich blood to the organs and tissues of the body. The systemic circuit around the body is much larger than the pulmonary circuit consequently the left ventricle is the most powerful chamber in the heart with a thicker muscle wall than the other three chambers. The heart is divided into left and right by a central wall called the septum and two thirds of its mass lies to the left of the body's midline. The heart weighs about 250 grams in adult females and 300 grams in adult males. It is able to contract independent of a nerve supply because it is stimulated by an area of specialised tissue in the right atrium called the sino-atrial node.

Blood vessels

The blood vessels are the transport network of the body. They allow blood to travel to every part of the body and return to the heart. The transport network consists of several types of vessels, as shown in Table 5.6.

Table 5.6: The vessels of the cardiovascular system.

Type of vessel	Description
Arteries	These are large vessels which usually carry oxygenated blood away from the heart to the rest of the body (the exception is the pulmonary artery). They subdivide to form smaller vessels called arterioles which then branch off again to form capillaries. These vessels are cylindrical and muscular and are able to contract and dilate in order to regulate blood flow.
Veins	These vessels are usually responsible for the movement of deoxygenated blood back towards the heart so that it can be sent on the pulmonary circuit once more, and back to the lungs. Vessels called venules connect the capillaries where the oxygen has just been deposited to the veins which then return it to the heart. The blood flow in the veins is under less pressure than the arteries and so they tend to be slightly less muscular.
Capillaries	These are the smallest blood transportation vessels in the body. They are incredibly thin which allows the exchange of gases through them. Organs and tissues which need a high amount of oxygen and nutrients, such as muscles and the brain, will have many capillaries.

Blood

Blood is a red fluid which carries oxygen, nutrients, hormones and disease fighting agents around the body. The typical human has around 5 litres of blood in their body. Blood is made up of several different substances:

- plasma
- red and white cells
- platelets.

Plasma. Plasma is what makes the blood a liquid. It transports the cells in the blood around the body. It is a pale yellow fluid made mostly from water and a small amount of protein.

Red blood cells (erythrocytes). Red blood cells are the most numerous type of cell in the blood. They are disc shaped with a depression in the centre (see Figure 5.11). They are created by the marrow in the bones and have a life span of approximately 3 months. They carry a substance called haemoglobin which helps transport oxygen around the body. It is haemoglobin that gives the blood its red colour.

White blood cells (leucocytes). White blood cells are the soldiers of the body as they are the cells that fight off bacteria and viruses. They are much bigger than red blood cells and are irregular in shape. Without them we would not be able to fight off infection or disease.

Platelets. Platelets play an important role in the repair system of the body. They help restrict blood flow to a damaged part of the body, such as a graze or a cut. They stick together at the site of an injury to plug gaps in broken blood vessels and so reduce bleeding. Also, they help form scabs over wounds. The scab prevents foreign particles entering the bloodstream and stays in place until the tissue underneath is repaired. It falls off once the tissue is healed.

The cardiovascular system performs a variety of functions in the body:

- Repair – platelets within the blood clot at the site of a wound and help to form a scab to protect the body from bacteria and repair the wound.

- Transport of oxygen – red blood cells are vitally important in transporting oxygen from our lungs to all the other parts of the body.

- Thermoregulation – blood vessels help control our temperature via a process called thermoregulation. When we are warm, blood vessels near the surface of our skin dilate (widen) and allow more blood to flow through to cool us down. When we are cold, the blood vessels near the surface of the skin constrict forcing more warm blood into the core of our body where it is needed most.

- Removal of waste products – the blood contains the waste products of the body. The waste products are transported to the kidneys that filter the blood around 36 times every 24 hours.

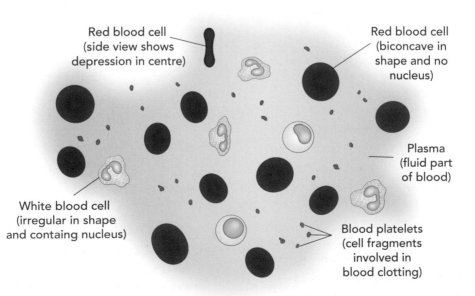

Figure 5.11: The main components of human blood are shown here. What is the major difference between red and white blood cells?

Assessment activity 5.2

(P2) **BTEC**

Understanding the basic structure and functions of the major body systems associated with health and fitness is very important if you are going to have the knowledge to be able to improve your fitness performance in order to pass the entry tests for the service of your choice. In the form of a large and engaging poster address the following task:

1 Describe the structure and functions of the muscular-skeletal, cardiovascular and respiratory systems (P2)

Grading tip

Make sure your poster contains lots of labelled diagrams which highlight the body systems as well as the explanation of their respective functions.

PLTS

Completing this assessment will help you develop your self manager skills.

2.5 Effects of exercise on the body systems

Exercise has many short-term and long-term effects across all the major body systems. Table 5.7 highlights the most important of these.

Table 5.7: The effects of exercise on the human body.

Short-term effects	Explanation
Blood flow	Blood flow around the body becomes faster and it is diverted away from areas such as the stomach, which are not essential to exercise and directed towards the heart, lungs and muscles. This is because the blood is required to carry more oxygen and take away more waste products.
Raised heart rate	The heart beats faster, fills up with more blood and moves blood around the body faster. Exercise increases not only heart rate but also blood pressure and stroke volume. Stroke volume is the amount of blood that can be moved with each beat of the heart.
Increased respiration	Respiration becomes faster and deeper as it responds to the need for more oxygen in the body. It also increases to remove a larger volume of carbon dioxide which is produced during exercise.
Long-term effects	**Explanation**
Muscle tone	Depending on the exercise, the muscles can become bigger and are more clearly defined.
Lowered heart rate	At resting state the heart is able to pump blood more efficiently, which means it needs to beat less to move the same volume of blood.
Blood pressure	Although the short-term impact of exercise is to raise blood pressure, the long-term effect is the opposite. Long-term exercise has the benefit of generally lowering overall blood pressure as the heart works more efficiently.
Strength	As muscles work hard during a programme of exercise they will become stronger. Again, this can depend on the type of exercise.
Stamina	Muscles are able to work for longer without becoming fatigued.

Table 5.7 (cont.)

Long-term effects	Explanation
Weight	A long-term exercise plan can have a varying effect on weight. Some exercise will increase muscle mass and lead to a weight gain while other types of exercise will help reduce or maintain original weight.
Cholesterol	Cholesterol can be reduced by a long-term exercise plan.
Digestion	Although the short-term impact of exercise is to direct blood away from the digestive organs, the long-term effect is the opposite. Long-term regular exercise helps to strengthen the muscles of the abdomen and digestive organs and reduces sluggishness by stimulating the muscles to push digestive contents through your body.

Assessment activity 5.3   P3 M2   BTEC

This is another practical activity that will be supervised by your tutor.

1   Undertake a fitness activity of your choice and record and identify the short-term effects of the exercise on your body systems **P3**

2   Once you have done this hold a discussion with your tutor where you explain the short- and long-term effects of exercise on the major human body systems **M2**

Grading tips

Remember to include the information in the table above in your discussion in order to achieve **M2**. For **P3** remember to record how your body reacted in the short term to the exercise that you did.

3.   The importance of lifestyle factors in the maintenance of health and well-being

Each of us makes lifestyle choices that can affect our levels of health and fitness. Lifestyle is the way we choose to conduct our lives from what we eat, to the jobs we do, to the types of relationships we choose to have. The following lifestyle choices impact upon our health and fitness.

3.1 Physical activity

It is a well-known fact that individuals who exercise regularly, either as part of their job or in their leisure time, have fewer heart attacks than those who don't. Exercise builds up the strength of the heart, which means it can cope better if you put a sudden physical demand on it. Exercise will also:

- help reduce blood pressure
- keep weight in check

- slow down the bone deterioration in older people (particularly important for women)
- keep muscles strong and joints flexible
- help you deal with stress and depression in more productive ways
- decrease the amount of bad cholesterol in the blood helping keep the heart and blood vessels healthy
- promote psychological well-being and positive self-image
- give you an opportunity to meet and socialise with other people, perhaps in the gym or as part of a sports team.

The government recommends we do at least 30 minutes of exercise three times a week in order to remain fit and healthy.

3.2 Alcohol

Alcohol has an impact on all of the major body systems and abuse of alcohol can lead to death. Some of the main effects of excessive alcohol are: blackouts, liver cancer, liver disease, diarrhoea, heartburn, cancer of the oesophagus, malnutrition, high blood pressure, loss of libido, reduced fertility, impaired decision-making and increased risk of accidents.

In terms of public service work, the abuse of alcohol can directly affect your working performance. Many public service jobs require the operation of complex equipment such as breathing apparatus, weapons and vehicles. The presence of alcohol in your system will impair your judgement, placing yourself and others at risk.

In addition, alcohol is very high in calories and without proper exercise this will lead to weight gain. Carrying excess weight places an additional strain on the body, especially the cardiovascular and respiratory systems, which have to work harder to perform their functions.

3.3 Smoking

Smoking is a major danger to your health. It can cause heart disease, numerous types of cancer and bronchial disorders. Over 100,000 people die every year in the UK from smoking-related diseases. Smokers have double the heart attack risk of non-smokers and, linked with the contraceptive pill, in women the risk may even be higher.

The body becomes addicted to nicotine, which is a stimulant, making the heart beat faster and the blood vessels narrow, causing a strain on the cardiovascular system. In addition, the blood becomes more 'sticky' with fats and sugars leading to a 'furring up' of the arteries. Carbon monoxide in cigarette smoke can drastically reduce the capacity of the blood to carry O_2 to the tissues, which again means that the heart must work harder. In the short-term smoking can also increase other problems, such as asthma, which might compromise your job performance in any public service work.

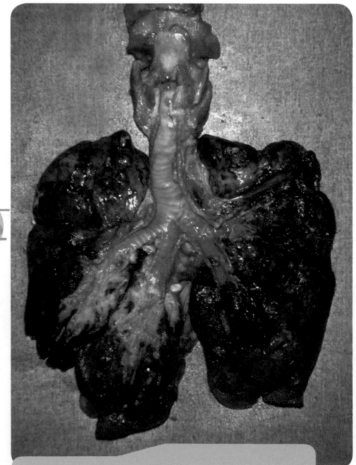

These are human lungs. Can you see evidence of inhaling cigarette smoke?

3.4 Stress

Stress is a constant part of our lives, whether it is worrying about getting assignments in on time or more serious worries such as divorce or bereavement. The kind of stress that is really damaging to your body is long-term stress, which can be caused by family problems, financial difficulties or being unhappy in your workplace.

Stress can show itself physically and emotionally through signs such as indigestion, fatigue, insomnia, feeling irritable or headaches. These symptoms are caused by the increased activity of the nervous system as it responds to your stress and the production of hormones such as adrenaline and cortisol, which trigger your **fight or flight** response. These hormones stimulate the heart to beat faster and to redirect blood to the brain, heart and muscles. This causes an increase in blood pressure, which can lead to the heart and blood vessels being placed under stress. If a blood vessel bursts in the brain it is called a 'stroke' and can have fatal consequences. In addition, the blood becomes 'sticky' with sugars and fats released from the liver in order to give the muscles more energy to power the fight or flight response. However, if you are sitting at a desk fuming at your boss, these fats and sugars are not utilised by the muscles and they can stick to artery walls clogging them up with fatty deposits which put you at greater risk of heart disease.

Stress has been linked with many other problems such as eczema, stomach ulcers and depression. The obvious way to deal with this problem is to tackle the cause of the stress so that it no longer exists or to change the way you react to stress. Techniques such as meditation and exercise can help an individual cope with stress more effectively.

It is also worth noting that public service officers may also be at risk of **post-traumatic stress disorder** (PTSD) if they experience stressful or traumatic events during their working life, such as a major disaster or war conditions.

3.5 Drugs

The abuse of different drugs will lead to a variety of effects on the short- and long-term health and fitness of an individual. These include:

- **Opiates (heroin)** – constipation, loss of libido, drowsiness, respiratory distress, an overdose is fatal. It is also linked to the spread of HIV and hepatitis through the sharing of contaminated needles
- **Amphetamines (speed, whizz)** – sleeplessness, anorexia
- **LSD** – sensory distortions, hallucinations, a feeling of panic or anxiety
- **Ecstasy** – hallucinations, heatstroke, dehydration, panic attacks and depression
- **Cocaine** – damage or loss of nasal septum, may cause paranoid psychosis
- **Cannabis (marijuana, weed, pot)** – may lead to feelings of depression, anxiety and apathy with long terms use. Possible linkage with some mental illness such as schizophrenia also has a negative effect on short-term memory. Smoking cannabis can be far more dangerous to your lungs than ordinary tobacco as most cannabis users roll their own cigarettes and don't use a filter.

Drug abuse may also lead to unwise sexual behaviour or involvement in crime.

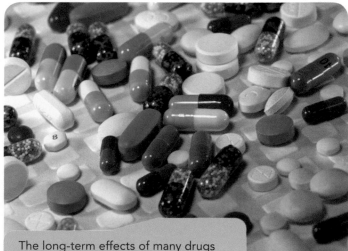

The long-term effects of many drugs can be damaging to health.

Key terms

Stress is the emotional and physical reaction our body shows to meet a challenge, this can be harmful and/or beneficial.

Post traumatic stress disorder (PTSD) is a severe anxiety disorder that can develop after a person experiences a traumatic event.

Fight or flight is an instinctive response to a threatening situation which prepares you to resist or run.

In any sports or fitness-related area of study there is also the danger from use of performance enhancing drugs such as anabolic steroids. Steroids are taken by some athletes and bodybuilders to increase their muscle mass and strength but these can have significant side effects such as:

- in men – shrunken testicles, baldness, higher voice, prominent breasts and infertility
- in women – a deeper voice, increased body hair and baldness.

3.6 Diet

Healthy eating is vital for all our body systems since they rely on the energy from food to run effectively. Diets in the Western world tend to contain too much fat, sugar, salt and dairy products, which can cause problems such as obesity, high blood pressure, coronary heart disease and dental decay. Food such as fresh fruit and vegetables, cereals such as rice and pasta can help fight against diseases such as bowel cancer and gum disease.

A well-balanced diet includes food from the five main food groups. These are:

- bread, cereal (including breakfast cereals) and potatoes (starchy foods)
- fruit (including fresh fruit juice) and vegetables
- meat and fish
- milk and dairy foods
- fat and sugar.

Dietary requirements and recommendations

A well balanced diet should contain enough of the five food components to keep the body running smoothly.

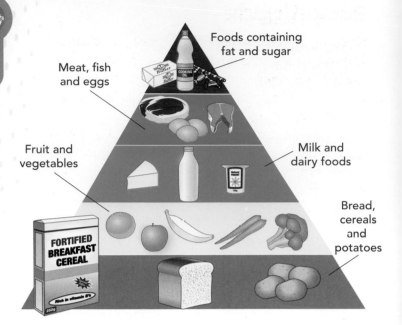

Figure 5.12: Does your diet include the five main food groups?

As you can see a well balanced diet would consist of enough of each of these components to satisfy the needs of the body. The portions outlined above are only an indication of the amount of food you should eat to stay healthy as it depends on your current weight, level of physical activity and health. As a general guide, a 10 stone woman should be aiming for around 2300 kcals per day and an 11.5 stone man around 3000 kcals per day.

A balanced diet can help to improve health and reduce the incidence of heart disease and cancer. A study by the National Audit Office found that nearly two thirds of adults in England are overweight. This costs the health services over £2.5 billion per year. Obesity is a growing problem across the western world. Obesity is a state in which the weight of a person is at a level where it can seriously endanger their health. It is on the increase due to the availability of high fat and sugar foods and snacks and a decrease in the amount of exercise we take. Obesity increases the risk of heart disease and strokes.

Your diet should reflect your lifestyle. If you are very active you will need more calories than if you are not active. This can have a big impact on the uniformed public services, which is why an average ration pack for the armed services contains food with an average of around 4000 kcals.

Personal hygiene

Keeping clean is an essential part of any lifestyle. Regular washing removes sweat and dirt, preventing unpleasant smells and, more importantly, reducing the risk of infections. This is especially important for service personnel operating away from their base for an extended period of time, for example, in jungle or desert conditions where bacteria can thrive. Emergency service personnel may also come into contact with contaminated environments where biological or chemical hazards are common in the line of duty, for example, a tanker spillage or a crime scene involving blood or other bodily fluids. These environments can pose a significant threat to health and safety if personal hygiene is not observed.

There are several easy ways of promoting your personal hygiene:

- Daily washing is essential for a healthy lifestyle.
- Wash your hands before eating.
- Shower after physical activity.
- Wash food before eating it if you suspect it may be dirty.
- Wear clean clothes every day if possible.
- Wear any protective equipment you are given, such as gloves or eye shields.

Case study: The effects of lifestyle

Narinda is a 21-year-old university graduate who is applying for a career in the Royal Navy. Her lifestyle at university was not best suited for promoting health and fitness. While at university she:

- predominantly ate takeaway food
- occasionally took illegal drugs
- drank alcohol at least three times per week to excess
- smoked heavily
- did little physical activity.

Fortunately the Royal Navy have given Narinda a start date for training which is six months away and she knows she has to clean up her act if she is going to be successful in training.

1 What should Narinda's first lifestyle change be?

2 Where could Narinda get help to improve her lifestyle?

3 What will be the consequences if Narinda does not change her lifestyle, both long-term and short-term?

4 What impact will Narinda's current lifestyle have had on her health and fitness?

5 Design a lifestyle action plan to help Narinda improve her chances of succeeding in naval training.

Assessment activity 5.4

 **BTEC**

It is important to understand the effects that your lifestyle choices can have on your overall health and your fitness for the services. For this activity you should produce a leaflet that addresses the following points:

1 Describe the lifestyle factors that can have an effect on health **P4**

2 Explain **M3** and evaluate **D2** the effects of identified lifestyle factors on health and fitness when applying for a public service and long-term employment

Grading tips

The lifestyle factors you should examine are things such as physical activity, smoking, alcohol, diet, drugs and stress. Describe how they impact on your health for **P4** and for the higher grades provide a more detailed explanation and evaluation of how these factors might influence your application for a public service and your chances of achieving the level of fitness required.

4. Advice on lifestyle improvement

You have examined lifestyle factors which may cause health and fitness problems (see pages 175–179). Now you need to examine the strategies that can be used to overcome these lifestyle problems and the advice you could give to those struggling to change their lifestyle.

Table 5.8: Advice on lifestyle improvement.

Lifestyle issue	Advice and strategies
Physical activity	• Increase levels of physical activity by following the government's guidance on levels of exercise. (If there are any underlying medical conditions, ensure that an exercise programme has been approved by a doctor.) • Aim for three 30-minute sessions of physical activity every week, this can include activities designed to suit your current level of fitness, such as yoga, walking, cycling or jogging.
Alcohol	• Many people find it very hard not to drink when they are socialising. One good way to reduce alcohol consumption is to change where you socialise, avoid going to the pub or club and head for the cinema instead where alcohol is not freely available. • If alcohol has become a significant problem then medical advice and counselling might be a route to follow, this can lead to therapy and rehabilitation. • If the problem is more severe then detoxification might be appropriate. • There are also self-help groups such as Alcoholics Anonymous, which can be a tremendous source of support.
Smoking	The NHS has a significant number of resources available to individuals who wish to stop smoking, such as the NHS smoking help-line, motivational videos, advice on nicotine replacement products and information and support to help you give up.
Stress	A certain amount of stress can be a good thing, but it can easily become overwhelming and upsetting. There are some strategies which can ease the situation: • Assertiveness training can help, many people become stressed because they have difficulty saying no to people and end up taking on too much responsibility with too little time to complete the tasks. Learning to be assertive and say no can help reduce this. • Also useful in reducing stress is making clear plans and goals which allow tasks to be completed in a set time. Many people find relaxation and breathing exercises to be effective, while others find an escape from stress in the form of physical activity.
Drugs	The best course of action for individuals with drug issues is to seek medical help and advice via the NHS. As with smoking, the NHS provides significant support for individuals with drug problems including the Talk to Frank help-line, rehabilitation and advice and guidance on how to quit. The NHS choices website contains a host of information to help.
Diet	Dieting can be very difficult for many people and obesity is a growing problem in the UK. An ongoing lifestyle change in eating habits will be more rewarding than a short-term diet. Again the NHS is a good source of guidance and your doctor or local practice nurse may be able to advise you on how to change your diet and even provide you with an eating plan to kick-start your efforts. Cooking food using fresh ingredients, menu planning and keeping a food diary to monitor your food intake will be helpful. It is important to know which foods to eat more of and less of, as well as timing your meals so that you have a slow release of energy all day (rather than skipping meals).
Personal hygiene	This can be a very sensitive issue both for you and for other people. Make sure you wash every day and change your clothes regularly, use a deodorant and brush your teeth as part of your grooming regime.

Assessment activity 5.5

P5 M4 BTEC

If your lifestyle isn't as healthy as it could be then you risk not being fit and healthy enough to pass the physical requirements of the entry test for the public service of your choice. Knowing what strategies and improvement you could make will be key to ensuring you are ready to apply. Create a lifestyle improvement leaflet that covers the following tasks:

1   Provide lifestyle improvement strategies that can have a positive effect on health P5

2   Explain the lifestyle improvement strategies to justify their positive effect on health M4

Grading tips

To achieve P5 your leaflet should cover the lifestyle improvement strategies outlined in the table above. To achieve M4 your explanation should be more detailed and you should make it clear how these lifestyle changes will improve the health of the person concerned.

5. Plan a health-related physical activity programme in preparation for the public services

5.1 Collecting information

Personal health improvement included assessing factors such as your nutrition, fitness and lifestyle to see if or where you need to make changes. A good way to do this is via an improvement action plan. However before you create your action plan you will need to collect information that will help you draw up your plan. The information you will need includes:

- personal goals
- lifestyle
- medical history
- physical activity
- attitudes
- motivation.

Collecting this information will help you tailor the programme more specifically to you or the person you are designing the programme for.

Goal setting

When you start your programme (or anything, for that matter) you need to decide on your aims and goals. To do this you need to give yourself achievable targets, which should lead to your ultimate goal, for example becoming a police officer or a Royal Marine Commando. Goals can be short term, medium term and long term. For example:

- Short-term goal – complete a 3 mile circuit, alternating walking and running (walk to a lamp post, run to the next one, walk to the next one, etc).

- Medium-term goal – run the 3 mile circuit (this should be achievable after walking and running the course three times a week for four weeks).

- Long-term goal – achieve level 5.4 on the bleep test (this should be achievable after running 3 miles three times a week for a month).

As you can see in the example, each step towards the ultimate long-term goal builds on what has gone before and uses a plan for success.

Activity: Health Improvement Action Plan

Think about your own personal information as listed above and draw up a personal improvement action plan that highlights where in your diet, fitness or lifestyle you need to make changes and exactly how you are going to change over a defined timescale.

Activity: Targets

What short-term, medium-term and long-term goals could you set for meeting the fitness requirements of your service?

List them and then speak to your health and fitness tutor about how best to put them into practice.

In order to be successful with your goal setting, use the SMART technique. Goals should be:

S – specific to your ultimate goal (Is this going to help me join the public service of my choice?)

M – measurable, for example, run 3 miles (Can I see what I've done?)

A – achievable (Is the task possible?)

R – realistic/relevant (Is this really going to help? Is it what I should be aiming to do?)

T – time-related, for example, 3 times a week for a month (Will I know when to be moving on with my goals?) or running a given distance in a certain time by a certain date.

You should try to stick to your goals as much as possible but sometimes life might get in the way or maybe your goals are too hard (or too easy). In this case, sit down and look at your plan; how can you change it to fit the problem?

It is also good practice to use a training diary. This can be used to log each session you have completed so that you can monitor your performance. This will motivate you when you see how you've progressed. You can also note how you felt you're you were training as this could have an impact on whether the programme should be changed (you won't do it if you don't like it). Ensure that your goals are outlined clearly – that way you can link performance to your progress in achieving your goals.

Principles of training

In order to build your fitness, you need to understand some of the principles that underpin your training:

- **Overload** – firstly, in order to see gains in strength, your muscles must be stimulated to do more work than they are used to.

- **Progression** – secondly, muscles must continually work against a gradually increasing resistance in order to maintain overload.

- **Specificity** – thirdly, the strength gains you receive from training depend on the particular muscle groups used and the particular movement performed.

- **Variation** – as with most things, familiarity breeds contempt. In order to stay motivated and interested in your training it is important to vary what you do. Don't keep to the same exercises year in, year out: your body will adapt to them and it will be more difficult to see improvements and it will be very easy to just go through the motions. Try something new instead – it will give you a new challenge and overload your body in a different way.

- **Reversibility** – the phrase 'use it or lose it' can be applied here. Improvements in performance start to disappear if you do not keep up the training. If you stop running, your cardiovascular stamina will gradually decrease; if you stop resistance training, you will gradually lose strength; if you stop stretching, you will gradually lose flexibility. This applies to all of the components of fitness, even the skill-based ones. Once performance is lost, you need to work hard to regain it.

Training can take many forms, but the most common types of training follow the FITT (frequency, intensity, time, type) principles. These are shown in Table 5.9.

Pyramid training is just one way to lift weights or engage in any strength building activity and involves changing your repetitions and added weights for each set of each exercise. In other words, you'll start light and end heavy or start heavy and end light.

Fartlek training is also called speed play and it involves a mixture of continuous and interval training.

Table 5.9: FITT principles for training.

Principle	Definition
Frequency 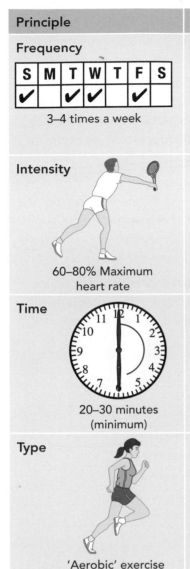 3–4 times a week	This is how often you train. For example, if you want to develop your cardiovascular stamina you can run up to 5 times a week. Once you've built it to the required level, you can change to running 3 times a week to maintain that level and use the rest of the time to concentrate on upper body strength. In another example, you may have been undertaking a simple strength circuit twice a week for the last 12 weeks and now want to devote more time to increasing strength – you decide to go to the gym Monday, Wednesday and Friday, instead of just twice.
Intensity 60–80% Maximum heart rate	This is how hard you train. It can be used to adapt training in many ways.
Time 20–30 minutes (minimum)	This is how long your session is. If you have increased the intensity, you may need to train for a shorter time but you have a harder work-out. Or you may be running further and therefore need a longer session. This will depend upon how much time is available, of course.
Type 'Aerobic' exercise	This is the type of training (you can change this). For example, to develop cardiovascular fitness, your first programme was to run continuously for 30 minutes. To improve your performance you may try **fartlek training** in order to improve your speed at completing your distance. In terms of strength, after completing a programme using a simple circuit of 12 exercises for 3 times a week, you may wish to develop more strength using **pyramid training**.

Essentially you run at different speeds over different distances, sometimes running slower and sometimes sprinting.

Activity: Training methods

Speak with your health and fitness tutor to find out which type of training they recommend for you in order to reach your goals.

Write a plan incorporating this advice.

Appropriate activities

In order to improve your fitness there are many activities you could undertake, but which one you choose will be based upon personal preferences, physical ability and medical history. You could consider activities such as:

- walking
- cycling
- hiking
- swimming
- jogging
- using the gym
- playing sports.

Cycling will improve your cardiovascular system. Have you measured your maximum heart rate reserve?

Exercise intensity

Exercise intensity is a measure of how hard your body is working while exercising. There are some common methods of measuring exercise intensity such as:

Rating of perceived exertion (RPE). This is how hard you think your body is working while exercising. It is based on the physical experiences of the person while they are exercising and their perception of how their body is reacting in terms of heart rate, tiredness and sweating.

The talk test. This is a really simple way of measuring how hard a person is working. If they are working at a moderate level they should be able to talk but not sing, if they are working very hard they will only be able to say a few words without pausing for breath.

Maximum heart rate reserve (MHRR). This is the difference between your maximum heart rate (MHR) and your heart rate (HR) when you are at rest.

Remember

Abbreviation	In full
HR	heart rate
MHR	maximum heart rate
RHR	resting heart rate
HRR	heart rate reserve
MHRR	maximum heart rate reserve
RPE	rating of perceived exertion

Assessment activity 5.6

This is another practical assessment that will be checked and supervised by your tutor. Taking into consideration the fitness test results you achieved in Assessment activity 5.1 (page 163), plan a six-week health-related physical activity programme based on your personal results. **P6**

Grading tips

Use your strengths and weaknesses chart from your fitness assessments to draw up an action plan, and then base your physical activity programme on this.

PLTS

Completing this practical assessment will help you develop your creative thinker, reflective learner, independent enquirer and effective participator skills.

Tessa Burns
Royal Marine Physical Training Instructor

My job is to ensure that the personnel in the Royal Marines are fit and ready for combat. This includes a whole range of things from sporting activities to improve teamwork and coordination, to individual training to improve agility and endurance, to the preparation for the series of combat fitness tests we have to do.

A typical day

A typical day for me could be spent in the gym where I supervise the health and safety of all the personnel who use it. I would start by checking all the fitness equipment for safety and cleanliness and report any faults. Then I would check the computer to see what type of sessions have been booked. I could be taking fitness assessments which means measuring heart rates and blood pressures and planning programmes to improve any aspect of fitness. Or I could be delivering scheduled fitness sessions or tests throughout the day, especially the PJFT (pre-joining fitness test). This test is performed in the gym on a running machine inclined at 2 degrees by all those wishing to join the Royal Marines.

The best thing about the job

One great thing is to see all the applicants who passed the PJFT come back for their PRMC (Potential Royal Marines Course). The PRMC lasts over a period of three days and, as a PTI, I feel it is important to take the test with them to give as much encouragement as I can. It's a mixture of running, swimming and gym tests. It is vital that all personnel are fit for combat and that they feel free to come to me for advice on health and fitness issues. Royal Marines personnel need to be physically and mentally fit for duty and it's my job to make sure they are. I'm very proud of the work I do and I hope to progress further in physical training.

Think about it!

What topics have you covered in this unit that might give you the background to be a physical training instructor in the Royal Marine Commandos?

What knowledge and skills do you think you need to develop further if you want to be involved in fitness training in the future?

Just checking

1 What are the four chambers of the heart called?
2 What are the parts of the respiratory system?
3 What is the effect of a lack of sleep on physical performance?
4 What are the effects of smoking?
5 What are the FITT principles?
6 How can you reduce your stress levels?
7 What are SMART targets?
8 What are the government guidelines for alcohol and exercise?
9 Describe the types of blood vessel
10 What are the health benefits of regular exercise?

edexcel

Assignment tips

- The service you want to join may be different from others in your class. Don't be concerned about this, your training programme is likely to be very different from people who want other services. Don't be tempted to do the same as they do because its easier that designing your own training programme. Remember you are getting yourself ready for your service, following a training programme for police fitness standards wont be of much help if you want to be a Royal Marine.

- Health and safety is a key component of this unit, remember to take care when training and if you have any medical problems or issues make sure you discuss them with your tutor and doctor as your training programme for your assessments should fit around your own personal needs.

- Keep a training diary throughout this unit. It will provide evidence for some of the criteria and help you monitor your progress towards your goals.

6 Fitness testing and training for the uniformed public services

The services will often support you in becoming fit and healthy and, because the recruitment process in the services can be lengthy, you will have plenty of time to improve your standard of fitness before they test you. However, the services do not want to recruit people who are not physically and mentally able to do the job so it is really important that when you are preparing to apply to the service of your choice that you include fitness training as part of your preparation.

The fitness tests vary for each service and some are much harder than others, so you will have to adjust your preparation to match the standard you need to achieve. This unit also allows you to develop a personalised training plan and review how effective it has been in improving your fitness.

Learning outcomes

After completing this unit you should:

1. know the fitness requirements for entry into the uniformed public services
2. know different methods of fitness training
3. be able to plan a fitness training programme
4. be able to monitor and review a fitness training programme.

Assessment and grading criteria

This table shows you what you must do in order to achieve a pass, merit or distinction grade, and where you can find activities in this book to help you.

To achieve a **pass** grade the evidence must show that you are able to:	To achieve a **merit** grade the evidence must show that, in addition to the pass criteria, you are able to:	To achieve a **distinction** grade the evidence must show that, in addition to the pass and merit criteria, you are able to:
P1 describe the entrance fitness requirements and tests of three different public services **Assessment activity 6.1 page 195**		
P2 outline a fitness test for the main components of fitness and compare results based on a public service entrance test **Assessment activity 6.1 page 195**	**M1** explain the strengths and areas for improvement of the fitness tests **Assessment activity 6.1 page 195**	
P3 describe one method of fitness training for the main components of physical fitness **Assessment activity 6.1 page 195**	**M2** explain one method of fitness training for six different components of physical fitness **Assessment activity 6.1 page 195**	**D1** evaluate methods of fitness training for the different components **Assessment activity 6.1 page 195**
P4 plan a six-week personal fitness training programme to incorporate the principles of training **Assessment activity 6.2 page 200**		
P5 undertake a personal fitness training programme, completing a fitness training diary **Assessment activity 6.2 page 200**		
P6 report on a fitness training programme including the strengths and areas for improvement **Assessment activity 6.2 page 200**	**M3** explain in detail strengths and areas for improvement following completion of the training programme **Assessment activity 6.2 page 200**	**D2** evaluate strengths and areas for improvement following completion of the training programme, providing recommendations for future activities **Assessment activity 6.2 page 200**

How you will be assessed

This unit will be assessed by an internal assignment that will be designed and marked by the staff at your centre. The assignment is designed to allow you to show your understanding of the learning outcomes for fitness testing and training. These relate to what you should be able to do after completing this unit.

Assessments can be quite varied and can take the form of:

- reports
- fitness assessments
- leaflets
- presentations
- posters

- practical tasks
- case studies
- diaries
- fitness records
- action plans.

Hazel's experience of fitness training

I liked this unit as it was very practical and allowed me the opportunity to build up my fitness across the unit so that by the end I was able to pass the police fitness test. It was also good fun as we got to do a lot of active things such as sport and spend time in the college gym.

I think the best part of the unit was being able to plan my own fitness programme. I did need a bit of support from my tutor but at the end of the six weeks of training there was a real difference in my approach to fitness and I was proud that I'd managed to stick with it.

Training is actually a lot more complicated than I thought it would be. I have developed new respect for the people who work in the college gym and support me in improving my fitness. I would never have believed it was so technical and scientific if I hadn't done this unit. I can see how the knowledge I have now about training methods will come in useful in my public service career.

Over to you!

- What areas of fitness testing might you find interesting?
- Have you ever completed a public service fitness test?
- Do you have any fears or concerns about your level of fitness?
- Are you currently fit enough to pass the fitness tests in the service of your choice?
- What preparation could you do to get ready for your assessments?

1. The fitness requirements for entry into the uniformed public services

Talk up

Thinking about fitness testing and training

Consider the fitness requirements for the service of your choice. Individually write down an honest assessment of your fitness and consider what steps you can make to improve.

Share your findings with the rest of your class. Did you come up with the same kind of things or was each person's assessment different? Why do you think this is?

All of the uniformed public services have some kind of fitness assessment that you must pass in order to be considered for employment. Fitness is really important to the public services as the nature of their work is very physically active. This section looks at the components of fitness, fitness tests and the reasons testing is done.

Link

This unit has very strong links and common content shared with Unit 5. The fitness requirements are covered on pages 156–163.

This Learning outcome is very similar to the first outcome in Unit 5 where the following topics are covered:

- **1.1** Fitness tests/Testing methods: pages 158–163

Outlines some of the tests that might be encountered in the public services and how they relate to the components of fitness.

- **1.2** Entrance requirements: pages 160–162

There is a wide variation in what is physically required in order to be a potential recruit to the services each of them performs a highly specialised role with its own set of interpersonal and physical fitness requirements.

- **1.3** Reasons for the inclusion of tests: pages 162–163

There are many reasons for the inclusion of fitness tests and one of them is to assess a candidate's current level of fitness.

- **1.4** Job-specific fitness tests: pages 160–162

Most uniformed services have a fitness test as part of their selection process, which is chosen to best represent the needs of the relevant service.

- **1.5** Benefits of tests: page 160
- **1.6** Reasons for repeated tests: page 163

This covers the first Learning outcome for Unit 6 in its entirety.

Strength is a component of fitness. Weight training improves dynamic strength.

2. The different methods of fitness training

Knowing how to train safely is a key issue when you are considering improving your fitness to meet the specific requirements of the public services entrance tests. This outcome covers components of fitness and methods of training.

2.1 Components of fitness

There are many factors that contribute to overall physical fitness. These are called the components of fitness and include cardiovascular endurance, muscular endurance, strength, flexibility and coordination.

> **Link**
>
> The different components of fitness are covered in Unit 5 on pages 156–158.

2.2 Methods of training

There are many ways to train and the methods you choose will depend largely on what aspects of your fitness you need to improve. Remember that you should take professional guidance before you undertake a training programme.

Flexibility

Flexibility is defined as the range of movement possible at joints. Up until the age of 40 ligaments, tendons and muscles are relatively elastic but after this age movement that is not used frequently can be decreased and eventually lost. This can cause problems and injuries if the body is suddenly asked to do something it has not done for a while. In terms of sports performance flexibility will help reduce the risk of injury, improve the execution of sports skills and reduce the likelihood of muscle soreness. It can be developed and maintained by stretching exercises or activities such as yoga and swimming. It is recommended that an individual should employ 5 or 10 minutes of stretching prior to beginning any sport or a physical activity in order to prepare the muscles for what is to follow. Stretching should also be conducted after physical activity since it helps to initiate the recovery process. There are several methods of stretching:

Active stretching. An individual moves a part of their body slightly beyond the usual range and holds for a few seconds.

Passive stretching. An individual's body is moved beyond the normal range of movement by a partner and held there for a few seconds.

Ballistic stretching. This involves moving the body well beyond the normal range of motion by way of swinging or bouncing movements.

Active stretching

Passive stretching

PNF

Figure 6.1: Flexibility can be developed and maintained by stretching exercises.

Proprioceptive neuro-muscular facilitation (PNF). An individual moves the body beyond the usual range of movement, contracts and releases the muscle involved and then moves a little further.

> ### Remember!
>
> Ballistic stretching uses the momentum of a moving body or a limb in an attempt to force it beyond its normal range of motion. An example might be bouncing down repeatedly to touch your toes. It is recommended that you *do not* incorporate ballistic stretching in your training at all. This is because the muscles are not able to adjust within the short period of time for which they are stretched.

Strength and resistance training

Resistance training develops strength. The muscles work against a resistance (weight) to develop size and strength. In addition to strengthening the muscles, all the other soft tissues in the area that is worked are strengthened too, that is the tendons and ligaments. It is dangerous to jump straight into strength training as it is easy to damage not only the muscles but also the surrounding tendons and ligaments. In order to avoid this, a lightly challenging programme should be put together that gets the body used to lifting weights. The resistance should be reasonably light and repeated about 10-12 times (reps); use a circuit of the gym and aim to work most of the body in between eight and ten exercises. Go around two or three times: this is a simple circuit. The weights can either be free or resistance machines can be used. Another method of building strength is **pyramid training**.

> ### Key term
>
> **Pyramid training** is just one way to lift weights or engage in any strength building activity and involves changing your reps and weight for each set of each exercise. In other words, you'll start light and end heavy or start heavy and end light.

Continuous training

This is running, walking, swimming, cycling and so on, at a steady continuous pace. For best gains this should be performed for at least 20–30 minutes and at least three times per week. Due to the nature of the muscles involved (the heart) training can be performed more regularly than anaerobic training and four to six times per week is acceptable. Running is seen as the most effective way of developing this kind of fitness although it does have a higher incidence of injuries than swimming or walking. Good running shoes are essential and they should be replaced every six months if used frequently. Certain activities can be used as alternatives to normal training to alleviate the boredom that can set in to training regimes. Such activities are often very good for continuous training:

- canoeing
- hill walking/mountaineering
- vigorous dance
- skiing.

As a rule of thumb, if you can talk while you are walking/running/cycling then you are training at the right level. However, beware of not working hard enough (you'll only be wasting your time). Your heart rate should be between 60 and 75 per cent of **maximum heart rate**.

> ### Key term
>
> **Maximum heart rate (MHR)** is calculated as 220 minus your age. It is important to know this so you can plan your cardiovascular training to work your heart hard enough to get some benefit, but not so hard that it might be dangerous.

The regular pace in running makes it an ideal form of continuous training. What are the drawbacks to running?

Interval training

This is a technique used by athletes to improve the heart's ability to deliver blood and oxygen. It involves training at a very high level followed by a period of light work. This cycle is then repeated. Interval training is usually associated with running but can be used in cycling and other activities.

During the intense period, work is done anaerobically and the heart works hard to pump oxygen around the body leading to an oxygen debt. In the recovery stage the heart is not working as hard, the oxygen debt is repaid and any poisons created are destroyed. This type of training improves the cardiovascular system, making better use of oxygen and more efficient removal of poisons.

This technique is obviously dangerous for those who are unfit or who have heart problems. Start with continuous training before moving on to interval training. Heart rates should be between 80 and 95 per cent MHR for interval training – take care when using this technique!

Circuit training

This involves going quickly from one exercise apparatus to another and doing a prescribed number of exercises or time on each apparatus. This ensures the pulse rate is kept high and promotes overall fitness by generally working all muscle groups as well as the heart and lungs.

Speed training

Speed is the ability to move a part of the body or the whole body quickly. Speed can be crucial in many sports where the activity is timed or you may be required to outpace an opponent. Speed is not just important for athletes, a quick physical reaction time might help you avoid injury in public service work or perhaps chase and run down criminal suspects.

press ups

star jumps

dorsal raises

shuttle runs

Figure 6.2: Circuit training can provide a whole body workout.

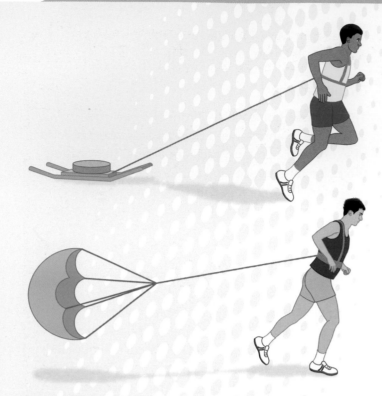

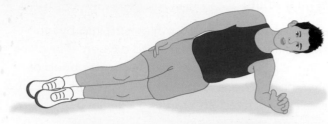

abdominal bracing for external obliques

abdominal bracing for rectus abdominis

Figure 6.4: Core stability training.

Figure 6.3: Speed training can involve dragging weights.

It is possible to improve speed with speed training methods such as **fartlek training** (also known as speed play).

Key term

Fartlek training (fartlek is Swedish for 'speed play') is a combination of both long slow distance and interval training. It involves changing speed, but at varying levels such as walking, sprinting and jogging.

Activity: Advantage of speed

In what services might it be a particular advantage to have speed?

Core stability training

This form of training involving working on the core torso and pelvic muscles, so that the pelvis, spine and shoulder girdle form a strong foundation on which the limbs can move. This can be very useful in correcting or preventing back pain and a strong core will help prevent injury from other exercises and activities. Core stability can be improved with activities such as medicine ball training or **pilates**.

Power

Power is the combination of strength and speed used together. Training methods which can be used to develop power include **plyometrics**.

Key terms

Pilates is an exercise system which focuses on developing core strength by using low impact stretching and conditioning exercises.

Plyometrics is a training technique designed to enhance power. It involves stretching a muscle and then immediately contracting it. An example would be a hill sprint or squats.

Assessment activity 6.1

P1 P2 P3 M1 M2 D1   BTEC

As a recruitment officer for a uniformed public service, you have been asked to measure the current fitness levels of new recruits and offer guidance to them on how they could improve their performance if required. The first thing you need to do is provide the recruits with an information booklet which covers the following task:

1 Describe the entrance fitness requirements and tests of three different public services **P1**
   This will allow the recruits to prepare properly for their fitness assessment and have the best chance of passing. The second key thing you need to do is demonstrate to the recruits how a service test is undertaken. Using a fitness record sheet complete the following task:

2 Outline a fitness test for the main components of fitness and compare your results to the public service entrance test **P2**

3 Also on your record sheet explain the strengths and areas for improvement of the fitness tests. **M1**
   It is possible that the public service recruits may not yet have the level of fitness required in order to pass the tests you have outlined and demonstrated so it is important to provide them with some training guidance on how they could improve their components of fitness Produce a series of training cards which address the following tasks:

4 Describe one method of fitness training for the main components of physical fitness **P3**

5 Explain one method of fitness training for six different components of physical fitness **M2**

6 Evaluate methods of fitness training for the different components of physical fitness. **D1**

PLTS

Carrying out this assessment activity will help you develop your independent enquirer, self manager and reflective learner skills.

Functional skills

When comparing pass rates of physical fitness test scores you will be developing your maths functional skills.

3. Planning a fitness training programme

In order to plan and create a fitness training programme you should be aware of the following issues:

- collecting information: see page 181.

This will help you draw up your plan, for instance your personal goals, lifestyle and medical history.

- health and safety considerations
- principles of training: see page 182.

This will help you in understanding some of the principles which underpin your training.

- periodisation
- training diaries.

Link

See pages 181–183 for more on collecting information and principles of training.

3.1 Considerations

Health and safety

The most important part of fitness training and testing is safety. If the activities are not carried out safely there is a high risk of injury, which at best can disrupt and interfere with the training routine or at worst can cause disability or death. Safety also includes checking that the venue and equipment are both in a suitable condition for the activities to be carried out. Last, but certainly not least, are the participants: they must be wearing appropriate clothing and footwear to perform the activities. Also participants need to be assessed for recent injuries and illnesses that may affect participation.

Warm-up

One of the most important, but often under-appreciated, components of the fitness session is the warm-up. It prepares the body and mind for exercise and helps to prevent injuries. Once you have checked the venue and all participants, it is essential to complete a warm-up. This should be done progressively, starting gently and increasing the workload. There are two phases to a warm-up:

- **Aerobic phase.** This is used to raise the heart rate. By stimulating the heart and the lungs, blood circulates around the body and literally warms the body up. This is important as muscles that are cold can easily be damaged. Any rhythmical activity that can be kept up for the required time is acceptable,

for example, running, cycling, rowing, stepping, skipping, and so on. This part of the warm-up should last about 5–10 minutes, but obviously varies on the individual and the environment. When you start sweating, you're ready for the next phase.

- **Stretching.** This follows the aerobic phase and uses the muscles that are going to be used in the session's activities. For example, if you are climbing you would stretch the arms, fingers, back and legs. Practising the actual skill you will be doing later can be included in the warm-up, so long as it is done gently and not at full speed. This part of the warm-up can prevent strain in the muscles that are going to be used in the session. The stretches should be held for about 10 seconds, with this phase lasting 5–10 minutes.

Once the warm-up is completed, your body will be ready to start working harder. You will also be ready psychologically to take part in the session as you've had 10 minutes getting used to working your body. This can be important if you haven't been particularly active prior to the session (for example, in bed or sitting in class).

Cool-down

This is just as important as the warm-up and follow on at the end of the session. The cool-down basically does the opposite of the warm-up by bringing the heart rate down to normal levels and preparing you for leaving the fitness environment. It is also very important in preventing injury and muscle ache. Again, there are two phases:

- **Light aerobic work.** This is essential in slowing the heart rate down. If you stop training abruptly, your heart rate will actually continue to increase, which is not healthy. By doing some moderate work the heart starts to calm down and blood flow returns to normal, preventing it from pooling in the muscles used. This has two advantages. Firstly, without a regular supply of oxygenated blood the brain ceases to function and shuts down leading to fainting. Secondly, the blood in the muscles will contain poisons created in the anaerobic energy process; oxygen breaks down these poisons. Any rhythmic activity like light jogging, walking, light cycling or rowing will work. Aim for 5–10 minutes to give the heart time to get used to the change in work rate.

- **Stretching.** This can help the muscles recover from the session and prevent aching. By stretching

Always incorporate a warm-up and cool-down in any exercise.

the muscles used, blood flow is stimulated and fresh oxygen is delivered. Flexibility training is also best done at the end of a session, when the muscles have been worked hard and can be stretched further resulting in an increased range of movement. Stretches in the cool-down should be performed for a minimum of 15 seconds. This part of the training session can be turned into suppleness training, adding another fitness factor into your session.

Cool-downs are also important psychologically as they allow your mind to calm down, removing any stress, aggression, competitiveness, etc. that may have built up during the session or test.

Activity: Warm-up and cool-down

Design a warm-up and cool-down routine for an activity of your choice.

Present this as a sequence of diagrams to the class.

Equipment

Training equipment should be:

- inspected regularly to ensure that it is in good condition and safe to use. If in doubt **do not use it**
- used in the correct manner, for the correct purpose. For heavy weights you may need a spotter (a friend to support the weights if you are struggling and to replace them safely if you cannot complete the repetition)
- put away properly when no longer needed
- checked before use, for example, collars are properly fitted to bar/dumbbells, suitable resistance (weight) is used, no frayed cables or loose parts, bar/dumbbells are equally weighted
- understood before it is used. Ask for an induction or read the instructions.

Link

Training programmes and a comparison of entry requirements for the public services can be found in Unit 5 on pages 160–163.

Periodisation

Athletes don't keep using the same training techniques all year round and neither should you. As we've seen from the principles of fitness there are benefits to changing the way you train. Another reason for change is to prepare yourself for different goals. This is what periodisation is all about: your training is split into a number of different phases or cycles. For an athlete the phases may be pre-competition, competition and post-competition. Training needs to take place in all phases, but it will be different in each phase and the principles of the FITT system can be used to manipulate sessions.

Link

The principles of the FITT system are outlined on pages 182–183.

The longest phase is the macrocycle and this usually covers the whole year, though it doesn't have to ('macro' simply means big). The macrocycle should take you to the year's long-term goal, for example, to complete and pass a uniformed service fitness test.

The training year is broken up into mesocycles, usually four of them ('meso' means middle). During each mesocycle you will be working to a different short-term goal, such as muscular endurance or strength. Each mesocycle lasts for a number of weeks during which the intensity of training gradually increases. The mesocycle will end in a peak where performance has been improved. All-round performance should peak in the third mesocycle, at the point of the long-term goal, whether it is a competition or a test. The final mesocycle is a recuperation phase, to avoid too much stress after the peak and excitement of the ultimate goal.

Between each mesocycle you need to build in one or two rest weeks to allow the body to recover from the increasingly intense training you've been doing. During the rest weeks you can adopt a lighter form of training or, preferably, do some other form of activity to give you a psychological rest as well. This could involve hill walking or canoeing or climbing: you will still be exercising, but in a different way. The mesocycles are divided into microcycles, which translate to your weekly training plans (see Figure 6.5).

macrocycle																				
mesocycle 1							mesocycle 2							mesocycle 3						
microcycle 1	microcycle 2	microcycle 3	microcycle 4	microcycle 5	microcycle 6	microcycle 7	microcycle 1	microcycle 2	microcycle 3	microcycle 4	microcycle 5	microcycle 6	microcycle 7	microcycle 1	microcycle 2	microcycle 3	microcycle 4	microcycle 5	microcycle 6	microcycle 7

Figure 6.5: Diagram of how periodisation can be used in training. A macrocycle usually lasts for one year.

4. Monitor and review a fitness training programme

4.1 Monitoring the programme

As you undertake your programme, remember to keep a training diary to log when you trained and what it was like. This will help you measure your progression, motivation, attitude and achievement of your training goals. You need to note the following:

- Date and time.
- Your attitude – did you feel in the mood for the session? Did you feel better afterwards?
- What did you do? Did you complete all of it or only a bit because you were distracted by something?
- Was it difficult or easy?
- Why was it easy or difficult? Does it need to be changed?
- Did you change anything? If so, what? Did it make the session better or worse?
- Did you work with a partner or alone? How did this affect your session?

You can also use your diary to log your performance in fitness tests. Using this data you can compare how you're doing with the public services fitness tests. Another useful source of information is from your tutor or gym instructors. What feedback have they given you on your programme and on your performance? Don't be afraid to ask – this is part of their role.

4.2 Reviewing the programme

Once you have completed your programme you can start to review it. This is where it's useful to have kept a training diary. There are several areas to review as shown in Table 6.1.

4.3 Evaluating the programme

Arranging your review strengths in this way will show your areas for improvement and you will clearly see how to modify and improve the programme for future use. This is essential to see further improvement and ties in directly to the principles of training. To evaluate the training programme, you need to look at the factors shown in Table 6.2.

Goal setting, planning, completing, reviewing and evaluating your training programme should be a continual process. All professional athletes and coaches use this system to continue improving fitness and performance. After a while it should become second nature and you will certainly be reviewing and evaluating your techniques and performance without conscious effort. Make sure that you continue to use a training diary, though. It can be very easy to forget the results of performance and reviews.

Table 6.1: Review of a fitness training programme.

Review	
Fitness training programme	**Results achieved**
• Was it relevant to the service you wish to join? • Was it specific to the required components of fitness? • Which components of fitness were used? • Which principles of training were used in the programme? • Was it set at the correct level for you? • Was it enjoyable? • Did it include fitness tests?	• Did you complete the programme or only do part of it? • Did you struggle with any parts? Which parts? • Why did you struggle? • How did you perform on the fitness tests? • What was your attitude to the programme? It may be that you didn't like it and therefore didn't carry it out. • Did you progress and see improvements in your performance? • Did your performance get worse?
Once you have reviewed these areas you can look at the strengths and areas for improvement for both.	
Strengths	**Areas for improvement**
• Things that worked well – why did they work well? • Good goals. Were they relevant to the service fitness test and specific components of fitness? • Was it well planned? • Improvements in performance. Which ones and why? • Improved results on fitness tests. Which results improved and why? • Used a range of components and principles of fitness. • Specifically used the FITT system. • Were you motivated? Why?	• What didn't work well? Why? • Maybe it wasn't relevant. • Unclear goals. • Not using SMARTER goal setting. • Not using a proper plan. • Maybe your performance got worse. Why? • You didn't include a fitness test. • The programme was too short. • The programme was boring.
The final question to ask is: to what extent did the training programme achieve your identified goals? Compare your original goals with the results of your review.	

Table 6.2: Evaluating a fitness training programme.

Evaluation	
Improvements	**Modifications**
• Use the areas for improvement to guide you. • Do you need clearer goals? • Was something missing? What was it? • How can you make the programme more interesting to motivate you more? • Can you make it more relevant?	• How can you change the programme so that you can carry on using it? • Do you need to change the components you used? • How about the principles of training? • Frequency? • Intensity? • Type of training? • Time spent training?

Assessment activity 6.2

(P4) (P5) (P6) (M3) (D2) :BTEC

As a recruitment officer for a uniformed public service, you will now plan and design a six-week fitness training programme for the new recruits and review their personal performance results. The first thing you need to do is:

1 Plan a six-week personal fitness training programme to incorporate the principles of training **P4**

However, in order to be sure you have devised an effective plan you need to test it on yourself to see it if it works, complete the following task:

2 Undertake the training programme, completing a fitness training diary **P5**

In order to get approval from your managers to provide the training programme to the new recruits you need to provide them with enough information that they can make a judgement on the programme you have designed and completed. Provide them with the following information in the form of a written report:

3 Report on a fitness training programme including the strengths and areas for improvement of the programme **P6**

4 Explain in detail strengths and areas for improvement of the programme following completion of the training programme **M3**

5 Evaluate strengths and areas for improvement of the programme following completion of the training programme, providing recommendations for future activities **D2**

Grading tip

Use your strengths and weaknesses chart from your fitness assessments to draw up an action plan, and then base your fitness training programmes on this. Use a periodisation chart to help you establish the macro-, meso- and microcycle events.

PLTS

As you carry out this assessment activity you will develop your self manager, reflective learner and effective participator skills.

Functional skills

By providing a written report you will develop your functional skills in English.

Corporal Michelle Farley

Army Physical Training Instructor

My job is to ensure that the personnel in the Army are fit and ready for combat. This includes a whole range of things from sporting activities, to improving teamwork and coordination, to individual training to improve agility and endurance, to the preparation for the annual combat fitness test we have to do.

A typical day

A typical day for me could be spent in the gym undertaking health fitness assessments including analysis of the psychological fitness of new recruits. I have to make sure the training I give will help them reach their goals and initially may include giving additional training sessions to individuals, such as circuit training.

The gym is equipped to undertake fitness measurements like heart rate and blood pressure as well as tests for stamina and muscular strength and endurance. I usually administer a range of fitness tests on each new recruit to obtain results across the different components. I can then devise the best training methods for a group and additional training that would benefit an individual. I monitor progress throughout training, altering the programme as we go.

The best thing about the job

Helping new recruits go from 'unfit' to 'fit' gives me a great sense of achievement. I've seen guys turn their lives around by ditching bad habits and getting into shape. This means that they not only become physically fit but their mental agility improves so they can look after themselves in combat. It's a great sense of personal satisfaction knowing I have improved their health, fitness and well-being.

Think about it!

What topics have you covered in this unit that might give you the background to be a physical training instructor soldier?

What knowledge and skills do you think you need to develop further if you want to be involved in fitness training in the future?

Just checking

1 What is pyramid training?
2 List the components of fitness.
3 How is BMI calculated?
4 Define fartlek training.
5 Suggest some activities for a circuit training session.
6 What is interval training?
7 Why do the services use fitness tests?
8 Describe a mesocycle.
9 What is periodisation?
10 What are the features required when planning a fitness training programme?

edexcel

Assignment tips

- The service you want to join may not be the same one as others in your class want to join. Don't be concerned about this even if it means your training programme is likely to be very different. Don't be tempted to do the same as they do because its easier than designing your own training programme. Remember you are getting yourself ready for your service, so following a training programme for police fitness standards won't be of much help if you want to be a Royal Marine.

- Health and safety is a key component of this unit, remember to take care when training and if you have any medical problems or issues make sure you discuss them with your tutor and doctor as your training programme for your assessments should fit around your own personal needs.

- Keep a training diary throughout this unit. It will provide evidence for some of the criteria and help you monitor your progress towards your goals.

7 International institutions and human rights

The uniformed public services are increasingly being deployed overseas on a variety of missions, including peacekeeping, humanitarian aid and disaster relief, as well as their more traditional combat and security role. This means it is essential that you keep up to date with what is happening outside our borders.

This unit is intended to provide you with a clear understanding of the importance of international affairs and how international events can impact on the operational work of the public services. You will examine a variety of international institutions, such as the United Nations and the European Union, and consider the impact these organisations have on the services and the ways in which our services support the work of these organisations. This unit also emphasises the importance of human rights issues, and discusses how human rights are protected internationally and how certain countries and regimes can infringe them.

Learning outcomes

After completing this unit you should:
1. know international institutions and their impact on UK public services
2. understand human rights and how the UK upholds human rights.

Assessment and grading criteria

This table shows you what you must do in order to achieve a **pass**, **merit** or **distinction** grade, and where you can find activities in this book to help you.

To achieve a **pass** grade the evidence must show that the learner is able to:	To achieve a **merit** grade the evidence must show that, in addition to the pass criteria, the learner is able to:	To achieve a **distinction** grade the evidence must show that, in addition to the pass and merit criteria, the learner is able to:
P1 describe the key international organisations and their impact on the UK public services **Assessment activity 7.1 page 217**	**M1** analyse how decisions made by international institutions affect the operations of UK public services **Assessment activity 7.1 page 217**	**D1** evaluate the role of international institutions in upholding human rights **Assessment activity 7.2 page 224**
P2 outline the key features of the Geneva Convention, Universal Declaration of Human Rights (1948), European Convention on Human Rights, Human Rights Act 1998 **Assessment activity 7.2 page 224**	**M2** analyse the role of the UK in upholding international human rights **Assessment activity 7.2 page 224**	
P3 outline how human rights may be violated and the ways international institutions respond to such violations **Assessment activity 7.2 page 224**		

How you will be assessed

This unit will be assessed by an internal assignment that will be designed and marked by the staff at your centre. The assignment is designed to allow you to show your understanding of the learning outcomes for international institutions and human rights. These relate to what you should be able to do after completing this unit. Assessments can be quite varied and can take the form of:

- reports
- leaflets
- presentations
- posters
- practical tasks
- case studies
- discussions.

Mae decides to join Amnesty International

I really enjoyed this unit – I hadn't really considered that our public services have such a varied role to play in the world. It was surprising to discover how much humanitarian and disaster relief work they do in addition to their more traditional role in combat. What I particularly liked was seeing how our public services fit into the international picture by working with international institutions such as NATO and the UN, and how the issues decided at those organisations have a direct impact on how our public services operate.

I found some aspects of the human rights part of this unit a bit upsetting to be honest. I can't believe how badly some people are treated and how their rights are taken away. The good thing was learning about how there are organisations that exist to monitor and prevent human rights violations and help the people who have been affected. I think this is a really worthwhile cause, and because of what I learned in this unit I decided to join Amnesty International and try to make a contribution to upholding human rights myself.

Over to you!

- What areas of international institutions might you find interesting?
- Have you heard of any human rights violations?
- Do you have strong opinions on human rights?
- What preparation could you do to get ready for your assessments?

1. International organisations and their impact on UK public services

Thinking about international organisations and human rights

The vast majority of information you receive about international institutions and human rights will be media based as they often report the most up to date events happening around the world. One of the best ways of keeping up to date is to read a broadsheet newspaper such as *The Times, Guardian*, or *Telegraph* at least once a week and more often if you can, and try and check the websites for the major international institutions. Try and make a point of doing this throughout your study of this unit – you will be surprised how many other units you are studying will benefit from your reading as well.

International organisations are large institutions that play a global role in matters such as defence, human rights and economics. The organisations we will examine include:

- the United Nations (UN)
- the European Union (EU)
- the North Atlantic Treaty Organisation (NATO)
- the World Bank
- the Red Cross
- Greenpeace
- Amnesty International
- Liberty.

1.1 United Nations

History

The UN was established in 1945, but it could be argued that its history began well before this with the establishment of the League of Nations in 1919. The League of Nations was created after the First World War to try and establish international cooperation,

peace and security between nations. The First World War was actually called 'The Great War' at the time, as never in the whole of human history had there been such organised and large-scale warfare; almost 70 million military personal went into action and over 15 million people died. The world had never seen a global conflict like it and never wanted to again.

The League of Nations was created by the Treaty of Versailles in 1919 and at the height of its influence had 58 members. For all its good intentions there were some significant problems with the organisation: it had no army or power of its own, and had to rely on the largest and most powerful states in its membership to enforce agreements and sanctions, something they were not always happy to do. This problem became particularly difficult during the 1930s when some of the largest nations, such as Germany and Italy, were the ones moving towards war and conflict, and the League had no real power or influence over their actions. The League failed to prevent the Second World War and was replaced by the UN in 1945.

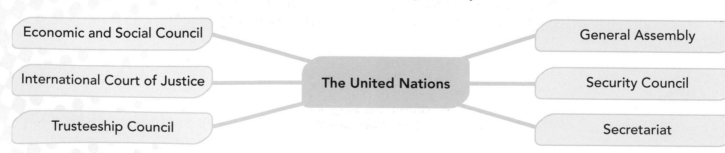

Figure 7.1: The structure of the UN.

Key term

Treaty is a written agreement made between two or more nations that is legally binding. It is like a contract between countries about a particular issue such as trade, conflict or territory.

Did you know?

The philosopher Immanuel Kant proposed a council of nations working together to promote peace as far back as 1795. It was in 1942 that the United Nations Declaration was signed and marked the start of the UN (see page 94).

The UN was created in very similar circumstances to the League of Nations after the Second World War came to an end. Political and social unity were seen as very important in the post-war climate, and as a consequence representatives from 50 nations met in the United States to debate the creation of a new global organisation to help maintain friendly international relations and promote peace and security. The new United Nations organisation officially came into existence on 24 October 1945 with 51 members.

The UN today has 192 members, all of whom must agree to and be bound by the UN Charter, a **treaty** that sets out the rights and duties of the member states in the international arena and also sets out fundamental practices in international relations. In 2008–2009 the UN had a budget of 4.171 billion dollars and employed over 40,000 staff.

Structure and institutions

The UN has many roles and performs many international functions. All of these divisions shown in Figure 7.1 are based at UN headquarters in New York, except for the International Court of Justice, which is based at The Hague in The Netherlands. Each division of the UN has responsibility for a variety of functions and tasks (see Figure 7.2).

International Court of Justice

This is the main court of the UN and it is located at the Peace Palace in The Hague. It was established in 1946 to fulfil two primary roles:

- to settle legal disputes between member states
- to provide opinions and advice on international legal issues.

Figure 7.2: Key roles of the UN.

In issues in dispute among the member states, participation in the proceedings is on a voluntary basis, but if a country does agree to take part then it must be prepared to abide by the decision of the court. Currently, the court has many cases pending, ranging from issues of territorial and maritime disputes, to oil, conflict and genocide.

Security Council

This division has responsibility for maintaining international peace and security. Members can bring complaints before it, but the council's first action is usually to encourage the parties involved to reach a peaceful agreement between themselves. However, it may act as a **mediator** in the dispute or appoint a special representative to oversee the process. If the conflict has led to violence, the Security Council has a responsibility to bring it to an end, and it does this by using measures such as negotiating ceasefires between hostile groups and deploying UN Peacekeepers to help reduce tension in troubled areas. In addition, the council may impose other sanctions such as trade restrictions, as with Iraq during and after the first Gulf War, or collective military action, such as in Kosovo. It

consists of 15 members of which five are permanent members and ten are elected for a two-year term. The five permanent members are:

- the United Kingdom
- the United States
- China
- the Russian Federation
- France.

Each member has one vote. On simple matters, a vote of nine members is needed for action to take place. On more serious issues, such as military action, nine votes are still needed, but all of the five permanent members must be in agreement. If they are not, then the action cannot go ahead. This is called the power of **veto**.

Key terms

Mediator is a person who is trained to liaise between different parties in order to resolve conflict fairly and peaceably.

Veto is the power to stop a piece of legislation or an action in its tracks.

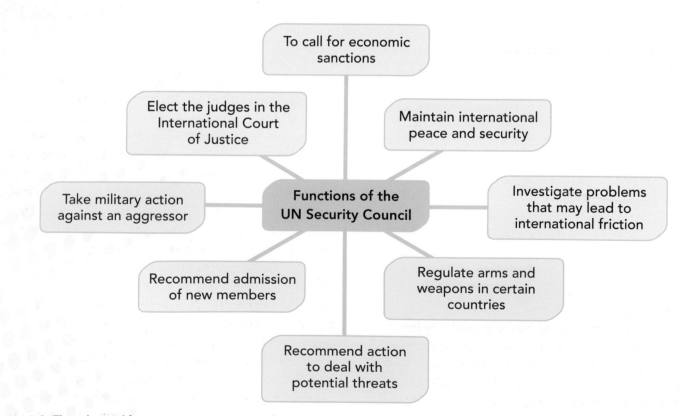

Figure 7.3: The roles and functions of the UN Security Council.

Activity: The power of veto

Why is a power of veto important when discussing serious matters like collective military action? Why might this be a problem to nations who are in conflict?

General Assembly

This is like the parliament of the UN in which representatives of the 192 member states sit. The assembly meets to discuss some of the world's most pressing problems, such as poverty, human rights and armed conflict. Each member state has a vote and decisions are made on the basis of a majority vote for routine matters and a two-thirds majority on important issues. The assembly has a variety of powers and functions, such as:

- making recommendations on disarmament and arms regulation
- promoting international political cooperation
- discussing threats to international peace and security
- supporting international respect for human rights
- approving UN budgets
- developing international law
- electing non-permanent members of the Security Council
- electing members of the Economic and Social Council.

The UN General Assembly deals with a tremendous amount of information and queries from all 192 member states, so rather than debate each issue between the 192 members in open forum, which would be very time consuming, the assembly has subsidiary committees which deal with many of the issues.

Economic and Social Council

This section comprises representatives from 54 member states who are elected for a three-year term of office. The council has responsibility for discussing economic and social issues, and developing recommendations and policies to help solve some of the more important international economic and social concerns. The council coordinates the work of 14 specialised agencies, such as:

- the World Health Organisation
- the International Monetary Fund
- the World Bank.

It also coordinates ten commissions, including:

- Commission on Human Rights
- Commission on the Status of Women
- Commission on Narcotic Drugs.

And it also coordinates the work of five regional commissions, including:

- Economic Commission for Africa
- Economic Commission for Europe.

These specialised agencies research complex issues such as protecting the global environment and the international status of women. The work of the Economic and Social Council accounts for over 70% of the human and financial resources of the whole UN.

Activity: Cost of the UN's work

Why does the work of the Economic and Social Council take such a large amount of the UN budget?

Trusteeship Council

This council was established so that member countries with other territories could have assistance in preparing them for independence or self-governance. It consists of the five permanent members of the UN Security Council and until 1994 it met annually. However, on 1 November 1994 the Trusteeship Council suspended its operations after Palau became independent; Palau was the last UN trust territory to gain its independence. Today the council meets only as and when required.

Secretariat

This is the administrative section of the UN. It is presided over by the Secretary General who is appointed for a five-year term of office, and it conducts the work and operations of the other UN bodies. The Secretariat has about 9,000 staff who are drawn from all of the member nations of the UN. They are expected to be independent of their home country and not be biased towards it. The Secretariat may fulfil tasks such as:

- administering peacekeeping operations
- organising international conferences
- public relations
- surveying economic and social trends.

Staff in the Secretariat can be stationed anywhere in the world; although the UN headquarters is in New York it has offices in many of its member states. The current UN Secretary General is Ban Ki-Moon from South Korea, who was appointed in January 2007.

UK service involvement in the UN

The UK services play a key role in UN peacekeeping operations and military action that has UN support, for instance in Afghanistan, Kosovo, Cyprus and Iraq. Being part of a collective of nations means that our armed and civilian public services can be utilised by the UN to help maintain peace and resolve conflict globally. The decisions of the UN can have a tremendous impact on UK public services: they may be required to support peacekeeping operations such as those listed above, or to provide and deliver **humanitarian aid** in times of large-scale overseas disasters such as the Asian tsunami in 2004 and the Haiti earthquake in 2010.

Key term

Humanitarian aid is the provision of food, shelter or medical supplies to areas of the world which are in a conflict situation or have been affected by a disaster. It can also include specialist personnel such as doctors or engineers.

Activity: The United Nations

Do we need an organisation like the UN in today's society? What might happen if the UN didn't exist? Conduct some independent research and make some notes on your findings.

1.2 European Union

The origins of the EU are similar to the UN, in that it was established after the Second World War with the idea of uniting European nations in trade and cooperation. From around 1950 the European Coal and Steel Community began to unite European countries economically and politically. This led to the Treaty of Rome in 1957, which created the European Economic Community (EEC); however, Great Britain

Case study: United Nations Peacekeeping Force in Cyprus

The Republic of Cyprus was created in 1960 when it gained independence from the UK. The island was largely split along ethnic lines between Greek Cypriots and Turkish Cypriots. After independence the government of the country was supposed to ensure that the interests of both the Greek and Turkish communities were protected and each group would be treated fairly. The tensions between the two communities grew, and there were outbreaks of civil violence in 1963. Also in 1963 the Cypriot government complained to the UN that Turkey was interfering in its internal affairs and behaving aggressively, a charge that Turkey denied.

The United Nations Peacekeeping Force in Cyprus (UNFICYP) was established in 1964 to preserve peace and security on the island. Unfortunately, the situation continued to deteriorate, and military action by Turkey in 1974 saw Cyprus divided into two parts, with the Turkish community holding the northern part

of the island and the Greek community the south. Because Cyprus was a British territory when it gained independence, the UK has had a direct involvement in the politics and military affairs of the island since 1960. It has contributed personnel and equipment to UNFICYP since 1964, and still maintains a troop and a military police contingent on the island as part of the peacekeeping mission.

UNFICYP has a current total strength of 909 uniformed personnel from eight nations.

1   Why would the UK have been invited to be a part of this peacekeeping mission?

2   Look up the UNFICYP mission on the UN website. What is its current purpose?

3   Conduct some research on UNFICYP. What is the total UK troop and military police commitment on the island?

did not join until 1973. The EEC later became the EC (European Community) and finally changed its name to the EU in 1994.

The EU performs a wide variety of functions; for instance, it is the world's largest trade body and it is one of the largest providers of funds and humanitarian aid for developing countries. It also sets out rules and guidance for member states on a whole range of important issues such as:

- monetary union
- agriculture
- fishing
- immigration
- human rights
- free trade
- public health
- transport.

The EU currently has 27 members and three additional countries have applied to join (see Figure 7.4).

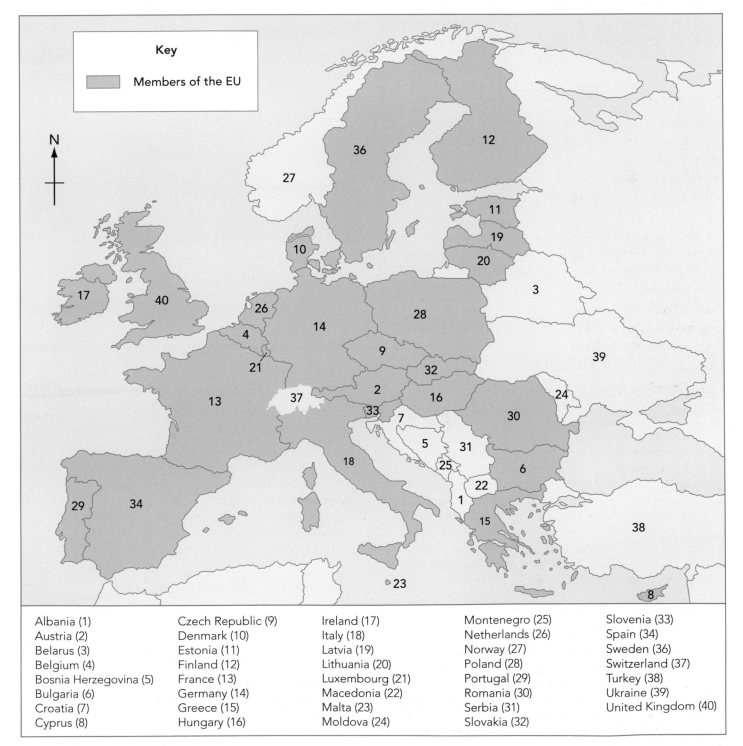

Key

Members of the EU

Albania (1)
Austria (2)
Belarus (3)
Belgium (4)
Bosnia Herzegovina (5)
Bulgaria (6)
Croatia (7)
Cyprus (8)

Czech Republic (9)
Denmark (10)
Estonia (11)
Finland (12)
France (13)
Germany (14)
Greece (15)
Hungary (16)

Ireland (17)
Italy (18)
Latvia (19)
Lithuania (20)
Luxembourg (21)
Macedonia (22)
Malta (23)
Moldova (24)

Montenegro (25)
Netherlands (26)
Norway (27)
Poland (28)
Portugal (29)
Romania (30)
Serbia (31)
Slovakia (32)

Slovenia (33)
Spain (34)
Sweden (36)
Switzerland (37)
Turkey (38)
Ukraine (39)
United Kingdom (40)

Figure 7.4: Map of Europe with members of the EU shown in green. Which are the other countries that have applied to join the EU?

Activity: Membership of the EU

The current members of the EU joined in the following order:

1952 Belgium, France, Germany, Italy, Luxembourg, Netherlands
1973 Denmark, Ireland, United Kingdom
1981 Greece
1986 Portugal, Spain
1995 Austria, Finland, Sweden
2004 Cyprus, Czech Republic, Estonia, Hungary, Latvia, Lithuania, Malta, Poland, Slovakia, Slovenia
2007 Bulgaria, Romania

There are currently three membership applications from:

• Croatia
• Turkey
• Republic of Macedonia.

What are the implications of allowing the EU to grow larger? What are the advantages to the nations who want to join of being members? Are there any disadvantages to growing larger? Research and produce a factsheet on EU enlargement that covers these questions.

Structure and institutions

Like the UN, the EU is divided into several different sections, each of which have specific tasks, as shown in Figure 7.5.

European Parliament

The Members of the European Parliament (MEPs) are elected every five years. Each member state elects its own set of representatives to send to the parliament and, just like in a British general election, MEPs come from a variety of political parties. The European Parliament has three main functions.

• It shares with the European Council (Council of Ministers) the power to create laws that apply to all the member states.

• It shares authority for the EU's budget with the European Council and can influence how European money is spent.

• It supervises the European Commission, and it exercises political democratic supervision over all of the other institutions shown above.

Activity: Your MEP

Find out who your local MEP is and what their role is in the European Parliament.

Council of the European Union (Council of Ministers)

This is the main decision-making body of the EU. It is made up of one minister from each of the member states who is answerable to their own national parliament and its citizens. The council discusses issues

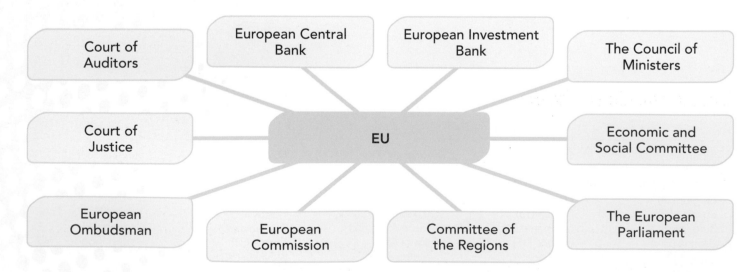

Figure 7.5: The structure of the EU. What are the main tasks of each body?

such as finance, education, health and foreign affairs. Like the European Parliament it has several key roles:

- sharing law-making power with the European Parliament
- coordinating the economic policies of the member states
- sharing authority for the EU budget with the parliament
- taking decisions on common foreign and security policies.

The council coordinates member states, and plays a special role in helping the police and judiciary of member states cooperate in criminal matters. Clearly, this is a matter of some importance for the British public services such as the police and customs and excise.

European Commission

This part of the EU is designed to uphold the interests of the European Union as a whole, and not of any one particular member state. Commissioners are expected to perform their duties without bias to their own member state. It has several responsibilities:

- drafts laws and proposals for the parliament and council to consider
- implements European laws
- along with the Court of Justice, makes sure that EU law is followed
- represents the EU in the international arena.

Court of Justice

This court has the task of ensuring that EU law is applied equally throughout the 27 member states. The majority of cases heard by the Court of Justice are referred by the national courts of the member states.

Decision making in the EU

Decision making in the EU is a complex and lengthy procedure; many bodies are involved, and the movement of policies and proposals between bodies as they are discussed and amended can be very difficult to track.

The three main bodies involved in EU decision making are the European Commission, the European Parliament and the Council of the European Union.

The European Commission proposes new legislation, but it is the council and parliament that pass the laws. There are three main ways by which the EU makes decisions:

- co-decision
- consultation
- assent.

Co-decision. In this procedure, the parliament and council share the power to make laws. The commission sends its proposal on law to both institutions and they each read and discuss it twice in succession. If for any reason they can't agree, it is put before a committee that tries to resolve the difficulties; the committee is composed of equal numbers of council and parliament representatives. Commission representatives also attend the committee meetings and contribute to the discussion since they were the ones to propose the law in the first place. Once the committee has reached an agreement, the agreed text is then sent to the parliament and council for a third reading, so that they can finally adopt it as law.

Consultation. Under this form of decision-making procedure, the commission sends its proposal to both the council and parliament, as described for the co-decision procedure, but it is the council that takes responsibility for consulting with parliament and other EU bodies, such as the Economic and Social Committee and the Committee of the Regions, whose opinions are an important factor in decision making. In all cases, parliament can:

- approve the proposal made by the commission
- reject the proposal
- ask for amendments to be made to the proposal.

Assent. This method of decision making means that the council has to obtain the European Parliament's agreement before certain very important decisions are taken. The procedure is the same as in the case of consultation, except that parliament cannot amend a proposal: it must either accept or reject it.

As you would expect, the countries of Europe must work together on a variety of issues and the decisions made at EU level can have a great effect on UK public services (see Table 7.1).

Table 7.1: EU decisions affecting UK public services.

Decision	Impact
Single currency	The European single currency is called the Euro; when introduced in 1999, it became the legal currency of 11 member states, but the UK and Denmark opted out of joining. Of the 27 EU members, 16 now have the Euro as their currency
	The British government argues that it is in favour of joining in principle, but that in practice five economic tests must be passed in order for the Euro to be the best option for the UK. Currently, the government does not believe these tests have been passed, and the UK will not join until they are. The single currency in Europe affects the public services despite the fact that the UK does not use the Euro. For instance, the exchange rate might affect decisions on peacekeeping initiatives
Terrorism and border control	EU members have faced the threat and reality of terrorist attacks for decades, with terrorist groups such as the IRA and ETA working within the borders of the EU. However, the Madrid train bombings in 2004 and the London bombings in 2007 brought new focus to the fight against terrorism. The European Union Counter Terrorism strategy places key responsibility on the member states themselves for the prevention of terrorism, but adds value to these national efforts by: • strengthening national capabilities • facilitating European cooperation • developing collective capability • promoting international partnership The EU was instrumental in creating the Schengen agreements, which allowed for a reduction in cross border checks to allow free movement of workers and goods; but the threat of terrorism has meant changes to these border controls, via increased passport security by the inclusion of biometric data, improvements to visa security, risk assessments of the EU's borders and border monitoring, and common standards at airports and seaports
European Security and Defence Policy (ESDP) and rapid reaction force	The European Council meeting in Helsinki in 1999 agreed that a European rapid reaction force to target trouble spots in Europe was needed. The situation in Kosovo in the mid 1990s highlighted the problems of European armed forces strategic cooperation and utilisation of equipment. Most of the equipment used in Kosovo was American as was most of the telecommunications technology. The rapid reaction force is designed to combat some of these problems. It is a 60,000-strong force, able to be deployed within 60 days and operate for up to a year. This also makes sense for economic reasons; it is better value for money to pool military resources across the EU nations and split the cost. This has affected the armed services by potentially enabling a faster, more coordinated response to European incidents of conflict
Europol	This is the EU cross-border police organisation. It coordinates cooperation between all the EU policing agencies, including customs and immigration. Europol has several key priorities in assisting the police forces of member states: it mainly deals with drug trafficking, illegal immigration, terrorism, vehicle trafficking, human trafficking. This has affected the police, customs and immigration by providing an information network across 27 nations that can be used to share intelligence and coordinate joint policing operations. This improves the operational effectiveness of the UK services on issues such as cross-border crime, drugs trafficking and counter terrorism
Eurojust	This is an EU organisation which was created to help judicial authorities such as courts in dealing with cross-border offences such as organised crime. Eurojust can help with extradition proceedings between member states. As you can appreciate, there are lots of language barriers in bringing someone to justice in a different nation; Eurojust supports investigations and prosecutions across the EU area. Its main aim is to develop Europe-wide cooperation on criminal justice cases

1.3 North Atlantic Treaty Organisation

The North Atlantic Treaty was signed in Washington on 4 April 1949, creating NATO. This arose because of the growing strength of the Soviet Union after the Second World War. The Communist Soviet Union had become powerful as a result of the part it had played in the defeat of Germany. In contrast, much of Europe in the post-war period was devastated and vulnerable to external attack. Although the United States implemented 'The Marshall Plan' which aimed to help with the rebuilding of Europe, it was recognised that any attack which came from the Soviet Union would have to be repelled by the Western allies until Europe was back on its feet. The treaty itself is not very long and conforms to the United Nations Charter. It states that:

- member countries of NATO commit themselves to maintaining and developing collective defence capabilities

- if one of NATO's member states is attacked in Europe or North America it will be considered to be an attack against them all
- members must contribute to the development of peaceful and friendly international relations
- members must eliminate conflict with the economic policies of other member states and encourage cooperation between them.

Did you know?

NATO currently has a membership of 28 countries: Albania, Belgium, Bulgaria, Canada, Croatia, Czech Republic, Denmark, Estonia, France, Germany, Greece, Hungary, Iceland, Italy, Latvia, Lithuania, Luxembourg, Netherlands, Norway, Poland, Portugal, Romania, Slovakia, Slovenia, Spain, Turkey, United Kingdom, United States.

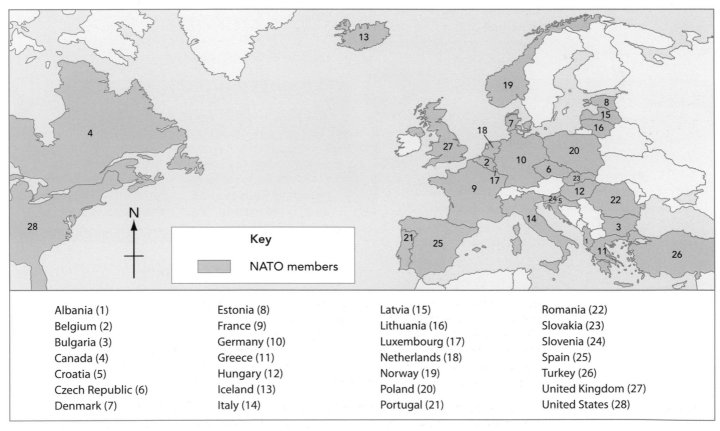

Albania (1), Belgium (2), Bulgaria (3), Canada (4), Croatia (5), Czech Republic (6), Denmark (7), Estonia (8), France (9), Germany (10), Greece (11), Hungary (12), Iceland (13), Italy (14), Latvia (15), Lithuania (16), Luxembourg (17), Netherlands (18), Norway (19), Poland (20), Portugal (21), Romania (22), Slovakia (23), Slovenia (24), Spain (25), Turkey (26), United Kingdom (27), United States (28)

Figure 7.6: Map of countries belonging to NATO.

Main NATO institutions

NATO has a distinct military and civilian structure (see Activity). NATO was originally designed to defend Europe against an attack from the **Warsaw Pact** (the USSR and its allies) after the Second World War; this developed into its more familiar role of being the first line of defence during the '**Cold War**' of the latter part of the 20th century. However, once the threat from the USSR disappeared at the end of the 1980s, NATO's role became unclear. There were calls for NATO to be disbanded, as the role that it was created to fill no longer existed; however, a new role has been adopted for NATO in collective defence against possible terrorist threats to the US, Canada and Europe, and peacekeeping missions.

Activity: NATO structure

Go to www.nato.int and examine NATO's military and civilian structure. It has three levels of command: strategic, tactical and operational. Where might you encounter that kind of structure among the UK emergency services?

Did you know?

The Union of Soviet Socialist Republics (USSR) or sometimes abbreviated to the Soviet Union was a group of nations that joined together to form a communist state in 1924; they were considered to be one nation after they had joined together. The nations included Russia and many surrounding countries. The Soviet Union dissolved in 1991 and the majority of countries that were part of the USSR are once again known by their individual country names.

Key term

Warsaw Pact was the Eastern European version of the NATO Treaty. It was a military treaty that bound together the USSR and its allies such as Albania, Poland and Czechoslovakia to come to the aid of each other if they were attacked.

Cold War is a term applied to the relationship between the US and USSR from the 1950s to the 1980s. The two superpowers were openly hostile and the threat of nuclear conflict was ever present. The situation improved dramatically with the fall from power of the communist Soviet regime and the disintegration of the USSR. Russia is now considered to be a friendly nation to NATO and no longer a military threat to Western nations.

Role of UK services in NATO

Because Britain is a committed and influential member of NATO, our armed services have to be ready to cooperate with NATO's decisions. This means that the British government must be prepared to send our armed forces personnel and equipment wherever NATO believes there is a need for them. This primarily means the deployment of peacekeeping forces in missions such as the NATO-led Kosovan force (KFOR) and the stabilisation force (SFOR), both of which used British troops as part of peacekeeping efforts in the former Yugoslavia in the late 1990s. The UK is one of the largest contributors of funds, personnel and equipment to NATO; in 2007 it gave £150 million to NATO's civilian and military budget. The UK is also currently involved in all five current NATO operations:

- the International Security Assistance Force (ISAF) in Afghanistan
- the Kosovo force (KFOR)
- the NATO Training Assistance Implementation Mission (NTM-I) in Iraq
- Operation Active Endeavour (OAE) in the Eastern Mediterranean
- counter piracy.

Activity: NATO operations

Research one or more of the five NATO missions listed above. What is the UK's commitment in terms of personnel and resources to the mission? What are the aims of the mission? Make notes on your research.

Security at world summits

World summits are occasions where world leaders can come together to discuss international social and economic issues. There are many different kinds of summit with different nations attending each. For instance, the G8 summit gathers the eight most powerful nations in the world together, the G20 sees the leaders of the largest economies and the EU meet, while the European Union Summit gathers the heads of the 27 member states together. In recent years, these summits have been the site of rioting and violence by anti-globalisation and anti-capitalism protestors, who believe the world economic system is unfair and unequal. These protestors can cause tremendous disruption to the towns and cities where the summits are held and cause severe problems for the local public services, to say nothing of the damage done to property and businesses in the city.

Assessment activity 7.1 P1 M1 BTEC

The work of the public services is not done in isolation; they have to work with many international institutions if they are going to be effective in their role. Knowing how the decisions made at international level affect the UK public services is a key aspect of this. Working in pairs, produce a large poster which addresses the following tasks:

1   Describe the key international organisations and their impact on UK public services **P1**

2   Analyse how decisions made by international organisations affect the operations of UK public services **M1**

Grading tips

The first thing you should do for task one is to research all of the international organisations described above, including their membership, history and structure, and describe how the decisions they make affect UK public services; this should help you achieve **P1**. To achieve **M1**, provide a more detailed analysis of how the decisions made affect our services.

1.4 Other institutions and organisations

European Court of Human Rights (ECHR)

The ECHR is an international court that was set up in 1959 to make judgements on breaches of the European Convention on Human Rights. This means it exists to ensure that European citizens who claim to have their human, civil and political rights broken have a court that will hear and rule on their case. This is particularly important because many human rights cases are breaches by the government against an individual citizen or group of citizens, and the government of the country involved may not be impartial on the issue in question.

The World Bank

The World Bank is not a bank in the traditional sense. It is made up of two organisations:

- the International Bank for Reconstruction and Development (IBRD)
- the International Development Association (IDA).

It is owned by a collective of 186 nations and was created in 1944. As with the EU and NATO, the World Bank developed as a consequence of the Second World War, and one of its main roles was post-war reconstruction in Europe. It currently has more than 10,000 employees in offices all over the world. The overall purpose of the World Bank is to reduce global poverty by providing loans to

Case study: Europe and homosexuality in the armed services

The ECHR decided in 1999 that the armed services ban on homosexuals serving in the forces was illegal. This was in response to two separate cases that had come before it: the case of *Smith and Grady v. The UK* and *Lustig-Prean and Beckett v. The UK*. The four service personnel had been investigated by the armed services, and when they were found or admitted to being homosexual they were discharged from the service. The individuals concerned had to go to the ECHR after the Court of Appeal in London rejected their claim that prohibiting homosexuals from serving in the forces was illegal. The armed services position on the private lives of the four was found to breach article 8 of the European Convention on Human

Rights, which grants individuals respect for their private and family lives; in addition, the court ruled that in the case of Smith and Grady the Ministry of Defence policy had breached article 13 of the convention which allows individuals the right to have their complaints dealt with in a UK court. The armed services now have no ban on homosexuality.

1   Why did the four service personnel have to go to the ECHR?

2   What were the legal problems with the Ministry of Defence policy?

3   Do you think the ECHR decisions were fair and appropriate? Explain your reasons.

countries to develop their infrastructure in key areas such as:

- agriculture
- education
- environmental development.
- healthcare
- industry

Remember!

Other organisations to consider include the International Red Cross (see page 219), the International Olympic Committee, the World Health Organisation, Human Rights Watch and Interpol.

Amnesty International

Amnesty International is a non-governmental organisation (NGO) that was established in 1961 by a British lawyer called Peter Benenson. Its symbol is a lighted candle surrounded by barbed wire, which was inspired by the Chinese proverb 'It is better to light one candle than to curse the darkness'. The main focus of Amnesty International is:

- to free **prisoners of conscience**. These are people who are illegally detained because of their beliefs, ethnic origin, sexuality, religion or political affiliation. Amnesty only works to free those prisoners who don't use or advocate violence.

- to ensure fair and prompt trials for **political prisoners**. These are people who oppose a ruling party or who a ruling party considers to be a threat. Often they may be held in prison for years without trial or access to justice.

- to abolish the death penalty, torture and other cruel, inhuman or degrading treatment of prisoners.

- to end **extra-judicial executions** and disappearances. Extra-judicial executions are where individuals are executed on behalf of the state, but without a trial or hearing. These executions are often conducted by the military or civilian police.

- to oppose those who advocate violence to oust a government.

Amnesty campaigns can take many forms, such as letter-writing campaigns on behalf of particular individuals. They also gather information on human rights abuses worldwide. Amnesty International pride themselves on their independence and they accept no government funds. Their finances are generated from membership fees and broad public support in the form of fundraising and donations.

Did you know?

Amnesty International has a website at www.amnesty.org which details human rights abuses worldwide. It also gives much greater detail on the origins and purposes of Amnesty, and it will be useful later in the unit when we discuss human rights.

Greenpeace

The Greenpeace Environmental Trust was set up in 1982, but its precursor had been investigating environmental issues for more than a decade prior to this. Like Amnesty International, it is a non-governmental organisation (NGO), which uses non-violent confrontation to highlight global environmental social problems and their causes through specific research and witnessing environmental problems. It was originally established to:

- examine the effect of human activities on the environment
- make information known to the public
- relieve sickness and suffering of humans and animals caused by environmental issues.

It has also campaigned on many issues such as:

- genetically modified crops
- international whaling
- promotion of renewable energy sources
- elimination of toxic chemicals
- nuclear disarmament
- driftnet fishing.

Here Amnesty is campaigning in Germany for peace in Sudan. What other causes do they support?

Greenpeace does not accept funding from governments and is independent of any political movement. It raises its funds from donations from the public and grants for research.

Liberty

Liberty is also known as the National Council for Civil Liberties and it has similar aims to Amnesty International, but Liberty only operates in England and Wales, not internationally. It was created in 1934 with the purpose of protecting civil liberties and promoting human rights. Liberty uses different methods to protect human rights, such as:

- public campaigns
- test cases
- lobbying
- policy analysis
- advice and information.

Activity: Liberty

Conduct some independent research using information on the Liberty website (www.liberty-human-rights.org.uk) and make a judgement on what are the most pressing human rights issues in England and Wales at the moment. Produce a wall display highlighting the key issues and cases.

2. Human rights and how the UK upholds human rights

2.1 Human rights

Rights are certain things that an individual is entitled to have or do based on principles of fairness and justice. In many countries the basic rights a citizen can expect are written down in a constitution. Other countries, such as Britain, do not have a formal constitution, but have the rights of citizens defined by legislation. In most democratic countries people have the right to do anything unless the law expressly forbids it.

Link

See Unit 3 (pages 75–110) for more about human rights in the context of citizenship, diversity and the public services.

Did you know?

Human rights are considered inherent, inalienable and universal. Human rights are **inherent** because they are the birthright of all human beings – they are not granted only to citizens, but belong to people simply because they are human. They are **inalienable** because no one can agree to give up their human rights, or have them taken away. They are **universal** because they apply to everyone regardless of their nationality, status, sex or race.

There are many organisations that examine human rights and monitor how people are treated across the world, such as Amnesty International, Liberty and the United Nations, which have already been discussed in this unit. There are also many charters or agreements that set out the rights countries should afford their citizens; we will now examine some of these agreements.

Geneva Convention

The Geneva Convention can trace its roots back to 1859, when a Swiss citizen called Henry Dunant witnessed the aftermath of the Battle of Solferino during the Second War of Italian Independence and was horrified at the numbers of soldiers who lay dying and wounded with no one to help them. This experience led him to call for medical relief societies to be set up to care for wounded soldiers and civilians in times of war. Dunant also called for an international agreement to be established which would protect those agencies and the wounded from further attack. This is how the voluntary relief society of the **International Committee of the Red Cross** and the Geneva Convention were established.

In 1864 a treaty was signed by 12 nations in which they agreed to care for all sick and wounded people regardless of nationality, and they also agreed to recognise the Red Cross agency as neutral in any conflict. This treaty was called the Geneva Convention. There are now four Geneva Conventions which most countries have signed; they cover a variety of issues such as armed forces on land and sea, treatment of prisoners of war and the treatment of civilians in times of war.

First and Second Geneva Conventions

These two conventions are very similar, and the main points are:

- the sick, wounded and shipwrecked must be cared for adequately
- each side must treat the enemy wounded as carefully as if they were their own
- the dead should be collected quickly
- the dead should be identified quickly and protected from robbery
- medical personnel and establishments should not be attacked.

Third Geneva Convention

This convention outlines what should happen if a member of the armed forces falls into enemy hands and becomes a prisoner of war (POW). Its main points are that POWs:

- do not have to provide any information other than their name, rank and service number
- must be treated humanely
- must be able to inform their next of kin and the International Red Cross of their capture
- must be allowed to correspond with their family
- must be supplied with adequate food and clothing
- must be provided with medical care.

Fourth Geneva Convention

This deals with the protection of civilian personnel in wartime, and its main points are given in Table 7.2.

Universal Declaration of Human Rights

As with many of the organisations and issues discussed in this unit, the UN declaration was a post-war initiative. Two major global conflicts had been fought in less than 30 years, and terrible atrocities had been committed against the European Jewish population and prisoners of war in the Far East. These atrocities had shocked the world, and it was felt that a better way must exist for dealing with international problems and treating people in times of both peace and conflict. This was the birth of the UN organisation and its charter, which emphasises the fundamental importance of human rights. The UN organised a commission to draw up a declaration that would state the importance of civil, political, economic and social rights to all people, regardless of colour, religion, nationality, gender or sexuality.

The Universal Declaration of Human Rights (UDHR) was agreed in December 1948 and consists of 30 rights or articles, although some of these are broken down into sub-sections. You can read the full list of rights on the UN website: www.un.org/en/documents/udhr/

Link

The UN declaration is also discussed in Unit 3 (page 94) where human rights in the context of citizenship, diversity and the public services are covered.

Table 7.2: Main points of the Fourth Geneva Convention.

Protected civilians MUST be	Protected civilians MUST NOT be
Treated humanely	Discriminated against because of race, religion or political opinion
Entitled to respect for honour, family and religious practices	Forced to give information
Allowed to practise their religion	Used to shield military operations
Specially protected in safety zones if:	Raped, assaulted or forced into prostitution
• under 15	Punished for offences they have not committed
• sick/wounded	
• old	
• expectant mothers	

Key features

Of the 30 articles in the declaration, it has been argued that articles 3 and 25 are key provisions. Article 3 states that all human beings are entitled to life, liberty and security of the person. These are core political and civil rights ensuring freedom and safety. Article 25 specifies that all people are entitled to an adequate standard of living for themselves and their families. This includes food, clothing, housing and medical care, which would seem to be fundamental rights on which the others are built. Articles 28 and 29 are also crucial although they are not often discussed. They overarch the others in that they emphasise the responsibility of the international community to put into place a political and social framework in which respect for human rights can flourish. Without this foundation the other articles cannot be effectively implemented. The declaration has achieved world-wide prominence and is probably the most important document of its type ever written. It has become an influential standard by which nations are measured.

European Convention on Human Rights

This treaty (the ECHR) was created in 1950, by members of the Council of Europe. It predates the EEC and the EU, but membership of the EU requires that the treaty is signed; this means all EU nations must abide by it. As with the UN Declaration of Human Rights, it arose from the atrocities Europe had experienced during the Second World War. It is deliberately set at a modest level to encourage EU nations to comply. The ECHR incorporates rights such as the right to:

- life
- freedom from torture or inhuman or degrading punishment
- freedom from slavery, servitude, enforced or compulsory labour
- liberty and security of the person
- a fair trial
- respect for private and family life
- freedom of thought, conscience and religion
- freedom of expression
- freedom of assembly and association
- freedom to marry and found a family.

Human Rights Act 1998

This piece of law is designed to incorporate the ECHR into domestic (British) law. This means that the principles laid out in the ECHR are now enforceable in English courts, and so people do not have to take their cases to the ECHR as they can be dealt with in our own courts. As with the ECHR, the main provisions of the act are as follows:

- the right to life
- freedom from torture and inhuman or degrading treatment or punishment
- freedom from slavery and forced or compulsory labour
- the right to liberty
- the right to a fair trial
- no punishment without law
- the right to respect for private and family life, home and correspondence.
- the right to freedom of thought, conscience and religion
- the right to freedom of expression
- the right to freedom of association and assembly
- the right to marry and found a family
- the right to property
- the right to education
- the right to free elections.

The major effect of the act was to put individual human rights at the centre of public life. Under the act, each citizen can expect the government and all public agencies to have respect for their human rights, and if they feel their human rights have been ignored they can take the agency to court and challenge their decisions or conduct. This had a significant impact on the public services as they are defined as a public authority in section 6 of the Human Rights Act. Section 6 states: *it is unlawful for a public authority to act in a way which is incompatible with a Convention right.*

This means the police and other agencies described as a public authority can now be subject to challenge in the courts over their conduct.

2.2 Violations

Human rights abuses are committed in every nation around the world (see Table 7.3). Many people think that such violations are the sole province of developing nations in Africa, the Middle East or South America, but they occur in developed Western nations such as the UK, Australia and the USA as well.

Activity: Human rights abuses

These can take many forms, such as torture, extra-judicial killing, ethnic cleansing and genocide. Go to the Amnesty International website at www.amnesty.org and look up a case of each of these human rights abuses. Write a short summary of each example.

International actions

When human rights breaches do occur there are several actions the international community can take to combat them or bring those responsible to justice.

War crimes tribunals

War crimes tribunals have been very difficult to organise and enforce because, to some extent, it is accepted that in war civilian casualties are often high

Case study: The CIA and waterboarding

The US Central Intelligence Agency (CIA) admitted to using waterboarding against suspected Al-Qaeda terrorists in order to gain information about terrorist plans and activities. Waterboarding involves a prisoner being stretched flat or hung upside down with a rag pushed in their mouth or a cloth covering the face, and water being poured continually over their face. The experience is a powerful simulation of drowning and causes extreme mental and physical distress.

The CIA did not consider waterboarding a method of torture; it was considered an 'enhanced interrogation technique'. When Barack Obama was elected as US president in 2008, one of his first acts was to admit that waterboarding had taken place under the previous president and to ensure it was banned across all US government agencies.

1 Why is torture an unreliable method of gathering intelligence?

2 Does waterboarding qualify as a torture method?

3 In your opinion, what impact might the US admission that it used torture on suspects have on its reputation worldwide?

and there is major loss of life and property. Also, some nations do not accept they have committed war crimes and will not cooperate with investigations, especially if

Table 7.3: Key violations of human rights.

Violation	Description
Violations by regimes	These are organised violations of human rights by a ruling government or regime. They can include the discrimination of minority groups, refusal to hold free elections and the imprisonment of opposition groups
Torture	This is when deliberate and severe pain and suffering is caused to an individual in order to obtain information or as a punishment. The pain and distress can be mental or physical, and the government or authorities may support the torture either publicly or privately
Extra-judicial killings	These are killings carried out by the police, armed services or security services of a nation that have not been approved or sanctioned by a court of law
Ethnic cleansing	This is the removal of an ethnic group from an area in order to make the population of the area homogeneous. The removal can be by force or by threats and intimidation
Genocide	This is the systematic destruction of an ethnic group. It usually means the physical destruction of the ethic group by mass murder, but has also been used to mean the destruction of culture and language, so that an ethnic group no longer exists after a generation or two
War crimes	Even during conflicts there are rules and codes that govern how military services should behave towards each other and towards the civilian population caught up in the conflict. War crimes are clear breaches of these guidelines, such as the deliberate massacre of unarmed civilians, mistreatment of POWs or systematic rape of the female population

they are the victor in the conflict. One of the first war crimes tribunals was conducted in 1945 in Nuremberg, and concerned the trials of Nazi officers involved in the atrocities against the Jewish population as well as other war crimes. Many former Nazi officers were hanged as punishment and the tribunal was replicated for Japanese officers who also committed war crimes in the Second World War. Tribunals have also existed after situations such as the Rwandan genocide and the conflict in former Yugoslavia. The International Criminal Court was established in 2002 to deal formally with very serious international crimes against humanity; it is located in The Hague in The Netherlands.

UN resolutions

A UN resolution is a formal text or declaration that sets out the UN's position on a matter of international interest or concern. Resolutions are designed to provoke change or action on an issue and have the support of UN nations.

Imposition of sanctions

The UN Charter gives the organisation the right to enforce measures in order to maintain international peace and security. These measures are called sanctions. Sanctions can be economic, social or military, and they are designed to put pressure on a country to abide by UN rules on a particular issue.

Activity: The Goldstone Commission

The UN Human Rights Council has supported a report by Richard Goldstone that investigated the Israeli offensive in Gaza that killed 1,400 Palestinians. The report alleges that Israel used disproportionate force, deliberately targeted civilians, used Palestinians as human shields and destroyed civilian infrastructure during the campaign. Hamas is alleged to have indiscriminately targeted civilians.

The report urges Israel and the Palestinian Authority to investigate their own involvement in war crimes.

Read a summary of the Goldstone Report (www2. ohchr.org/english/bodies/hrcouncil/docs/12session/ A-HRC-12-48.pdf) and consider what the problems might be in a country investigating its own alleged war crimes. Would an independent investigation be more appropriate? What can be done if nations refuse to accept responsibility for their actions? How can the UN deal with these issues?

Humanitarian role of international institutions

The international institutions, such as the UN, the EU and NATO, discussed earlier in this unit provide a great deal of humanitarian assistance to civilian populations in times of disaster or conflict. Some of their key roles are outlined in Table 7.4.

Case study: Radovan Karadzic and crimes against humanity

Radovan Karadzic is a former Bosnian Serb leader who is accused of the worst atrocities in the Bosnian war in the 1990s. He is currently facing 11 counts of genocide, war crimes and crimes against humanity at the International Criminal Court in The Hague.

The key charges include being responsible for the shelling of Sarajevo during a two-year siege in which over 10,000 civilians were killed, and the massacre of over 7,000 Bosnian Muslim men and boys in Srebrenica as part of a plan to ethnically cleanse Bosnian Serb areas. After the war, Karadzic went into hiding and was found disguised and living under another name in Belgrade, Serbia in 2008. His trial is expected to last until 2012.

1 Why do the charges against Karadzic during the Bosnian conflict qualify as war crimes rather than just the usual horrors of war?

2 Why would Karadzic go into hiding?

3 Why would a trial such as this take until 2012 to complete?

4 What is the need for an international criminal court in instances such as these? Explain your answer.

Activity: The use of sanctions

Using the UN website (www.un.org) conduct some independent research on how sanctions have been used against member states. What are the advantages and disadvantages of the use of sanctions? Are they the best method of encouraging members to obey resolutions? What else could be done?

Table 7.4: Key humanitarian roles of international institutions.

Key role	Explanation
Humanitarian aid programmes	Humanitarian aid is the provision of food, water, shelter, medical supplies and personnel to poverty-stricken, war-torn or environmentally damaged areas with the intention of saving lives and relieving suffering. The UN agency responsible for aid programmes is the UN Office for the Coordination of Humanitarian Affairs
Disaster relief	This is the organisation of food, shelter, water, medical supplies and other humanitarian aid, such as specialist personnel, which may be needed in the aftermath of a disaster such as the 2004 Asian tsunami, when the EU donated over $600 million, the World Bank $250 million and the UK $96 million
Peacekeeping	Restoring and maintaining international peace and security is a key goal of many international organisations. The UN is currently involved in 16 peacekeeping missions, including Cyprus, Sudan and Lebanon; NATO has an involvement in Afghanistan, Iraq and Kosovo
Reconstruction	Reconstruction is the rebuilding of a country or region's infrastructure after it is has been destroyed or damaged by disaster or conflict. Examples include the Haiti earthquake 2010, Asian tsunami 2004, Pakistan earthquake 2005, and the damage done by Hurricane Katrina to New Orleans in 2005
Providing for refugees and asylum seekers	Many international organisations also provide help and assistance to asylum seekers and refugees; the UN does this through the Office of the United Nations High Commissioner for Refugees. The assistance can take the form of military protection for people who have been displaced from their homes as the result of disaster or conflict, as well as the more usual forms of support such as shelter and water

Assessment activity 7.2

P2 **P3** **M2** **D1**

BTEC

Dealing with the issue of human rights is a key aspect of international organisations and our own public services. You need to be aware of the guidance and legislation in place to protect human rights, how organisations uphold the rights of others and how rights may be violated throughout the world.

1 Produce a factsheet that describes the key features of the Geneva convention, the Universal Declaration of Human Rights, the European Convention on Human Rights and the Human Rights Act 1998 **P2**

2 Using the Amnesty International website, select three human rights violation case studies and use them to outline in a short report how human rights may be violated and the ways international organisations respond to such violations **P3**

3 At the end of your report on human rights violations, include a section which analyses the role of the UK in upholding international human rights **M2** and evaluates the role of international institutions in upholding human rights **D1**

Grading tips

Your factsheet for **P2** is very straightforward; just ensure you cover all the required content about the ways human rights are protected in guidance and law. For **P3**, the Amnesty website will present you with case studies on a wide variety of violations all over the world – choose ones from different countries and involving different violations, and outline what happened in the cases you have chosen and how international organisations responded to them.

To achieve the higher grades, additional detail is needed in your human rights report to analyse how the UK in particular upholds international rights, as well as to evaluate the role of international institutions.

Carla Darwin
Volunteer with the Refugee Council

I work as a volunteer with the Refugee Council. The purpose of the refugee council is to provide asylum seekers and refugees with advice and guidance on their application to stay in the country.

We don't offer legal advice, but we do offer training, language classes, guidance to other services such as housing and education, and support for children who have been separated from their families.

A typical day

I work full time as a teacher, so my typical day volunteering for the refugee council is at the weekend. I'm an English teacher in a large comprehensive school and I wanted to use those skills to help others, so I trained as an ESOL teacher, which means I can teach spoken and written English to speakers of other languages.

I give three classes on Saturdays that involve teaching English to small groups of asylum refugees, so that they can start to interact with the rest of society and understand what is being said to them. It really makes a difference to the quality of their lives when they know enough English to start to adjust to their new environment.

The best thing about the job

The best thing about the job for me is seeing people settle into a new life and a new community after they have been through some of the most horrific circumstances you can imagine. I think that we have a duty to help people fleeing from war-torn countries to make the best of a new start.

Think about it!

What topics have you covered in this unit that might give you the background to work with refugees or asylum seekers?

What knowledge and skills do you think you need to develop further if you want to be involved in human rights issues or international organisations in the future?

Just checking

1 When was the UN established?

2 What is the key principle of the NATO treaty?

3 How does the EU make decisions?

4 When did the UK join the EU?

5 What is the role of the World Bank?

6 How was the Geneva Convention created?

7 What is a UN resolution?

8 What are sanctions?

9 What is ethnic cleansing?

10 Briefly describe a current UN peacekeeping mission.

edexcel

Assignment tips

- In a unit like this, which focuses on international organisations and human rights, one of the best things you can do to help improve your grade and your knowledge is to make sure you keep up to date with current events by reading a reputable news source on a daily basis. This means using your lunch hour or an hour after school/college to read the BBC news website or picking up a broadsheet newspaper such as *The Times*, *Guardian*, or *Telegraph* (these have websites where you can read the news if you can't get hold of the paper). Not only will you become more informed about government policies and the public services, but you will pick up lots of information that can be used across all of your BTEC National units.

- Another good tip is to make sure you regularly check human rights websites such as Amnesty International; they often have headline cases which might make a good start for your assignment. The same is true for the websites of international organisations, which will often send you email updates on issues if you register to receive them.

- This may sound very basic, but make sure you have read your assignment thoroughly and you understand exactly what you are being asked to do. Once you are clear about this then you can move on to your research. Doing your research well and using good sources of evidence is essential. Lots of students rely too much on the internet and not enough on other sources of information such as books, newspapers and journals. The internet is not always a good source of information. It is very easy to use information from American or Australian government websites without noticing – but your tutor will notice. Always double check the information you find; don't just accept it at face value. Good research and preparation is the key to getting those higher grades.

8 Understand the impact of war, conflict and terrorism on public services

This unit is designed to provide you with an insight into the issues surrounding war, conflict and terrorism. These are key issues that our uniformed public services must deal with both at home and abroad: the UK is a terrorist target for several terrorist groups, we are involved in overseas conflicts in Afghanistan, and political instability in many parts of the world calls for our public service personnel to operate as a peacekeeping and reconstruction force.

You will examine in detail the causes of war and conflict, the types of conflict commonly dealt with by the public services, and the possible public services response to national and international conflict. In addition, you will examine the causes of terrorism, the impact of terrorism on the public and the public services, and the effectiveness of counter-terrorism measures; this is particularly important in the current international climate as the fight against terrorism is taking an increasingly larger share of public services resources.

Learning outcomes

After completing this unit you should:

1. know the impact of war and conflict on UK public services
2. understand how UK public services deal with terrorism.

Assessment and grading criteria

This table shows you what you must do in order to achieve a pass, merit or distinction grade, and where you can find activities in this book to help you.

To achieve a **pass** grade the evidence must show that the learner is able to:	To achieve a **merit** grade the evidence must show that, in addition to the pass criteria, the learner is able to:	To achieve a **distinction** grade the evidence must show that, in addition to the pass and merit criteria, the learner is able to:
P1 describe the causes of war and conflict **Assessment activity 8.1** **page 238**	**M1** analyse the impact of war and conflict on one UK public service **Assessment activity 8.1** **page 238**	**D1** evaluate the impact of war, conflict and terrorism on one UK public service **Assessment activity 8.3** **page 246**
P2 describe the impact of conflict on UK public services **Assessment activity 8.1** **page 238**		
P3 outline the terrorism methods used by key terrorist organisations **Assessment activity 8.2** **page 244**	**M2** analyse the measures used to combat national and international terrorism **Assessment activity 8.3** **page 246**	
P4 discuss the methods used by UK public services to counter both national and international terrorism **Assessment activity 8.3** **page 246**		

How you will be assessed

This unit will be assessed by an internal assignment that will be designed and marked by the staff at your centre. The assignment is designed to allow you to show your understanding of the learning outcomes for the impact of war, conflict and terrorism on public services. These relate to what you should be able to do after completing this unit. Assessments can be quite varied and can take the form of:

- reports
- leaflets
- presentations
- posters
- practical tasks
- case studies
- discussions.

Mitch considers the impact of war, conflict and terrorism

This unit was really interesting to me – our armed services are currently under threat abroad and I heard news stories about the casualties, but I didn't really understand why our troops were there until I did this unit. I also learned a lot of history about other wars and conflicts as well, and what caused them. I think this is really important because if you are going to resolve conflicts in the future you need to know what caused them in the past.

I also was really interested in the terrorism aspect of the unit – I hadn't really considered why people turn to terrorism and the stress it places on the resources of our public services when they try to combat it. It has made me more aware of how our services protect us even when we don't know they are doing it, both at home and abroad.

Over to you!

- What areas of war and conflict might you find interesting?
- Have you heard of any terrorist attacks?
- Do you have strong opinions on how terrorists should be dealt with?
- What preparation could you do to get ready for your assessments?

1. The impact of war and conflict on public services

Thinking about war, conflict and terrorism

Conduct some independent research into recent terrorist attacks, such as those on the World Trade Centre in 2001, the Madrid train bombings in 2004 or the London bombings of 2005. What possible reasons could terrorists have to commit acts like these? Make a list of as many reasons as you can think of and feed back to the rest of your group. Once you have done this, examine each reason in turn and consider what strategies the public services could use to combat it.

War and conflict have a significant impact on our public services, particularly the armed services, which are often at the forefront of international efforts to maintain peace and resolve conflict. This section will examine the issues of war and conflict in more detail.

1.1 Definitions of war and conflict

War has been given many definitions, but loosely it could be considered to be one of the responses a society can make to reduce the capacity of another society to achieve its objectives. Very simply put, war is a clash of interests that results in a violent armed struggle. These clashes usually involve increasing tension between nations and competition between countries for territory or resources. Traditionally, wars normally have a formal declaration so that the citizens of the countries and the governments involved are in no doubt that they are actually at war.

A war is always a conflict, but a conflict isn't necessarily a war. Conflicts do not have to involve armed hostilities or **battles**, or indeed any **active military operations** at all. Conflicts can range from the trading of insults between politicians from different nations or aggressive posturing all the way through to a full-blown war. This is called the 'spectrum of conflict' and it will be discussed later in this unit.

War and conflict are of vital importance in understanding the role of domestic and international public services.

Did you know?

Neville Chamberlain's declaration of war 1939

At 11.15 am on 3 September 1939, the Prime Minister Neville Chamberlain made a radio broadcast to the nation that formally declared war on Germany:

'This morning the British Ambassador in Berlin handed the German government a final note stating that unless we heard from them by 11 o'clock that they were prepared at once to withdraw their troops from Poland a state of war would exist between us.

I have to tell you now that no such undertaking has been received and that consequently this country is at war with Germany.'

Key terms

Active military operations are any active operations where military personnel are deployed, such as in combat or peacekeeping.

Battle is a meeting of opposing forces in a war or conflict, and their engagement in violence against each other.

This is because conflicts of an ethnic, religious, political and cultural nature are continuing to dominate world attention. Although most of these wars occur within countries rather than between countries, the role of the public services is still crucial in a peacekeeping rather than an offensive capacity. The United Nations University notes that since about

90 per cent of countries are made up of different ethnic and cultural groups, this level of conflict shows no sign of decreasing. In fact one of the major changes in conflict over the last 40 years or so has been the tendency of wars and conflict to occur within nations rather than between nations.

Activity: Examples of war and conflict

How many wars and conflicts have you heard of? Make a list and see how many you come up with; compare your list with others in your group.

1.2 Spectrum of war and conflict

The spectrum of conflict is a sliding scale of types of war and conflict that can range from small-scale terrorist attacks to large-scale international conflict. All conflict, instability and war in the globe can be placed somewhere on this spectrum to highlight its severity in relation to other previous or ongoing conflicts. The spectrum of conflict shows high intensity at one end and low intensity at the other (see Figure 8.1 and Table 8.1).

The vast majority of conflicts are at neither the low-intensity nor high-intensity end of the spectrum;

Low intensity	High intensity
Intra-national conflicts	International conflicts

Figure 8.1: Spectrum of conflict.

instead they can be placed somewhere between the two. For example, the 'Cold War' that existed between the USSR and the United States for most of the latter half of the twentieth century was characterised by the breakdown of the relationship and development of mistrust between the two nations rather than an armed conflict.

Activity: Low or high intensity

Using your list of wars and conflicts from the last activity, decide based on the information above whether they are low intensity or high intensity.

Table 8.1: Conflict can be loosely categorised into low-intensity conflicts and high-intensity conflicts.

High intensity	Low intensity
These are conflicts in which military action may come in the form of an alliance of nations or a superpower using their military resources to obtain objectives in a highly organised and lethal manner. High-intensity conflict tends to have a limited life span and rarely exceeds 6–10 years. With the end of the cold war and the decline in the influence of the superpowers, these wars are becoming less common. Examples of high intensity conflict over the last 100 years include: • The Great War (First World War) • Second World War • Vietnam War • Falklands War • Iraq	Low-intensity conflicts, in contrast, can last many decades and often have roots in cultural and religious issues going back hundreds of years. They tend to involve military skirmishes, low-intensity attacks and retaliation. This is common in areas of ethnic tension, border disputes and as rebellion against a government via terrorist action. This kind of conflict is becoming more common. Examples of low-level conflict have been seen in the following areas: • Northern Ireland • Middle East • Kashmir

Case study: Low-intensity conflict in Northern Ireland

Anglo-Irish relations have always been characterised by instability. The conflict in Northern Ireland was a result of disagreement between the Catholic nationalist minority (Republicans) who wanted to be independent of British rule and the Protestant unionist majority who wanted to maintain British rule.

In 1921 Ireland was partitioned into six counties that remained under British control (Northern Ireland), and 26 Southern counties that were independent (Republic of Ireland). However, this arrangement was seen as betrayal by some Irish Republicans, who were prepared to fight for a united and independent Ireland free from British rule. They formed the Irish Republican Army (IRA) and campaigned in the 1920s, 1940s and 1950s. The British government created emergency legislation which produced a predominantly Protestant Unionist police service and systems of economic and electoral discrimination against the Catholic minority in Northern Ireland.

Catholic dissatisfaction with their treatment led to civil rights disorders in the 1960s. There were protests modelled on US civil rights protests, such as marches, sit-ins and the use of the media to publicise grievances. The police often responded brutally. By 1969 the Northern Ireland administration could not cope and the British government sent in troops to re-establish order. After riots in which Catholic areas were attacked by Protestant mobs, younger members of the IRA formed a more militant breakaway group called the Provisional IRA, which soon became bigger than the original IRA. The Provisional IRA began a campaign of violence against the British Army and Protestant targets. Loyalist terrorist groups were also formed and attacked Catholics. The violence reached a peak in 1972 when 468 people died.

The British government suspended the Northern Ireland government and began direct control of the province from Westminster, a situation that continued into the 1990s. During 'the Troubles' over 300 police officers from the Royal Ulster Constabulary (RUC) were killed, mostly by the Provisional IRA. The police force

in Northern Ireland is now called the Police Service of Northern Ireland (PSNI) and contains a much higher percentage of Catholics.

Causes

- Political differences between the British government and the Irish Republicans, and also between the Irish Republicans and Northern Irish Loyalists.
- Religious conflict between Protestants and Catholics.

Effects

- An average of about 100 people died each year in the troubles, both Catholic and Protestant and both British and Irish.
- Northern Ireland was a divided society with religious and political differences leading to hatred and mistrust.
- Irish culture and language had been in decline, replaced by English language and culture.
- There were negotiations between Loyalists, Nationalists and the British and Irish governments in an attempt to prevent terrorism and to re-establish a devolved government for the six Northern counties. There were also secret negotiations with the Provisional IRA and loyalist terrorist groups. Eventually, these negotiations became the peace process that largely ended 'the Troubles.' The terrorist groups agreed to dismantle their weapons. Former members of terrorist groups now serve in the devolved government.

British involvement

British public and security services had been operating in Northern Ireland for over 30 years. Their presence in nationalist areas caused resentment, hatred and violence, placing the lives of troops and support staff at risk from terrorist attack. Indeed, many British soldiers and intelligence personnel have lost their lives on the streets of Northern Ireland. However the brutality is not a one-way street, and the British public services have been accused of colluding with loyalist terrorist groups in order to assassinate republican terrorists. In addition, there have been many instances where the conduct of the British Army has been called into question for their treatment and sometimes killing of nationalist individuals, such as the Bloody Sunday incident.

1 Research the terms Nationalist, Unionist, Republican and Loyalist in the context of Northern Ireland. Write your own definitions and use pro-British rule or anti-British rule in your descriptions.

2 Why would Republicans want a united and independent Ireland?

3 Why would Unionists want to remain part of UK?

4 Northern Ireland now has a devolved parliament; do you think terrorist activities helped secure this change?

Case study: High-intensity conflict in the Falkland Islands

The Falkland Islands are restored to British control, 1982.

The Falkland Islands are located in the South Atlantic Ocean about 400 miles from the South American coast and around 8000 miles from the UK. They have been a British territory for over 150 years, although this is disputed by the Argentine government. On 2 April 1982, an Argentinean military force invaded the Islands. This was done for more than one reason: firstly the fact that the Argentineans saw the Falklands as part of their national territory; but secondly and more importantly the Argentinean dictatorship led by General Galtieri was in significant political trouble, and needed a cause to unite the people of Argentina behind it or risk losing power.

The British government led by Prime Minister Margaret Thatcher made an immediate decision to fight for the return of the Islands to British control and secure the safety of the Falklands citizens, the majority of whom were of British descent. A British task force of 28,000 troops and over 100 ships sailed for the islands and retook the island of South Georgia on 25 April with an offensive following on the capital of Port Stanley in early May. After several fierce battles, such as the battle for Goose Green, in which British troops were often outnumbered, the Argentine forces surrendered on 14 June and the capital was restored to British control.

Diplomatic relations between the UK and Argentina resumed in 1990, and although Argentina still makes a peaceful claim to the islands, the UK has made it clear that there is no room for negotiation on the issue.

Causes

- Disputed historical sovereignty of the Islands.
- Unstable political situation in Argentina including a major economic crisis and large-scale civil unrest.
- Feelings of nationalism and national pride.

Effects

- 655 Argentinean deaths, 255 British deaths; and three Islanders also died as a result of the conflict. The UK lost a total of 10 ships, and the conflict is estimated to have cost the UK alone £1.6 billion.
- The failure of the Argentinean government to win the conflict made their downfall come much quicker.
- The Conservative government of Margaret Thatcher was strengthened and won the 1983 general election, and the Conservative Party went on to win the next two elections.
- The UK government re-evaluated its role towards the Falklands and offered more support in developing its political and economic infrastructure. The Islands are self-sufficient and have several thriving industries, such as fishing and tourism.

1 Why would the Argentineans believe they have a claim to the Falkland Islands?

2 What were the political and economic causes of this conflict?

3 What were the political and economic effects of this conflict?

4 What was the impact of this conflict on UK services?

Areas of instability and risk

There are several factors to indicate that war and conflict may appear in a region. Some of these are:

- competing territorial claims between different groups of people
- a government with an oppressive and unaccountable regime
- gross human rights violations
- economic distress
- military seizure of power from a civilian government
- demographic pressures such as an increase in population coupled with limited access to food and water.

The Middle East remains a major source of instability, with friction over oil, religious differences, land and military superiority set to increase. There are long-standing religious, political and territorial conflicts in the area, such as between Palestine and Israel, which remain unresolved. There are ongoing tensions in Iraq and concerns over the development of nuclear capabilities in Iran.

Many African nations have been left politically instable in the aftermath of European colonialism. This can lead to civil wars being inflicted on already poverty-stricken societies and populations; currently there are ongoing conflicts throughout Africa, with particular problems in Somalia and Zimbabwe. There is also significant conflict throughout Afghanistan, and political and nuclear tensions between North and South Korea.

Identifying sources of global instability is very important for the public services. This is because areas of the world which are politically and economically unstable are more likely to become breeding grounds for terrorist groups whose ideologies can seem very appealing to citizens who are oppressed by their own or external governments. The consequences of terrorism can be very wide ranging as the September 11 terrorist attacks in 2001 have shown. We will examine this in more detail later in this unit.

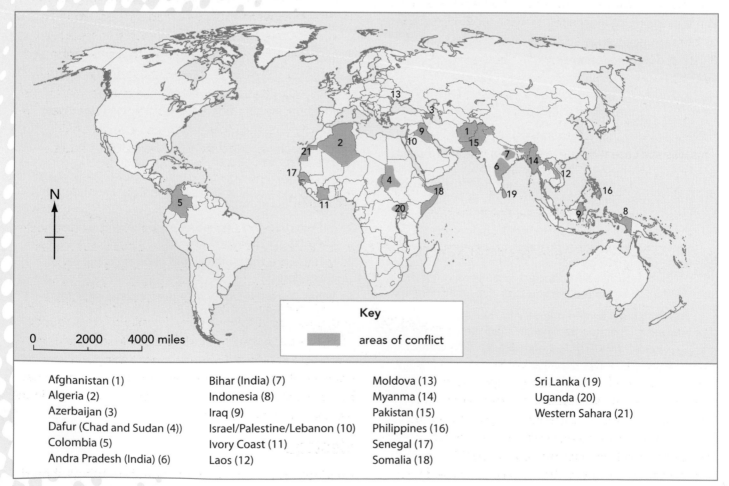

Key

areas of conflict

Afghanistan (1)	Bihar (India) (7)	Moldova (13)	Sri Lanka (19)
Algeria (2)	Indonesia (8)	Myanma (14)	Uganda (20)
Azerbaijan (3)	Iraq (9)	Pakistan (15)	Western Sahara (21)
Dafur (Chad and Sudan (4))	Israel/Palestine/Lebanon (10)	Philippines (16)	
Colombia (5)	Ivory Coast (11)	Senegal (17)	
Andra Pradesh (India) (6)	Laos (12)	Somalia (18)	

Figure 8.3: Areas of global conflict.

1.3 Causes of war and conflict

Figure 8.4: Some of the main causes of war and conflict.

Politics

International politics. The international political arena is rife with potential sources of war and conflict, such as border disputes and disputes over territory, as illustrated by the ongoing conflict between India and Pakistan over Kashmir. It must also be remembered that many countries exist as part of a greater political and military alliance, such as NATO. An attack on one of these countries may be seen as an attack upon them all. This was the case with the German invasion of Poland that started the Second World War. Britain had an alliance with Poland and so was obliged to enter into conflict even though it had not suffered an attack.

Link

See Unit 7 (page 215) for more about NATO and other international institutions.

Internal politics. Wars can be caused by internal power struggles between sub-groups and divisions in a society, such as classes and tribes. They may also involve certain geographical regions wanting autonomy and self-determination or even full independence from a larger nation. Conflict can also be caused by the tactics and politics used by a government against those who it seeks to represent.

Nationalism

Often people feel so passionately about their way of life that they want to protect it against pollution or dilution by the culture of other groups or societies. Sometimes this feeling may apply to a small tribe and sometimes it may apply to a whole country. When it applies to a country it is called 'nationalism' and it can lead to the persecution of people who do not belong to the dominant culture. It can also cause conflict if the leaders of a society have a different cultural background to the population they lead.

Religion

Religion can be a great source of stability and cohesion in society by providing moral and ethical guidelines on appropriate ways to conduct one's day-to-day existence. However, conflicts between different or competing religions can lead to hatred and mistrust, and cause political instability. Equally the distribution of power between civil and religious leaders can be a source of conflict if either are not happy with the balance of power. An example of religious differences being a contributing factor to conflict is apparent in the Northern Ireland situation.

Ideology

An ideology is a set of ideas about how things should be organised; for instance, a political ideology is a set of ideas about politics and a religious ideology is a set of notions governing how a belief system may be organised and implemented. Groups of people may have competing thoughts on many different issues and some of the issues are considered so important that the differences can lead to conflict. For instance, the USA and the Soviet Union had competing political and economic ideologies after the Second World War leading to a state of mistrust and hostility that became known as the Cold War.

Land and resources

Nations often involve themselves in war over a variety of natural resources, such as oil, gas and water. These assets are immobile – they cannot be moved to another location so preserving them is a matter of enormous political and economic concern. In some cases, the income generated from natural resources can constitute the majority of money entering a country; without these resources the economy would collapse. Countries that rely on immobile natural resources are found particularly in the Middle East and Africa, where the land is rich in oil and precious stones and minerals. An example of this kind of war is the Gulf War – Iraq invaded Kuwait in a dispute over oil pipelines. Wars can occur because one group desires to acquire the industrial wealth and influence of another. This wealth can take the form of cities or ports, trade routes, manpower, manufacturing industries or financial centres. We live in an information age, and conflict over the control of information is not uncommon. Control of such data is usually in the form of computer technology and scientific advancement. Conflict can develop particularly over the development of military technology.

Historical rivalry

Sometimes there is historical rivalry between nations or territories that may lead to conflict. In situations like this, you often see a repeating pattern of conflict between the nations that never quite gets resolved, and is always ready to flare into life again.

Ethnic differences

This factor can cause war and conflict if one ethnic group is denied access to resources and the mechanisms of government. There have been instances of some ethnic groups being denied access to facilities that other groups take for granted, such as education, healthcare and political suffrage. Clear examples of this are the Jews under the Nazi regime and non-whites in South Africa under Apartheid. In certain circumstances, relations between ethnic groups can deteriorate to such an extent that genocide and 'ethnic cleansing' can occur. Genocide is where the dominant ethnic group undertakes the wholesale extermination of another group, as happened in Rwanda. 'Ethnic cleansing' is where one group violently expels another from the previously mixed territory, as happened in the former Yugoslavia.

Link

See Unit 7 (page 222) for more on these examples of ethnic conflict.

1.4 Impact of conflict on UK uniformed public services

The role that the British public services play in these conflicts is not always the same; this means that the effects on service personnel will vary from one type of involvement to another (see Table 8.2).

It is also important to remember that involvement in some of the areas mentioned in Table 8.2 is not the sole job of the armed services. During the Hong Kong riots of 1966 and 1967 there were many British police officers serving as part of the Hong Kong police force. Similarly, the situation in Northern Ireland has tremendous implications for all of those involved in any public service, including people like postal workers who have been recent targets in the troubles. UK police officers are also present in Iraq training a new Iraqi police force.

Table 8.2: Effects on the public services of different roles in conflict areas.

Role	Effects on the individual and the service
Direct military combat	The effects of engaging in direct military combat are well documented Individuals may lose their lives; be severely and permanently injured; witness traumatic scenes leading to psychological difficulties, including post-traumatic stress disorder (PTSD), alcoholism, depression and suicide. They may witness the deaths of friends, colleagues and civilians. There may be after-effects from exposure to chemical or biological agents The service will need to replace lost personnel and equipment and be able to reflect on weaknesses in strategy and equipment and improve for next time; it may also re-train personnel in light of the results of a conflict. This can happen after any conflict such as the situation in Iraq. Military combat is often a source of pride for individuals and military units. A victory increases the prestige of the armed forces.
Peacekeeping	Public services involved in peacekeeping operations also run the risk of being involved in direct military combat. Peacekeepers are not deployed until there is a ceasefire in place, but this does not mean they are safe. Between 1948 and 2007, over 2300 peacekeeping personnel have been killed in action Deployment to peacekeeping operations may be a source of pride to an officer as they are helping a community rebuild itself and ensuring the safety of vulnerable civilians The effect on the services is the deployment of personnel and equipment to the command of the UN or NATO, which may have an operational impact on British responsibilities elsewhere. An example of this would be the UK's involvement in the Kosovo peacekeeping operation
Evacuation and security of UK nationals	If there is civil war or major civil unrest in a nation then our services may be called upon to ensure the safety and security of British nationals living or working there by evacuating them. This may involve direct combat to protect the lives of civilians. British nationals overseas are still the responsibility of the British government and they use the Army, Navy or Air Force to fulfil this responsibility
War crimes investigation	This can be a complex and difficult part of service life. War crimes such as genocide, massacres, systematic rapes and 'disappearances' are often only brought to light by the stories of survivors or by discoveries made by a liberating or peacekeeping force This can have long-term impacts on service personnel: firstly, they may be accused of war crimes themselves and have a responsibility to ensure that their conduct is of the highest possible standard and conforms with all recognised legislation and conventions such as the Geneva Convention; secondly, they may be called upon to preserve evidence and secure witness testimony to the war crimes of others An allegation of war crimes against service personnel can be devastating to a public services organisation as it will lose credibility and respect both nationally and internationally
Disaster relief and refugees	Responding to major incidents and disasters and dealing with the flow of refugees can have a large impact on service personnel. They may experience PTSD as a result of what they witness, or be subject to long-term health problems due to contamination at the site of an incident. They may also experience an enormous sense of pride from being able to contribute to aid efforts The service itself will have to liaise with other agencies and there may well be a significant financial cost. The UK services were among the first to send aid after the Asian tsunami in 2004 and Hurricane Katrina in the US in 2006
Training military and civilian personnel	Our emergency and military services are often called in to re-train security personnel in other nations, particularly in the case of instances of civil war or ethnic tensions This can be a very rewarding job for individuals and many take great satisfaction from the work they are doing. However, the job is not without danger and service personnel may be put at risk; in November 2009 five soldiers were shot dead in Afghanistan by a rogue police officer from a group they had been training The services will have to release the person concerned and ensure operational effectiveness here in the UK is not compromised by their absence. The UK services are currently a key part of the re-training of Iraqi and Afghan civilian police forces

Assessment activity 8.1

P1 **P2** **M1**

BTEC

You need to show that you understand the types of war and conflict our services are likely to become involved in overseas, their different causes and impacts. Produce a factsheet that addresses the following tasks:

1 Understanding why wars happen can be the first step in helping to prevent them or restore peace once they have started: describe the causes of war and conflict **P1**

2 Describe the impact of conflict on the UK public services **P2**

3 Analyse the impact of war and conflict on one UK public service **M1**

Grading tips

In order to achieve **P1**, describe the common causes of war as listed above, such as ethnic conflict, religion and resources. For **P2**, clearly state the impact of war on our own public services. To achieve the higher grade of **M1**, you should provide a detailed examination of how war and conflict have affected one service, such as the British Army or the Royal Navy.

PLTS

This assignment may be useful in giving you the opportunity to develop your creative thinker skills when you describe the causes of war and conflict.

Functional skills

This assessment activity may help you to show that you can describe and analyse the impact of war and develop your functional skills in English, and ICT by word processing your report.

2. How UK public services deal with terrorism

Terrorism can be a difficult concept to define, but it includes the idea of violence against a civilian population to inspire fear for political purposes. There are many terrorist groups that operate worldwide; some are national organisations and operate within or near to the borders of their own country and some are global organisations able to strike at foreign targets great distances away.

2.1 Terrorist organisations and areas of instability

National and regional groups

There have been hundreds of terrorist groups over the world in the last few decades. Some are still active, others have won power, been defeated or turned to peaceful means. Table 8.3 summarises the aims of some past and present groups.

The armed and emergency services undergo training in a variety of possible terrorist scenarios, including controlled explosions with suspected car bombs.

Table 8.3: Terrorist organisations worldwide.

Regional terrorist groups		
Name	**Location**	**Aims**
Euskadi ta Askatasuna (ETA)	Northern Spain	The creation of an independent Basque nation in north-west Spain and southern France
Irish Republican Army (IRA) and offshoots (Provisional IRA, Real IRA)	Northern Ireland/UK	The creation of an Irish Republic free of British influence. Responsible for numerous terrorist attacks, including the bombing of a Brighton hotel where the Conservative party were having a conference and bombings in Manchester, Birmingham and Omagh. The IRA and Provisional IRA have now renounced violence.
Khmer Rouge	Kampuchea (also called Cambodia)	To overthrow the government of Kampuchea. They are an extreme communist group that had political power in Cambodia in the 1970s and were responsible for a genocide that killed over one million Cambodians
Armed Islamic Group (GIA)	Algeria	To overthrow the Algerian government and replace it with an Islamic regime
National Liberation Army (ELN)	Colombia	To replace the Colombian government with a Marxist one. Responsible for politically motivated kidnappings in the 1990s
Aum Shinrikyo	Japan	Global domination, small cult responsible for the sarin gas attack on the Tokyo subway in 1995
HAMAS (Islamic Resistance Movement)	Occupied territories of the West Bank and Gaza Strip in Israel/Palestine	The establishment of a Palestinian state under Islamic law. Has carried out terrorist attacks against Israel. Also uses legitimate means to seek power via elections

Global terrorist groups	
Name	**Aims**
Al-Qaeda	To overthrow governments in Islamic countries for a unified Islamic Caliphate and expel Westerners. Responsible for global activities such as the bombings of embassies, and attacks on US military and civilian targets such as the World Trade Center
Abu Nidal Organisation (ANO)	The establishment of a Palestinian state in the Middle East. Has carried out terrorist attacks in over 20 countries
Hezbollah	To establish an Islamic government in Lebanon. Has carried out terrorist attacks in Israel but also uses legitimate means to seek power in Lebanon via elections

Case study: Regional terrorist group

Euskadi ta Askatasuna (Basque Fatherland and Liberty)

The Basque region is located in the north-west corner of Spain and across the border into the south-western French provinces of Labourd, Basse-Navarra and Soule. ETA was established in 1959 with the aim of creating a Basque homeland, independent of Spanish rule, based around Marxist principles. It arose partly as a reaction to the right-wing rule of General Franco in the 1950s and 60s.

Activities include political bombings and assassinations of Spanish government officials, including judges and opposition leaders. ETA was also responsible for the car bombs on the island of Majorca in 2009, which killed two police officers. It finances its activities from extortion and armed robberies, and also claims ransom on kidnap victims.

ETA has killed more than 800 people since the early 1960s. Members of ETA are thought to have received training or assistance from Libya and Lebanon, which are countries with a history of sponsoring terrorist activities. It is also possible that the organisation had links with the Provisional IRA in Northern Ireland due to the similarity of their political aims and methods. Although many people in the Basque region are in support of self-determination for their region, the vast majority of them reject achieving it by terrorist means.

1 What are ETA's main aims?
2 What are ETA's preferred terrorist methods?
3 What are the effects of ETA's actions on the Spanish public services?
4 Why are they compared to the Provisional IRA?

Case study: Global terrorist group

Al-Qaeda (The Base)

Al-Qaeda has become one of the world's best-known terrorist groups since it claimed responsibility for the destruction of the twin towers of the World Trade Centre on 11 September 2001. It is an international terrorist group that funds and organises the activities of Islamic militants worldwide. It developed in the early 1980s to fight against the Soviet invasion of Afghanistan. After the war against the Soviets came to a successful conclusion, the organisation's primary goal became the overthrowing of corrupt governments of Muslim states and their replacement by true Islamic law (Sharia).

Al-Qaeda is intensely anti-Western with particular emphasis on the United States; there are several reasons for this:

- the US support for Israel at the perceived expense of Islamic Palestine
- the US being seen as providing support for Islamic countries that are enemies of the group, such as Saudi Arabia and Egypt
- the involvement of the US in Islamic affairs, such as the Gulf War in 1991–2 and Operation Restore Hope in Somalia in 1992–3, and the current US presence in Iraq and Afghanistan.

The group is led by Osama bin Laden among others, and it was originally based in Afghanistan and the Peshawar region of Pakistan. It moved its base of operations to Sudan in 1991 and returned to Afghanistan in 1996, where it was the subject of a campaign by the US and its allies in 2002 to seek out and destroy its infrastructure and operations in response to the September 11 attacks on the US.

Al-Qaeda is implicated in a whole string of terrorist attacks in many nations, such as the killing of US military personnel in Somalia and Yemen, attempted assassinations of the Egyptian president and the Pope, and car bombings against US and Egyptian embassies worldwide. It is thought to have several thousand members, but it also acts as a focal point for other Islamic extremist groups. It is well funded, with access to the 300-million-dollar fortune bin Laden had before he went underground; the organisation also maintains many profitable businesses and collects donations worldwide.

1 What are the reasons Al-Qaeda exists?
2 What are its primary aims?
3 Why is the US a particular target?
4 What are the implications of Al-Qaeda activity on the UK public services?
5 What are the favoured terrorist methods of Al-Qaeda?

Remember!

Terrorists can use a variety of methods, but they are all intended to do the same thing: cause the civilian population to be frightened and cause the government to meet the terrorist group's demands.

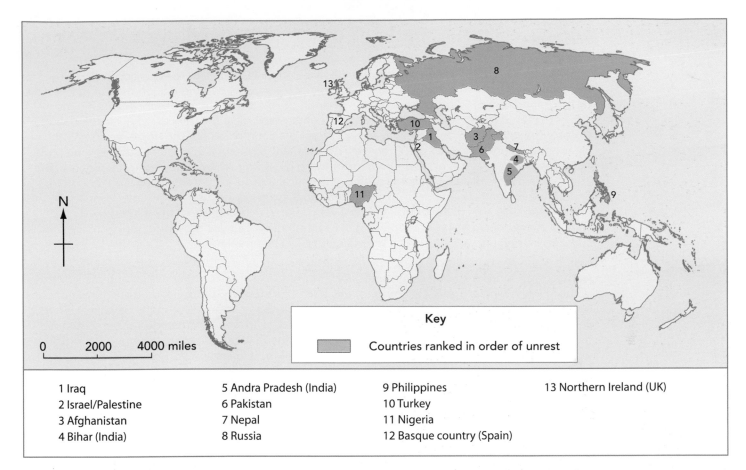

Figure 8.5: Map showing areas of the world under terrorist threat. Do you know which terrorist groups are operating in the different areas?

State-sponsored terrorism

This is when a terrorist group forms to attack the enemies of another nation. Although they seem to be independent, they actually receive funds and resources from countries that are sympathetic to their aims. Countries that sponsor terrorism are often found in the Middle East and their targets are usually powerful Western nations.

Areas of terrorist activity

Figure 8.5 shows areas of terrorist threat globally. As you can see, there are areas of the globe such as the Middle East, Pakistan and Northern Ireland where the threat is higher than elsewhere.

2.2 Methods used by terrorists

Terrorist groups use a variety of methods to inspire fear and achieve their political goals, such as bombings, assassinations and suicide attacks. These have been the traditional tactics of most terrorist groups in the twentieth century, but increasingly there is the threat of the use of non-conventional methods as well. Table 8.4 highlights a variety of terrorist tactics.

Table 8.4: Tactics of terrorist groups.

Method	Explanation
Chemical terrorism	This is the use of a toxic chemical agent released into the atmosphere or water system in order to create casualties and demoralise the population. In 1995, a terrorist group called Aum Shinrikyo (Supreme Truth) released the chemical nerve agent sarin gas on the Tokyo underground, killing 12 people and injuring hundreds of others. Chemical substances are much easier to manufacture or obtain than either nuclear or biological substances. They are also safer to carry, meaning they can be readily transported from country to country. However, chemical weapons are very difficult to use effectively because environmental conditions such as wind and rain interfere with their progress. Often just moving out of the area will be enough to counter the immediate effects of a chemical toxin. To put chemical attacks in context, when Aum Shinrikyo conducted their attack on the Tokyo underground they had perfect environmental conditions, but even so only 10% of the people present were injured and only 1% of the injured died. Chemical attacks are not very effective at mass destruction, but like biological terrorism they succeed in their primary aim, which is to generate fear and panic
Biological terrorism	This is when biological organisms, such as microbes and viruses, are spread in civilian populations in order to cause casualties and lower morale. The terrorist use of anthrax spores in the US in 2001 is a perfect example of this particular strategy. Biological terrorism cannot be used for pinpoint attacks and often the results may be unnoticed for many days, making it very difficult to track down the perpetrators. However, such weapons can be rendered almost harmless by a quick and organised medical response and vaccination programme. Biological weapons are weapons of terror and panic rather than mass destruction. Their primary aim is to demoralise and frighten a civilian population and distract a government from other, more effective, attacks
Assassination	This is the targeted murder of individual(s) perceived to be a source of threat to a group or whom the group hold responsible for perceived or actual oppression. A high-profile or famous person could be assassinated to generate publicity and increase fear in the civilian population. The Provisional IRA was responsible for the assassination of Lord Louis Mountbatten, the great uncle of Prince Charles, in 1979. Lord Mountbatten and several others, including his 14-year-old grandson, were murdered by a radio-controlled bomb attached to their boat. Lord Mountbatten was a target who fitted into both categories of usual assassination targets, as he was a high-profile member of the Royal Family and part of the British establishment
Suicide attack	In this technique it is the intent of the terrorist to die in the attack. The most common form is to become a 'human bomb' and detonate explosives carried upon the person where there is a high likelihood of many others being injured or killed, such as in a crowded place (the attacker does not need to get away so the maximum number of victims can be targeted). One of the worst examples of a suicide attack was the hijacking of four planes by 19 terrorists on September 11 2001. The planes were then used as missiles against several US targets, most notably the twin towers of the World Trade Center in New York
Bombing	Bombs are a tried and tested terrorist technique. They have the advantage of being able to be placed in a location and detonated from some distance away, ensuring that the bomber is not injured. They have the disadvantage of being detectable if people are observant, and also they may fail to detonate on command. An example of this method is the worst bombing ever carried out by the Real IRA: a bomb was detonated in the town of Omagh in Northern Ireland in 1998, killing 29 people, including a woman eight months pregnant with twins, and several children. The attack was an attempt to derail the Northern Ireland peace process by provoking retaliation but it did not inspire fear in the public; instead it created grief, anger and outrage
Hijacking	This is usually, but not always, the taking over of a civilian aircraft by a terrorist group. The pilot is forced to fly where the terrorists say, or alternatively the flight crew are killed and the terrorists themselves fly the plane. The most common reason to hijack a plane is to use the passengers as hostages to gain transportation to a particular place, or to hold them ransom until certain political demands are met. An example of a terrorist hijacking occurred in 1970 when terrorists from the Popular Front for the Liberation of Palestine (PFLP) hijacked four aircraft and flew them to Jordan. The Jewish passengers and flight crew were held hostage until exchanged for PFLP members who were being held in prison

2.3 International counter-terrorism

Combating terrorist networks can be a very difficult job. By their very nature, terrorist groups operate in secret and often in small groups that cannot implicate the wider organisation if they are apprehended. The British security service spends well over half its annual funding allocation on combating domestic and international terrorism. Table 8.5 details some of the counter-terrorist measures listed by the United Nations that can be implemented by governments and agencies seeking to end terrorism.

Not all groups will respond to all of these methods and not all countries will be prepared to utilise all of these strategies. It takes more than one counter-terrorism measure to disrupt a terrorist organisation, and in reality governments will employ multiple tactics to achieve the result they want.

Effectiveness of measures

Financial measures and sanctions. Sanctions can be used as an anti-terrorism measure by both individual countries and the UN. The US has imposed economic sanctions preventing US trade with Iran on grounds of Iranian sponsorship of terrorism; however this does not stop Iran's trade with other countries. Anti-terrorist sanctions against states can raise the cost of state sponsorship of terrorism, but at the cost of harming the general population. In addition, international governments are able to seize money they believe to belong to terrorists; although this may halve a particular

Table 8.5: Counter-terrorism measures (see www.un.org/terrorism/strategy-counter-terrorism.shtml).

Method	Detail
Through mechanisms of politics and government	• Address the specific political grievances of the terrorists • Engage publicly or privately in discussion to resolve conflict • Offer political concessions to terrorist groups or to the political parties representing them • Offer amnesty to active terrorists • Apply diplomatic pressure on the countries sponsoring terrorist groups • Control and regulate immigration/asylum
Through economic and social policy	• Address the specific socio-economic grievances of the group • Ban terrorist fundraising • Create a socio-economic climate that disinclines people to violence, by having good standards of living for all • Apply economic sanctions to countries which sponsor terrorism
Through psychological and educational strategies	• Establish common values with opponents • Allow freedom of expression • Ban interviews and publications by terrorist groups • Provide training in dealing with terrorist threats • Conduct media campaign to condemn group's methods • Educate the public on awareness of terrorist threats
Through the use of military tactics	• Use strikes/operations to undermine/destroy groups • Use public services to protect potential victims and property • Recruit and train counter-intelligence personnel
Through the use of the judicial and legal system	• Agree and abide by international treaties which denounce terrorism • Expand extradition treaties • Introduce and update laws prohibiting terrorist activity • Give harsh sentences to convicted terrorists • Provide witness protection • Increase the speed of justice for terrorists
Through the effective use of the police prison service and border control service	• 'Target harden' (put up physical defences) objects or people at risk from attack • Improve international police relations and coordination • Run training simulations of terrorist attacks • Encourage informants and infiltrators • Ensure terrorist networks cannot recruit in prisons • Control and regulate those entering and leaving the country
Through the use of intelligence and security services	• Effectively use technology to monitor terrorist groups • Improve and maintain links with other intelligence services • Infiltrate terrorist organisations • Use detective measures to arrest terrorists

strategy or attack it will not resolve the reasons why the terrorists are prepared to kill in the first place.

Direct attack. The US favoured direct military strikes as a response to September 11 in order to destroy Al-Qaeda. This was the beginning of the US-led 'War on Terror'. This tactic is expensive and time consuming and can cost many lives with few visible results. Al-Qaeda is an international terrorist group with independent cells across the world that are well funded and well trained. A military strike against one part will not destroy the organisation, and may in fact recruit new members to the cause because of their resentment of US counter-measures. There have been times when terrorist groups have been militarily defeated. In May 2009 the Sri Lankan army launched a final assault on the terrorist group Liberation Tigers of Tamil Eelam (LTTE or Tamil Tigers) which killed practically all their leaders and resulted in their surrender. However, there was a huge loss of civilian life in the course of this attack. Terrorist groups have also been effectively destroyed when most of their members were captured by police, as happened to the far-left Red Army Faction in West Germany in the 1980s.

Extra-judicial killing of suspects. This tactic has short-term success in that the immediate threat from a particular terrorist is removed. However, in some societies the terrorist can become a matyr leading others to follow in their footsteps. Extra-judicial killing by the state is also subject to international condemnation; if a government suspects someone of being a terrorist they have a duty to abide by the law and try them – not murder them.

Diplomacy and political compromise. In Northern Ireland, this tactic has brought a measure of security to the region in recent years and established a devolved political system. The strongest reason for negotiating is that it stops the killing. Some terrorists resort to violence because they feel they have exhausted all political measures to have their issues heard. By re-opening a dialogue with terrorists it may be possible to reach a compromise on their political goals. However negotiation with terrorist groups does mean that acts of violence have succeeded in getting the attention of those in power. This, many fear, will encourage more terrorism, not just from that terrorist group but also from others.

In essence, the effectiveness of counter-terrorist measures is variable and depends largely on the type of strategies employed by a particular government; negotiation and compromise is generally a far better tool of resolution than direct military action. This is because the root cause of most terrorism lies in the perceived oppression of one group by another; negotiation can help lift this feeling of oppression while violence may simply reinforce it. The problem with this is that governments cannot be seen to be forced to the negotiating table by groups who use violence to threaten them and their citizens; it would be a licence for any group with a grievance to commit atrocities simply to get the ear of those in power.

Activity: Counter-terrorism measures

What is your view on the fact that most governments refuse to negotiate officially with terrorists?

What counter-terrorist measures do you think are most effective and why?

Assessment activity 8.2

P3 **BTEC**

This assessment focuses on terrorist groups and their methods. Since a proportion of public service time is taken up with counter-terrorism issues, it is essential to have a good knowledge of these if you are going to be successful in your chosen public services career. Working individually, conduct some research into the key terrorist groups operating in the world today and address the following task:

1 Produce a wall display that outlines key terrorist organisations and their methods **P3**

Grading tip

Your wall display can include maps where the groups operate as well as their history, development and activities. Be sure to discuss the most common methods used by the groups as well.

Measures to prevent domestic or international terrorism in the UK

Since the attacks of 11 September 2001 the UK has been on a high state of alert with regard to a possible terrorist threat on our own soil. The UK was targeted by Islamic extremists on 7 June 2005, who conducted four concurrent bombings on the transport system in London. A total of 52 people plus the four bombers were killed in the explosions with hundreds more injured. Since this time UK services have undergone extensive training and preparation in order to firstly prevent another attack taking place and secondly ensure a swift emergency response if we are targeted again.

The UK uses many of the counter-terrorism measures described in Table 8.6 including:

- education
- awareness/vigilance campaigns
- promoting freedom of speech
- building relationships with communities who might feel oppressed
- extensive training and exercising of simulations
- control of immigration/asylum
- ensuring the safety of public buildings by 'target hardening' them, that means making them less vulnerable to attack.

Table 8.6: Counter-terrorism measures used in the UK.

Measures	Description
Education	Good education is one of the key aspects of preventing terrorism. A good level of education means you have the ability to question any misinformation you are given by people who might want you to commit terrorist attacks
Threat assessments	A threat assessment is the realistic evaluation of whether a terrorist attack is imminent and where it is likely to be. It also concentrates on likely targets and assesses likely suspects. It is dependent on information collected by the public services and particularly the intelligence services
Awareness/ vigilance campaigns	Campaigns that encourage the public to be vigilant are essential in combating terrorist activity. This includes being aware of the dangers of unattended luggage in airports or train stations, and reporting strange or suspicious behaviour. Such campaigns include posters, TV/radio advertisements and leaflets
Promoting freedom of speech	In many parts of the world, individuals and groups have to resort to violent behaviour because they are not allowed to speak out about their circumstances or the oppression and discrimination they face at the hands of others. A culture where free speech is valued can alleviate some of this frustration and make people more likely to seek peaceful solutions to conflict
Building relationships with communities who might feel oppressed	Communities who feel isolated, misunderstood and victimised are more likely to have a culture of anger against the government and may respond with violence to their treatment. It is therefore essential that the government and public services build strong and effective relationships with all sections of our society
Extensive training and exercising of simulations	The services are required to train extensively for a variety of possible disaster scenarios, of which a terrorist attack is just one. This includes training for chemical or biological attack and practising a combined service response.
Control of immigration/ asylum	This measure assumes that terrorists come from outside our nation to target us. As the London bombings showed, terrorists are as likely to be British citizens as foreign nationals. However, controlling entry into the UK of individuals who may pose a threat is a sensible precaution
Security of public buildings	This involves making a specified building such as a government office or airport a much harder target for terrorists to reach and destroy. It can include measures such as banning certain substances, such as liquids at airports, installing barricades, increased security personnel, CCTV and identity checks for visitors

The Police Ambulance and Fire Services outside the Edgeware Road tube station, London, on 7 July 2005. The emergency services are continuously updating their emergency procedure to offer a swift coordinated response in the event of a terrorist attack.

Assessment activity 8.3 P4 M2 D1 **BTEC**

The public services work very hard and in collaboration to reduce the risk to the UK from terrorists. The methods they use to reduce terrorism are important to know, and an assessment of how effective the methods are is also needed. Produce a written report that addresses the following tasks:

1 Discuss the methods used by UK public services to counter both national and international terrorism **P4**

2 Analyse the measures used to combat national and international terrorism **M2**

3 Evaluate the impact of war, conflict and terrorism on one UK public service **D1**

Grading tips

P4 requires a simple outline of the methods used to fight terrorism such as direct retaliation or political measures. **M2** is an extension of this task and requires more depth and detail about the measures that can be taken. **D1** is a task which involves coverage of the whole unit, and requires you to consider how one particular public service deals with the effects of war, conflict and terrorism.

Did you know?

Three of the London bombers were British citizens and the fourth was born in Jamaica. Our risk from terrorism may be more from 'home-grown' terrorists than individuals who try and cross our borders.

PLTS

This assignment may be useful in giving you the opportunity to develop your independent enquirer skills when you discuss the methods used by the UK public services to counter terrorism.

Activity: Terrorism and human rights

Should the human rights of ordinary citizens ever be compromised to combat terrorism? Explain your reasons.

WorkSpace

James Durham

British soldier

I'm a soldier with an infantry battalion that has just returned to the UK from a six-month tour of duty in Afghanistan. I was based at Camp Bastion, which is the UK's forward base in Afghanistan, located in Helmand province, and is the largest British military camp built since the Second World War.

A typical day

There isn't really any such thing as a typical day in Afghanistan as you have to be prepared to respond to the circumstances on the ground and events as they happen.

You could have a really quiet couple of days then all hell breaks loose, and you are out on patrol or re-taking territory for weeks at a time. It's dangerous work – the risk of encountering improvised explosive devices (IEDs) made by terrorists is high and you are constantly on the lookout for danger, which makes it difficult to unwind or relax back at the camp.

The best thing about the job

Just being in the army is the best thing about the job for me. I knew it was what I always wanted to do. I love the lifestyle and the camaraderie of my fellow soldiers, and even though the environment is dangerous I am pleased to be serving my country. Afghanistan is misunderstood. The majority of the people here are friendly and very hospitable; they want peace just as much as we do. It's our job to deal with the Taleban forces preventing that peace, so the ordinary citizens can rebuild their lives. The worst thing is knowing how much my mum and family worry about me; I wish there was some way I could make it easier on them.

Think about it!

What topics have you covered in this unit that might give you the background to work with the armed services?

What knowledge and skills do you think you need to develop further if you want to be involved in dealing with conflict or counter-terrorism in the future?

247

Just checking

1   Name three low-intensity conflicts.

2   Name three high-intensity conflicts.

3   Describe how ethnic conflict can lead to war.

4   What is the UK services' role in evacuating UK nationals?

5   What do the UK services provide in the way of disaster relief?

6   What is the difference between national and global terrorist groups?

7   What is state-sponsored terrorism?

8   How effective is direct retaliation against terrorists?

9   List frequently used terrorist methods.

10 List common counter-terrorism measures.

edexcel

Assignment tips

- In a unit like this which focuses on war and terrorism, one of the best things you can do to help improve your grade and your knowledge is to make sure you keep up to date with current events by reading a reputable news source on a daily basis. This means using your lunch hour or an hour after school/college to read the BBC news website or picking up a broadsheet newspaper such as *The Times*, *Guardian* or *Telegraph* (these have websites where you can read the news if you can't get hold of the paper). Not only will you become more informed about war, conflict and terrorism, but you will pick up lots of information that can be used across all of your BTEC National units.

- This may sound very basic, but make sure you have read your assignment thoroughly and you understand exactly what you are being asked to do. Once you are clear about this then you can move on to your research. Doing your research well and using good sources of evidence is essential. Lots of students rely too much on the internet and not enough on other sources of information, such as books, newspapers and journals. Always double check the information you find; don't just accept it at face value. Good research and preparation is the key to getting those higher grades.

12 Crime and its effects on society

Crime happens everywhere and it is the responsibility of public service providers to bring it under control. Crime and disorder legislation is the backbone of the work of a large number of public services, which play a vital role in how society deals with crime and how crime affects society. Public services such as the police, probation and prison services are responsible for not only catching the criminals and supporting the victims of crime but also for making sure that offenders are managed effectively and that crime figures are reduced.

Catching the criminal is only one part of the story. Crime needs to be controlled effectively by taking measures to combat crime, to reduce public anxieties and fears about crime, and to manage and punish offenders. When working in the public services it is important to understand crime and its effects on society, and how to deal with the victims of crime in a sensitive and responsible way.

Through this unit you will develop an understanding of crime and disorder legislation, as well as the effects crime has on a victim and on society as a whole. An understanding of why people commit crime is important, so you will look at a range of theories behind crime for part of this unit. You will also develop an understanding of approaches to crime reduction and ways to address anti-social behaviour. In the final part of this unit, you will investigate service providers that offer support to both victims and witnesses of crime.

Learning outcomes

After completing this unit you should:

- know crime and disorder legislation, sentences and orders
- know the effects of criminal behaviour on communities
- understand approaches to reduce crime, disorder and anti-social behaviour
- understand how the public services support victims and witnesses of crime.

Assessment and grading criteria

This table shows you what you must do in order to achieve a pass, merit or distinction grade, and where you can find activities in this book to help you.

To achieve a **pass** grade the evidence must show that you are able to:	To achieve a **merit** grade the evidence must show that, in addition to the pass criteria, you are able to:	To achieve a **distinction** grade the evidence must show that, in addition to the pass and merit criteria, you are able to:
P1 outline current crime and disorder legislation **Assessment activity 12.1 page 262**	**M1** analyse the impact of two pieces of crime and disorder legislation **Assessment activity 12.1 page 262**	**D1** evaluate the impact of one piece of crime and disorder legislation **Assessment activity 12.1 page 262**
P2 state the main sentences and orders criminal courts can impose **Assessment activity 12.1 page 262**		
P3 describe two theories of criminal behaviour and the factors that contribute to them **Assessment activity 12.1 page 262**		
P4 describe the effects crime has on communities and the individual **Assessment activity 12.2 page 280**	**M2** analyse the effects crime has on communities and the individual **Assessment activity 12.2 page 280**	**D2** evaluate a local public service initiative designed to address crime and its impact on the community **Assessment activity 12.2 page 280**
P5 identify approaches used by public services to reduce crime, disorder and anti-social behaviour **Assessment activity 12.2 page 280**	**M3** analyse how the strategies used by the local community public services, work to reduce crime, disorder and anti-social behaviour **Assessment activity 12.2 page 280**	
P6 outline how public and third sector organisations support witnesses and victims of crime **Assessment activity 12.2 page 280**		

How you will be assessed

This unit will be assessed by an internal assignment that will be designed and marked by the staff at your centre. The assignment is designed to allow you to show your understanding of the learning outcomes for crime and its effects on society. Assignments can be quite varied and can take the form of:

- small group discussions
- posters
- leaflets
- reports
- booklets
- presentations.

Colin trains new police cadets

This unit helped me to see that crime has a massive impact on society as well as individual people's lives. It was really interesting to find out about all the different types of sentences that there are and which organisations are involved in keeping an eye on the offenders to make sure they do as they are told! It was especially interesting when we went on a visit to the Crown Court and got to sit in on several different court cases where offenders were sentenced. When the judge give out sentences, it was interesting to hear the reasons they gave in their verdict.

When I finish this course I am hoping to go to university to study law and criminology and this unit has really helped open my eyes on a number of things. I was fascinated by the effects of criminal behaviour and the 'nature versus nurture' debate. We had several heated debates on this topic in our lessons!

As a police cadet I work with new recruits in training, and understanding how crime can impact people has really helped me with this. It was good to explore different approaches to managing crime, disorder and anti-social behaviour because I was able to see how these can really help people in the area that I live in.

Looking ahead to a career in law and criminology, I found the work we did on how public services support both victims and witnesses of crime the most enjoyable. I think it is really important that people who give evidence in court feel supported and therefore are not afraid to tell the truth, the whole truth and nothing but the truth, especially if I am appearing in court with them as part of the same case!

Over to you!

- How do you think crime and disorder legislation relates to the area in which you live?

- Do you think criminals are born, or are they made? Discuss this with a partner and see if you still think the same at the end of the unit.

1. Crime and disorder legislation, sentences and orders

What is anti-social behaviour?

Think about where you live. What is the area like? What is your street like? Are the police often in your area dealing with problems? Try to identify the anti-social behaviour that occurs in your area.

Make a few notes individually then pair up with someone who lives in a different area from you, share your notes and discuss your local areas in more detail. Did you identify similar problems? If not, why?

Come together as a class and share your thoughts with your classmates and your tutor. Your tutor should make notes on the board of your discussions. Are there big differences between where people live? Are there other things that we class as anti-social behaviour that have not been identified?

1.1 Crime and disorder legislation

The Crime and Disorder Act of 1998 is a major piece of **legislation** that has introduced both the public services and society to a number of strategies designed to support victims of crime, help agencies work together to fight crime, and ensure appropriate **sentences** and orders are issued to **offenders**. There are several reasons for this, such as:

- making communities safer for people to live in
- reducing the financial cost of crime to the taxpayer
- working as a team across the services to improve detection rate.

Key terms

Legislation is the act of making or enacting laws.
Sentence is the punishment that is given to a person who is found guilty by a criminal court.
Offender is a person who has committed a crime.

Since the introduction of this act a number of other pieces of legislation designed to strengthen the Crime and Disorder Act have been introduced,

their main focus being to reduce crime and disorder.

Crime and disorder legislation as you would expect is amended and updated on a regular basis to meet the needs of our ever-changing society. Current legislation is detailed below.

Crime and Disorder Act 1998

The Crime and Disorder Act 1998 created 376 crime and disorder reduction partnerships in England and Wales. This legislation means that local authorities, police and other agencies work in partnership to develop and implement strategies to reduce crime and disorder. The partnerships carry out an audit of crime and disorder every three years and publish a strategy for dealing with the problems found.

The intention was that these strategies would reflect local needs and priorities, which means different partnerships around the country could be tackling different things. The Crime and Disorder Act 1998 covers such areas as anti-social behaviour, sex offences, parenting orders, child safety orders and racially aggravated offences. The orders created as part of the act will be discussed in more detail (see page 255). The partnerships are made up of many different organisations, such as:

- the police
- community safety officers
- youth offending teams
- local authorities
- health trusts
- probation services
- the National Association for the Care and Resettlement of Offenders (NACRO)
- victim support
- educational establishments
- businesses
- housing associations.

Police Reform Act 2002

This act received Royal Assent in 2002 and its content was brought into force in a number of stages. The fundamental aims of the act are to improve things like supervision, administrative functions and conduct of police forces, police officers and other people who carry out police-related functions. It also made some amendments to police powers and provided powers for non-police officers relating to anti-social behaviour.

Activity: Police Reform Act 2002

Undertake some internet research into the main provisions of the act and then research your local police force and try to find out the different ways the Police Reform Act impacted them.

Criminal Justice Act 2003

This act was designed to look at a wide range of measures to modernise areas of the criminal justice system in England and Wales and, to a lesser extent, Scotland and Northern Ireland. It looked at a number of things including amending the law relating to police powers, bail, disclosure of evidence, prosecution appeals, what counts as evidence and sentencing. It also permitted judges to sit alone without a jury in certain cases.

Activity: Criminal Justice Act 2003

Undertake some internet research into the main provisions of the act, particularly looking at which cases a judge can sit alone to hear, and the introduced exceptions to the double jeopardy rule.

Find out in what circumstances a judge can try a case without a jury and when the double jeopardy rule does not apply. Write down one reason for and one reason against this change.

Anti-social Behaviour Act 2003

This act was designed to strengthen the rules around **anti-social behaviour** and **fixed penalty notices**. It also banned the sale of spray paints to under-16s and gave local councils powers to remove graffiti from private properties. The other feature of the legislation was to address other issues including truancy, gang activity and public drunkenness, to name a few.

Key term

Anti-social behaviour refers to a set of behaviours by some people that have an adverse affect on other people in society.

Fixed penalty notice refers to a notice issued for a minor offence of a fixed amount of cash that must be paid or the offender will be taken to court.

Until recent years it has only been possible to access legal documents through printed material but many documents may now be viewed online.

1.2 Sentences and orders

Once an offender has been apprehended, it is important to understand the process they go through, what happens when they go to court, etc. The courts are governed by their own guidelines and they must ensure that the sentence they give is suitable for both the crime and the offender. These guidelines are important because they help to ensure consistency across the country. It would be unfair for an offender to be given a fine in one part of the country and another offender a custodial sentence in another part of the country for committing the same offence. There are a number of sentences and **community orders** that are used and these are detailed below.

Key terms

Community orders are a range of punishments given to an offender to serve in the community.

YOT stands for Youth Offending Team.

Sentences

The word 'sentence' has more than one meaning. For this purpose we are referring to 'sentence' as the final judgement of guilty in a criminal case and the punishment that is imposed.

Sentencing for young offenders

Sentences are designed to be supportive as well as a punishment and therefore vary in style for young offenders. For example, young offenders (those under the age of 18) are often given sentences designed to support them in turning their behaviour around, which can include:

- the **Child Curfew Scheme**, which applies to unsupervised children under 10 and prohibits them from being in specified public places between 9pm and 6am. The police can remove children breaching their curfew and take them home or to a place of safety. In many cases social services are also involved.

- **truancy orders**, which are designed to support young people back into education. It is widely believed that truancy is something that without intervention is a factor in why young people re-offend in the future.

If measures like these do not work, the **YOT** will use other strategies as pre-court measures. These include:

1 **Reprimand** – a formal verbal warning given by the police to a young person who admits they are guilty of a minor first offence. In some cases the young person will work with the YOT and take part in a voluntary programme to help them address their offending behaviour.

2 **Final Warning** – a formal verbal warning given by the police to a young person who admits guilt to a first or second offence. Unlike a reprimand, the young person is assessed to determine the causes of their offending behaviour and a programme of activities are put together to address these. This means giving offenders a final chance of changing their behaviour. If these are unsuccessful then any future offences will be dealt with by the courts.

Anti-social behaviour measures

Anti-social Behaviour Orders (ASBOs) are intended to control the nuisance elements in a community to improve the quality of life for all of the other residents. These orders generally last for a minimum of two years and contain certain conditions which must be obeyed. ASBOs impose restrictions or conditions on someone, such as:

- restricting access to a residential area

- not committing the same behaviour again

- not associating with certain people.

If someone breaches an ASBO they can be given up to five years in prison, but this is rare.

Other sentences

Other sentences imposed on offenders are wide ranging and include:

- financial penalties (fines), where an offender is required to pay a certain amount of money to the court
- community sentences, which often require the offender to give a certain number of hours to serving the community. This could be removing graffiti or helping landscape waste ground, etc.
- custodial sentences, which mean spending a period of time in prison
- restorative justice, which gives victims the chance to tell offenders the real impact of their crime, to get answers to their questions and to receive an apology. It gives the offenders the chance to understand the real impact of what they've done and to do something to repair the harm.

Orders

As part of the Crime and Disorder Act of 1998, anti-social behaviour orders were developed. They were designed to sit alongside the legislation as another way of supporting the act by working with the public services as well as the community to find ways of reducing anti-social behaviour. Under the act a wide range of measures were designed to address anti-social behaviour committed by adults and young people, such as those outlined in Table 12.1.

Table 12.1: Types of anti-social behaviour order.

Order	Description
Compensation order	The offender pays an amount of money to the court as a consequence or punishment for the crime they have committed
Child safety order	Designed to protect children under 10 who are at risk of becoming involved in crime. The child is then put under the supervision of a social worker. Issued if the child has previously breached a curfew
Parenting order	Requires a parent to control the behaviour of their child. Can be imposed by a magistrate when a child aged 10–17 is convicted of an offence or subject to an ASBO. This means a parent may be convicted if the child fails to adhere to the order
Reparation order	Requires the young offender to make specific reparation either to an individual or a community. Can last for a maximum of three months and must have full consent of the victim. Referred to a Youth Offender Panel who will produce a programme to allow the offender to face up to the consequences of their behaviour
Supervision order	Can last up to three years and often has a range of conditions attached, such as a drug treatment programme, curfew, residence requirement, etc. The young offender is also required to take part in activities set up by the YOT which can include repairing the harm done by their offence, either to the victim or to the community, as well as addressing their offending behaviour through programmes such as anger management. Can be imposed until a person's 18th birthday
Restriction of liberty order	Also known as a curfew – requires young person to remain for set periods of time at a specified place and can be given alongside other community orders. The time period can be between 2 and 12 hours per day and the sentence can last no more than six months for those over 16 years of age, and three months for those under 16
Community rehabilitation order	Available to courts for young people aged 16–17 and equivalent to a supervision order, but for this specific age range. Supervised by the YOT and can include activities such as repairing the harm caused by an offence and programmes to address the offending behaviour

1.3 Impact of this legislation

As you would expect, legislation, sentences and orders have an impact on all those that are affected by them but in different ways, as outlined below.

Impact on public services

Not only do public service staff have to keep their knowledge up to date on changes in legislation, but they also need to ensure they use their knowledge wisely. This will go towards building good relationships within the community they police and reassuring the public that the public services are working and supporting society. The changes in legislation have also had a significant impact on regular police officers with the introduction of PCSOs. PCSOs provide a reassuring presence within the communities

Judges pass sentences in a Crown Court. Who decides on innocence or guilt?

Impact on offenders

ASBOs, for example, do provide an instant punishment that may in some cases shock offenders out of a pattern of criminality before they become hardened criminals. However, the flip side of this view is that trivial behaviour may be seen to have become criminalised, and that some may see an ASBO as a badge of pride, especially within criminal subcultures.

Impact on individuals

The impact of current crime and disorder legislation on individuals varies depending on a number of factors, including whether they have been or know a victim of crime or if they live in a high-crime area. In most cases the impact is positive as people see that legislation is designed to protect them and punish those that break the law. Victims in particular are encouraged to contact the organisations set up to offer emotional support and advice, on protecting their home for instance. The legislation has also introduced a Witness Charter (see page 279) designed to support the witness both before and after they attend court.

Impact on communities

Communities are also affected by crime and disorder legislation in many ways. For example, if ASBOs are issued in your community, it might become a more orderly place. However, because ASBOs are made public it may be that the area where you live might get a reputation as a place of frequent trouble. The impact on communities is by no means equal however, as some members of the public do not see police community support officers (PCSOs) as 'real police officers' due to their limited training and legal powers. In some cases they are not feared or respected by criminals.

Activity: Are ASBOs effective?

Working in groups

Do you think the police see ASBOs as an effective punishment? Discuss this issue in your group. How do you think having penalties such as these has changed their daily work? What has been the cost of employing PCSOs, and issuing ASBOs?

2. The effects of criminal behaviour on communities

2.1 Criminal behaviour: theories

It is important when looking at crime that we explore definitions of crime and the theories that attempt to explain why crime happens and how this affects both individuals and communities. The study of crime is known as 'criminology' and is drawn from many other disciplines such as sociology, psychology, biology, geography, law and anthropology. It is generally accepted that there are three main categories that are used to explain why crime happens. These are biological, sociological and psychological (Figure 12.1).

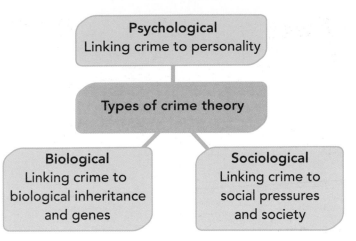

Figure 12.1: Theories of crime.

Biological

The burning question when we look at biological theories is: *are people born evil?* What possesses people to rape or kill someone in cold blood? The only way to get any sort of answer is to try to get inside the minds of the criminals. Evidence suggests that there are many similarities in serial killers which include: ritualistic and compulsive behaviour; suicidal tendencies; history of serious assaults; history of drug/alcohol abuse; alcohol- or drug-abusing parents; cruelty to animals; unnatural liking for firearms; emotional behaviour signs, such as chronic depression; abuse as a child.

The work of Cesare Lombroso (1835–1901) included research that looked at the physical measurements of Italian prisoners and non-criminal military personnel. From this research he argued that the physical shape of the head and face determined them as being 'born criminal'.

As with any theory, it can only be proved or disproved by replicating the research with different groups. This was done in 1913 by Goring, who compared physical measurements of 3,000 English convicts and 3,000 non-convicts. Goring found nothing to support the work of Lombroso and was very critical, as the sample used by Lombroso included people with severe learning difficulties and ignored that fact that poverty could be a cause of physical appearance rather than genetics. The problem with hunting for the 'criminal face' is the existence of stereotypes of what a criminal looks like. Despite these discussions, the work of Lombroso was at the time seen as groundbreaking and even now still has a place in the work of criminology.

In the 1940s research done by William Sheldon proposed that the general body shape was the key determinant of personality and behaviour. His research was done by collecting over 4,000 photos of male students and 650 possible personality traits. From this he was able to determine three basic body builds: endomorph, mesomorph and ectomorph (Figure 12.2).

Based on these types, Sheldon looked for correlations including temperament and body shape, and delinquency and body shape. After eight years of detailed studies he concluded that the average delinquent tended to be heavily mesomorphic and rarely ectomorphic. More studies followed by Glueck and Glueck (1950) who found mesomorphs were over-represented in a delinquent population of 500. More recent work in the UK concluded that those who commit serious crimes are generally smaller in size than non-delinquents. Having said this, a further study in 1973 by West and Farrington found no association between body shape and delinquency.

More modern theories concerning biological explanations for crime concentrate less on physical shape and more on genetics.

Genetic determinism is the belief that it is the genes alone that decide the physical features, such height, hair colour, intelligence and so on, of a human being (or any organism). The chromosomes are the cell structures that carry the genetic material contained in the nucleus of the cells of all living things. The molecules of DNA that make up the chromosomes carry the information that allows organisms to function, repair and reproduce themselves. Cells in normal females contain two X chromosomes and those in normal males contain an X and a Y chromosome. A genetic anomaly can occur that results in an extra Y chromosome. It has been suggested that it is this that accounts for high levels of aggression in certain individuals. There is the possibility that the extra Y chromosome can influence the brain's chemistry (neurochemicals) and this may account for criminal behaviour. More recently researchers have discovered links between a version of a male gene and criminal behaviour. Scientists believe that they may be able to treat these conditions, and therefore potential criminality, with drugs. The danger is that youngsters may be labelled as potential criminals before they have committed any crime. In addition, governments might be swayed to fight crime with drugs rather than addressing some of the more fundamental social problems.

Biological determinism is similar to genetic determinism but a much wider (and much more controversial) idea – that all features of a human being,

Figure 12.2: The three basic body builds proposed by Sheldon.

Sheldon's somatotype			
Body build	Endomorph	Mesomorph	Ectomorph
Character	relaxed, sociable, tolerant, comfort-loving, peaceful	active, assertive, vigorous, combative	quiet, fragile, restrained, non-assertive, sensitive
Shape	plump, buxom 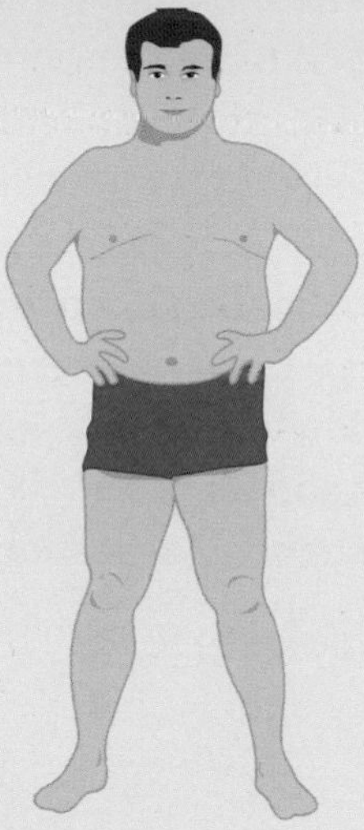	muscular 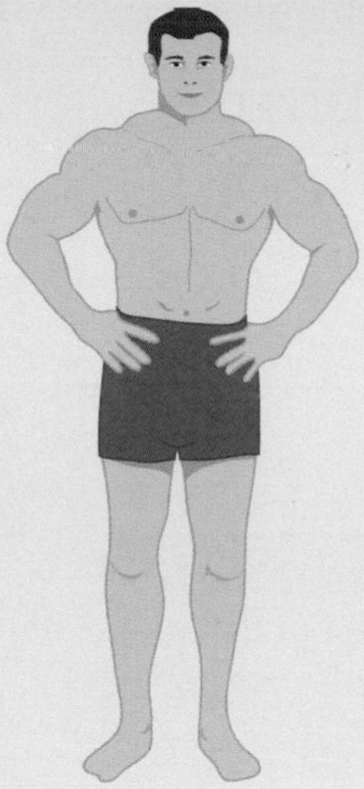	lean, delicate, poor muscles 

including behaviour, are controlled by biological factors. This means that any influences from other people or the environment are ignored. So, biological determinists would say that the children of criminals are likely to be criminals themselves.

In contrast, the '**blank slate**' view treats a newborn baby as a blank slate with no **innate** characteristics. What the baby learns and experiences as he or she grows up decides how he or she will turn out. This view is often linked to a strong belief in free will. Criminals are criminals because they choose to be.

Not many experts take either extreme view but the question of 'nature versus nurture' is an ongoing debate.

Activity: Biological theories

Working in groups

Undertake some research into biological theories and the work of Lombroso, Sheldon and others. As part of your research find out more information about how their theories describe criminal behaviour and the factors that contribute to these theories. Produce a presentation on your findings to share with your colleagues.

As you can see from these biological studies, there is some evidence to suggest that biology plays a part in criminal activity, but this is by no means cut and dried. There is plenty of evidence to support the sociological and psychological theories of crime discussed below.

Sociological

These theories focus on society as the main cause of crime. There are a number of sociological theories that suggest this. The four main theories are briefly discussed below.

Functionalism was developed by Emile Durkheim (1858–1917) who was an active social theorist. He was one of the first people to analyse crime and **deviance**. Many later criminologists have built on his work to develop this theory further. Durkheim believed that for society to exist and work effectively there had to be a strong sense of social order. His theory was based around an agreed set of rules and values within society that he called a '**collective conscience**'.

Marxism was born out of the work of Karl Marx (1818–1883). Marx's theory covered economics, politics and history but the root of it was the idea of 'class struggle'. This referred to the tendency of each class in society to jostle with all the other classes in order

Key terms

Determinism is the theory that a person's actions are controlled by outside causes and that people do not have free will.

Innate means inborn or natural.

Deviance is often defined as a behaviour that is not normal and goes against morals and values.

Collective conscience is the feeling of people in a group of what is right and wrong; a group of people sharing the same morals and values with similar views of deviant behaviour.

Labelling is the process of giving people a 'label' based on their behaviour. This can be both positive and negative and can greatly influence how you are treated by others.

to gain maximum advantage. Marx saw crime as a product of society and believed that the various class struggles in each different society would produce its own type and amount of crime. Two classes that were evident in Marx's time were the urban middle class and the urban working poor. Marx's theory of crime concentrated on the struggle between these two classes. He felt that the working poor committed crime as the only way to escape the misery that their powerless position caused.

Labelling theory sees crime as a result of people **labelling** an act or a person as a criminal. In other words an act is not wrong or criminal unless society says it is. This theory was researched by Howard Becker (from 1928 onwards) but was prominent in the 1960s and 1970s. The basis of the theory is that:

- acts are only criminal because society says so
- society's reaction to the crime is more important than the crime itself
- criminals are ordinary people who have simply received a label.

Labelling theorists argue that being stigmatised with a label because you broke a rule can encourage a person to see themselves as deviant and therefore behave in a more deviant manner.

The **Chicago School** emerged in the 1920s and 1930s and focuses on human behaviour as determined by social structures and physical environmental factors rather than genetic or personal characteristics. It is based around the idea that societies and individuals adapt to circumstances in a similar way to biological evolution. The theory centred on conceps such as the changing patterns of crime in different zones of

a city. The Chicago School introduced the idea of socialisation as an explanation for criminal activity. These theories hold that people are not simply born good or bad; they are influenced by the people, social situations and other external forces that surround them.

Sociological determinism is a name given to a belief that nurture (the care and upbringing the child receives as he or she grows up, and also the society he or she lives in) is overwhelmingly important in deciding how the adult turns out, and that inherited factors are unimportant. According to this view crime is caused by society. Some theories of exactly how society causes crime are discussed (see page 260). (It is more than 'nature versus nurture' in that it is a three-way debate where the extremes are biological determinism, sociological determinism and the view that it all depends on the experiences of the individual.)

Activity: Sociological theories of criminal behaviour

Working in groups

Undertake some research to find out more information about the different sociological theories identified above, and produce a presentation to share with your colleagues that describes a theory of criminal behaviour and the factors that contribute to it.

Your tutor will divide you into four groups to work on this activity.

Psychological

Psychological theories are designed to examine the reasons why an individual becomes a criminal. They are not looking at it from the perspective of society, but concentrating on the individual. This could involve looking at an individual's mental state, how they have learned to be a criminal, and even how an individual was raised (nurtured) by their family. As you would expect, there are a number of psychological theories that attempt to explain criminal behaviour and we will briefly examine two of these below.

Psychoanalytical theory was the theory discussed in great detail by Sigmund Freud (1856–1939). He argued that as humans we all have natural urges and desires, which could develop into criminal activity unless they are repressed, but that repression itself can cause new problems. He argues that as children we are socialised to suppress these instinctive impulses by those around us (generally our parents/carers). Freud claims the human personality consists of three parts: the **id**, the **ego** and the **super-ego**. The relationship between these three parts is key. The ego is the part of our personality that balances the demands of the id without causing offence to the super-ego. Freud felt that crime occurred when a child was not socialised effectively, resulting in a poorly developed ego that lacks control over the id, and leading to anti-social and destructive behaviour.

Misuse of controlled drugs is dangerous and may promote unwanted side effects. What are some possible side effects?

Key terms

The id is the demanding and child-like side of a person, which responds directly to instincts such as hunger, thirst and the need for sexual gratification. The id does not respond to social norms and values, and according to Freud is the part that must be repressed.

The ego is the rational, logical part of us, governed by reality. It is the part of the id that has been modified by the world around us. It tries to satisfy the id in a socially acceptable way.

The super-ego is the moral part of our personality that judges things as right or wrong, good or bad. It develops around the age of 5 years old, and is effectively what we call our conscience.

Activity: Psychological theories of criminal behaviour

Working in groups

Undertake some research to find out more information about the different psychological theories identified above, and produce a presentation to share with your colleagues that describes a theory of criminal behaviour and the factors that contribute to it.

Your tutor will divide you into groups to work on this activity.

Social learning theory is based around the principles of behaviour. The theory suggests that an individual's behaviour is learned and maintained by rewards and punishments. From this theory, crime is seen as either a learned behaviour (usually as a result of being brought up in a criminal environment) or a failure of the socialisation process which teaches children right from wrong. This theory is based on the notion that crime is a learned behaviour that does not differ from any other learning experience that we have. Theorists believe that deviant or criminal behaviour can be reduced by taking away the reward value for the behaviour and replacing it with a punishment.

Causal factors

When looking at theories of criminal behaviour it is also very important to take into account other factors that may contribute to whether an individual becomes involved in criminal activity. Some of these factors are described below.

Peer pressure is the influence of a friend or peer group and is important when considering the beginning of a criminal career. Evidence suggests that young people commit most of their offences in a group with their peers. In many cases the pressure from friends to adopt common behaviours or fit in can be overwhelming. A young person may be drawn into criminal behaviour by the need to feel connected to others.

Drugs/alcohol taken regularly can often lead to an addiction, which requires increased amounts of cash to fund it. Drugs in particular are an expensive habit to maintain on a daily basis; therefore, in order to feed

Link

For more information on drugs and health see Unit 5, page 177.

Case study: Sonia and Nicky turn to crime

Sonia and Nicky had been friends for many years; they went to school together and became friends around the age of five. Nicky's parents split when she was young due to her mum's alcohol problems and her dad spent much of his adult life in and out of prison. As a consequence of this she spent a lot of her childhood being cared for by her elderly grandparents who had their own health problems and consequently Nicky brought herself up from a young age. In contrast Sonia's parents owned a chain of stores and she lived in a big house with both parents and enjoyed regular holidays abroad.

Despite their different upbringings their friendship was strong and they would often go shopping into their local town centre. On most occasions Sonia would buy clothes, CDs, make-up, and Nicky would just window shop as she did not have any money. One afternoon as Nicky tried on some clothes Sonia dared her to steal them – after initially refusing Nicky thought why not! She decided it was time she had nice things like Sonia and stole a shirt by taking the tag off and wearing it under her clothes as she left the shop.

The girls ran from the shop and didn't get caught. They had a chat and decided it had been fun, and from then they both stole items from shops for several weeks, Nicky so she had all the things she wanted and Sonia just because she could! That was until one week they were caught by a store detective …

Think about the points below. How do you think theories of criminal behaviour explain this?

- Who is to blame for this crime? Nicky? Sonia?
- Was it nature or nurture that persuaded Nicky to commit crime?
- Why did Sonia commit crime?
- What casual factors do you think made Nicky commit crime?
- How do you think the parents of the girls would react? Will this make them stop committing crime?

their habit individuals are often forced to turn to crime. In addition to this, using these substances on a regular basis can lead to poor social behaviour, and promote aggression and violence.

Education that is not engaging or interesting can often lead students to play truant and become involved in low-level criminal activity such as criminal damage or graffiti, or just generally causing a nuisance. A person who is a persistent truant is at increased risk of giving a poor academic performance, which can often make it more difficult for a young person to move away from criminal behaviour.

Family is one of the biggest causal factors to consider for a number of reasons.

- If the family itself is involved in criminal activity, it can be a learnt behaviour (e.g. it is accepted as 'normal' behaviour).
- If the family is broken or just large, a child may not receive the socialisation they need to help them understand right from wrong, good from bad, etc. and have to rely on friends and peers as models of appropriate behaviour.

- Similarly, within a dysfunctional or larger family a child may exhibit poor behaviour in order to get some attention from their parents.
- The stress or disruption involved in a family breakdown can often lead a young person to crime as they may feel isolated or torn between parents.
- Boys growing up with absent fathers can turn to gang leaders as role models.

Political and socio-economic factors – some studies suggest that there is a clear link between people on low income and criminal activity whereas other studies say the exact relationship between poverty and crime has not been fully explored. It is argued that some commit crime as they are jealous of the wealth of others (wealth referring to material things) but this is still a topic of much debate. The political climate can also influence crime – the government may introduce new legislation on crime that criminalises acts that were previously acceptable, for example raising the age a young person can buy cigarettes from 16 to 17 years of age.

Assessment activity 12.1

P1 P2 P3 M1 D1 **BTEC**

1 Using your discussions from the initial 'Talk up...' as well as your individual research into a variety of legislative acts, produce a report that outlines current crime and disorder legislation **P1**

2 Using the activities above as well as independent research on the criminal justice system, produce a poster that states the main sentences and orders the criminal courts can impose **P2**

3 Using what you have discussed in the case study of Nicky and Sonia, the other activities you have completed and your own personal research, produce a factsheet that describes two theories of criminal behaviour and the factors that contribute to them **P3**

4 To support your report, undertake some individual research on two specific pieces of crime and disorder legislation in order to analyse the impact of the legislation **M1**

5 Ask your tutor to invite a guest speaker from the Police Service. This guest speaker would ideally be a PCSO who can then help you evaluate the impact of the crime and disorder legislation **D1**

Grading tips

To support your work it is important that you understand the verbs for each task:

P1 Outline – write a clear description but not a detailed one.

P2 P3 Describe – give a clear description that includes all the relevant features. Think of it as 'painting a picture with words'.

M1 Analyse – identify separate factors, and say how they are related and how each one contributes to the topic.

D1 Evaluate – review the information then bring it together to form conclusions. Give evidence for each of your views or statements.

PLTS

This assessment activity may be useful for practising your skills as a reflective learner when outlining current crime and disorder legislation, an effective participator when stating the main sentences and orders criminal courts can impose, and a creative thinker when describing two theories of criminal behaviour and the factors that contribute to them.

Functional skills

This assessment activity may also help you to develop your functional skills in ICT if you word process your report and include images or tables.

2.2 Effects of crime

Crime has a massive impact on society. It can impact individuals in many different ways as well as affecting whole communities, minority groups and businesses. In many cases, the crimes that most affect the public are crimes that we class as anti-social behaviour.

Impact of anti-social behaviour

As you would expect, there are often impacts of anti-social behaviour. These can include criminal damage to both private and commercial property, such as houses, shops, schools and even the highway, which costs money to repair. Graffiti, for example, costs local authorities large amounts of money every year to

Activity: What is anti-social behaviour?

Working in pairs

Think about crimes that fall into the category of 'anti-social behaviour'. Make a list of as many as you can. Share your list with the rest of your class and your teacher will record these on the board.

Discuss the list. Have you seen these behaviours where you live? How do you think they impact on the public? Think about both the social and financial costs of these crimes for the individual as well as the community.

Did you know?

Crime costs households in England and Wales an estimated £60 billion a year!

remove. Anti-social behaviour, however, can and does cover a multitude of things such as:

- vandalism including fly-posting, graffiti
- dumping rubbish in the streets, abandoning cars
- begging and drinking in public
- buying and selling drugs on the street
- yobbish behaviour which includes intimidating others
- rowdy behaviour, for example groups of people congregating together in bus stations, throwing stones, etc.
- nuisance neighbours, for example being noisy or aggressive.

Public perception of crime

The types of behaviour identified above can make the public very fearful of crime and disorder, and give the perception that crime is everywhere and something we should fear always. In most cases our fear of crime is much higher than the likelihood of us actually being a victim of crime.

Activity: Public perception of crime

Working as a whole class

Ask your tutor to help you put together a simple questionnaire to give to five people each, to see how fearful they are of crime in your local area.

Ask your tutor to collate the results.

Working individually

Using the data you have collected, produce a short report that looks at the public perception of crime in your area.

Community support officers work on the front line of the local police force. In what ways would you like them to help your community fight crime?

The media

This term refers to television, radio, newspapers, the internet and magazines to name but a few. When looking at crime, the media can often present a distorted view of reality which can in turn make us more fearful of crime. In essence, the media need to have newsworthy stories for us to read and so will select the most shocking stories to report on. This can give the public the impression that such crimes are much more common than they actually are.

Fear of crime

As mentioned above, when the media and public perception of crime are high this leads to a heightened fear of crime. People are often frightened of crime for a variety of reasons, such as:

- we live in a high crime area
- we have already been victims of crime
- we feel poorly informed about policing in our local area
- our local environment is in a state of disrepair
- there is poor public transport in our local area.

Impact of crime on victims

The impact of crime on victims can be wide ranging. This is discussed in much greater detail later in this unit (page 274).

Impact of crime on lifestyle

Strong fear of crime has an impact on the lifestyle of many people. A study by Hough (1995) found that between 1 and 2 per cent of people *never* go out at night as a result of being fearful of crime. This becomes a vicious circle because crime is more likely when there are fewer witnesses. Many other people no longer feel safe walking alone at night, and more and more people carry personal attack alarms to help them feel safe. It could be argued that the fear of crime may affect people's health due to stress-related illnesses brought on by anger and resentment towards criminals. A study by Simmonds in 2002–3 found that:

- 5% of people carry weapons
- 5% of people carry personal attack alarms
- 30% of people usually travel in groups for safety

- 40% of people avoid walking near people who they feel might be a threat.

Collective cost of crime

This can be looked at in three different ways.

In anticipation of crime – this refers to the money we spend 'just in case' we are a victim of crime. It can include things like security expenditure (burglar alarm, security staff, CCTV, and so on), insurance costs (such as insuring our home contents), other crime prevention costs which may be incurred to protect your property or business.

As a consequence of crime – this refers to the costs associated with being a victim of crime, for example the cost of property stolen and damaged, losing pay at work to sort things out after the crime, the cost of replacing locks, and losing pay while recovering if a victim of violence.

In response to crime – this refers to the costs associated with investigating the crime, which could be the costs for the police (deploying police officers to crime scenes, taking statements, solving crimes, use of resources), prosecution (costs of hiring solicitors) and legal aid to the offender if they are able to claim it. Other costs include the cost of holding an offender in prison if they are found guilty and the costs of the probation services monitoring them through the criminal justice system. Costs are also incurred for the clear-up operations by the local authority for graffiti, fights, criminal damage, damage to roadways after a road traffic accident, and so on. Health services in many cases incur costs to look after victims of crime in hospitals, to provide ambulances to attend at the scene, and at local doctors' surgeries for aftercare.

When looking at the cost of crime we should always remember the physical and/or psychological costs there may be to the victim and their families.

Physical injury – as a result of a crime a victim may sustain minor/major physical injuries, which can take many months to recover from, and in some cases a full recovery physically is not possible.

Psychological impacts – attacks on a person, and sometimes burglaries, can leave lasting damage such as panic attacks, exhaustion, depression and flashbacks/nightmares. Many victims suffer a lack of confidence or are afraid to go out at night. This has an impact on their quality of life: they sometimes feel it has been downgraded because they are worried and feel insecure. These types of problem can be made worse by the fact that statistically they are likely to be a repeat victim.

Did you know?

In 2005–06 the British Crime Survey indicated that 16% of victims were repeat victims of burglary offences over a 12-month period.

3. Approaches to reduce crime, disorder and anti-social behaviour

Crime occurs in all areas of society. While it may differ from region to region in its type, quantity and severity, there is no part of society that does not have some degree of crime within it. It is important therefore that strategies are in place to reduce crime, disorder and anti-social behaviour. In order to develop strategies, crimes are recorded and then they can be categorised and investigated using a standardised system. This allows the police to compare crime statistics across forces and establish crime patterns. Recording crime highlights the volume of work the police have to deal with and enables them to work with other agencies to target specific crimes in certain areas and to implement crime reduction strategies more effectively.

3.1 Intelligence-led policing

The National Intelligence Model (NIM) is a code of practice governing the way the police use **intelligence**. It came into operation in January 2005 and the overall aim is that all police forces have the same ways of classifying and storing information so it can easily be shared and used by other forces. The NIM is primarily used for allocating police resources, to plan and work in cooperation with partnerships in the community, and to manage performance and risks. It enables forces to standardise and coordinate the fight against crime at all levels. As part of the NIM, it is important that there is cooperation across and between different police forces. A senior officer is usually given the responsibility of ensuring that cross-force coordination meetings are held regularly in order to ensure crime hot spots are identified and that the intelligence gathered can then lead officers to work more effectively.

Identification of crime trends

Intelligence-led policing is central to the NIM strategy. It is a policing model that has emerged in recent years in which intelligence gathering is central to police operation. It was felt that too much of police time was being spent responding to crime and not enough time was used to target offenders. Using the data collected by forces on crimes that have occurred, it is possible to then scrutinise this information in great detail. This process allows the police to look for **trends** in the data which they can then target.

Key terms

Intelligence is information about crimes and offenders that the police and other authorities can use to reduce crime.

Crime trends are increases or decreases in crime over a period of time.

Targeting of prolific and priority offenders

Police use surveillance, informants and intelligence to detect repeat criminals; this enables officers to target those offenders as a result of the intelligence gathered. Analysis of where and when crimes have occurred shows that a small number of offenders are responsible for a large number of crimes. Intelligence-led policing is an effective way of catching criminals in the act, or preventing a crime from happening. Intelligence-led policing became a more significant policing practice globally following the September 11 terrorist attacks in the United States.

Creating problem-solving policing initiatives

To help tackle crime and implement more effective crime reduction strategies, within the NIM crimes are

classified into three levels.

Level 1 – local crime and anti-social behaviour. Usually the crimes, criminals and other problems are affecting a basic command unit or small force area. The scope of the crimes can be wide ranging, from low value thefts to more serious crimes such as murder.

Level 2 – regional criminal activity usually requiring additional resources. This is usually the actions of a criminal or other specific problems affecting more than one basic command unit, neighbouring forces or a group of forces.

Level 3 – the most serious organised crime, usually operating on a national and international scale, requiring identification by proactive means and response primarily through targeting operations by dedicated units and a preventative response on a national basis.

By classifying crime in this way, forces are then able to look at level 1 crime locally to establish crime trends or problem areas that they can focus their attention on to deal with the problem. As already identified, target policing is about problem-orientated and intelligence-led policing, that is analysing and understanding the real crime or anti-social behaviour problem and its underlying causes, and then tackling it by effective, efficient and focused deployment of the resources needed. This type of targeted policing is not aimed at any particular type of crime. It is aimed at helping the police to develop and implement a problem-oriented approach to policing. Within this, there is also an opportunity to evaluate each programme, so that lessons can be learnt allowing local crime and disorder partnerships to benefit from the findings.

This police car is fitted with ANPR technology. This assists in the arrest of road and vehicle criminals but also assists in the detection of other crimes.

Activity: Cracking down on offenders with interception intelligence

In recent years there have been significant developments in the use of Automatic Number Plate Recognition (ANPR) technology within the policing environment. The technology provides police forces with the ability to do the following:

- capture images of vehicle registration plates
- analyse these images to resolve and recognise individual Vehicle Registration Marks (VRMs)
- compare the VRMs against a number of databases and hot lists, and as a result
- bring vehicles of interest to the attention of officers.

In summer 2002 the Home Office supplied each police force in England and Wales with a mobile ANPR facility. The aim of the strategy is to stop road criminals from driving by exploiting the full potential of ANPR, acting where appropriate in partnership with others.

In April 2005 work began with all 43 police forces in England and Wales, ensuring that ANPR intercept teams were put in place and effective strategies and structures were supporting their operations. By December 2005 all of the forces had implemented ANPR operations, with the British Transport Police implementing theirs early in 2006. The aim is to integrate ANPR into mainstream police business.

During an evaluation carried out on ANPR between April 2005 and March 2006, forces reported:

- 18,643 arrests
- 40,704 document offences
- 20,744 vehicle seizures

- 75,648 fixed penalty notices issued with a fine value of £4.2m
- 1,437 stolen vehicles recovered.

The seizure of vehicles contributes to the objectives of the Home Office and partner agencies. Research has shown that drivers without insurance are six times more likely to drive a non-roadworthy vehicle and up to nine times more likely to be involved in an accident.

Offenders caught through ANPR activity include an instance where Customs and Excise had put an information marker on a minibus regarding possible illegal immigrants. The vehicle was stopped and 11 persons were detained and handed over to the immigration service.

Between 1 April 2008 and 31 March 2009, North Yorkshire's ANPR Unit reported:

- £646,361 worth of stolen property, cash and drugs were recovered
- 225 arrests were made
- 817 people were reported for summons
- 474 fixed penalty notices were issued
- several hundred intelligence feeds were obtained.

These are examples of how using technology alongside intelligence-led policing can have good results.

Working in groups

Think about the use of ANPR technology. Do you think this is a good idea? Undertake some research into examples of this and other intelligence-led policing in your local area and share your findings with the rest of the group.

3.2 Safer communities and multi-agency partnerships

Crime has a very high cost and impact on society. Although fighting crime and dealing with crime once it has occurred is important, of equal importance is the emphasis given to actually preventing crime and reducing the number of offences committed in the community. Police alone cannot be responsible for fighting and preventing crime. Preventing and reducing crime requires much more widespread involvement and support. Increasingly, it has been the role of local crime reduction **initiatives**, which involves different agencies working together to deal with crime and social problems that affect a particular area.

Key term

Initiative means a new venture.

Crime reduction initiatives

Link

For more on anti-social behaviour and the Crime and Disorder Act 1998 see page 252.

The Crime and Disorder Act 1998 created 376 crime and disorder reduction partnerships in England and Wales. The idea was that these partnerships would develop a number of strategies that should reflect local needs and priorities. This means different partnerships around the country may be tackling different things. The partnerships are made up of many different organisations as shown in Figure 12.2.

Neighbourhood Watch – this is one of the biggest and most successful crime prevention schemes. It is based on simple ideas and values that are shared by many people around the country: *Getting together with your neighbours to reduce local crime and disorder in the bid to make your neighbourhood a safe*

Signage is used in local Neighbourhood Watch areas to deter criminal behaviour.

Figure 12.2 Partnerships fighting crime.

and better place to live, work and play. The aims of a Neighbourhood Watch scheme are to:

- cut crime and the opportunities for crime and anti-social behaviour
- provide reassurance to local residents and reduce the fear of crime and anti-social behaviour
- encourage neighbourliness and closer communities
- improve the quality of life for local residents and tenants.

It does this by:

- being a community-based organisation, involving residents and tenants who are working together
- working in partnership with the police, local authorities and other agencies to reduce crime and disorder
- sharing information and advice with the police and other agencies concerning crime and other incidents.

There are other community action teams that exist to support both communities and partnership initiatives. Their main aim is to be 'community led'. This means they will support the residence and service users in their local area. The teams are designed to work with other agencies and the community to take the lead in showing how services can be improved. They will then work in partnership with agencies to monitor, evaluate and develop service improvements.

More recently to assist the police in reducing crime, disorder and anti-social behaviour, Police Community Support Officers (PCSOs) and Community Wardens have been employed. Their main role is in response to public demand for more highly visible patrols. As part of Police Reform the government provided this additional service to better meet the demands of what communities expect and deserve.

PCSOs – employed directly by the police and compliment and support regular officers. Their primary purpose is to improve the community and offer greater public reassurance. They work with a number of partner organisations to address anti-social behaviour, the fear of crime, environmental issues and other factors which affect the quality of people's lives.

Activity: Community support in Broxtowe Borough Council

There are over 20 Community Action Teams (CATs) now meeting regularly throughout the Borough.

The meetings are open to all residents and offer a friendly environment in which to make suggestions about how to improve your area and raise any issues that concern you.

Community Action Teams were originally developed to address issues concerning crime and disorder in Broxtowe. This proved so successful that the meetings have been opened up to all residents as a forum to discuss any issues that affect the community. If you would like to raise an issue at a CAT you can have it put on the agenda by contacting your local Councillor in advance, or you can simply attend the meeting and raise your issue then.

Community Action Team meetings are chaired by local Councillors, and attended by Council officers, the police and representatives of other organisations and local groups. This means that local residents and representatives from these organisations can work together to make a real difference to issues that affect the area.

Working in pairs

Think about the work of the Community Action Team in Broxtowe. Do you think this is a good idea? Undertake some research into Community Action Teams in your local area and share your findings with the rest of the group.

Crime and Disorder Act 1998 discussed earlier in this chapter. This legislation meant that local authorities, police and other agencies should work in partnership to develop and implement strategies to reduce crime and disorder. The partnerships carry out an audit of crime and disorder every three years and publish a strategy for dealing with the problems found. The idea was that these strategies must reflect local needs and priorities, which means different partnerships around the country will be tackling different things.

Community safety partnerships – alongside the Crime and Disorder Act, Safer Community Initiatives were developed. These are more local initiatives that involve multi-agency partnerships intended to make areas safer and nicer places to live, by beating crime and tackling drugs. Police, local authorities and key partnerships work together to deliver more coordinated services. These initiatives focus on anti-social behaviour and associated violence and criminal damage.

Third sector organisations – other organisations also exist with the purpose of reducing crime, disorder and anti-social behaviour, such as **NACRO**. The aim of the charity is to set up practical services to help ex-offenders resettle in the community. They work with individuals at risk of getting involved in crime and with communities to help prevent crime. The charity was

PCSOs offer a visible and reassuring presence on the streets. How does the work of a PCSO differ from the role of a police officer?

Community wardens – these are similar to PCSOs but are employed by the local council. Their aim is to help the people within the local authority area to live safely and independently in their neighbourhoods and communities. They again provide a visible uniformed presence to tackle anti-social behaviour and are often a focal point for communities.

Crime and Disorder Reduction Partnerships – these partnerships were set up as a direct response to the

Key term

NACRO stands for National Association for the Care and Resettlement of Offenders.

Case study: Saneka finds help

'NACRO's Discuss Family Support Project helped get my mum into rehab for her drug problem. She was self-harming, cutting her arms and using heroin. There were loads of needles in the house, so it was upsetting. My Dad was not around, so it was up to me to do something.

I went to see one of the project workers about a year ago and mum had an interview. I didn't have to force her, she was glad to go, and now she's in rehab. It really helped because she's stopped self-harming – she's got a long way to go with her drugs problem but she's better than she was. I've got my own flat now but I see her and she has visits.

I knew of the NACRO project because I used to go to their girls' group when I was younger and we did things like sex education. It's different to school because there are no boys around and you can concentrate. It kept us off the streets – if we hadn't gone to the group we would have been hanging around on the streets drinking.'

Working in groups

The case study above explains one area of NACRO's work. Undertake further research into the work of NACRO (www.nacro.org.uk) and identify examples of at least two other areas of their work to share with the rest of your class.

originally established in 1996 but re-branded in 1999 to reflect its work. Around 50% of their work is supporting the resettlement of offenders, 45% concerned with crime prevention and 5% looking at criminal justice reform. The primary aims of NACRO are:

- resettling ex-offenders and prisoners
- education and employment
- housing
- mental health issues
- youth crime
- race issues and the criminal justice system.

Criminal justice agencies

There are a number of agencies that are designed to work together within the criminal justice system (CJS) to support its effectiveness to deal with crime efficiently and fairly. These agencies between them are to ensure the smooth running of the CJS for all members of society.

Police

The role of the police is vital within the CJS. They provide a great deal of support to the victim: they are usually first on the scene as well as the first agency to make contact with the victim. This initial contact is crucial in collecting enough evidence to pursue a suspect.

Within the police service there are specialist family units as well as officers trained to deal with many other aspects of crime, such as sexual crimes or crimes involving children. A family liaison officer is often appointed in the most serious cases so that there is a stable point of contact for the victim and their family. The police can also refer victims to other specialist agencies that exist to support victims of all types of crime. The police service spend large amounts of their time working on crime prevention strategies and a wide variety of campaigns designed to reduce specific crimes, such as drink driving.

Prison

Within England and Wales there are 138 prisons that look after in excess of 80,000 prisoners each year. The CJS uses imprisonment for the most serious offences and when no other punishment is appropriate. It is used to keep the public safe from those who have committed the crimes, as well as to punish the offenders. Prisons are categorised based on the level of risk to the public the offender poses if they were to escape.

- **Category A** – this is for the most dangerous prisoners who would pose a real threat to society if they escaped. These are maximum security prisons and house offenders who are guilty of the worst crimes such as murder, rape or terrorism.
- **Category B** – this is for prisoners who are dangerous but less so than those in category A. Security is tight.
- **Category C** – these prisons are for prisoners who cannot be left in the community but who will probably not try to escape.
- **Category D** – these prisons are for prisoners who can be reasonably trusted in open conditions; sometimes they are allowed out during the week to work, etc. They are a very low escape risk and they are not considered a danger to the public.

Courts

The courts system in England and Wales has a long history and is designed to deal with all areas of law, both **civil** and **criminal**.

> ## Key terms
>
> **Civil law** is the area of British law that is concerned with the private affairs of citizens, such as marriage and property ownership.
>
> **Criminal law** is the area of British law that deals with crimes and their punishment.

The structure of the courts system is complex. Figure 12.3 will help you to see how they link together.

This diagram shows the County Court deals with the majority of civil cases, as well as some family and bankruptcy hearings, whereas the Magistrates' Court deals with over 95 per cent of cases. Additionally magistrates' courts can deal with some civil cases, mostly family matters, liquor licensing, betting and gaming work. Cases in the magistrates' courts are usually heard by panels of three magistrates who are also known as Justices of the Peace.

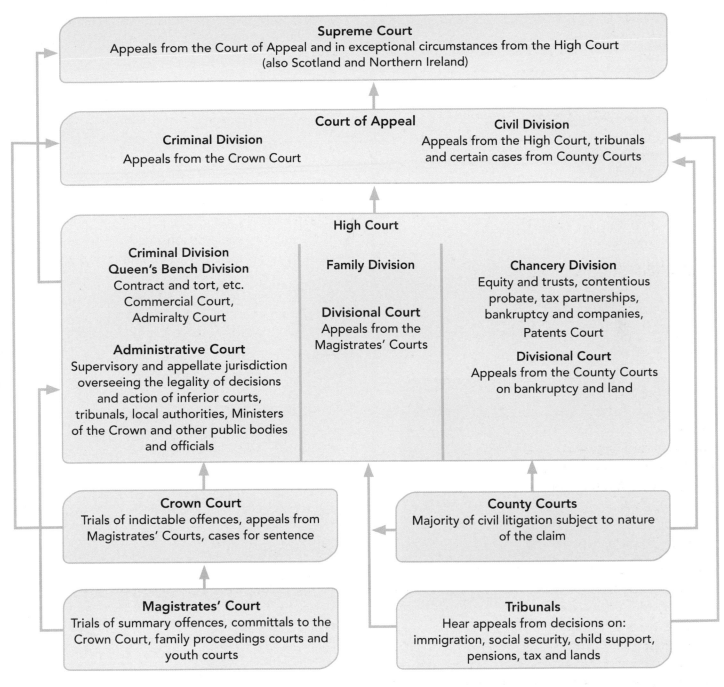

Figure 12.3: Relationship between the courts.

The Crown Court deals with major criminal cases; it also hears appeals against decisions made in the magistrates' courts and deals with cases sent from magistrates' courts for sentence. The next layer of court is the Court of Appeal; this is split into two sections, the criminal division and the civil division. The most senior court is the House of Lords; this is the upper house of Parliament and is also commonly referred to as 'the Lords'.

If a case cannot be appropriately dealt with nationally, it can be referred to the European courts. The

European Court of Human Rights is an international court based in Strasbourg which consists of a number of judges equal to the number of member states of the Council of Europe. The European Court sits to protect the human and fundamental rights of every citizen, and cases it deals with are referred from all over the world.

Crown Prosecution Service

The Crown Prosecution Service (CPS) is the Government Department responsible for prosecuting

Activity: The courts system

Working in groups

Undertake some group research to find out more information about the courts and produce a presentation to share with your colleagues on the following:

- Civil Court
- Magistrates' Court
- Crown Court
- Court of Appeal
- Supreme Court
- European Court

Your tutor will divide you into six groups to work on this activity.

criminal cases investigated by the police in England and Wales. It was set up in 1985 to take over from the police the job of prosecuting offenders. The CPS is responsible for:

1 giving advice to the police on cases for possible prosecution
2 reviewing cases submitted by the police to ensure there is enough evidence to prosecute
3 deciding the charges (if any) in all but minor cases
4 preparing the cases for court (making sure all the evidence is available and reliable)
5 presenting the case in the Magistrates' Court and instructing council in the Crown Court.

There are a number of advantages to an independent organisation taking charge of all the evidence that the police collect for an offence and then charging the person. It can reduce the workload of police officers, allowing them to hand over the files to the CPS and return to front-line duties. The prosecution of cases is seen to be more consistent and fair as the CPS is independent of the police. The decision made by the CPS as to whether to prosecute is based on two main 'tests':

- **evidence test** – is there enough? Is the case likely to succeed? If not the CPS is likely to discontinue with the case.
- **public interest test** – if it is decided there is enough evidence to pass the first test, they will then consider whether it is in the interest of the public to prosecute. There are a number of factors that have to be considered which are laid out in the document 'The Code for Crown Prosecutors'.

Activity: The Public Interest Test

Undertake some personal research to find out more information about the CPS code regarding the public interest test. Share your findings with the rest of your class.

Class discussion

Do we agree with the public interest test? Discuss …

Probation Service

The Probation Service is an organisation designed to supervise offenders. Of those supervised approximately 90% are male. Of these, 70% will be supervised on a community sentence and the remaining 30% imprisoned with a period of **statutory licence supervision** in the community as an integral part of the sentence. Working with offenders requires a combination of continuous assessment and expert supervision programmes designed to reduce re-offending and ensure enforcement of any conditions on the order or licence. Another important role of the Probation Service is assisting magistrates and judges with their sentencing decisions through the provision of pre-sentence reports and bail information reports. Other elements of their work include contributing to the decisions on early release of prisoners and running 100 approved probation hostels providing controlled environments for offenders on bail, community sentences and **post custody licences**.

Key terms

Statutory licence supervision is a legal document giving official permission for the probation service to supervise your movements.

Post custody licence is a legal document giving you official permission to leave custody under strict guidelines about re-offending.

Did you know?

Each year the probation service deals with about 175,000 offenders.

Youth Offending Teams

YOTs exist within every local authority in England and Wales. These teams are made up of public service colleagues from a wide range of services, including the police, probation, social, health, education, drugs and alcohol misuse, and housing. This is so that the team can draw upon a wealth of knowledge and experience across a wide range of services in order to support the young offender in the best way possible. For example, if a young offender has a drug problem, as part of their sentence they will be

Activity: Probation hostels

Probation hostels or approved premises provide structured, supervised, temporary accommodation for offenders who would in any case be living in the community. They play an important role in protecting the public.

Rules of residence are very strict and contribute to the smooth running of the hostel and to protecting the public. There are strong links with the local police service, and specialist police officers visit the premises almost on a daily basis. There is also extensive CCTV coverage at the hostels.

Probation hostel rules of residence include:

* a night-time curfew which is rigorously monitored; many residents, depending upon their risk factors, will have earlier curfews and extra times during the day when they must report back to the hostel
* room searches, to check offenders' rooms weekly at random
* a total ban on alcohol and solvents as well as illegal drugs; residents are tested for drug and alcohol misuse.

Offenders who do not comply will receive a warning and can be returned to prison or court.

Key workers undertake initial assessments with residents, and produce individual, structured programmes of work. They work with offenders to help them address their offending behaviour, recognise the impact of their offending on victims and members of the community, acquire basic skills to change their lifestyle, boost employment opportunities and address their accommodation needs.

Working in groups

Undertake some group research to find out more information about a probation hostel in your local area and produce a fact sheet to share with your colleagues.

required to undertake some kind of drug rehabilitation programme in order for them to be able to overcome their addiction which will in turn reduce the chances of the young person re-offending.

4. How the public services support victims and witnesses of crime

Crime can affect individuals in many different ways, as well as affecting whole communities, minority groups and businesses. The impact can be emotional. In the case of a house break-in, the **victim** might feel very upset that personal or valuable objects have been taken. The impact of crime may also be practical. In the case of a house break-in, there may have been forced entry where a window is broken and the victim of crime is left to replace the window. This may cause the victim inconvenience as well as having a financial impact.

Key terms

Victim is a person who has been targeted in a crime.

Witness is someone who saw what happened, i.e. was present when a crime occurred.

4.1 Victims of crime

All kinds of people can be vulnerable to crime for different reasons. In general terms, we can categorise the victims of crime as detailed below.

Businesses

This can be any kind of premises run as a business, such as a shop, pub, hotel, warehouse, factory or restaurant. Businesses can be victims of a wide variety of crime. Think about a small newsagent's shop. They could be the victims of a theft because a customer steals a bar of chocolate. An employee might steal cash from the till or steal some stock from the shop. They could also be victims because of vandalism or damage to the shop or the victim of fraud if someone uses a stolen credit card to pay for goods. Businesses can suffer from crimes such as burglary, damage to vehicles, structural damage (such as vandalism or arson), disruption to trade, loss of business, staff morale being affected and increased insurance costs.

Communities

In this context, a community can be a number of things: the nation as a whole, a town or city, a suburb or housing estate, a street or village, or a minority group

Activity: How is a business a victim of crime?

Working in pairs

Think about different types of businesses; some examples to help you are given below. Complete a table like the one below which explains some of the different ways that businesses can be victims of crime.

Type of business	How might they be a victim of crime
Restaurant	1 Customer may leave without paying bill 2 Employee may steal food or money 3 There could be a break in and the property vandalised and therefore unable to open (lost business)
Hotel	
Supermarket	
Small shop	
Warehouse	
Factory	

Share your findings with your classmates to see how many different ways you can identify that a business could be a victim of crime.

such as an ethnic or religious group. A community can even be your local scout group, community centre or local football team, who have had their equipment stolen or club house burgled.

A community cannot be a victim of crime in the same way that a business can. For example, if a business was to lose all of its stock, this would have a financial impact on the owners as they would be unable to open until the stock was replaced. This could lead to the business having to close down. A community may lose items but they are able to pull together as one to deal with the consequences much more easily.

All people can be vulnerable to crime but an elderly person can be more vulnerable to certain types of crime such as mugging or burglary.

If an area has been affected by a high rate of crime, it will have a negative impact on the area. A high crime rate may affect how an area looks – an area with higher levels of crime may look more neglected and run down. Home and car insurance may be higher in this area. If an area in neglected and run down, it will affect the price of property. This will in turn affect the type of people the area attracts to live there, the type and nature of businesses that it attracts, and the quality of life of the people in that area.

Minority groups

A minority group is a smaller group in society with less power or control over their lives than the majority. A

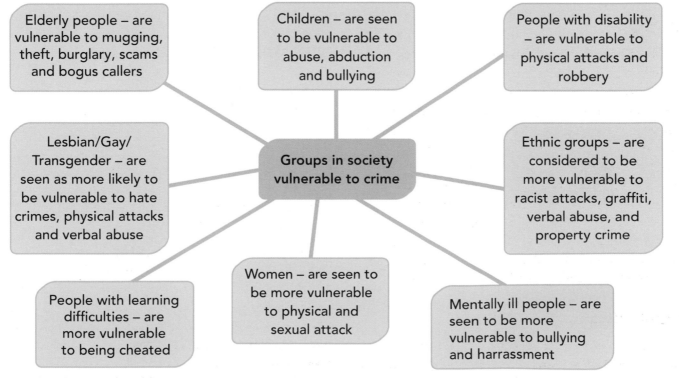

Figure 12.4: Groups vulnerable to crime.

Text within Figure 12.4:

Elderly people – are vulnerable to mugging, theft, burglary, scams and bogus callers

Children – are seen to be vulnerable to abuse, abduction and bullying

People with disability – are vulnerable to physical attacks and robbery

Lesbian/Gay/Transgender – are seen as more likely to be vulnerable to hate crimes, physical attacks and verbal abuse

Groups in society vulnerable to crime

Ethnic groups – are considered to be more vulnerable to racist attacks, graffiti, verbal abuse, and property crime

People with learning difficulties – are more vulnerable to being cheated

Women – are seen to be more vulnerable to physical and sexual attack

Mentally ill people – are seen to be more vulnerable to bullying and harrassment

minority group does not necessarily mean a smaller percentage of the population. It refers to groups such as people living with disabilities, religious minorities, ethnic groups, economic minorities (such as unemployed people) and people with different sexual preferences. For example, asylum seekers and migrant workers are a minority group and police have found that they can often be the targets of harassment, victimisation and violence.

Vulnerable members of the community

People are vulnerable for all sorts of different reasons. Vulnerable people can include: the elderly, children, the disabled, ethnic groups, women, lesbian/gay/transgender (see Figure 12.4).

As well as reasons linked to belonging to a vulnerable group, people can become vulnerable due to particular circumstances such as being harassed by an angry spouse or partner, being a drug addict, living in an area where there is violent rivalry between gangs, or working in a job that involves travelling through high-crime areas at night. An elderly person can be more vulnerable to certain types of crime such as mugging or burglary.

Individuals

All victims of crimes are individuals and many victims of crime do not belong to a vulnerable group. They may simply have something that someone wants to steal, or become the target of drunken violence. People can become victims of crime simply because they are in the wrong place at the wrong time.

Repeat victimisation can have devastating consequences on the victims; therefore it is important for all police forces to tackle this as part of their crime management strategies. This should be done by:

1 ensuring crime recording systems are accurately identifying repeat victims so this can be both measured and monitored

2 ensuring a prompt response to repeat victims

3 ensuring that appropriate resources are allocated to include a strategy of prevention and detection to reflect local victimisation patterns, which includes a graded response for repeat victims.

> **Key term**
>
> **Repeat victimisation** refers to a person being the victim of the same crime on more than one occasion.

4.2 The role of public services to assist and support victims of crime

Understanding how crime can impact people and society is very important in most public services. By understanding which members of society are most vulnerable, they can think about how to protect them from crime and how to offer support when they become victims of crime.

There are a large number of organisations both locally and nationally who exist to assist and support victims of crime. Some examples of these are listed below.

The Police Service

The police will respond to your call and investigate the crime as well as provide crime prevention advice. Their role is one of rescue, crime prevention, crime investigation, crime detection, referral to victim support, acting as a witness in court, and providing advice and guidance as well as reassurance.

Social services

They provide a number of invaluable services and support in many cases for older people and people with learning disabilities, physical disabilities or a mental illness. They also provide services for people with wider social problems, including alcohol, drugs and being affected by HIV. The support they give is designed to help people live as fulfilled lives as possible, helping them with care and support in their own homes, etc.

> **Link**
>
> For more information on the Probation Service see page 273.

Probation services

A probation officer may make assessments and recommendations to the courts about the risk posed by an individual offender. They manage and enforce community orders. Probation officers work with prisoners during and after their sentence to help with rehabilitation back into the community and to minimize re-offending. They work with offenders to change behaviours and reduce the risk of harm that they pose, and work to reduce the impact of crime on the victim.

Local authorities

Local authorities exist across the country and they are designed to supply a wide range of services for the area they cover and they can support you in many ways. The typical support available to victims and witnesses of crime from your local authority includes general advice on finances, such as benefits, or community safety schemes designed to benefit society and reduce crime.

Link

For more information on local authorities see Unit 1, page 8.

Education services

Despite first appearance, this sector has an important part to play in assisting and supporting crime. They are often leaders in carrying out research into things like 'repeat victimisation' and use their research to suggest ways to reduce crime levels.

Third sector organisations

Third sector organisations are not part of the government, the private sector or the public sector and do not aim to make a profit. They re-invest their surplus into social, environmental or cultural objectives. Examples of third sector organisations are given below.

Key term

Third sector organisations are non-governmental organisations such as voluntary and community organisations and charities.

Shelters for abused families – agencies like this are designed to help break the cycle of domestic violence by providing facilities that allow women (chiefly, but also men) the ability to make choices about their home life, and give families the opportunity and support to get out of abusive environments.

The Samaritans – victims often experience significant emotional trauma in the aftermath of a crime committed against them. They may develop feelings of anxiety, depression, etc. or more serious post-traumatic stress disorder. This is a voluntary organisation that operates a 24-hour service designed to help and support individuals who feel desperate or suicidal.

Help the Aged – This is an international charity that is designed to protect older people from poverty, isolation and neglect, including helping them if they have been victims of crime.

Did you know?

Help the Aged and Age Concern have plans to join forces and be known as Age UK. Look out for an announcement in the near future.

Survive – is run as a not-for-profit organisation. It is designed to help raise the awareness of rape, but in particular it provides a support network of counsellors who can assist victims with things like reporting the crime to the police, getting medical treatment and support, as well as talking through their ordeal with others in a safe, confidential environment.

Rape Crisis – This is a similar organisation to Survive. It is a registered charity to support the work of Rape Crisis Centres in England and Wales and works to raise the awareness of the issues surrounding sexual violence in the wider community. Rape Crisis acknowledges all forms of sexual violence so has a wider remit than Survive.

Agencies bound by code of support for victims of crime

There are a number of agencies bound by a set of rules to support victims of crime. Two examples are briefly described below, and a more detailed description is given later in this chapter.

Victim Support – this is a registered charity which focuses on helping victims of crime in terms of emotional support and practical tasks, such as helping with insurance or compensation claims. It receives support from the police who refer victims, and it receives funding from central government.

Witness Service – this ensures that the process of giving evidence in court is as comfortable an experience as possible. Established in 1989, it is managed and organised by its parent charity Victim Support. There is a witness service in every crown court in England and Wales which provides information on courtroom procedure for witnesses and helps and reassures them.

Link

We will look at the work of the Witness Service in more detail in this unit (page 279).

METROPOLITAN POLICE Working together for a safer London

LOCAL COMMUNITY
INFORMATION

ROBBERY ALERT – 'HUGGER MUGGERS'

Be vigilant, watch out for unsolicited approaches from people you do not know.

Be careful when engaging with strangers who wish to hug or dance with you.

Please help us by keeping your mobile phone and other valuables safe.

If you need emergency police assistance, call 999

Police warnings and public notices help reduce the fear of crime and warn the public to be vigilant.

Multi-agency cooperation and partnerships

Since the introduction of the Crime and Disorder Act of 1998 (which has been discussed in detail earlier, page 252), agencies that support victims of crime, as well as agencies that fight crime and deal with suspects, have been urged to work together to try to reduce crime as a whole.

Reducing the fear of crime

Public services have introduced a number of strategies:

- police and local government measures to counteract the exaggerated perceptions of the level of crime in an area with more visible policing on the street
- Community Action Trust groups to set up Neighbourhood Watch systems aimed at improving safety on public transport
- architectural improvements in community areas to remove places for muggers to hide, within multi-storey car parks, for instance
- ongoing crime and disorder initiatives to reduce crime and also reduce the fear of crime.

It is important, however, to remember that purely cosmetic measures to reduce the fear of crime won't work for long unless crime is really controlled.

Activity: Reducing the fear of crime

Working in pairs

Produce a mind map with as many ideas you can think of about what members of the public could do to help reduce the fear of crime. Share your findings and ask your teacher to draw up a list on the board.

4.3 Victim and witness support

As identified above, there are agencies that exist to support victims of crime throughout the court process and beyond. They are regulated by codes of practice that monitor how they support the victims and ensure certain standards are maintained.

Code of Practice for Victims of Crime

This piece of legislation comes directly from the Home Office and is designed to set out the service that a victim can expect to receive from the criminal justice system. There are a number of areas that are covered by these codes, such as:

- in the case of a bereavement the relatives are given a dedicated family liaison police officer

- there is flexibility to opt in and out of the services provided to ensure each victim receives the level of service they want

- being kept up to date about how the investigation of your crime is progressing, including timescales and being notified if people are arrested and sent to court as a result of the crime

- all victims are informed about the services offered by Victim Support, and offered their support

- giving accurate information about the Criminal Injuries Compensation Authority (CICA) to those who are eligible to claim under the scheme

- a more supportive and enhanced service in the cases of victims who are vulnerable or feel intimidated.

This legislation covers all criminal justice bodies, which includes all police forces in England and Wales as well as the Prison Service and the CICA. The government aim is to ensure that every victim and their relatives (including the relatives of those who have died) have access to information on all the support services available in their local area.

Witness Charter

This charter is designed to complement the code of practice discussed above. It sets out standards of service for all prosecution and defence witnesses. The idea behind this charter is to raise public confidence in the Criminal Justice System as well as supporting the needs of both victims and witnesses. The services provided by the charter include:

- minimising unnecessary attendance and waiting times in court

- an opportunity to visit the court building before the trial

- information about the process of investigation, a court case and key stages of the process

- emotional and practical support before, during and after the court case.

In extreme cases it becomes necessary for people to be taken into a victim or witness protection scheme. This is treated as a last measure, as it requires the people who are going into the scheme to change everything about themselves. This often includes leaving their homes, family, job, etc. and changing their name. Schemes such as these are only used if the life of those involved is in serious jeopardy as a result of their involvement in the court case. This is usually as a result of them being witness to a serious crime, when those guilty of that crime do not want the witness to give evidence in court.

Case Study: Helen discovers she's a witness

Helen has just turned 18. Her friends arranged a 'girls' night out' and after a few drinks they went on to a club. While at the club a couple of her friends had an argument. Helen tried to intervene and calm the situation down. One of her friends did not take kindly to her involvement and pushed her out of the way. She fell into a group of other girls. She tried to apologise but one of the girls was very drunk – she smashed a glass and hit Helen on the arm resulting in a serious cut.

The police and paramedics were called, Helen was taken to hospital and the girl responsible was arrested. As the police investigated the crime and took statements, it became clear that the girl responsible had been in trouble before and is in fact waiting to appear in court for a similar offence.

As the date of the court case approaches, Helen begins to worry about what will happen and how the case will turn out. She decides to have a chat with

you, her friend who works as a court attendant, to find out some more information. Help Helen to find out:

1 more information on the Code of Practice designed to support victims of crime

2 how the Witness Charter can support her when she attends court to give evidence.

Share your findings with the rest of your class.

Assessment activity 12.2

(P4) (P5) (P6) (M2) (M3) (D2) **:BTEC**

1 Using the activities completed as well as your independent research, produce an essay that describes and analyses the effects crime has on communities and the individual (P4) (M2)

2 Using what you have discussed in the case study of Saneka, the other activities you have completed and your own personal research, produce a factsheet that identifies approaches used by public services to reduce crime, disorder and anti-social behaviour. You should then extend your factsheet to ensure that it analyses the strategies used by the local community public services to reduce crime, disorder and anti-social behaviour (P5) (M3)

3 Using what you have discussed in the case study of Helen, the other activities you have completed and your own personal research, produce a report that outlines how public and third sector organisations support witnesses and victims of crime (P6)

4 Undertake some research on a specific public service initiative that has been ongoing in your local community. Use www.crimereduction.gov.uk to assist with this. You should also ask your tutor to invite a guest speaker from a local initiative who can then help you to evaluate the initiative and how it addressed crime and its impact on the community (D2)

Grading tips

To support your work it is important that you understand the verbs for each task:

(P4) Describe – give a clear description that includes all the relevant features. Think of it as 'painting a picture with words'.

(P5) Identify – point out (choose the right one) or give a list of the main elements.

(P6) Outline – write a clear description but not a detailed one.

(M2) (M3) Analyse – identify separate factors and say how they are related and how each one contributes to the topic.

(D2) Evaluate – review the information then bring it together to form conclusions. Give evidence for each of your views or statements.

PLTS

This assessment activity may be useful for practising your skills as a self-manager, when you describe the effects crime has on communities and the individual, as an independent enquirer when identifying approaches used by the public services to reduce crime, disorder and anti-social behaviour, as a team worker when you outline how public and third sector organisations support witnesses and victims of crime.

Functional skills

This assessment activity may also help you to develop your functional skills in ICT if you word process your report and include images or tables.

Liz Winn
Police Community Support Officer

I have worked as a PCSO for almost two years and I love my job! I joined because I wanted to make a difference to my local community. I am a very social person so I find going to work really enjoyable. I get to talk to lots of different people because the uniform is like a magnet! People come and talk to you about anything and everything but its nice to have the one-to-one contact with the public.

A typical day

At the start of a typical day, you attend a briefing with your team. One of the community response sergeants updates you on crime and disorder problems and you are given an area to patrol with a colleague or police officer.

The sergeant may task you to assist people who have contacted the police. You will have to record information accurately and concisely, completing paperwork for other officers or departments. This can include taking statements from members of the public and local businesses so your writing needs to be neat and legible, as others will depend on this information.

On a typical shift you may be tasked with patrolling a large retail area. This is certainly a job for someone who likes meeting people, as people approach you for all manner of things. You will assess each individual person you meet and decide on the appropriate response. You may have to use your first-aid training to assist an injured member of the public. You will use your radio to obtain further assistance, for example when dealing with a drunken man aggravating shoppers. When you are waiting for officers, you ensure you make notes in your personal notebook, in case you should be called to attend court.

The best thing about the job

I really enjoy crime prevention initiatives because you get to meet so many people and are able to give them lots of advice to help them feel safer in their communities. Part of my work is also to visit victims of crime to show our support as well as allowing them to put a face to a name that they can contact at any time. The public really appreciate this.

Think about it!

What are your thoughts on the typical work undertaken by a PCSO? Do you feel their work is of benefit to society?

A regular duty of a PCSO is taking statements from members of the community who have either been victims of a crime or a witness. This can free up regular officers to deal with other issues. Is this a good thing? Discuss your views for and against this.

Just checking

1   What is anti-social behaviour? What current legislation is there to deal with this? Explain at least two.

2   It is important to deal with different offenders in a different way; can you identify the main sentences and orders a criminal court can impose? I will give you a clue: Prison!

3   In the 'red corner' nature (your biology). In the 'blue corner' nurture (your upbringing). Which side do you think will win and why? What are the theories of criminal behaviour? What other casual factors should you consider?

4   Why am I scared to go out after dark? How and why has crime affected me in this way, explain?

5   Do the police and other agencies do enough to reduce crime, disorder and anti-social behaviour? Can you list and explain five examples of what these organisations do?

6   I have been a victim of crime and now I need to go to court to tell them what happened. What will happen? Will I be looked after? Will I come face to face with the person who committed the crime? What support can I expect to receive from third sector organisations and other agencies?

Assignment tips

- Get on the internet – the internet has a wealth of information on many key areas in this unit. When looking for current crime and disorder legislation see www.crimereduction.homeoffice.gov.uk.

- Use the library – your library will have access to daily newspapers as well as specialist magazines such as *Police Review*. There will also be a wide selection of books on psychology and sociology that you can use to describe theories of criminal behaviour.

- Think about the impact of crime on people that you know. Speak to your family; has anyone been a victim of crime? How did they feel? Are they more scared now?

- Watch the television! There is a wide and diverse range of programmes that can help you to identify approaches used by the public services to reduce crime and disorder.

- Ask your tutor to arrange a court visit if possible; this will help you understand the main sentences and orders they can impose. If this is not possible try to see if you can get a guest speaker in from the Probation Service.

- Speak to your local Victim Support – ask your tutor to see if they can arrange for someone to come and talk to you about the help they can give to both victims and witnesses.

13 Command and control in the uniformed public services

Command and control is the underlying principle by which all the uniformed public services operate; it is essential to the way they perform their tasks. It is vital that those responsible for command and control are trained and prepared, as well as being experienced in the necessary skills, since there are many situations that call for immediate and decisive action.

This unit will allow you to develop your knowledge of the command and control structure and the skills required to exercise command and control. You will see that all uniformed public services have a chain of command, with different levels of responsibility, which is identified by ranks or titles. You will be able to compare ranks and responsibilities within the uniformed public services and see the importance of wearing clearly visible badges of rank. You will also develop an appreciation of leadership and teamwork that contribute to command and control.

You will see how different situations are managed through command and control and how different services handle those situations, paying particular attention to a specific uniformed public service.

Finally, you will realise that command and control requires specific skills, which are acquired through training, practice and experience, though personal qualities are equally important. You will be able to put into practice and develop the skills you have learnt by participating in command task role-plays.

Learning outcomes

After completing this unit you should:

1. Know how the principles of rank, responsibility and the chain of command relate to the command structures of the uniformed public services
2. Understand the skills and personal qualities required for command and control
3. Understand how an individual can exercise command and control
4. Be able to demonstrate command and control skills through command task activities.

Assessment and grading criteria

This table shows you what you must do in order to achieve a **pass**, **merit** or **distinction** grade, and where you can find activities in this book to help you.

To achieve a **pass** grade the evidence must show that the learner is able to:	To achieve a **merit** grade the evidence must show that, in addition to the pass criteria, the learner is able to:	To achieve a **distinction** grade the evidence must show that, in addition to the pass and merit criteria, the learner is able to:
P1 identify the rank structure in two contrasting uniformed public services including responsibilities **Assessment activity 13.1 page 293**		
P2 describe the chain of command for one public service, including its uniform structure **Assessment activity 13.1 page 293**	**M1** analyse the importance and use of command and control within a uniformed public service **Assessment activity 13.1 page 293**	**D1** evaluate the importance and use of command and control within the uniformed public services **Assessment activity 13.1 page 293**
P3 explain the skills and personal qualities required for command and control **Assessment activity 13.2 page 303**	**M2** assess the skills required for given practical command and control scenarios and compare these to own performance **Assessment activity 13.2 page 303**	
P4 explain how an individual can exercise command and control **Assessment activity 13.3 page 312**		
P5 demonstrate with support the use of command and control skills in different situations **Assessment activity 13.4 page 316**	**M3** demonstrate practical command and control in different situations within uniformed public services **Assessment activity 13.4 page 316**	**D2** evaluate own performance in command and control situations, identifying areas for personal development **Assessment activity 13.4 page 316**

How you will be assessed

This unit will be assessed by an internal assignment that will be designed and marked by the staff at your centre. The assignment is designed to allow you to show your understanding of the learning outcomes for command and control. These relate to what you should be able to do after completing this unit. Your assessments might include some of the following:

- portfolios of evidence
- wall displays
- learning journals
- video diaries
- role-plays
- presentations
- leaflets
- reports.

Kesia works to develop her skills

This unit was very helpful for me because it taught me a lot about myself and has helped me to think a little more clearly about my future. I would like to join one of the uniformed services, probably the police, and now I have a better understanding of what's needed for promotion. I like to think I have some of the qualities required to be a leader but I need to work on some of them. At least I know now how to set targets and plan for the future, and even if I don't join the Police Service I can still use the techniques I have learnt to develop myself and reach my targets.

We often have visits from the uniformed services at our college, as well as going on trips with the army or to visit the Fire Service. Since doing this unit I've started to think more about the qualities and skills that the senior officers have, and I try to picture myself in their position, but I know it'll be a long time before I get to their standard. I enjoy teamwork and problem-solving activities but I'm not sure I could make some of the tough decisions that senior officers have to make. This is why I need to work on my skills so that I'll be better prepared. Studying this unit has helped me identify my strengths and weaknesses.

Over to you!

- What areas of command and control might you find interesting?
- Have you ever been involved with issues of rank and responsibility before?
- What are your opinions on the principle of the chain of command?
- What preparation could you do to get ready for your assessments?

1. How the principles of rank, responsibility and the chain of command relate to the command structures of the uniformed public services

Thinking about command and control

On 7 July 2005 London came to a standstill when three bombs exploded on three trains on the London Underground during the morning rush hour. The first bomb exploded at 8.50 a.m. and two more exploded within a minute of the first. A fourth bomb exploded on a bus almost an hour later. The explosions were believed to be the work of suicide bombers.

A total of 56 people, including four suspected terrorists, were killed and 700 people were injured. London's transport system was closed down for the day while the emergency services undertook the huge task of dealing with the incident.

This is an example of the implementation of command and control, without which the operation would not have been concluded as swiftly and successfully as it was.

Have you ever wondered how the uniformed public services organise themselves to control situations like this?

How do they know who is responsible for taking overall charge of the incident and how do they know who is responsible for which task?

Have you thought about the personal skills and qualities that make commanders effective in such situations?

Do you have the necessary skills and qualities to make quick and vital decisions?

This unit will help you to answer questions like this, as well as giving you a good insight into the command structures of different uniformed public services. Even if you do not apply for the uniformed public services you will acquire personal development and leadership techniques that could benefit you in any career.

1.1 Rank structures

Identifying which uniformed public services have a rank structure

Rank structure is the way in which the hierarchy of authority is arranged within an organisation. A rank is a position within the hierarchy, and the higher the rank or position, the greater the authority and responsibility. The uniformed public services include the emergency services (police, fire and ambulance) and the armed forces, which are comprised of the Royal Navy

(including the Royal Marines), Royal Air Force (RAF) and British Army. They all have rank structures to ensure that orders and instructions are followed, thus making the services efficient (see Table 13.1).

Link

You should note that the rank structure of the police service in the provinces is slightly different to that of the Metropolitan Police (see Unit 4, page 115).

Table 13.1: The rank structures of uniformed public services, with the highest ranks at the top of the table (please note that ranks across each row are not at a comparable level).

Army	Royal Air Force	Police	Fire
Field Marshall (honorary rank or wartime only)	Marshall of the RAF	Chief Constable	Brigade Manager
General	Air Chief Marshall	Deputy Chief Constable	Area Manager
Lieutenant General	Air Marshall	Assistant Chief Constable	Group Manager
Major General	Air Vice-Marshall	Chief Superintendent	Station Manager
Brigadier	Air Commodore	Superintendent	Watch Manager
Colonel	Group Captain	Chief Inspector	Crew Manager
Lieutenant Colonel	Wing Commander	Inspector	Firefighter
Major	Squadron Leader	Sergeant	
Captain	Flight Lieutenant	Police Constable	
Lieutenant/2nd Lieutenant	Flying Officer/Pilot Officer		
Warrant Officer Class 1	Warrant Officer		
Warrant Officer Class 2			
Staff Sergeant	Flight Sergeant/Chief Technician		
Sergeant	Sergeant		
Corporal	Corporal		
Lance Corporal	Leading Aircraftman/woman		
Private	Aircraftman/woman		

Badges of rank

"Badges of rank allow members of the public services to identify the rank of fellow-members."

It is important for you to realise that not all badges (or insignia) are badges of rank. For example, each regiment and corps within the British Army has its own badge (which is usually worn on a cap, beret or belt) but they are not badges of rank. Similarly, different police services throughout the country have different badges. Insignia for depicting rank are usually worn on epaulettes, sleeves or a shoulder slide (in the army), although they are also shown on the helmets of some uniformed services. The identifying insignia are often called role collar markings. Look at the rank badges for senior officers of the Police Service in Figure 13.1.

All of the public services have rank badges on their uniform so that they can be identified and individuals can recognise where they fit into the hierarchy; they know whether they are senior or subsidiary to a particular rank even if they do not know the person of rank.

Some of the rank badges of several of the uniformed public services are very similar. In many cases, it is only the colour of the epaulettes that distinguishes the badges of one service from another, although different services sometimes have the same colour epaulettes (for example, the police and the Royal Marines' dress uniform).

However, even though the rank badges of different services are similar, you should remember that they do not identify the same rank in different services. The armed forces are different from the emergency services, which are different from the Prison Service and HM Revenue and Customs. Any similarity in rank badges is merely coincidental, and you cannot identify someone as the same rank as another in a different service simply because they have similar rank badges. The only exception to this is the Royal Marines, which is the Royal Navy's infantry, yet it has the same rank insignia as that of the army.

Chief Constable   Deputy Chief Constable   Assistant Chief Constable   Chief Superintendent   Superintendent

Figure 13.1: Rank badges for senior officers in the Police Service. How do these compare with those of the other emergency services?

1.2 Responsibility

While the responsibilities of different uniformed public services vary, there are similarities. For example, in the emergency services, it is the primary responsibility of the police, fire and ambulance services to save lives, but each service has other responsibilities, especially when working together at major incidents (see Figure 13.2). Senior officers from the emergency services form incident command and control personnel.

Activity: Comparing rank insignia

Go to the website www.uniforminsignia.net where you will find rank badges for the Royal Marines, Royal Navy, RAF and British Army.

Look at the rank insignia of the Royal Marines and the army – the only difference is the colour of the epaulettes and the 'RM' up to and including the rank of lieutenant colonel. However, in combat dress, the insignia would be worn on a slide and the colour would be the same as for the army and more difficult to identify. This is to make it difficult for the enemy to target officers.

Now look at the army ranks of major, lieutenant colonel and field marshall and see which of the police ranks are very similar. Remember, though, that the responsibilities and job roles for each service are very different and so are the ranks. You do not have the rank of superintendent in the army, just as you do not have the rank of warrant officer in the Police Service.

Produce a brief report comparing the roles of three equivalent ranks in the army and the police.

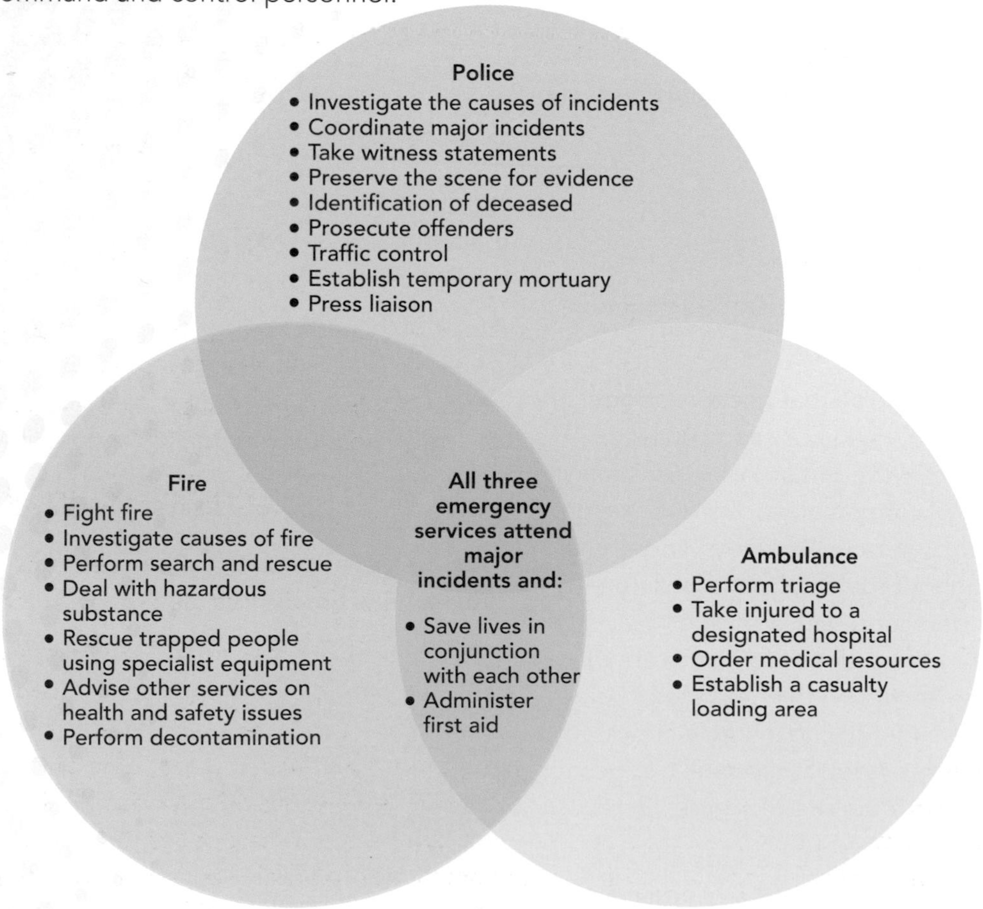

Police
- Investigate the causes of incidents
- Coordinate major incidents
- Take witness statements
- Preserve the scene for evidence
- Identification of deceased
- Prosecute offenders
- Traffic control
- Establish temporary mortuary
- Press liaison

Fire
- Fight fire
- Investigate causes of fire
- Perform search and rescue
- Deal with hazardous substance
- Rescue trapped people using specialist equipment
- Advise other services on health and safety issues
- Perform decontamination

All three emergency services attend major incidents and:
- Save lives in conjunction with each other
- Administer first aid

Ambulance
- Perform triage
- Take injured to a designated hospital
- Order medical resources
- Establish a casualty loading area

Figure 13.2: Each of the emergency services has its own responsibilities when they are working together at a major incident. Why is it important for them to work together?

Case study: The Kegworth Air Disaster

At 7.52 p.m. on 8 January 1989 a Boeing 737 was en route from London's Heathrow Airport to Belfast International Airport, carrying 126 people (including flight staff). It developed engine trouble as it climbed to over 28,000 feet. The captain closed down what he believed to be the faulty engine and, on the suggestion of British Midland Airways Operation, attempted an emergency landing at nearby East Midlands Airport.

Unfortunately, the captain shut down the remaining working engine and as it descended on approach to the runway, the aircraft was, in effect, gliding. With only a few hundred yards to the airport's runway, the aircraft crashed onto the M1, narrowly missing the village of Kegworth. On impact with the ground, the aircraft broke into three pieces; a total of 39 passengers died and 74 received serious injuries.

All the emergency services attended the scene and, before rescue operations could begin, the fire service sprayed the fuselage with foam to minimise the risk of fire from leaking fuel. The motorway was closed and remained so for a week while the wreckage of the aircraft was removed. The army and the RAF assisted in recovering and transporting the wreckage.

1   Which of the emergency services would you expect to be responsible for coordinating the Kegworth Air Disaster?

2   Which service would be responsible for having the dead identified?

3   Apart from transporting the injured to hospital, what else would the ambulance service be responsible for?

4   How would the wreckage of the plane be removed, and who would be responsible for arranging this?

5   Would the scene need to be examined by Scenes of Crime Officers (SOCO)?

Table 13.2 shows a breakdown of the ranks and responsibilities within the British Army.

In the Police Service, the Chief Constable is the ultimate commander and is assisted by a deputy chief constable and two or three assistant chief constables. Officers above the rank of chief superintendent are considered to be non-operational officers. This means that they are not involved in a hands-on approach to policing; they are strategic commanders whose main role is to implement service policy and plan strategies, such as how to meet Home Office targets. They also form the senior command when dealing with major incidents.

The Chief Superintendent is the commanding officer of a divisional police headquarters (sometimes referred to as district), which would contain somewhere in the region of 400 officers, depending on the size of the division. A chief superintendent would be expected to implement the force's policy regarding the safety of the community, maintain discipline over those under their command, and ensure the welfare and professional development of their staff.

Table 13.2: Ranks and responsibilities within the British Army.

General Officers (these are administrative commands and these officers would not normally lead soldiers into action)	
Rank	**Typical command**
Field Marshall	British Expeditionary Force
General	British Army
Lieutenant General	Corps (two divisions)
Major General	Division
Brigadier General	Brigade
Colonel	Usually an administrative command

Field Officers (these lead troops in the field of battle)	
Rank	**Typical command**
Lieutenant Colonel	Infantry or cavalry regiment or artillery brigade
Major	Company (four platoons)
Captain	Battalion's adjutant
Lieutenant	Infantry platoon (four sections)
2nd Lieutenant	Same as for Lieutenant

Other ranks in the British Army	
Rank	**Appointment or role**
Warrant Officer (1st Class)	Regimental Sergeant Major (in charge of discipline for a regiment)
Warrant Officer (2nd Class)	Company Sergeant Major (company discipline)
Colour/Staff Sergeant	Company Quartermaster (supplies and pay)
Sergeant	Platoon or troop administration
Corporal	Infantry/cavalry section commander
Lance Corporal	Infantry/cavalry 2nd in command
Private	A rifle-armed soldier

Relationship between posts and ranks

In the context of the uniformed public services, a post can mean an area where personnel perform their duty (for example, a posting to Iraq if you are in the army), or it can mean being assigned to a specific task (such as a weapons instructor). Some posts carry a lot of responsibility, and there is a relationship between the post and rank whereby seniority of rank does not always take command. For example, at a crime scene, a detective sergeant would take seniority over a higher ranking uniformed inspector, because the detective sergeant has had the necessary training to protect and examine crime scenes. Hence, the officer in charge of a crime scene is not necessarily the highest ranking officer at the scene. Similarly, the commander of a RAF aircraft is not necessarily the most senior rank on board.

1.3 Chain of command

The command structure

The uniformed public services consist of a collection of units that can join with others to form larger units or can operate independently within the command structure. Each unit has a leader or commander, and when units combine to form larger units, the larger unit has a higher commander. For example, an infantry regiment is a unit that can work alone or join with other regiments to form a brigade. The 7th Armoured Brigade, also known as the Desert Rats, is comprised of 12 regiments and supporting units.

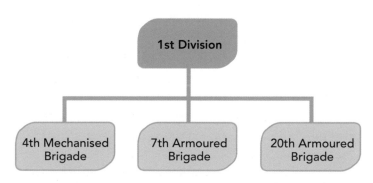

Figure 13.3: The army command structure. Are there any similarities between the army command structure and that of the fire service?

The army is organised into five divisions: two fighting divisions and three administrative support divisions. A fighting division is a complete, self-sufficient force consisting of soldiers, support staff, cooks, medics, clerks and a headquarters. It is traditionally comprised of three or four brigades, with each one containing approximately 5000 men (see Figure 13.3).

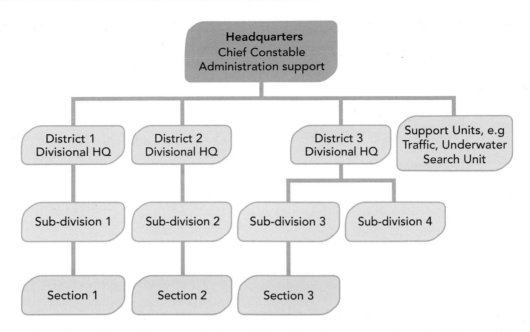

Figure 13.4: The organisation of a police headquarters, showing divisions/districts, support units, sub-divisions and sections. What is the difference between a division/district of the police service and a division of the army?

Did you know?

Battalions, regiments, brigades and divisions are links in the chain of command that operate within the command structure of the British Army. Each brigade is made up of regiments, which are a collection of battalions, each containing about 700 soldiers.

The command structure of the 43 police services throughout England and Wales is very different from that of the army, although they do have a chain of command. Like the army, our Police Services have divisions (or districts), but these usually refer to a city or town within the county for which the Police Service is responsible; and each division will have a police station. If, for example, a county has four towns within its boundary, then the Police Service will usually have four divisions or districts; that is, one division for each town, though a large city may well have two divisions.

Unlike the army, Police Services do not have a headquarters within each division, but they do have a divisional headquarters that provides administrative support for each division (see Figure 13.4). This is usually a separate building which contains administrative support and special services, such as the Criminal Records Office, Scenes of Crime Department, Fingerprint Department, Underwater Search Unit and so on, though some support units might be based in a central location other than at headquarters.

The outlying areas of the towns, especially the heavily populated areas, will also have police stations, although these will be smaller establishments than divisions and will be known as sub-divisions. Depending on the size of the Police Service area (in terms of geography and population) a division could have more than one sub-division. Sub-divisions can be further divided into sections, which are smaller police establishments (more like small offices than police stations) which serve the more rural areas. Section stations are not always staffed 24 hours a day, and they serve the smaller communities which, because of distance, could not practicably be served by sub-divisions or divisions.

Activity: Public service command structures

Carry out some research on the command structures of:
- the Royal Air Force
- the Royal Navy
- the Royal Marines
- HM Coastguard
- HM Revenue and Customs.

Produce an illustrated guide showing your findings.

Relative levels of control

Each unit of the uniformed public services, whether it is one of the armed services, emergency services or other uniformed services, has a commander. The rank of the commander will depend upon the size of the unit.

In the army, a general will be in command of a division, while a brigadier is in command of a brigade. A regiment is commanded by a colonel and the officer in charge of a battalion is a lieutenant colonel. In a battle group, some smaller units are used:

- company – a unit of about 100 soldiers and commanded by a major
- platoon – a unit of about 30 soldiers and commanded by a second lieutenant or lieutenant
- section – a unit of between 8 and 10 soldiers and commanded by a corporal.

In the Police Service (see page 291), a division is commanded by a chief superintendent with a sub-division commanded by a superintendent. A section station would normally be commanded by a police sergeant.

Government control of the public services

You have seen how the uniformed public services operate within a chain of command, but there is a higher authority to which they are accountable.

Ministry of Defence

All of our armed forces are controlled by the Ministry of Defence (MoD), which is a department of central government. The cabinet minister in charge of the MoD is the Secretary of State for Defence, who is the person ultimately responsible for making and carrying out the UK's defence policy. The Secretary of State for Defence is also the Chairman of the Defence Council which has three boards: the Admiralty Board, the Army Board and the Air Force Board.

To assist in the huge task of organising defence, the Secretary of State is supported by three junior ministers, one of whom is the Minister of State for the Armed Forces (see Figure 13.5).

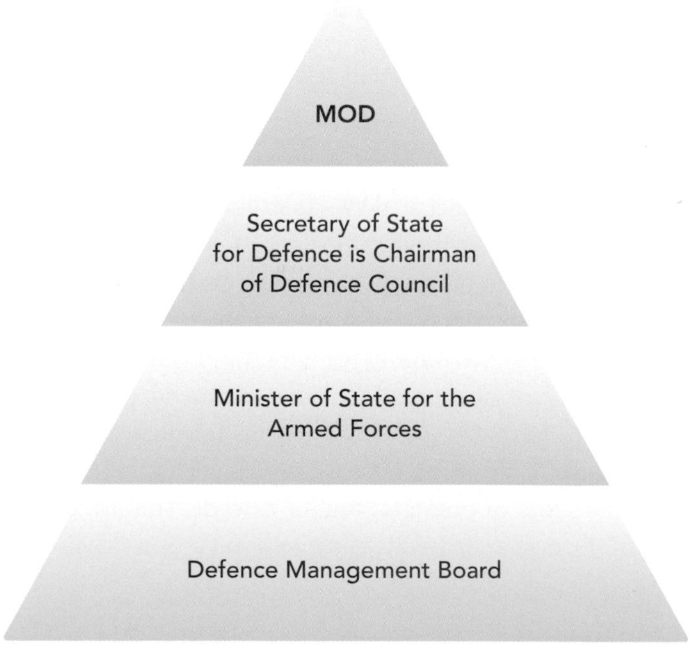

Activity: Names of units

Carry out some research, individually, and answer the following:

1. In the RAF, what is a squadron and who is in command of one?
2. In the RAF, what is a wing and who is in command of one?
3. How many divisions are there in the London Fire Brigade?
4. What is the rank of the officer in charge of a division in the London Fire Brigade?

Functional skills

Completion of this task will show that you have selected and used a variety of sources of information independently for a complex task, using your ICT functional skills.

MOD

Secretary of State for Defence is Chairman of Defence Council

Minister of State for the Armed Forces

Defence Management Board

Figure 13.5: The Secretary of State for Defence is supported by the Minister of State for the Armed Forces and the Defence Management Board. Do you agree that the armed forces should be accountable to a civilian authority, namely, the MoD? Explain.

Home Office

Just as it is the government's responsibility to defend the UK's interests at home and abroad, it is also their responsibility to provide us with a safe and secure environment in which to live and work. The government department in charge of ensuring our safety in the community is the Home Office, headed by the Home Secretary. The Home Office is responsible for providing us with an efficient Police Service and, prior to government restructuring in May 2007, was responsible for the Prison and Probation Service.

While it is chief police officers who are responsible for their individual services in terms of control, discipline and direction, it is the Home Office that funds and coordinates the 43 Police Services within England and Wales. Our Police Services are monitored by HM Inspectorate of Constabulary, which reports to the Home Secretary and makes recommendations for their increased efficiency.

Assessment activity 13.1

P1 P2 M1 D1 **BTEC**

Identifying rank structures is important so that individuals can recognise those in authority and know where they fit in to the organisation's hierarchy. It is also important for an effective chain of command that uniformed public service personnel know their place within the overall rank structure of a particular service.

Address the following tasks in the form of a presentation:

1 Identify the rank structure in two contrasting uniformed public services including responsibilities **P1**

2 Describe the chain of command for one public service, including its uniform structure **P2**

3 Analyse the importance and use of command and control within a uniformed public service **M1**

4 Evaluate the importance and use of command and control within the uniformed public services **D1**

Grading tips

P1 requires you to identify the rank structures of two contrasting services, e.g. the police and the army. You could do this by showing the different rank structures on either a handout or slide.

P2 requires you to describe the chain of command in one service, e.g. the Fire Service, and include the role played by non-uniformed personnel. This could be a government department or other authority.

M1 requires you to look in detail at the importance of the use of command and control in one uniformed public service.

D1 requires you to say what is positive and negative about the importance and use of command and control within the uniformed public services, followed by a balanced conclusion.

PLTS

This assessment activity may help you to develop your independent enquirer and creative thinking skills.

Functional skills

Completion of this assessment will show that you have the skills to develop, present and communicate information.

2. The skills and personal qualities required for command and control

'Command and control' is used by the uniformed public services to deal effectively with many situations. For example, a major incident, such as a plane crash, would require proper command and control in order for the emergency services to respond quickly and efficiently to deal with the incident. The armed forces also rely on command and control for successful military exercises, especially in a war or conflict situation.

Did you know?

Command and control is the term used when instructions are given to control or manage certain situations, or to achieve objectives.

2.1 Skills and qualities

Technical skills

We live in a very technical age, and the uniformed public services have access to some of the world's most advanced equipment, which helps enormously in a command and control operation.

Technology allows high ranking officers to make informed decisions and prepare battle strategies which, before the development of science and technology, were unavailable. For example, a naval captain and warfare officer can draw up a tactical strategy based on the information from an operations mechanic, who has tracked the position of enemy ships, aircraft and submarines on the ship's computers.

It is the responsibility of commanders to keep up to date with new technology and know how to use it effectively.

Specialist skills

As well as having good technical skills, specialist skills are often required in command and control for a variety of reasons. For example, in the Royal Marines, a landing craft officer must be skilled in seamanship, sea survival, navigation, boat handling, communication and management. In times of conflict these specialist skills could prove vital in safeguarding personnel.

Case study: High technology in the Navy

The Royal Navy has recently acquired three nuclear-powered attack submarines (to be named Astute, Artful and Ambush). The submarines will have on board newly-developed combat managing systems, which will receive and interpret data from sonar and sensors through advanced algorithms and data handling.

Propelled by nuclear power, each submarine will never need refuelling throughout its service history and will be capable of circumnavigating the world 40 times. The submarines are equipped with Tomahawk cruise missiles and Spearfish torpedoes, as well as having the latest in electronic counter-measure technology.

1 Would you expect the commander of such a submarine to be familiar with it just because he has technical skills?

2 The crew would also need technical skills, but do you think you have to have an interest in such advanced technology before you could become a vital crew member or would it just be a case of receiving some training?

3 What are the advantages of a nuclear-powered submarine?

In the RAF, a regiment officer who is responsible for defending a base must be skilled in military tactics, communications, signalling, weapons handling and deployment. Without these specialist skills, RAF bases would be vulnerable.

The armed forces have certain members who are trained in mountain leadership; they are able to navigate and lead groups safely through dangerous mountain regions, using specialist climbing and belaying equipment. Furthermore, the Special Air Services (SAS) are renowned for their success and professionalism because of the specialist skills they possess, such as communications, survival in extreme temperatures, explosives, negotiation skills and even foreign languages.

As well as having good technical skills, specialist skills are often required in command and control for a variety of reasons. It would be unreasonable to expect commanders to possess lots of specialist skills, but it is important that they can deal with a situation by calling on the people who do have the necessary skills.

Activity: Using specialist skills

Look at the following examples and say what specialist skills would be required to successfully resolve these situations:

- a hostage situation where the hostage-takers do not speak English
- a shopping complex evacuated because a suspect package has been found by a shop assistant.

Leadership qualities

Leaders are usually people who have been selected for the qualities they possess and for their ability to bring out the best in others (see Table 13.3).

Activity: Born to be a leader?

Consider which of the uniformed public services you would like to join. Research some jobs within that service and see if you can find reference to leadership skills.

- Do you think someone is born with leadership skills or do we all have the potential for leadership skills to be developed?
- How could you develop leadership skills?
- Do you have a favourite leader? Explain.

Functional skills

Completing this activity shows that you have selected and used different sources of information, practising your ICT functional skills.

Table 13.3: The personal qualities of leaders.

Personal quality	Description
Role model	Someone who is regarded by others as a good example for a particular role; this is someone who is admired and respected by others, and very often others measure their performance by comparing themselves to a role model
Courage	Someone who is brave and disregards fear in order to do their duty, even in the face of great adversity
Confidence	Someone who is self-assured and bold in their manner and execution of duty
Integrity	Someone who is honest, of sound judgement and morally upstanding
Determination	Someone who is firm and resolute in what they do, and who will overcome obstacles to succeed in a task
Decisiveness	Someone who can make a decision quickly and effectively without having to rely on or consult with others
Mental agility	Someone who has an active and quick mind with the ability to read situations and know exactly what is required to achieve a positive result

Qualities instilled by a good commander

Good commanders are well informed about people, especially those under their command – they know how people react to certain conditions and they know how to instil qualities in others.

Trust

If you trust someone, then you have a strong belief in their reliability; you can depend upon them without fear or hesitation. However, that trust has to be justified in the first place. You should remember that if a person holds the rank of a commander, that in itself is justification that they can be trusted; they will not ask lower ranks to do something that they have not done or are not capable of doing themselves. However, good commanders will not always take this for granted. They will give those under their command good reason to trust them, through words and deeds, and by displaying the qualities listed in Table 13.3.

Trust is a mutual thing, especially in the uniformed public services, and it is only because trust is reciprocated that command and control is successful.

Loyalty

In the context of the uniformed public services, to be loyal means to be faithful to your duty and to remain committed to your task. The very nature of the work of the uniformed public services means that there are many occasions when members of the services are under extreme pressure. For example, soldiers in Iraq have witnessed hostile resistance by insurgents when, no doubt, they would rather be at home with their families and friends. However, they remain committed to their duty and responsibilities because they have commanding officers who understand their feelings and, besides leading by example, make them realise the value of their work.

Discipline

Discipline in the uniformed public services is needed for many reasons but, in a command and control situation, it is especially necessary for maintaining order and for ensuring that rules and regulations are followed and orders are carried out. Without this assurance, there would be no command and control because the hierarchical structure would collapse, leading to chaos. A good commander has the skill of ensuring that discipline is maintained so that operations run smoothly and effectively.

Link

For more information on the need for and role of discipline see Unit 4 (page 118), and for leadership and teamwork skills see Unit 2 (page 57).

Morale

Morale is a state of mind that can affect the way you and the team, or even the service, work. Low morale can be unproductive and is one of the worst things for the uniformed public services, because it leads to poor team spirit and lack of motivation. It is part of the commander's role to maintain high morale to ensure that the lower ranks are effective in their tasks.

A good commander, because they have a good understanding of people, knows what causes low morale amongst lower ranks and will take steps to ensure high morale is maintained.

Remember!

It is particularly important to maintain order in a command and control situation.

Discipline is essential in a command and control situation. This ensures that operations run smoothly and orders are carried out.

Case study: Raising morale

Prior to the war with Iraq in 2003, the MoD conducted an attitude survey into the morale of British troops about to be deployed in Iraq. The survey revealed that more than a third (36 per cent) of the army's soldiers suffered from low morale. The survey of Royal Navy personnel showed that 27 per cent were dissatisfied with the conditions of their service and 22 per cent stated that their own morale was poor.

A politician said the cause of low morale was concern over jamming SA-80 rifles and ineffective personal equipment. They added that: 'The MoD has a great deal to do if we are to have the motivated and satisfied armed forces that we require, particularly in view of their current obligations.'

Low morale due to ineffective equipment might not matter so much if it were not reinforced by a wider problem. This was that many serving personnel felt that they were not fully supported by the public due to widespread doubt over the justification for the wars in Iraq and Afghanistan.

1   How would commanding and controlling the troops maintain control?

2   What problems would low morale cause in the situation just mentioned?

3   Imagine you are a platoon commander deployed in Afghanistan and your platoon is constantly under threat from violent attacks. Many soldiers in the platoon have not seen active service before and they have seen some of their friends seriously injured. How would you keep morale high?

Motivation

Lack of motivation, just like low morale, can be very damaging to the uniformed public services because it means that there is no interest in the job to be done. Even if the lack of motivation is experienced by an individual (and not the whole team), this can have an adverse effect on team spirit because not everyone is trying their best and a burden is placed on the remainder of the team.

A good commander will motivate individuals and teams to ensure they maintain an interest in their work, thus ensuring the smooth operation of that particular service.

Respect

Lack of respect for those of a higher rank in the uniformed public services can lead to low morale and lack of motivation that, for the reasons just given, can affect the smooth operation of a service. You may have heard the phrase 'respect has to be earned', which means that someone has to show that they are of a certain quality in order to gain the esteem of others. In the uniformed public services, promotion to a particular rank is given for that very reason – because the member of that service has shown qualities that are to be admired and which make them a leader.

You should remember that it is the rank that is respected, not necessarily the person who carries that rank. While it is natural not to want to respect someone you do not like, you must respect the authority of the rank.

2.2 Motivational strategies

Instigate and maintain command

By virtue of their higher rank, commanders in the uniformed public services have the authority to demand that lower ranks carry out their orders, and it could be said that as long as orders are carried out then the end justifies the means. That is to say that it does not matter how people feel as long as they do what they are told. However, this authoritarian style does nothing for individual or team morale; it can make members of the lower ranks feel as though they are not valued at all.

A good leader would not 'pull rank' in order to have their orders carried out, unless it was absolutely necessary. Instead, they would stimulate their colleagues into complying with the line of command by recognising and appreciating their individual talents and skills. By instigating command in this way, leaders enable others to feel valued while achieving their organisation's objectives. And if morale and motivation are high, then it is easier to maintain command.

Key term

Instigate means to bring about or make something happen by persuasion or urging someone to do something.

Inspire loyalty and obedience

Just as command can be maintained by an authoritarian style of discipline, both loyalty and obedience can be enforced in the same manner. However, a good leader does not force someone into being loyal and obedient by threatening punishment. A good leader is inspirational and makes others feel proud to belong to a particular service. Again, this raises morale and team spirit, and makes members of the lower ranks want to be loyal and obey orders.

However, to maintain morale and team spirit under adverse conditions requires skill on the part of the commander.

Did you know?

It is an offence to attack firefighters or to stop them doing their job under the Emergency Workers (Obstruction) Act 2006, which also covers National Health Service workers.

Case study: Attacks on firefighters

Attacks on fire crews have become commonplace in the UK over the last five or six years, and the problem has become worse. In April 2005 the media revealed that attacks on firefighters in Greater Manchester were being hugely under-reported, and government figures have shown that attacks on fire crews in England and Wales have risen from 1,300 in 2006 to 1,500 in 2007.

On one occasion, firefighters in Stockton were called out to what they believed to be a burning wheelie bin, but found a full gas canister concealed inside. In a separate incident, one firefighter received a broken elbow when he was attacked by a gang of youths.

Similar behaviour has occurred in Wales, with a number of attacks on firefighters reported in recent years.

The Fire Brigades Union (FBU) called for adequate funding to allow a national strategy to be implemented;

they asked that incidents involving violence or abuse be recorded more accurately and that training be provided to help deal with the associated problems. They also called for the government to assist fire brigades in educating the public.

1 How would you feel if you were a firefighter having to cope with such situations?

2 As a fire officer, how could you motivate your team and inspire loyalty?

3 There is no evidence that the firefighters retaliated to the attacks. Why do you think that is?

4 Would educating people about the dangers of interfering with the emergency services doing their job make it easier for the firefighters to carry out their work?

Case study: Safer Neighbourhood Team

A team of Police Constables and Community Support Officers make up the Safer Neighbourhood Team and work in an area where there is a lot of youth crime and antisocial behaviour. When they apprehended the youths responsible they gave them a caution, but this did not stop the trouble. The youths were then issued with anti-social behaviour orders (ASBOs) but nothing seems to have changed. Team morale is very low and the general feeling is that the police are fighting a losing battle.

1 If you were a commanding officer, how would you motivate your team and ensure loyalty?

2 If you were a member of the Police Service in the above example, would you expect your commander to be strict or sympathetic with you?

3 Would the behaviour of the youths make you wish you had joined another service?

2.3 Maintenance of authority

Need for authority

Authority is needed to ensure the smooth and efficient running of the uniformed public services. It gives certain ranks the right to make decisions and give orders, which should be carried out as directed by lower ranking personnel. If orders are not obeyed, then authority becomes undermined and the entire hierarchical structure could collapse. For

example, if a corporal in the infantry orders a private to clean his dirty weapon, then the private is obliged to comply with that order. If the private refuses to obey the order and the corporal has no means of enforcing it, then there would be no point in having the rank of corporal since the rank would carry no authority.

Practical consequences of orders not obeyed

There are many practical consequences of failing to obey orders. Orders are not given for fun or to flaunt authority – they are given for a reason. They could be given for health and safety reasons, where failing to obey could endanger a member of the uniformed services or members of the public. Orders are also given to ensure that the good name of the uniformed public services is not brought into disrepute.

Activity: Failure to obey an order

Imagine what would happen if you were in the Fire Service and you were ordered to check that the recently installed smoke alarms in a residential home were fully operational. However, you merely assumed that because they were fine when they were last inspected, they would still be in good working order. During the night a fire broke out in the home and, because there was no warning of smoke, the residents' lives were put at risk.

1 How would you feel if anyone died as a result of the fire?

2 What would it do for the name of the fire service when it transpired that the smoke alarms had not been properly inspected?

3 What would it do for team morale?

You should remember that all the uniformed public services have a purpose, and that purpose can only be fulfilled by having a hierarchy of authority whereby orders are given and carried out correctly. The practical consequences of not obeying orders are that the services' purposes cannot be fulfilled effectively and the hierarchy of authority will have little effect.

Course of action if orders not obeyed

Failing to carry out a lawful order amounts to misconduct, and any member of the uniformed public services who is reported for misconduct will have their case considered by a senior officer and may be called to a disciplinary hearing, which is usually presided over by a commanding officer. However, in a military hearing, known as a court martial, serious cases are presided over by a judge advocate.

Disciplinary hearings follow similar lines to that of a court hearing and the person accused can have legal representation if they so require. If the case is proven, then a range of punishments can be administered, including: a caution, a fine, reduction in rank, reduction in pay, dismissal from the service or, in armed forces cases, imprisonment.

2.4 Credibility as a commander

Be fair

All good commanders should have, and be able to demonstrate, a sense of fairness, either when commanding situations or when dealing with the welfare or discipline of colleagues. It is essential for the integrity of a commanding officer, as well as the morale and trust of the lower ranks, that they are seen to be fair. However, you should recognise that to be fair does not necessarily mean that everyone should be treated in the same way – to do so would could mean that no consideration has been given for individual circumstances.

Do not favour individuals

Good commanders do not have favourite individuals; everyone should be given the same consideration, regardless of gender, religion, colour or creed. If a commander were to show favouritism, this would undermine their integrity as well as the morale and trust of the team.

In the uniformed public services, promotion comes from merit, loyalty and devotion to duty, amongst other things; it is not simply given to someone who is a favourite of the commanding officer.

Activity: Consequences of favouritism

Explain how favouring individuals could lead to:
- resentment (of the individual who is being favoured and of the commanding officer)
- lack of motivation
- low morale
- low productivity.

Case studies: A sense of fairness

Firefighters Jordan and Greenslade were both ten minutes late for the start of their shift. Firefighter Jordan had overslept, whereas firefighter Greenslade was delayed because she assisted with a road traffic accident and did not have access to her mobile phone.

Should the watch manager treat them both in the same way in terms of disciplinary proceedings? Explain.

Private Muscroft's application for 48-hour leave was turned down by the company sergeant major (CSM), even though he knew how much Muscroft wanted to watch his favourite football team playing in a cup competition. Private Mumby's application was also turned down so he could not go and visit his newborn son. The CSM told him: 'I refused Muscroft so, to be fair, I have to refuse you.'

Was the CSM being fair? Explain.

Police Constable Waring was a very bright woman with a flair for detecting crime and, after just two years in the service, her application to join the Criminal Investigation Department (CID) was accepted on the recommendation of her inspector. However, Police Constable Burton, who had five years' service and showed an aptitude for criminal investigation, had applied to the CID six months ago and on this occasion had his application rejected. The reason why Police Constable Burton was not successful was because his inspector had stated in the reference, quite truthfully, that Burton had taken more than average sick leave in the last 12 months. The constable pointed out that the sick leave was because of various sports injuries he had received while playing rugby for the Police Service.

Was the inspector who gave the reference being fair? Explain.

Know the strengths and weaknesses of direct reports and managers

A good commander makes the time to get to know the people they command, including those who report directly and those who manage others on the orders of the commander. Only by doing this can a leader command effectively, because by knowing the strengths and weaknesses of lower ranks, the leader can form a strategy that takes these into account. Furthermore, the commander will know who is best suited to execute the plan.

Understand the group's role or function

It seems quite obvious to say that a commander should understand the group's role or function, but this is not simply a case of understanding what the group has to achieve.

> **Remember!**
>
> What you may regard as weaknesses could, in some situations, be seen as strengths, and vice versa – it depends on the task.

It is important for the commander to understand the task or function of the group because, with their knowledge of the individual group members, they will know if it can be achieved without further resources and in the time that has been allocated. In deciding this, the commander must consider if the group has the mental, physical and technical capability to perform the task, as well as considering the impact of the task on the welfare and morale of the group.

Activity: Choosing your team

Look at the following scenarios and select from the grids one person who you would like to be in the team under your command. Give reasons for your answers.

1   You are an army lieutenant serving in a country where law and order has broken down. You command a platoon from which you need to select a team to rescue a colleague who is being held in a makeshift prison ten miles away. The prison is guarded by six members of a local militia, who are armed with rifles.

Rank	Strength or weakness
Private	Extremely courageous and expert rifleman but does not work well as part of a team
Corporal	Likes to be one of the boys and gets on well with privates but not very assertive
Private	Good team player but soon loses interest if things aren't going as planned
Corporal	Renowned for disciplining privates who do not obey promptly but has the respect of the section

2   You are a chief inspector in the police service and you need a team of police officers to carry out a fingertip search of a playing field and hedgerows for a button that is vital evidence.

Rank	Strength or weakness
Police Constable	Desperately wants promotion and is very capable but likes to take all the glory; once received a commendation for an act of bravery when he rescued a child from a burning car with no thought for himself
Police Sergeant	Ready for retiring and still dedicated but would sooner work inside; however, if called to do something he is very dependable
Police Constable	Still on probation but can follow orders to the letter without distraction; she does not get on well with some female team members
Police Sergeant	A newly promoted female sergeant who is destined for a high rank; knows all the rules and regulations but lacks people skills, especially with colleagues

Furthermore, the group's function may be a small part of a larger plan, and while it is important for the commander to know the group's role, it is equally important for them to know how that role contributes to the overall plan. It is only by understanding the role or function of the group, as well as the individual characteristics of the members, that the commander can match the roles to the individual members best suited to them. Without these considerations, the group, and the commander, could fail.

Demonstrate confidence

Commanders are only human and have feelings like anyone else, but they must demonstrate confidence for the good of morale, team spirit and to maintain the team's trust and belief. One of the qualities that good commanders possess is to think and make decisions quickly, even though they may have had no time to plan; it could be that something has happened unexpectedly. It is the confident manner in which commanders conduct themselves, both verbally and non-verbally, that instils confidence in the team and enables them to take the right course of action at the right time.

Ensure information is shared and orders disseminated

In a command and control situation, it is important for commanders to share information with the team so that everyone knows exactly what is happening and is aware of any progress. This gives the team a sense of purpose, especially when they are becoming tired; news that their efforts are having a positive effective on the organisation's overall objectives can be motivating. It would be bad for morale if a commander continued to make demands of a team without keeping them informed of developments – they would have no idea whether or not they were working in vain. However, the commander must decide which information is relevant, what the team needs to know and at what point they should be told – information overload could have a negative effect on the team's performance.

While the commander may be selective in the information they share with the team, they must ensure that all orders are passed on promptly and accurately. This is especially important when a leader is commanding a team or unit as part of a higher or strategic command involving lots of units. The success of the operation is wholly dependent upon every unit following orders from senior command promptly.

Case study: The sinking of the *Sir Galahad*

On 8 June 1982, during the Falklands conflict, two naval vessels, *Sir Galahad* and *Sir Tristram*, were anchored off Fitzroy in the Falkland Islands. They were unloading equipment, ammunition and military personnel so that an advance could be made on the occupied eastern side of the island. However, before the personnel and supplies could be unloaded, both ships were attacked and bombed by Argentine Air Force A-4 Skyhawks.

Both ships caught fire and were engulfed in flames and thick, choking smoke, with *Sir Galahad* sustaining the most damage, which resulted in the ship being abandoned.

A total of 50 personnel, mainly Welsh Guards, were killed or missing, and this might have been worse had it not been for the helicopters and boats that had been unloading the ships but which quickly turned their efforts to rescuing and treating survivors.

It is very difficult for anyone to imagine the horrendous experience of that event, but even in all the confusion a rescue operation still had to be attempted and it needed coordinating.

1 Besides the agencies just mentioned, can you think of three more that might be required to respond to an emergency incident?

2 From a survivor's point of view, what might have been most reassuring during those terrible moments?

3 From a rescuer's point of view, what would have been most important about the coordination of the rescue operation?

4 From the point of view of the officer who was commanding and controlling the operation, what would have been one of the most important aspects?

Activity: Personal skills inventory

Carry out an inventory of your own skills and check it with your peers to see if they agree with you. You could list the skills in a table like the one shown below (but make it larger so you can include more skills and qualities). Ask your peers to use a scale as shown, to show how much they agree with your own assessment of your skills.

I believe I have the following skills and qualities	Rate your agreement from 1 to 5 where 1 is 'strongly agree' and 5 is 'strongly disagree'				
Communications					
Assertiveness					
Strength of character					
Creativity					
Fairness					
I can instil trust					
I can instil loyalty					
I can boost morale					
I can instil respect					
I can motivate					
Courage					
Decisiveness					
Mental agility					
Determination					
I am a good role model					
I can instil discipline					

Assessment activity 13.2

P3 **M2** **BTEC**

In any of the uniformed public services, command and control is essential for the efficiency of that service. However, to be in a position to ensure proper command and control, a leader must possess certain skills and qualities.

In the form of a report, address the following tasks:

1 Explain the skills and personal qualities required for command and control **P3**

2 Assess the skills required for given practical command and control scenarios and compare these to own performance **M2**

Grading tips

P3 requires you to look at the personal skills and qualities that have been covered in this unit, and explain why each one is important.

M2 is an extension of **P3** where you should explain those skills and qualities in more detail, and compare them to your own skills and qualities.

Functional skills

Successful completion of this task may show that you can write documents, including extended writing pieces, communicating information, ideas and opinions, effectively and persuasively and develop your functional skills in English.

PLTS

In completing this task you will be practising your independent enquirer and creative thinker skills.

3. How an individual can exercise command and control

3.1 Sequence of events

In the uniformed public services, there are several occasions when command and control need to be established. While it is generally assumed that the senior officer takes command of a situation, this does not necessarily mean they take control of everything. For example, the first police officer to respond to a crime scene, regardless of rank, would be in control of the scene and responsible for preserving it until it could be forensically examined and until supervisory officers arrived.

In the uniformed public services, individuals are able to exercise command and control by virtue of rank and status within the hierarchy of a particular service. Command and control scenarios are widely practised so that the services know how to respond efficiently during a real situation.

A good example of a command and control situation is where there is a major incident on land. It is usually the police who have overall control in these situations and who are responsible for coordinating all the emergency services and other organisations. However, there is a lot of individual control and command which combines to form a chain of command. The case study below is a fictitious scenario but it will illustrate how command and control can involve several organisations and individuals.

Who is responsible for assuming control and how they would do it

As we have already established, it is universally accepted that the police have overall command in such incidents, and this is outlined in the Emergency Procedures Manual published by the Association of Chief Police Officers. However, in a fire situation or situation involving hazardous materials or unstable structures, the Fire Service are specialists and would, therefore, have control.

The first member of the uniformed public services to attend an incident is usually a police officer who then, regardless of rank, assumes the role of initial police incident officer. He or she assesses the situation, contacts their control room and a major incident is declared, drawing a coordinated response from all of the emergency services. The initial police incident officer will then protect the scene, unless conditions dictate otherwise, and will remain with their supervisor to maintain continuity of procedures and to act as staff officer.

In the scenario described above, the immediate area would be cordoned off by the police in order to establish control of it, ensuring there is access to and from the area for rescue work to be carried out. Command vehicles would be brought to the scene and sited in a safe location on the advice of the Fire Service.

Case study: Dealing with disaster

During the early hours a commercial airliner has crash landed in fields, four miles from an industrial town in northern England. Just before it landed and broke up, the airliner demolished a chemical processing plant causing toxic fumes to be released into the atmosphere. Debris from the airliner seems to be confined to 200 metres of open land and there are several small fires where aviation fuel has ignited on impact with the chemical plant. Power lines serving the local town have been brought down and it is feared that local drinking water supplies may be contaminated.

The airliner's fuselage is broken in half, and while it is believed that several of the 200 passengers could not possibly have survived the landing, there is a strong chance that many are still alive and require urgent medical attention.

It is not known at this stage what long-term effects the chemicals could have on humans, animals and the environment but it is known that they cause respiratory problems and skin irritation, as well as mineral damage to soil.

1 If you were the first member of the uniformed public services to arrive at the scene, apart from radioing for help, what would be your initial actions?

2 What sort of information would you communicate to your control room to ensure the right response was activated?

3 Once you had called for assistance, would it be wise to attempt a rescue by yourself? Explain.

The Chief of Police for the area, in liaison with chiefs of other services and organisations, would act as incident coordinator from strategic headquarters, away from the immediate area. They would formulate a plan of how best to deal with the incident.

At the scene, a Fire Service officer could decide that the incident is likely to escalate and, therefore, an outer cordon is required to secure the site. The incident coordinator, in conjunction with the Fire Service, would decide who should enter the inner cordon together with authorisation identification, as well as the safe routes for entering and exiting the cordon. All personnel entering the inner cordon must be briefed about hazards, an evacuation signal, control measures and other issues relevant to the incident. It is important, therefore, to designate a member of the uniformed public services to record all personnel entering and leaving the inner cordon. The officer in charge of this task, regardless of rank, has the authority to admit or refuse personnel into the inner cordon.

Where it is known that people have died, it is essential to inform Her Majesty's Coroner before the bodies are removed from the scene. The bodies require formal identification and documentation and this is carried out by the police – usually a police constable – who act as agents on behalf of the coroner and are known as coroner's officers. Depending on the size of the incident, there could be more than one coroner's officer – they have the authority to ensure that bodies are not disturbed or moved unnecessarily. Hence, coroner's officers can control members of the uniformed services of a higher rank when it comes to dealing with fatalities.

Remember!

In a major incident on land the Police Service have overall control in coordinating the emergency services.

3.2 Comparison of the methods used by the services

The emergency services use similar methods of command and control, especially where a large incident calls for a combined response. The initial command and control of each service is initiated by the first vehicle to attend at the scene. The police would use the first police vehicle until a specially designed command and control vehicle was brought in as the incident developed; this would form the incident control post and be located with other command and control vehicles.

The Fire Service forward control vehicle would be the first fire tender to arrive at the scene, and this would be identified with a red flashing beacon. As more resources arrived, this would be replaced with a command support unit, which would serve as the formal command support point.

The Ambulance Service uses specially equipped communications vehicles, identified by a green flashing beacon. This provides the focal point for all ambulance, medical and voluntary personnel. St John Ambulance personnel volunteer their services at major incidents and are coordinated by the ambulance service.

Activity: Coordinating an incident

1 In the case of a major incident involving hazardous chemicals, why would it be dangerous to allow rescue workers to go into the inner cordon without personal protective equipment?

2 If you were coordinating the incident, would you take any precautionary measures regarding the toxic chemicals before you allowed any rescue work to commence? If so, what would they be?

3 Why is it necessary to keep a register of all those who enter and leave the inner cordon?

All the control vehicles for each of the services are parked together and are recognisable by the fact that they are the only vehicles displaying flashing lights.

A chain of command is established by dividing the incident into sectors or levels of command (see Figure 13.6). Each of the emergency services appoints a sector commander who operates in that sector with a team of personnel from their service. Hence, there will be three sector commanders and at least three teams of emergency service personnel. The sectors are known as:

- strategic (also known as gold)
- tactical (also known as silver)
- operational (also known as bronze).

The armed forces use a different type of command and control, especially during a huge military operation such as war. It very much depends upon the type of war as to who will command the armed forces. This means that if

the conflict is mainly a land-based operation then the army will take control, but if the conflict is mainly a sea battle then the Royal Navy would be in command.

The Falklands War of 1982 was commanded and controlled by the Admiral of the Fleet, who was situated in Whitehall. He was assisted by other commanders located outside London. Overall control was taken by the Royal Navy, not because the operation was a naval one, but because the war mainly involved a conflict at sea. Over 30,000 armed forces personnel were engaged in the conflict, including a large proportion of the Royal Navy, five army battalions and RAF squadrons. Operational command was carried out by the commanders at the scene, under the control of the commanders in the UK.

However, as stated, where the conflict is predominantly a land battle, the commander of the operation would

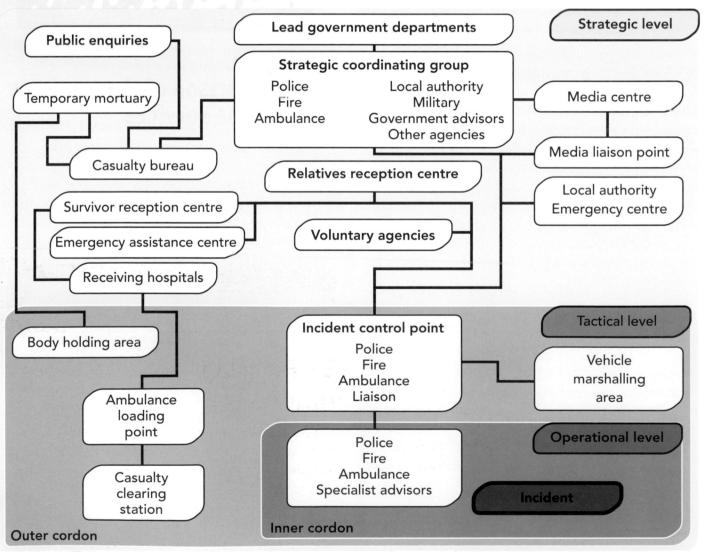

Figure 13.6: The gold, silver and bronze levels of command and control are not hierarchical but signify functions.

be an army officer, as in the Gulf conflict. In the case of the conflict in Iraq, strategic command is controlled away from the conflict zone by several commanders who form the Multinational Force – Iraq, while tactical command is headed by a US army general.

3.3 Levels of command and control

It is important to understand that while the term 'levels of command and control' seems to imply a hierarchy of command, the following levels of strategic, tactical and operational command do not represent seniority, they signify functions. The senior officers in charge of each level could all have the same rank.

Strategic command

A strategic commander is involved in formulating plans or strategies in order to decide on the best way to achieve an organisation's objectives. The strategies could include such things as planning for war, combating terrorism, reducing crime or dealing with a major incident.

Strategic command usually involves several chiefs of different uniformed public services because some plans affect more than one service. For example, the conflict in Iraq would have taken meticulous planning and meant months of collaboration with senior officers from the British Army, Royal Navy and RAF, since the conflict entailed a combined response from our armed forces.

Strategic command in a major incident would involve the heads of the emergency services formulating a plan of how best to deal with the incident. This level of command is also known as 'gold command' by the police and ambulance services.

Strategic command headquarters are normally established away from the incident, or spread over one or two locations. For example, during a major incident, strategic command might be located at a local police headquarters or local authority council offices, or both. Strategic command for the armed forces would normally be established in London.

Tactical command

A tactical commander is involved in implementing the plan formulated by strategic command. There

may be several tactical commanders, especially where there is more than one service. Tactical commanders are responsible for ensuring that members of their service are aware of the strategy and how to put it into operation. Tactical command is not involved in direct hands-on operations; that is to say, they are not involved directly at the scene of an incident. Theirs is more of a planning and coordinating role, and in a conflict situation it is important that tactical commanders should remain detached and not allow themselves to become personally involved. They would be located away from the front line because it is their job to support and liaise with strategic command on any issues or changes that may develop and to ensure these are carried out.

In a major incident situation, tactical command is also known by the Police and Ambulance Services as 'silver command' and serves the same function outlined above.

Operational command

In a conflict situation, this would be the front line where operational commanders would deploy and control the resources of their respective services, implementing the tactics relayed to them by their tactical commander, and thus following the plan set by strategic command.

In a major incident situation, this is known as 'bronze command' by the police and ambulance services. It is the area within the inner cordon where rescue work is being carried out or measures are being taken to prevent the incident from escalating.

> **Link**
>
> See Unit 2 (page 40) for more on leadership.

3.4 Planning
Clear objectives

Successful strategies are formulated by individuals who have clear objectives that can be realistically achieved in a given time. This does not necessarily mean that they have to be leaders of organisations; individuals can formulate strategies for a variety of reasons, including personal development. One of the most popular models for formulating successful plans has the mnemonic (an aid to memory) SMART.

SMART objectives are:

- **Specific** – objectives must be specific and clearly set out. Vague objectives are difficult to follow and could be ambiguous. For example, a specific objective in your plan could be to pass the promotion exam.

- **Measurable** – objectives must be measurable so that you can gauge the progress of your plan and see how far you have travelled towards achieving it. If you cannot measure progress, then you have no way of knowing if you are heading in the right or wrong direction. For example, you could measure your progress by passing the promotion exam.

- **Achievable** – objectives must be achievable otherwise there would be little point in setting them as goals. When something is achievable it means it is capable of being accomplished or reached, even though it might involve lots of hard work and dedication. Something that is achievable can motivate a person to strive towards it, whereas if something is impossible or impracticable to achieve then there could be no motivation.

- **Realistic** – objectives must be realistic, which means you must be reasonable in what you want to achieve. If you set your targets too high they might not be realistic and you will lose heart when you cannot achieve them. Would it be realistic for you to have passing the promotion exam as one of your targets?

- **Time-related** – objectives must be achievable over a certain period of time. You cannot measure success if there is no time limit on your objectives. You could set a realistic target to pass your promotion exam within two years.

Activity: SMART

Devise a SMART plan for the course you are doing at the moment.

1 What would be your specific objective?
2 How would you measure it?
3 Is it achievable?
4 Is it realistic?
5 What is the time scale?

This model is used in the uniformed public services, as well as other organisations, to empower individuals to achieve their potential. It allows individuals to set their own targets and plan their development within an organisation, thus enabling them to be in charge of their own future.

3.5 Briefing

In the uniformed public services, a briefing is very important as it can mean the success or failure of an operation. For example, a briefing could be in the form of a bombing plan for the RAF, and if the instruction is not understood then civilian lives could be at risk. This would be devastating, not to mention the discredit and disrepute brought upon the service.

Key term

Briefing is a meeting where instructions or information is given; for example, a briefing about a mission to gather information on enemy positions.

SMEAC

There are several points that constitute an effective briefing, and another mnemonic that will help you to remember those points is SMEAC.

- **Situation** – an explanation of the state of affairs and the reason why the forthcoming operation is necessary. The situation could be that a unit of soldiers have been cut off from their section by the enemy, and they need to be rescued from their current position.

- **Mission** – the assignment or task is explained; for example, a rescue party may be required to penetrate enemy lines in order to rescue their colleagues.

- **Execution** – the means of carrying out the mission is explained in great detail. It would include coordinates, timings, rendezvous points, etc.

- **Any questions** – to give personnel the opportunity to clarify any queries about the situation, mission or execution; for example, 'What if we miss the rendezvous point?'

- **Check understanding** – to allow the officer giving the briefing the chance to test the understanding of the personnel who have been briefed. The officer will ask questions and judge understanding from replies to questions, as well as making a note of body language. If there is any doubt that everyone has understood, the briefing will be repeated.

Remember!

A mnemonic (pronounced nim-onic) is an aid to memory. Remember SMART and SMEAC.

Activity: Clear and concise

Why is it important that briefings have clarity?

Why is it important that briefings are accurate and concise?

3.6 Effective control

Receive and give orders directly

The most effective way for a commander to control is by receiving and giving orders directly. In other words, there is no go-between or relaying of orders through another person. However, this is not always possible.

For example, where there is a breakdown in radio or electronic communication, a system of runners might be used to relay orders and instructions. If they are not written down at the time they could be misinterpreted or distorted, resulting in something like 'Chinese whispers'!

There is a well-known story that, while probably false, perfectly illustrates the point of receiving and giving orders directly. During the First World War, an instruction was passed verbally along the trenches to the radio operator to: 'Send reinforcements, we're going to advance.' However, by the time the message reached the operator, he sent: 'Send three and fourpence, we're going to a dance.' Not the original instruction at all!

Noise, stress, hunger and lack of sleep can affect people's perceptions and they may hear incorrectly, or they may not relay the message clearly enough for people to understand. This can lead to ineffective command and control, so the best way to ensure that orders are carried out correctly is for the commander to receive and give orders directly.

Monitor teams effectively

Monitoring a team means checking that it is fulfilling its function in accordance with objectives. However, to monitor effectively includes checking that the welfare of the individual team members is as it should be. This would include checking that team spirit and enthusiasm are maintained because, while the team

Activity: Giving instructions

In your class, pass an instruction from one person to another by whispering: does the last person to receive the instruction give the correct version? You will be surprised how quickly it becomes distorted.

Working in pairs, see how few words you can use to direct each other to your homes and then repeat the directions.

You could try an exercise (under supervision from your teacher) where you are blindfolded and have to achieve an objective by following the directions of one person. When you have completed this, consider how you felt about the person giving the directions. For example, did you trust the person? Were the directions clear and concise?

might be fulfilling its function, low morale could quickly lead to an unsettled team.

The manner in which a commander monitors a team is also important. It would have a bad effect on the team if they thought they were being watched to see if they were doing their job correctly.

Maintain a physical position of control

Maintaining a physical position of control serves two purposes:

- it allows the commander a direct view of the operation where they can assess and reassess progress and make changes where necessary
- it is good for team morale to know that the leader is there to offer support and guidance when required.

Commanders in certain organisations have a natural position of command where they can view progress. For instance, the captain of a ship has a good position of control from the bridge, and a squadron leader has an excellent position of control over a squadron, as a squadron leader or wing commander is usually located at the front and centre of a formation.

Not all commanders have such advantageous positions (as they might then be exposed to enemy fire) but this does not mean they are not maintaining a physical position of control. A good commander would want to be with their team, whether this means hiding in a swamp with them or swimming across an icy cold river with them in the middle of the night.

Essentially, a commander is there for the team, and the team can rely on their commander to help achieve its objectives.

Issue clear orders and commands

Orders and commands are not invitations for a discussion; they are instructions or directives given by those in authority with a view to meeting objectives. The person issuing orders and commands knows exactly what is required to meet those objectives, and expects the person at whom the order is directed to carry it out efficiently and without question. However, for a person to respond correctly to an order or command it must be given clearly and concisely, which means the directive must be unambiguous with a sufficient but minimum amount of words, so as not to cause confusion. Instructions can easily become distorted and lose their meaning if they are too long, or if they have to be passed from one person to another, rather like 'Chinese whispers'.

Maintain a strong command presence

You should not confuse this with maintaining a physical position of control. To maintain a strong command presence means to maintain a strong personality – the type of personality that befits a good commander. A good commander speaks with confidence and conviction while looking people in the eye, which gives team members belief and trust in their commander. A commander with a weak presence or character will lose trust and respect.

Influence the tempo

The tempo of something is the speed at which it is being done – it could be slow, moderate or fast. Doing something too quickly could lead to errors; for example, taking the wrong decision because the problem was not given enough thought. On the other hand, doing something too slowly can also have a negative effect, especially in an emergency situation where lives may be put at risk. A good commander recognises when the tempo of a task is wrong and skilfully alters it for the good of the group, the organisation or the general public.

Delegate

To delegate means to pass on a task to another person. This is a good management tool, and a commander can motivate a team by delegating tasks to the team or individual members. It gives them a sense of responsibility and value, as well as being recognition of the fact that the commander trusts them. However, the commander has to be sure that the team is capable of carrying out the delegated task otherwise this can make the group feel inadequate or incompetent.

Functional command methods

Functional command methods are practical ways of ensuring commands are carried out effectively. For commands that involve a task, it is sometimes easier to break it down into manageable stages and one such

Case study: Floods in South Cumbria 2009

In November 2009 around 200 people were rescued from the Cumbrian town of Cockermouth when extraordinary amounts of rainfall caused severe flooding.

Floodwater in the centre of the town was over eight feet deep and the Environment Agency had issued four severe flood warnings for the county. In nearby Workington, a bridge collapsed claiming the life of a police officer, Police Constable Bill Barker.

The rescue effort was a joint operation involving the RAF, army, emergency services, RNLI Lifeguard and Coastguard teams. Five RAF Sea King helicopters were used to airlift 50 people to safety, some of whom had to break through the roofs of their homes to escape the floodwaters, while around 150 were rescued by RNLI lifeboats. Hundreds of homes were flooded and had to be evacuated, and around 1200 homes were left without power. Local schools were used to provide shelter for around 200 evacuees.

Wing Commander Peter Lloyd said, 'We are concentrating on getting people away from imminent danger and delivering them to what is comparative safety.'

1 If you were the commander of the rescue operation described above, what tempo would you implement?

2 What factors would you take into account to help you decide on the tempo?

3 How would you know if the operation to evacuate was succeeding?

4 Would you, as commander, become physically involved in the evacuation process? Explain.

5 How would you tell your team to approach the people they were evacuating in the early hours of the morning?

---

method has another mnemonic to help you remember those stages – PICSIE.

- **Plan** – a strategy or plan is drawn up, either by a team or by the leader, with the purpose of achieving a mission. It will contain aims and objectives and means of measuring progress. For example, the mission might be: 'Rendezvous with 4 Section at 749046 at 0230 in one week and construct a rope bridge over the River Fury between 0300 and 0330 at 751049. You must not be discovered.' The plan will involve measuring the distance of the coordinates from the present location and estimating the travelling time, including arrangements for travelling, bearing in mind the instruction stated that the team should not be discovered. It is the responsibility of the leader to ensure that proper steps are taken so that the mission is accomplished.

- **Initiate** –the first stage in carrying out the plan would begin with a full briefing to the rest of the team (remember SMEAC).

- **Control** – the plan is put into operation and the leader, who is aware of every stage of the plan, controls the task by ensuring each member of the team knows their role. A good leader should not become personally involved in the task but should maintain a supervisory role.

- **Support** – the leader, besides ensuring that team members support each other, will maintain morale and team spirit by praising and encouraging, as well as maintaining discipline.

- **Inform** – effective sharing of information within the team and with the leader. The team needs to be informed of any change in the plan or mission and the leader needs to be informed of any changes that the team thinks are necessary.

- **Evaluate** – an assessment by the leader of the team's progress, both in terms of objectives achieved and overall team performance. If targets are not being met and the team is performing badly then the leader may alter the plan and reassess at intervals.

Functional skills

Completion of this task may demonstrate your functional skills in English, showing that you can make a range of contributions to discussions and make effective presentations in a wide range of contexts.

Assessment activity 13.3

P4 **BTEC**

Not all leaders are born with the attributes that make them effective in command and control situations. There are certain methods and techniques that can be developed to enable people to take control, having regard to team members and the specific situation to be dealt with.

Address the following task in the form of a discussion:

1 Explain how an individual can exercise command and control **P4**

Grading tip

P4 requires you to familiarise yourself with the content of the section just covered, and discuss at some length how people can exercise command and control. It would be a good idea to make notes and then practise with members of your group, so that you know what to say without reading your notes. It is always a good idea to illustrate your points with examples.

4. Command and control skills using command task activities

4.1 Command and control skills and qualities

There is a difference between understanding the required command and control skills and qualities, and demonstrating them. Good leaders not only understand the skills and qualities, they are also able to demonstrate them through command task activities.

Personal qualities

We have already looked at some of the personal qualities required for command and control (page 295). Have another look at those qualities to refresh your memory and then add the following.

- **Knowledge of people.** A good leader can command and control effectively because they are knowledgeable about people and know how to bring out the best in them. They have the wisdom to understand what makes people happy, what motivates them, and what upsets them. Knowledge of people enables a good leader to demonstrate patience and understanding because they are aware that people make mistakes, especially when under pressure, and they help and encourage them to improve.

- **Belief.** A good leader will truly believe in their organisation and all that it stands for. This belief gives them commitment and loyalty to their service, and the conviction to command and control with confidence. Without this fundamental belief, a leader would be unable to demonstrate dedication and enthusiasm, which are vital in command and control.

- **Strength of character.** Leaders, like anyone else, are accountable for their actions, and a good leader has the strength of character to accept responsibility for their actions without having to apportion blame.
- **Creativity.** Good leaders are creative and resourceful. Their mental agility enables them to think of original ideas to solve problems where others might fail. This is one of the reasons why leaders should not get personally involved in team tasks; they are required to see the whole picture without becoming distracted.
- **Personality.** A good leader has a personality that can adapt to any situation. For example, there may be times when a leader has to be assertive because being forceful might be the only way forward. However, at other times, the leader might have to show compassion or appear charismatic. This is because situations and moods can be very different, including the mood of the team. A good leader can read a situation in terms of atmosphere and mood and can demonstrate personality by adapting to it.

Effective control

By utilising their personal skills and qualities to their best advantage, leaders should be effective in commanding and controlling. To be effective means to bring about a successful outcome to the task in hand. No matter how many skills the leader possesses, they will not be of use unless they can complete a

successful mission. Figure 13.7 shows the elements of effective control.

Effective communication

Effective communication involves many things. It is not only the ability to speak clearly and at the right pace and tone, it also includes non-verbal communication such as body language, eye contact and correct body posture. Negative body posture and lack of eye contact can contradict words of praise and encouragement; body language is often more powerful than the spoken word. A good leader will appreciate the importance of demonstrating positive body language, especially when they encounter someone who does not speak the same language.

Good communication also entails sending the right message at the right time to the right person. Messages sent too late are ineffective, and messages sent too early can be forgotten or cause a backlog.

Activity: Practical and non-practical activities

Some leadership skills and qualities are more practical than others; for example, a pleasing personality is a quality, but with no practical application. A commander might be a nice person to work with but, unless they can demonstrate practical skills and qualities, they will be no good at command and control.

Look at the various skills and, as well as thinking of some of your own, try to classify them as practical or non-practical.

4.2 Types of command task activities

Combat

To engage in combat means to engage in a fight or battle and, in a conflict situation, combat usually means an armed encounter. Therefore, out of all the different command tasks, this is perhaps the most important for both the commander and those being commanded and controlled. In this type of command task, a commander must use all their skills and qualities – courage, mental agility,

Figure 13.7: The elements of effective control. Which do you think is the most important?

decisiveness, creativity and commitment – to ensure the safety, as far as possible, of all those under their command.

While strategies and objectives will have been drawn up, in a combat situation there will certainly be events that have not been planned for. This is where mutual trust between the leader and the team will be at its greatest. The team will trust the leader to command and control and the leader will trust the team to respond promptly to commands.

Rescue

All of the uniformed public services take part in rescues of some form or another. For example, HM Coastguard personnel regularly perform rescue operations at sea, as well as the RAF and RNLI (Royal National Lifeboat Institution). The Fire Service frequently rescues people from burning buildings, road traffic accidents and train crashes, in conjunction with the police. And all the emergency services cooperate to rescue people during major incidents.

In all these situations, the uniformed public services are professional and dependable because, apart from the personal skills and qualities they possess, they know their role within the command and control system.

Containment

Containment refers to the policy of preventing hostilities or a bad influence from spreading through a country. While this could involve the Police Service in a riot situation, it is a procedure that is usually carried out by the armed forces, who act in a peacekeeping capacity. Such operations have been taking place in Northern Ireland, Kosovo, Iraq and Afghanistan to name but a few. These manoeuvres are very dangerous, especially in highly volatile areas (for example, Iraq at the time of writing), and strategies have to be carefully drawn up to minimise casualties.

Here again, the skills of a commander are tested to the full because the operations can involve innocent civilians and children who become embroiled through no fault of their own. This can serve to worsen an already grave situation and can cause even greater hostility to our uniformed public services. A commander has to exercise diplomacy, compassion and understanding, as well as remaining focused on the task in hand; knowing that an insurgent could take on the guise of an innocent civilian and thereby threaten the safety of one or more of their team.

It is important to know your role within the command and control system in a rescue situation. The firefighters in the yellow hard hats follow instructions from the firefighter in the white hat.

Situation control

There are many situations that call for control by the uniformed public services. These can either be civilian or military situations. For example, a prison riot would be a civilian situation that requires control, while a natural disaster, like flooding, could involve the military and the civilian police, as well as other agencies. Situations like these call for command and control so that the situation can be monitored, controlled and returned to normal.

Accident

Unfortunately, road traffic accidents are all too frequent, and multiple-vehicle accidents invariably call for command and control because of the amount of work involved in dealing with them. For example:

- roads need to be blocked while the emergency services rescue the injured from the scene
- relatives need to be informed and told which hospitals their relatives have been taken to
- property at the scene needs safeguarding
- photographs of the scene will be required, etc.

However, accidents do not only involve traffic – chemical explosions, accidents on oil rigs, mining disasters, etc., all require command and control to be dealt with effectively.

Recovery

Recovery entails restoring the community to normality after, for example, a major incident. The community is often the centre for social, leisure and spiritual life, and any upheaval can devastate its fabric. It usually falls to the uniformed public services to help the community to recover. This is particularly difficult in the event of, say, a flood, where properties, including houses, shops and community buildings have been destroyed. To restore a community is a huge operation and requires proper command and control.

Lead and support people to resolve operational incidents

It is an unfortunate but true fact that operational tasks can themselves result in incidents. For example, military aircraft have been known to develop technical problems and crash. In the Falklands conflict, some Royal Navy vessels came under enemy fire, resulting in fires and horrendous burns to crew members.

In such incidents, the commander has the task of organising and leading teams to deal with them. Again, the skills of the commander are crucial because, as you can imagine, the morale of the team can suffer greatly.

Activity: Planning an expedition

You and four of your friends live in the south of England. You are going on a three-day hill-walking and camping expedition to the Lake District in July and you haven't worked out how to get there. Furthermore, you're not sure what food to take and how it will be affected by the anticipated warm weather. You will also need to consider getting home.

Working in small groups, consider the problems presented by this scenario and test your skills at solving them, using the following points to guide you:
- define the problem
- gather all the relevant information
- list the possible solutions

- test the possible solutions
- select the best solution.

Other operational incidents call for lead and support even where serving personnel have not been injured. For example, the alleged manner in which prisoners of war are treated during a conflict situation could bring about low morale. The ill-treatment of Iraqi prisoners a few years ago brought the good name of the US Army into disrepute, which called for leadship and support to resolve the incident.

4.3 Problem-solving techniques

As we have already seen, commanders routinely solve problems in a whole range of situations. It is not by accident that commanders do this; they expect problems as part of their responsibilities and solving them becomes second nature to them, although some situations are more complex and involved than others. Whatever the problem, it is easier to solve if you use some sort of plan and, while not everyone uses the same techniques, the manner in which a problem can be solved successfully usually involves a number of stages; as you will see in the following activity.

Assessment activity 13.4   P5 M3 D2   BTEC

For this assignment you are required to take part in several group scenarios where you will identify and demonstrate the skills and qualities required for command and control.

Address the following tasks in the form of practical activities:

1 Demonstrate with support the use of command and control skills in different situations **P5**

2 Demonstrate practical command and control in different situations within uniformed public services **M3**

3 Evaluate own performance in command and control situations, identifying areas for personal development **D2**

Grading tips

P5 requires you to identify and demonstrate the skills and qualities you have covered in this section, so you need to ensure that you know what they are in order to demonstrate them in the tasks. If you need support with the tasks then that is fine, but you should understand that your grade will be limited to a pass.

M3 is an extension of **P5** but you must complete at least three different tasks without support.

D2 requires you to assess your performance in the tasks you completed and be critical of yourself, so that you can identify where development is needed for the future.

PLTS

Completion of this task may show that you have demonstrated self manager and teamworking skills.

Sue Wilson
Detective Sergeant

I'm rapidly approaching 13 years' service in the job. I've had some scary moments, but I can't think of a better career. After two years' probation in a busy town, I did three years on area patrol before applying for CID. I must have been involved in every incident possible, including hostage situations and multi-road traffic collisions. When you're involved in a large incident you see the different levels of command operate, and it makes you feel good to be part of such an efficient organisation.

Whatever job you do within the Police Service you need lots of personal skills and qualities to deal with the diversity of things you get called to. It's also amazing how you develop different skills. You need to know your role and understand where you fit into the organisation, because everyone relies on one another, and you have to respect rank and authority in order to be efficient. We have a great team spirit and mutual respect for each other, but at times I have to be a motivator as well as a sister, brother, auntie…

A typical shift

There is nothing typical about a shift. We normally work from around nine in the morning and finish about six, but it depends what happens during the day or night; we do whatever we have to, even if that means doing without time off. Paperwork takes quite a lot of our time, but we normally spend a shift making enquiries and collating information to see what evidence we've gathered for a case.

Most of the crimes are major ones – burglaries, serious assaults, fraud and even murders. We have to do a thorough job to ensure the evidence measures up and isn't flawed. We can be called out at any time, day or night, to assist with a serious crime, and it's not the type of job where you watch the clock.

The best thing about the job

Without a doubt, the best part is detecting a crime and getting the offender put away. I know it shouldn't matter to us about the sentencing but we are only human and we need protecting from criminals just as members of the public do.

I find my job particularly rewarding because I have responsibility for the team and I love it when we get good results because the entire team gets a real buzz. Even if I'm feeling under pressure I try not to show it to the team in case this rubs off on them and de-motivates them. Besides, we are always so busy that you don't have time for self-pity.

Think about it!

What topics have you covered in this unit that might give you the background to become a member of the uniformed public services?

What knowledge and skills do you think you need to develop further if you want a career in the uniformed public services?

Just checking

1. The Royal Marines have the same rank insignia as the army, but which of the armed forces do the Royal Marines belong to?
2. Who is responsible for army discipline?
3. Which rank in the Police Service would command a division or district?
4. Why is integrity a good quality to have for command and control?
5. Give three qualities that a good commander can instil in others.
6. What does 'disseminate orders' mean?
7. What are the three levels of command and control?
8. What does the acronym SMART stand for?
9. When would you use the acronym SMEAC?
10. PICSIE is an acronym for a functional command method. What does it stand for?
11. List five command tasks.
12. What are the five stages of good problem-solving techniques?

edexcel

Assignment tips

- This unit gives you the basic outline of how command and control operates within the uniformed public services. You have looked at rank structures and the responsibilities that go with a particular rank, as well as the skills and qualities required to effectively carry out those roles and responsibilities. In order to further your knowledge and understanding, it would be a good idea to take particular notice of any news items on television or in the press that relate to command and control and follow this up by carrying out your own research into the stories; then see if you can apply the principles you have learned in this unit. Researching a topic for yourself gives you a greater insight into a subject, as well as giving you a better chance of achieving the higher grades in your assignment.

- Any of the services outlined in this unit require certain qualities of character, and because of this they have quite demanding selection and recruitment procedures. Some of those qualities are to do with teamwork, problem solving and working with others, which are excellent skills to have in any career, but especially in the uniformed public services. Other qualitites include strength of character, motivation, leadership and integrity, especially if you are considering the higher ranks. How could you develop these qualities? Can you make the right decision when under pressure? How could you practise and develop such a thing? You could set yourself a SMART target for the duration of your current course and review it on completion.

Credit value: 10

25 Public service data interpretation

The public services are increasingly reliant on the information provided by data collected in surveys, observations and government studies. This information is used to guide funding, human resources, strategic operations and target setting. Increasingly, public service workers have to meet statistical targets and write evaluative reports on the performance of their teams, of their service and of themselves.

This unit exists to provide you with skills in the field of data analysis and evaluation as it applies to the public services. You must be able to locate, process, analyse and evaluate data, and be able to present the results in a variety of formats. It can help you gain skills that will need in any career you decide to go into, whether you choose to wear a uniform or not. One of the first things you need to examine if you are considering conducting some data interpretation or research is where your basic information can be found.

The public services are actually seeking individuals who understand that a service career is a dynamic field of work, which requires skills in real world problem solving. This is where the field of data interpretation and research methods can provide you with skills such as problem identification, analysis and evaluation.

Learning outcomes

After completing this unit you should:

1. know the nature and sources of information relevant to public services and how they are used
2. know how to interpret and present information to aid decision making in public services
3. be able to gather, use and present data.

Assessment and grading criteria

This table shows you what you must do in order to achieve a **pass**, **merit** or **distinction** grade, and where you can find activities in this book to help you.

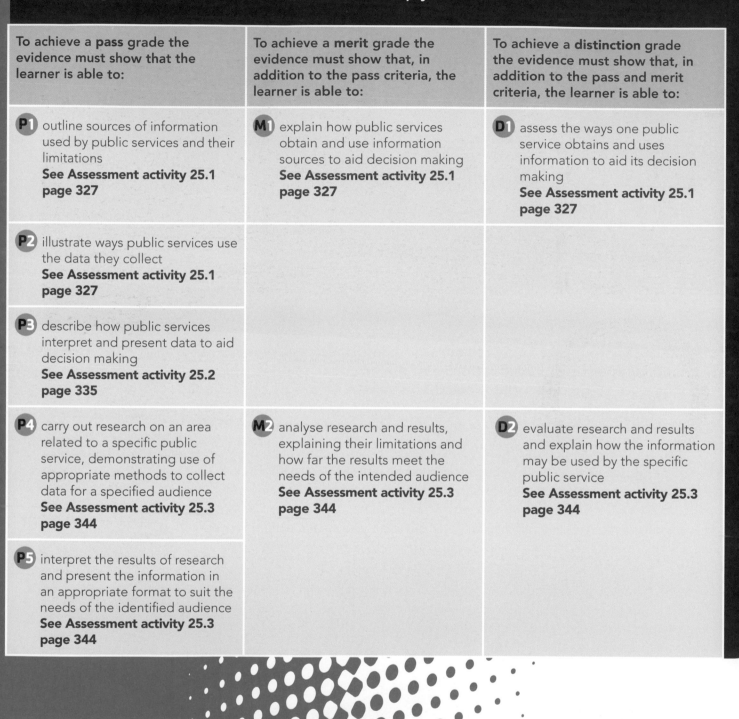

To achieve a **pass** grade the evidence must show that the learner is able to:	To achieve a **merit** grade the evidence must show that, in addition to the pass criteria, the learner is able to:	To achieve a **distinction** grade the evidence must show that, in addition to the pass and merit criteria, the learner is able to:
P1 outline sources of information used by public services and their limitations **See Assessment activity 25.1 page 327**	**M1** explain how public services obtain and use information sources to aid decision making **See Assessment activity 25.1 page 327**	**D1** assess the ways one public service obtains and uses information to aid its decision making **See Assessment activity 25.1 page 327**
P2 illustrate ways public services use the data they collect **See Assessment activity 25.1 page 327**		
P3 describe how public services interpret and present data to aid decision making **See Assessment activity 25.2 page 335**		
P4 carry out research on an area related to a specific public service, demonstrating use of appropriate methods to collect data for a specified audience **See Assessment activity 25.3 page 344**	**M2** analyse research and results, explaining their limitations and how far the results meet the needs of the intended audience **See Assessment activity 25.3 page 344**	**D2** evaluate research and results and explain how the information may be used by the specific public service **See Assessment activity 25.3 page 344**
P5 interpret the results of research and present the information in an appropriate format to suit the needs of the identified audience **See Assessment activity 25.3 page 344**		

How you will be assessed

This unit will be assessed by an internal assignment that will be designed and marked by the staff at your centre. The assignment is designed to allow you to show your understanding of the data interpretation outcomes. These relate to what you should be able to do after completing this unit on public service data interpretation.

Assessments can be quite varied and can take the form of:

- reports
- leaflets
- presentations
- posters
- practical tasks
- case studies
- simulations
- projects.

Marshal works with data as a part-time shop assistant

I was a bit nervous about this unit as my maths isn't brilliant, but my tutor was really good at supporting me through it and it linked in really well with my Maths functional skills so I had a lot of support if I needed it. A unit like this is really useful for the public services because they have to make decisions all the time about how to use their resources and what targets to achieve and they couldn't do that if they didn't understand information and data.

This is a unit that is really useful in any job or profession, not just the public services. I work part time in a shop and the content we looked at helped me understand the manager's decisions on stock, pricing and sales performance much better than before. Understanding information and data is a transferable skill and will be useful whatever you do for a living.

Over to you!

- What areas of data interpretation might you find interesting?
- What sources of information are you already aware of?
- What preparation could you do to get ready for your assessments?

1. The nature and sources of information relevant to public services and how they are used

Talk up

Thinking about data interpretation

Consider the service you wish to join – how would the research and data interpretation skills help you progress in your service?

In order to understand how the public services can use data to improve their efficiency and performance, it is necessary to know where to find sources of information and how to evaluate their quality.

Table 25.1: Sources of information.

Sources	Advantages	Disadvantages
• Internet	• May be lots of information available • Easy to use and download • Information available on a variety of levels from easy to hard • Up-to-date information and archive	• Requires access to IT equipment • Can be difficult to locate specific information • Can be difficult to verify that the information is correct • May not be able to identify the author • You have to decide which information is relevant and which is not
• Journals	• Up-to-date information available • Only deal with specific topics and so more likely to be relevant • Usually well respected and experienced authors • May provide primary statistical data	• May be written in complex academic language • Can be difficult to get hold of • Limited number of articles per journal; it may not have what you require • Time consuming to search through back issues
• Books	• Usually written by experts in the field • Usually written for a specific group of people • May be based around a specific topic or issue • High likelihood that the information is accurate and correct	• May be out of date • Time consuming to read • Usually written for a specific group of people which may not include you • Expensive to buy • Good books are often difficult to get hold of in libraries because they are so popular
• Newspapers	• Up-to-date and archive material available • Good coverage of current events • Inexpensive • Easy to read and understand	• Not written by experts • May be politically biased • May be difficult to locate back issues • May lack depth and detail • May be factually inaccurate
• Local/ Government statistics	• Usually primary first hand information • Usually conducted by experienced and qualified researchers • May provide very detailed information on a specific topic • May help provide support for a theory or idea	• May be politically biased • May not be easy to understand because of the statistical nature of the data • Does not highlight wider or related issues • Can be hard to track down specific information

1.1 Sources of information

The public services use many different sources of information to inform their decisions and strategies, such as:

- books
- journals
- internet reports
- databases
- government statistics
- primary and secondary data
- newspapers.

Table 25.1 shows some of the key advantages and disadvantages of these sources of information.

Primary and secondary data sources

The sources of information you are likely to come across when you are conducting research or interpreting data fall into two main categories:

- primary data
- secondary data.

The use of primary data

Primary data are collected by or on behalf of the people who are going to use the data (usually for a particular purpose), so if you went out and conducted your own survey for instance, you would be collecting primary data. There are several general advantages and disadvantages to using primary data (see Table 25.2).

Table 25.2: Use of primary data.

Advantages	Disadvantages
• Data can be collected on an exact topic • The researcher knows exactly how the data have been collected and what has been done to the data	• Time consuming • Expensive

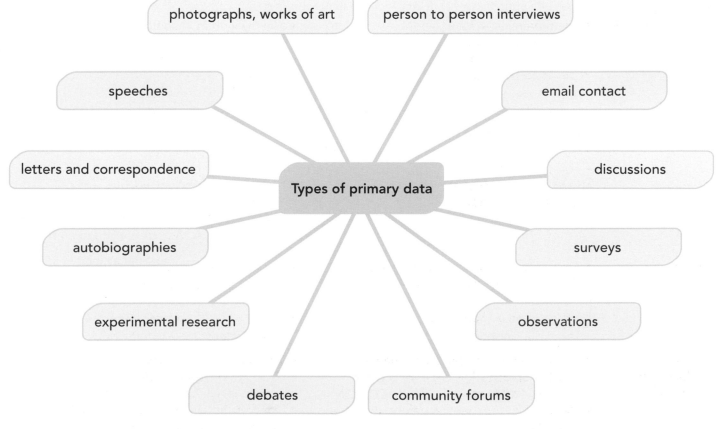

Figure 25.1: Types of primary data.

Activity: Primary data

Working in groups

Can you think of any other source of data that would be considered primary? Try to come up with as many sources of information as you can that are original.

Table 25.3: Use of secondary data.

Advantages	Disadvantages
• Economical • Can be relatively easy to locate • Large quantities/variety	• Someone else's interpretation • May not have exactly what you're looking for • Little information on accuracy or how data was handled

Primary sources are often original materials on which other research is based. The information tends to be presented in its original and unabridged format, and it is often conducted at the same time as the event it is studying, which helps make the research more valid.

The use of secondary data

Secondary data are second hand data; they represent someone else's thoughts and findings. Secondary data can also mean data collected on someone else's behalf or collected for a different purpose than your own. They tend to occur in work that reinterprets or summarises a primary data source, and they are often of a more recent time frame than the event that they comment upon. Some general advantages and disadvantages of using secondary data are outlined in Table 25.3.

Confusion can occur because it is not always easy to distinguish between primary and secondary sources. For instance, a journal article may contain the results of a survey, which would make it a primary source, but it might also comment or analyse the work of others, which would indicate that it is a secondary source. Similarly, a newspaper might publish an article from a foreign correspondent outlining the current situation in Iraq, which is a primary source; but if the article is abridged or edited or a commentary on the political or historical causes of the conflict are included it becomes a secondary source. There are no hard and fast rules to distinguish primary and secondary sources, but in general terms the sources you are most likely to come into contact with, such as the internet and books, will be secondary. If in doubt ask your tutor for advice.

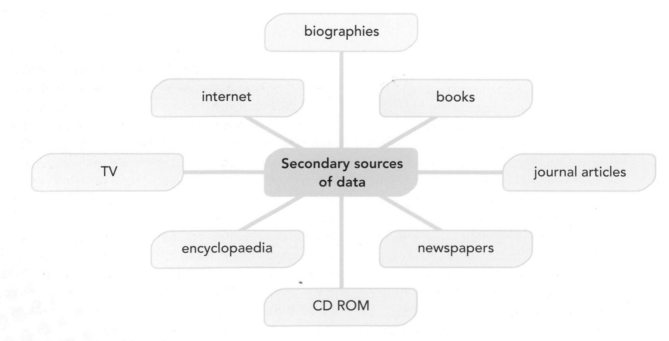

Figure 25.2: Examples of secondary sources.

Assessment activity 25.1

P1 P2 M1 D1 · BTEC

Knowing how public services data are collected and how they are used is crucial in understanding why data interpretation is so valuable to the public services. For this assessment, you are working as part of a local council education unit and you have been asked to go into a class of Y9 school pupils to explain how the public services collect and use data. You have decided to do a set of presentation slides to accompany your talk to the students. Your slides and your talk should be structured as follows.

1 Outline the sources of information used by the public services and their limitations P1

2 Illustrate the ways public services use the data they collect P2

3 Explain how the public services obtain and use information sources to aid decision making M1

4 Assess the ways one public service obtains and uses information to aid its decision making D1

Grading tips

For P1, your talk and slides should cover the sources of information available such as journal articles, books and the internet, and discuss the limitations of these sources such as accuracy, delayed publication and errors. For P2, you should discuss how the services actually use the data for purposes such as decision making and measuring performance. To achieve the higher grades, your talk should be more detailed and cover how the services use the data to make decisions.

1.2 Problems with information

Whether you use primary or secondary data from any of the sources above, you must realise that there is no guarantee that the data are valid or accurate. Even experienced researchers make mistakes which means their data are flawed. Some of the most common areas for error in research are as follows.

Errors and omissions. An error is an inaccuracy in your research. Errors in research are very common and can range from something as simple as an incorrect calculation in the results, to a flawed sampling choice, to a biased perspective on a topic. If you were biased you might only see what you wanted to see when conducting your investigation, or see only information that confirmed your existing beliefs. For example, if you were conducting a study on whether primary school boys were more aggressive at play than girls, you might watch the boys more than the girls and therefore see more instances of aggressive play amongst them. Your research would then be flawed because you have committed the error of being biased and have omitted to watch the girls equally so that your results would paint the full picture.

Degrees of accuracy. This is an assessment of how accurate the data are that you have collected via your primary research. There are lots of factors that can affect the accuracy of your data, such as the type of research methods you used to collect it, the types and number of people you asked to participate, the topic you are studying, and the way you apply the data. One classic mistake that is often made in terms of accuracy is overgeneralisation. Overgeneralisation involves taking a 'fact' or something you think you know and applying it to a situation or a groups of individuals as a whole. For example, if you had the misfortune to be mugged by a member of an ethnic minority group you might then overgeneralise and assume that all muggers were from an ethnic minority group – clearly nonsense. If you apply this to research you may find that 8/10 of your subjects prefer brown bread to white and infer from this that 80% of the British population prefer brown bread to white – how true is this likely to be when the original sample was only 10 people? You have used a sample of 10 people to extrapolate to a population of 60 million people – your degree of accuracy will be low.

Internet research

A literature review is when you examine what has already been written on the topic you are investigating by looking at the subject in textbooks, reading journal articles or looking on the internet. While textbooks and journals tend to be relatively reliable sources of academic information, the internet is often full of incorrect and unreliable data. If you over rely on the internet to investigate a subject, it is likely that you will come across sites that may look professional and convincing, but actually have no academic merit whatsoever. Even worse than this is cutting and pasting from these sites to create work that you then go on to call your own – this is known as **plagiarism**.

Delays in the publication of data

Research topics or problems can change very quickly. If a researcher investigates a particular issue such as hate crime in a small town but doesn't publish the research for a long period of time, then it is likely that the research will no longer be valid as the situation in the small town may have changed. This is why it is important to publish research as close to the time it was conducted as possible. This also gives the public services the best chance to act on the findings and improve the situation.

There are advantages and disadvantages of using the internet for research. What are they?

Key term

Plagiarism is when you take work that someone else has already done and claim it as your own. It is very easy for your tutors to find out what web page you have taken it from – all they have to do is put in a phrase from your copied work into an internet search engine and see what pops up. If you have plagiarised your work you cannot pass your assignment. If you use the work of others you must summarise it in your own words and reference it clearly – it is never acceptable to cut and paste large passages from the internet or books and then just put the website or author's name at the bottom – this is still not your work, it is the work of another person and it will not be acceptable to your tutor.

Freedom of Information Act 2000

The Freedom of information Act 2000 actually came into force in January 2005. It provides the public with the right to request information from public authorities in England, Wales and Northern Ireland. Public authorities include:

- central government and government departments
- local authorities
- hospitals, doctors' surgeries, dentists, pharmacists and opticians
- state schools, colleges and universities
- police forces and prison services.

The public authority must tell you whether it holds the information you are looking for and if it does it should supply it within 20 days of receiving your request. There are exemptions to the disclosure of public data – information which might harm national security or be against the public interest won't be provided, but the organisation does have to tell you why it won't give you the information. If it doesn't have the information it should tell you which public authority does have it.

Data Protection Act 1998

The Data Protection Act gives people the right to know what information is held about them and provides legal rules on what can be done with the information and how it should be handled.

1.3 Use of data by public services

All of the sources of data mentioned above are used by the public services in order to improve their service to the public. Some of the key uses are described below.

To inform

The public services need to be aware of issues as they happen in order to respond to them in the correct way. This includes trends in crime, demographic changes, changes in immigration, changes to funding and changes in human resources, to name but a few. The types of information we have discussed are some of the ways the services stay informed about their area of expertise. The services can also use the information to inform decision makers in local or national government or inform the public if necessary.

In provision of services

Public services use data to be able to make decisions about the level of services they provide the community. This might include the opening or closing of facilities, such as fire stations or prisons, in response to the problems in the area or nationally. If the services were poorly informed they may not be able to provide the right level of services in the right areas at the right times, which could potentially lead to a failure to protect the community.

Planning for future services

As well as planning to provide the current level of services required, the public sector must also plan for the services we will need in the future so that they can adapt to changing community, political or funding requirements. For example, investing heavily in a school in an area where the demographics show that in five years there will be fewer young people may not be the most sensible use of resources, if there is a school in another area where the research predicts an increase in the numbers of young people. The use of research information is crucial in making these decisions.

Uses in deciding performance

The public services also use research information to help them decide how effective their performance is. By gathering research data on how a specific public service performs across the country, local public services can compare their performance to other similar services. For example, National Health Service (NHS) trusts can compare their ambulance 999 response times to all of the others in the country to see whether they are comparing well or if they need to improve. Police services can compare arrest rates for certain crimes between similar constabulary areas. This happens a great deal in education where the research produces league tables on educational achievement, and in health care where infection rates and patient recovery rates are compared.

Links to funding

The public services and the government also use sources of research information and data to influence the funding of public services. This means that if the research shows there will be a greater need for a service there is an argument to increase the funding, and if the research indicates a reduced need then there is an argument to cut funding.

2. How to interpret and present information to aid decision making in public services

Knowing how to interpret data and being able to present it in such a way that others can understand it easily is a key skill in public service data interpretation. Here, we look at how this skill can be developed.

2.1 Interpretation of data

There are several ways in which data can be interpreted. Table 25.4 highlights some of the key issues.

Table 25.4: Interpretation of data.

Key issues	Description
Performance	Data can be used to measure performance against national or local benchmarks. If your service scores below the national average for a particular service, such as 999 response times, patient infection rates or number of GCSE passes, it may be the case that there is room for improvement in the performance of the service
Efficiency	Efficiency is the effective use of time and resources to achieve a goal. Data can tell you if your staff are productive or if they are wasting their time, and can also tell you if the money you put into a project is worth the investment. Data can help you make choices about which services and which staff are working to the best of their ability and which are not
Achieving targets	Data can tell you whether you are on track to meet set targets, or if you are going to miss the targets data can tell you by how much. Using this information you can then devise strategies to correct any problems that arise
Financial planning and accountability	Data is a key factor in financial planning – without data on how much money you have to spend and what you are expected to spend it on you cannot provide a service to the public. Equally important is recording data on how the money was spent – the public services receive their money from the public via taxation, and so the public has a right to know that their money is being spent sensibly
Management decision making	Having access to accurate data enables managers to make decisions that benefit the service the public receive. If the data they have indicate that the public is dissatisfied with a particular aspect of service they can address it. If the data show that that there is no demand for a service then managers can look at how to redeploy the funds to a service which has more take up
Inspection and audit purposes	The public services are required by law to produce data that can be inspected and audited by the government. This includes how money is spent, performance against targets and a whole range of other measures. The full data for the service must be available for inspection upon request
Public accountability	The public services are so named for a reason – it is because they are public servants. They receive all their funding from the government who in turn receive it from the public via the taxes you pay on your salary, on goods in shops or on your savings. They must be accountable to the public for the money they spend and the decisions they make. The public has a right to a certain level of data and information so they can judge how well the service is performing

2.2 Presentation of information

How you present your data is at least as important as how you collect and process it. If no one can see the point your data is making then it will not be much use to anyone. This is where good presentation becomes a key aspect of data interpretation.

Methods and format

There are many methods of presenting data such as those listed below:

- bar charts
- pie charts
- histograms
- linear graphs
- tables
- time series
- moving averages
- seasonal adjustment.

In order to demonstrate how some of these methods work and how you could employ them in your academic studies and later on in your chosen career, examples are given below. Each of the first three examples uses exactly the same raw data.

Raw data (example)

A public services disaster management committee gathered to discuss the possibility of a major incident occurring in the UK in the wake of the 2001 World Trade Center attacks. The committee was made up of representatives from the services, as follows:

Fire Service	10
Police Service	8
Ambulance Service	3
Army	1
Government representatives	6

In graphical form the data could be presented in different ways.

Bar chart. This is one of the most common forms of representing data graphically. A bar represents a variable. There are several types of bar chart, such as compound, simple and component. Bar charts can be vertical or horizontal.

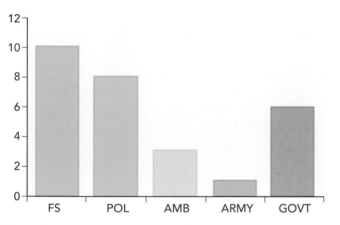

Figure 25.3: A vertical bar chart of the data.

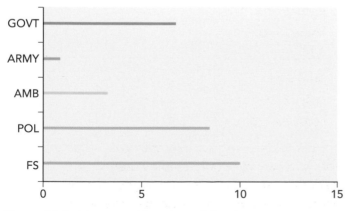

Figure 25.4: A horizontal bar chart of the data.

Pie chart. This is a circle, which is divided into sectors. Each sector represents an item or variable and should have an area in proportion to the percentage that the variable makes up of the whole.

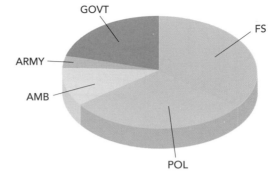

Figure 25.5: A pie chart of the data.

Formula used to calculate sector size is:

$$\text{angle of sector} = \frac{\text{number of items}}{\text{total}}$$

For Fire Service: $= \frac{10}{28} \times 360° = 128°$

$$\text{percentage} = \frac{128}{360} \times 100 = 35.5\%$$

%n = percentage of one variable of the whole.

The advantages of pie charts are that they can be eye-catching and give an overview of data at a glance, but they can sometimes be difficult to interpret and are regarded by some as inefficient at illustrating nominal data.

Histogram. This consists of a series of blocks or bars, which have a width proportional to the class interval and an area proportional to the frequency. Histograms are usually used to show how frequently different results occur, and how the results are distributed across a range, such as the pattern of scores in an exam.

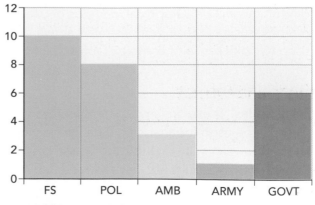

Figure 25.6: A histogram of the data.

It is important to consider how best to present your data. Does the method display the information?

Remember!

The main difference between a histogram and a bar chart is that each column on a bar chart represents a category while each column on a histogram represents a continuous quantity.

Linear graphs

A linear graph is used when you are trying to show the relationship between two variables. On this type of graph the relationship between the variables forms a straight line.

Tables

Another primary method of data representation is in tabular form. Tables are excellent at grouping data together in order that conclusions may be drawn from them, but the more complex the table is the more difficult this will be. Graphical methods of data interpretation, such as those demonstrated above, are often used to make sense of complex tabular data or to draw out specific conclusions, which may not be readily visible in a large table.

Frequency tables. These are among the simplest of tables that can be used for analysing data. Frequency tables show how values are distributed in a sample, i.e. how common certain results are. For example, Table 25.5 shows how satisfied 50 members of the armed services are with their current service assignment.

Table 25.5: How satisfied are you with your current service assignment?

Answers given	Count (50 in total)	Percentage
Very Satisfied	7	14%
Satisfied	13	26%
Neither Satisfied nor Dissatisfied	5	10%
Dissatisfied	20	40%
Very Dissatisfied	5	10%

Cross tabulation. This is where two or more variables are put into a table to show the relationship that might exist between them. For instance, age might be cross tabulated with frequency of illness, or gender might be cross tabulated with income. From these tables it is possible to see whether your data show any patterns, particularly if your table is used as a stepping stone to graphs and charts. Table 25.6 cross tabulates the income and gender of 20 public service employees.

Table 25.6: Gender and pay in the public services.

Employee	Gender	Pay (£000s)
1	Male	34
2	Male	42
3	Female	16
4	Male	24
5	Female	24
6	Female	12
7	Female	38
8	Male	28
9	Male	17
10	Female	20
11	Female	17
12	Male	26
13	Male	54
14	Female	35
15	Female	19
16	Female	21
17	Male	27
18	Female	11
19	Male	32
20	Male	25

It is very easy to examine these data and draw conclusions from them. If you re-tabulate the data in ascending order of salary, are the highest earners male or female? What else does the table show? Using tables like this you can include as many variables as you wish, such as age, ethnicity, length of service and so on. Each variable introduces the potential for a new relationship to be seen and explored.

Time series

This consists of numerical data recorded at intervals of time. It is a useful measuring technique when the development of an issue over a period of time is key. For example, monitoring of crime figures over a period of 10 consecutive years to see if there has been an increase or decrease in crime, or the measuring of the polar ice caps over a period of several years to monitor the impact of rising sea temperatures.

Moving averages

This is a method of repeatedly calculating a series of different average values along a time series to produce a trend line. This technique is of great use to measure performance in businesses and public service organisations. It is a relatively straightforward calculation (see below) and helps organisations see improvement or decline in a year on year (or month on month) pattern (see Table 25.7).

Table 25.7: Calculation of a moving average.

Year	Sales (£millions)		5-year moving average (£millions)
92	5		
93	2		
94	4		
95	9		
96	12	$\frac{32}{5}$	6.4
97	17	$\frac{44}{5}$	8.8
98	18		

1 Add up the figures for the first five years (to 1996) and divide by 5 to obtain the mean: 32 ÷ by 5 = 6.4
2 Subtract the first year and add the sixth (1997), and recalculate: (32 – 5 + 17), 44 ÷ 5 = 8.8.
3 Proceed through the rest of the figures, for as many years as you have data for.

Activity: Moving averages

Consider the following three public services:
- Police
- Local Council
- Ambulance Service.

Provide at least two examples of how each of these public services might use moving averages.

Although the example above shows sales data, the public services would use it to calculate trends in all kinds of performance data from response times to budgetary matters.

Seasonal adjustment

The effects of seasonal variations are often eliminated from data in order to clarify the underlying trend. The resulting figures are termed *seasonally adjusted*. What this means is that some forms of data have seasons where they will be stronger and weaker; for example, if you were looking at the sales figures in the month of December you would see an inflated picture due to people buying Christmas goods. Seasonal adjustments smooth out the differences in figures throughout the year to provide an overall average.

Communicating results to a range of users

Your data are only as good as their presentation. If no one can understand your data then there is very little point in having taken the time to collect the data in the first place. This means you should ensure you can communicate your results to a variety of people and a range of audiences. This might mean producing reports, and adjusting the tone, language and style of your work to suit your audience.

Structuring data and reports

Generally reports are written in a very formal and professional style. They are clearly structured and don't wander from the subject at hand. They are often broken down into easily referenced sections and paragraphs that enable specific points and comments to be found easily. For example, a report on the numbers of suicides in prison may begin:

Section 1 – The Prison System in the UK

Subsection 1.1 – Prisons in the North East

Paragraph 1.1.1 – Numbers of deaths in custodial institutions in the North East.

This format makes the information much easier to understand as you don't have to wade through a 10,000 word report to find the particular section you want to read. This is supported by a detailed contents page and an index that allows ease of reference for specific topics.

The language of a report should be written at a level which would make it straightforward for the educated person in the street who has no prior knowledge of the subject to read and understand. The only time a report would be written in highly complex language is if it was written for a specific reader such as a medical professional or an academic.

Producing reports

Reports should always be produced using a word-processing package such as Microsoft Word. This makes your report look professional and well produced. A hand-written report looks amateurish and unless it is photocopied it cannot be read by multiple individuals. However, even if you word process a report it can still look amateurish if you don't follow some basic rules:

- double space your report
- ensure your spelling is accurate
- use formatting appropriately
- use sensible margins
- ensure paragraphs are not too short or too long
- justify or left align your text
- number your pages
- punctuate accurately.

One of the key things about word processing a report is that it can be electronically stored so that if you lose a copy you can simply print off another. Equally, it is convenient for electronic transmission via email or uploading on to the web if required.

What is your preferred method for presenting data?

Visual methods

A report is a useful way of communicating information, but it is not the only way information can be presented. If you are going to be presenting your data in person then a formal presentation can be an excellent method of communicating your findings. A series of presentation slides with images, diagrams, graphs and tables can illustrate your data and information to a large audience simultaneously.

Decision making

Understanding data and information allows the services to make informed decisions about how they target their services and plan for current and future provision. This includes issues such as:

- allocation of services to people and groups
- maintaining service provision
- increasing service provision
- making decisions between alternative services.

Link

For more information on use of data by public services see page 327.

Case study: NHS treatment

The National Institute for Health and Clinical Excellence (NICE) has judged the liver cancer drug Nexavar as too expensive to be provided on the NHS. The drug, which can prolong the lives of individuals with advanced liver cancer, costs around £3,000 per month to provide to patients.

Andrew Dillon, the Chief Executive of NICE, was quoted: *The price being asked by the manufacturer is simply too high to justify using NHS money which could be spent on better value cancer treatments.*

1 If Nexavar is provided to patients what impact might it have on other NHS services?

2 How do organisations like NICE make decisions such as this?

3 What is the impact on patients of decisions such as this?

Assessment activity 25.2

Knowing how the public services interpret and present data so they can make informed decisions about issues that affect them and the public they service is a key aspect of this unit.

1 Produce a leaflet that describes how the public services interpret and present data to aid decision making **P3**

Grading tip

Consider how the public services make sense of the information they collect or are given, and how they present data to help them make decisions about their provision.

Functional skills

If you use word processing to produce your leaflet for this assessment activity you will be developing your ICT functional skills.

3. Gather, use and present data

As we have already discussed, the ability to gather, use and present your data in an appropriate format is a key skill needed in the public services. This learning outcome looks at some of the research methods that can be used to help you develop these skills.

3.1 Research methods

Research methods are the tools you can choose between to help you gather and analyse your data.

Link

For more information on primary data see page 323.

Primary data sources

Primary data sources include:

* surveys
* questionnaires
* observation.

Activity: Data

Consider whether during your course you are most likely to deal with primary or secondary data. Why is this?

Methods of survey

There are many ways in which surveys and questionnaires can be carried out – some of the main methods are briefly described below.

Observation

Participant observation is when the researcher takes part in the activity they are in the process of surveying or monitoring. So, for example, if a researcher was conducting a survey on how football hooligans behaved, they might go to the football ground concerned and become part of a group which causes trouble (although they wouldn't become involved in the violence, they would simply observe how the group worked and what they did and draw conclusions based on their findings). Participant observation can either be covert, when the individuals being observed don't know that the observer is a researcher, or overt, when they are made aware that the researcher is observing them.

Systematic observation is the meticulous monitoring of a behaviour or group in a very clearly laid out and rigid way. It is considered more scientific than participant observation because the researcher doesn't necessarily interact with the subjects; they may simply monitor how many times a particular behaviour occurs.

Mechanical observation is observation via mechanical means, such as CCTV or traffic-monitoring measures.

Interviews

Formal interviews are also known as structured interviews, and contain a set list of questions that are repeated in exactly the same way to everyone who is interviewed. Generally the answers that are allowed are yes / no / don't know. There is no scope to follow up on issues that may be interesting to the subject or researcher, but the data you get from formal interviews are usually much easier to process than from informal interviews.

Informal interviews are often called unstructured interviews, and the researcher has the scope to find out about a person's opinion in much more detail because they can follow up on tangents or interesting comments made by the subject. However, although the data are usually a lot more detailed and rich than from formal interviews, it can be much more difficult to tabulate the results or make structured sense of your findings.

Questionnaires

Postal questionnaires. A questionnaire is a document that has a list of questions on it that the researcher uses to find out what people might think about an issue. Postal questionnaires are posted out to homes and businesses, the individuals concerned return them and the researcher interprets the results. The main advantage of postal questionnaires is that you can send thousands of questionnaires relatively cheaply. The main disadvantage is that most people don't bother to complete and return the questionnaire, they simply put it in the bin, so there is a low response rate to this kind of survey. Another disadvantage is that the people who do reply are likely to be especially interested in the subject of the questionnaire, so you cannot assume that their opinion is typical.

Questionnaires completed under guidance. This is when the researcher hands the questionnaire out and collects it in by hand. As you can imagine this takes a lot of time so it will involve a smaller number of results. The bonus of using this method is that with a researcher present the subjects are far more likely to actually complete the questionnaire.

By handing out questionnaires or asking the public questions directly you will be able to record responses immediately.

Activity: Questionnaires

It is important to design effective questionnaires or you will have flawed data, which will not answer the questions you initially set out to investigate. In designing questionnaires you must bear in mind the following points:

- keep questions simple
- avoid long words and complex sentences
- avoid 'sensitive' questions
- ask only one question at a time
- questions should not invade privacy
- the questionnaire should not be time consuming
- avoid too many open-ended questions
- begin with basic questions such as age/sex/geographical location
- use unambiguous and unemotive language.

Your questionnaire should be short and to the point. You need to decide between open and closed questions. Open questions allow the respondent the chance to answer freely. This can take a great deal of time and be difficult to statistically process but affords the advantage of more detailed information. Closed questions restrict answers to a simple yes/no/don't know or a rigid categorisation such as a **Likert scale**. They have the advantage of being quick to answer and being very easy to statistically analyse but the downside is a lack of detail.

A Likert scale is a psychometric scale that is commonly used in surveys and questionnaires. An example would be:

How do you rate the performance of your local council?

1 Very Good
2 Good
3 Average
4 Poor
5 Very Poor

Public service skills	1	2	3	4	5
Confidence					
Public speaking					
Coping with new situations					
Making friends					
Talking to strangers					
Making eye contact with others					
Communication					
Vocabulary					
Clear speech					
Body language					
Respect for diversity					
Honesty and directness					
Teamwork					
Ability to work with others					
Ability to take orders					
Ability to listen and respond to others					
Respect for the opinions of others					
Ability to participate in discussions and offer suggestions					
Interpersonal skills					
Sensitivity to others					
Ability to cope with the distress of others					
Diplomacy					
Ability to be fair and impartial					
Able to read body language of others					
Conflict management					
Ability to keep your temper					
Ability to calm others					
Ability to resolve a situation without shouting or violence					
Confidence to step in to help others who are in conflict					
Ability to liaise with all different kinds of people					

Use this questionnaire with the Likert scale to rate your suitability for work in the public services.

Case study: Binge drinking

You have been asked to conduct a survey on binge drinking in your local town centre, including the average amount of alcohol consumed, the impact on local businesses, the cost of public service time to deal with the impact and the reasons for excessive drinking among the 16–24-year-old age group. You know that you cannot use just one survey method to gather all of this data, you must use a combination of survey methods.

1. Which survey method could you use to find out the average amount of alcohol consumed by each person in the town centre?
2. Which survey method could you use to discover the impact binge drinking has on local businesses?
3. What is the most suitable method to find out the financial cost to the public services of dealing with binge drinking?
4. How could you discover the reasons for excessive drinking?

Activity: Training evaluation

You are a new recruit to the fire service, and as part of your training you are asked to help senior officers conduct an evaluation of the training new recruits receive. Which of the primary data collection methods described above might be suitable for this task and why?

Sampling methods and uses

Sampling is the technique of choosing whom you will get data from – a sample of the population will be on average representative of the characteristics of the population as a whole. The sample must be chosen to be of such a size and composition that it will yield the best possible results. There is no point conducting a survey on men if you are aiming to find out women's opinions on a subject, equally if you are aiming to gather the views of the population as a whole then simply surveying your neighbours won't give you representative data. A sample is a small, medium or large group of individuals who have been specially selected to take part in a study or survey because of their personal characteristics, such as:

- age
- geographical location
- gender
- ethnicity
- employment status
- educational status
- religion
- number of children
- family income.

In theory, the larger the sample the more likely your results are to be correct. However, there are lots of drawbacks to having a large sample, such as cost and the time it takes to survey or interview them all. In addition, the more subjects you have the longer it takes you to process your data and the more complex your report will be.

Activity: Sampling

Why is a good sample crucial in undertaking effective research?

Sampling strategies

There are several methods of selecting your sample of individuals to survey, and some of the most widely used methods are described below. In general, sampling is either random or non-random and each category can contain different types of sampling within it (Figure 25.8 and Table 25.8).

Samples of individuals are drawn from lists called sampling frames. A sampling frame is a list of all the people who are eligible to take part in your survey. Examples of sampling frames might be the electoral roll that is kept at your local town hall and contains the names and addresses of all registered voters.

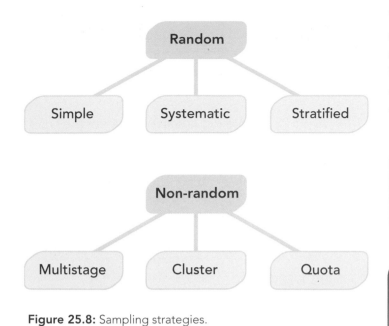

Your college may use the enrolment list of new students as a **sampling frame** if they want to survey students about a topic. Sampling frames do contain inaccuracies though; the electoral roll may contain the details of individuals who have moved out of the area or who have died.

Figure 25.8: Sampling strategies.

Key term

Sampling frame is a list of all the people who are eligible to take part in your survey.

Link

For more information on secondary data sources and their advantages and disadvantages see page 324.

Table 25.8: Description of sampling strategies.

Random sampling types	
Simple sampling	This is when every single person in a population has an equal chance of being randomly chosen
Systematic sampling	True random sampling can only be achieved if there is a good sampling frame and the population is fairly small. Most researchers resort to quasi-random sampling such as every 'nth' on the list. It is important to make sure there are no cyclical patterns that occur in systematic sampling which will affect the sample, such as every 10th house being a corner house
Stratified sampling	Ensures all the important views are represented in the sample. Each social group is represented by the same proportion as they exist in the population at large. Groups can be subdivided by age, race, gender, class. So, if the general population, is made up of 8% ethnic minorities, then 8% of your sample will be ethnic minorities
Non-random sampling types	
Multi-stage sampling	Rather than interview 2000 people at random in a country, instead interview 100 people each in 20 selected areas
Cluster	A few geographical areas are selected and every household interviewed; the areas must be relatively small in order to save time and cost. However, the population as a whole is heterogeneous (this means different), but the population of a few local streets in a particular area is likely to be homogeneous, i.e. hold the same opinions, morals, lifestyles, which may bias your results
Quota	The interviewer has a set quota of questionnaires to complete and they fulfil the quota with a certain number of females or males, and specified age ranges or ethnicity. They are otherwise free to choose whom they stop in the street, so this method is open to abuse and bias, but it is cheap

3.2 Using and presenting data

In order to use and present data in a format which can be easily understood, there are some basic mathematical techniques that you need to master before you draw up your results. If you have GCSE maths the chances are that this area is familiar to you, and you may not need the refresher. However, if maths isn't your strong point, the instructions and activities below will help you along.

Link

More information on presenting data to meet the needs of the audience and different presentation methods, including written reports, ICT and visual methods can be found on pages 328–332.

Finding a percentage

It is often necessary in research to discuss the percentage of subjects who agree or disagree with a statement or who have done or not done an activity, such as committing a crime. Finding percentages can be tricky if you don't know how. Consider these examples:

£7 as a % of £50 $\frac{7}{50} \times 100\% = 14\%$

5% of £450 $\frac{5}{100} \times 450 = 22.5\text{p}$

If you apply this formula to your research you might come up with something like the following example.

You have interviewed 35 subjects on whether they have ever committed a crime – 14 of them have, and you need to convert this figure into a percentage. The way to do this is as in the first example above:

$$\frac{14}{35} \times 100\% = 40\%$$

Therefore, you can conclude that 40% of your subjects have committed a crime, which is a better way of saying 14 out of 35 have committed a crime – it helps the reader of your research to understand it in more depth.

You have discovered that 15% of your subjects do not know whether they have committed a crime or not. You need to find out the actual number of individuals this represents. The way to do this is as in the second example above:

$\frac{15}{100} \times 35 = 5.25$ people did not know whether they had committed a crime.

Converting percentages

Fractions to percentages:

To change a fraction to a percentage multiply it by 100%

For example ½

$\frac{1}{2} \times 100\% = 50\%$

Decimals to percentages:

To change a decimal to a percentage multiply it by 100%

For example 0.55

$0.55 \times 100\% = 55\%$

Percentages to fractions:

To change a percentage to a fraction divide it by 100.

For example 50%

$\frac{50}{100} = \frac{1}{2}$

Percentages to decimals:

To change a percentage to a decimal divide by 100 *or* move the decimal point two places to the left.

For example 13.96%

$\frac{13.96}{100} = 0.1396$

Activity: Percentages

Complete the following conversions:
- change ¼ into a percentage
- change 0.45 into a percentage
- change 35% into a fraction
- change 89% into a decimal.

Statistical averages

An average is the middle, typical or expected value of a data set. There are several different types of average, such as:

- a summary of a group or a dataset
- a way of describing data concisely.

Generally speaking there are three types of statistical average (see also Table 25.10):

- arithmetic mean
- mode
- median

Mean

You find the mean by using the formula below. Add up all of the values that you have and divide the result by the number of individual values:

$$\text{mean} = \frac{\text{sum of all values}}{\text{number of individual values}}$$

For example, you have five subjects with differing ages:

Subject 1   11 years

Subject 2   22 years

Subject 3   33 years

Subject 4   44 years

Subject 5   55 years

In order to find the mean you must add up all of the ages and divide by the number of subjects:

$11 + 22 + 33 + 44 + 55 = 165$

$\frac{165}{5} = 33$ years is the statistical mean.

Median

The median is another form of average, but is much simpler to establish, it is simply the value of the middle item, when the items are listed in order of size. So if you consider the list of ages above the value that is in the middle is subject 3 who is 33 years old, this figure would become the median value. You can also apply the following formula where you have too many values to easily see where the middle one is.

$$\text{median} = \text{middle value } (n\text{th value})$$
$$n = \frac{(\text{number of items} - 1)}{2}$$

Mode

This form of average is found by locating the most frequently occurring value in a distribution. For example, you have conducted a survey which shows how often individuals have been a victim of crime and you have data as shown in Table 25.9.

Table 25.9: Example of the mode of a distribution.

Subject No.	How many times have you been a victim of crime in the last year?
1	3
2	1
3	0
4	1
5	2
6	5
7	2
8	1
9	8
10	1

As you can see from the table, the value that occurs most often in your data is 1, and therefore the mode of this distribution is 1.

Table 25.10: Types of statistical average.

	Advantages	Disadvantages
Mean	Widely used Mathematically precise Uses all data	Distorted by extreme values May not correspond to any actual value
Median	Often an actual value Useful when extreme values would distort the mean	Not as widely used Gives the value of only one item
Mode	Commonly used Represents a typical item Usually a real value	Does not include all values Less mathematically correct

Data processing systems

Using research methods and data organisation systems such as those outlined above and earlier in this unit allows a researcher to retrieve, analyse and make comparisons with their data very quickly and easily. Use of ICT is also invaluable in this area.

Manual processing

This is where you work out the patterns and relationships in data by hand without the benefit of computer assistance. This is not a particularly efficient way of producing information from a dataset as it is very time consuming and prone to error. The vast majority of individuals and all organisations and services prefer ICT-based processing because of its speed and efficiency.

ICT-based processing

There are many methods of utilising computer software in analysing data, for example using a database or spreadsheet, as well as specific software for data analysis such as the Statistical Package for the Social Sciences® (SPSS). Software such as this can help organise and sort data, perform calculations and data analysis, and help represent the data graphically. It is a real advantage to be familiar with software such as this as it can make data analysis very speedy and the results are less subject to human error. If you have thousands of different sets of results from a questionnaire, it can be extremely difficult to manage them and understand the patterns in them. IT packages can show these patterns very quickly and can cross reference data to find relationships between different variables much quicker than a researcher could do by hand.

The types of software you are likely to come across are as follows.

Databases. These are software products which allow lots of data to be stored and retrieved very quickly. Databases can also cross reference data and produce reports on the data they contain. In essence, a database is like an electronic filing cabinet. You are likely to come across databases such as Microsoft Access® (see Figure 25.9) on an average PC that you might have at home or at college. Microsoft Access has very good help and tutorial facilities, which will enable you to become familiar with how databases work. The word database is also used to describe all the data held (for example, all the answers of a questionnaire) as well as the software used to analyse it.

Spreadsheets. A spreadsheet is a tool for performing calculations and analysis on large amounts of numerical data. A spreadsheet also allows the data to be represented in graphs and charts. Common spreadsheet packages you are likely to encounter are Microsoft Excel® (see Figure 25.10) and Lotus 1-2-3. Like database packages most spreadsheet packages have help and tutorial facilities available.

Statistical Package for the Social Sciences (SPSS). This is a package widely used in colleges and universities to perform statistical analysis on collected data. It analyses and produces statistics from large amounts of raw data to assist with the prediction of trends and identifying categories. This is more specialised statistical analysis software than databases and spreadsheets and so would be used when you want to derive specific meaning from a large dataset.

Link

More information on tables, time series and how to organise data can be found on pages 330–332.

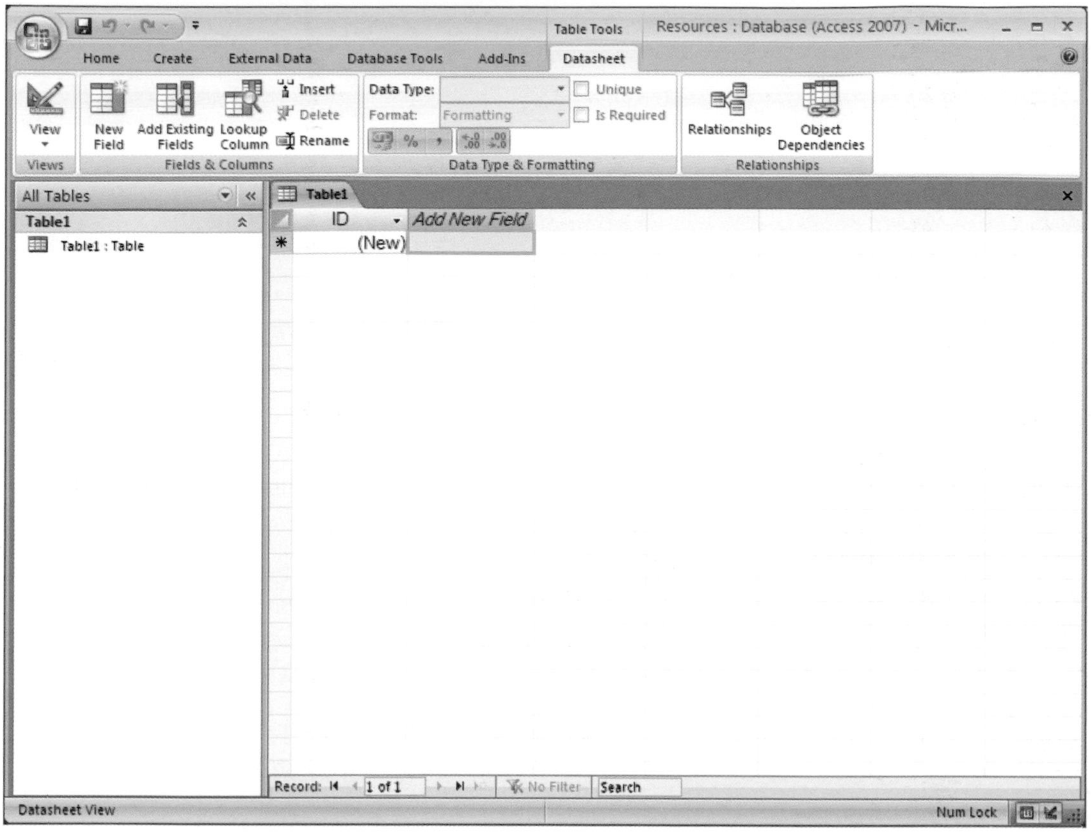

Figure 25.9: Data can be stored and retrieved very quickly from a database program such as Microsoft Access®.

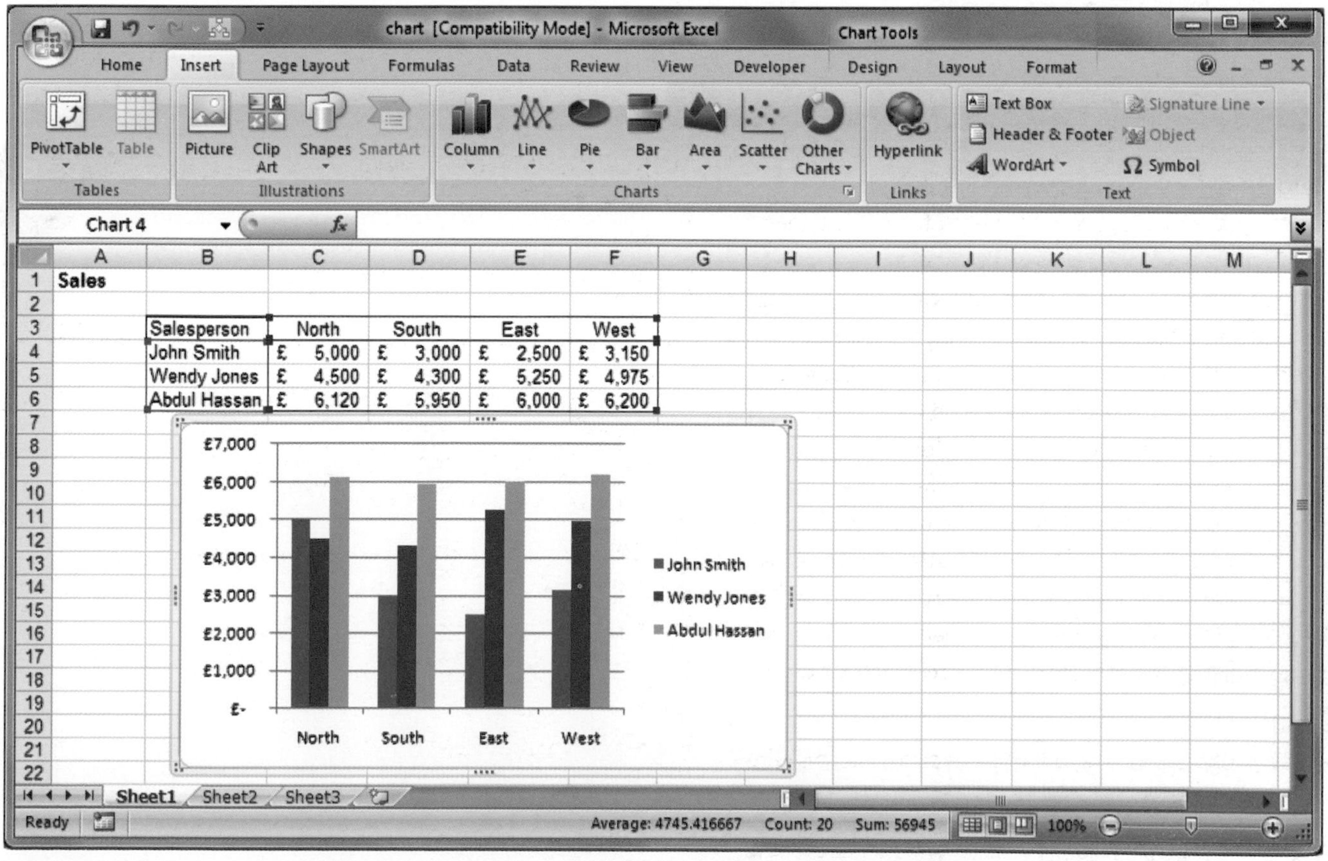

Figure 25.10: A spreadsheet program such as Microsoft Excel® is able to display data as graphs or charts.

Assessment activity 25.3

P4 P5 M2 D2 **BTEC**

After having learned about research, data collection and interpretation in this unit, you now need to demonstrate that you can put what you have learned into practice by completing your own research project.

1 You are working for the local council's crime reduction partnership and you have been asked by your line manager to conduct some research into the fear of crime in a particular area of your town. You will present this research to the multi-agency team who work in partnership with the local council at the next full partnership meeting. While conducting your research you need to demonstrate the use of appropriate methods to collect data for a specified audience, in this case the multi-agency partnership team **P4**

2 Once you have completed your research, you need to interpret the results and present the information in an appropriate format to suit the needs of your intended audience. This could be a report or a presentation showing clear evidence of data interpretation such as tables, charts and statistical analysis **P5**

3 Once you have interpreted your results, you need to analyse your research, and explain the limitations of the results and how far they meet the needs of the partnership **M2**

4 You then need to evaluate the research and results and explain how the information may be used by the partnership in tackling fear of crime **D2**

Grading tips

You need to select appropriate methods to collect your data, so consider if a questionnaire, survey or observation might be the most useful method and explain your reasoning. Once you have collected your data, consider how it can be converted into useful information by using tables, graphs and charts to highlight the key issues. Present your information in the most useful way for the partnership team, so consider the value of a report or a presentation.

PLTS

Completing this Assessment activity will give you the opportunity to practise your skills as a reflective learner and independent enquirer.

Functional skills

This research activity requires you to collect and use data and interpret the results, so using your maths, English and ICT functional skills.

Lily George
Police data analyst

I work as a data analyst for a police service in the south of England. The role involves collecting and analysing primary and secondary data to provide usable information that will help senior officers to make strategic and operational decisions about resources and priorities in the force area.

A typical day

I spend most of my time office based, working with data and turning it into a usable format such as a report which then gets forwarded to senior officers for consideration. The data I usually work with is crime based as you would expect in the police service. Sometimes my colleagues and I are required to collect primary data, which is usually done via interviews and questionnaires.

The best thing about the job

One of the best things about my job is turning raw data that barely anyone can understand into usable information that can be used by the police and their partner agencies to combat crime and anti-social behaviour. The information I collect and produce helps them make informed decisions about how to spend their resources and support the public, I like knowing I've had a hand in that.

Think about it!

What topics have you covered in this unit that might give you the background to work in your chosen service?

How does the service of your choice use data interpretation?

What knowledge and skills do you think you need to develop further if you want to have a career in data analysis?

Just checking

1 What are primary data?

2 What are secondary data?

3 What are the limitations of data?

4 Can you summarise the Freedom of Information Act 2000?

5 Can you explain what a time series is?

6 How do you work out a moving average?

7 What is seasonal adjustment?

8 Can you describe three different sampling methods?

9 What is a sampling frame?

10 How would you design a good questionnaire?

advancing learning, changing lives

Assignment tips

- This unit requires a lot of research into the public services so making sure you use the right sources will be essential. Your school or college should order in journals and publications about the services such as *Police Review* or *Soldier* magazine. These often contain issues arising from changes in the services that you will need to be aware of if you are going to get the best grades in your assignment work. If your centre doesn't stock them, speak with your tutor or librarian about getting them in.

- In a unit like this which focuses on data interpretation and primary and secondary data services, one of the best things you can do to help improve your grade and your knowledge is to make sure you keep up to date with current events by reading a reputable news source on a daily basis. This means using your lunch hour or an hour after school/college to read the BBC news website or picking up a broadsheet newspaper such as *The Times*, *Guardian* or *Telegraph* (these have websites where you can read the news if you can't get hold of the paper). These are valuable and easily accessible secondary sources.

Glossary

Active military operations are any active operations where military personnel are deployed, such as in combat or peacekeeping. A battle is a meeting of opposing forces in a war or conflict, and their engagement in violence against each other.

Alienation is a feeling of being withdrawn or isolated from those around you.

Anarchy literally means 'without rule' and is used to describe a state of political or social disorder.

Anti-social behaviour refers to a set of behaviours by some people that have an adverse affect on other people in society.

Apartheid was the policy of racial segregation in South Africa that ended in 1990. It was used to keep the black and white populations separate. The South African black majority were forced into racially segregated living areas, education and healthcare, all of which was significantly inferior to the facilities provided by the government for the white minority.

Asylum seeker is an individual who has fled their own country due to conflict or persecution and has applied to stay in another country until their own country is safe to return to. If an asylum seeker is successful in their application they become a refugee. If they are unsuccessful they are deported to their country of origin.

ATP (adenosine triphosphate) is a molecule that carries energy and is the only direct source of energy for all the processes in the body.

Authoritarian leadership is a very direct leadership style where the leader tells the team members what they must do.

Body mass index is defined as the individual's body weight divided by the square of their height:

Brief is a verbal process of getting information to people quickly and efficiently, very similar to a meeting but with less open discussion.

Briefing is a meeting where instructions or information is given; for example, a briefing about a mission to gather information on enemy positions.

Broadsheet newspaper traditionally has larger pages which cover more serious news content. Examples include *The Times*, *Guardian* and *Telegraph*.

Bureaucratic leadership is a style of leadership that focuses on rules and procedures to manage teams and projects.

By-election is an election that happens in a specific constituency due to the retirement, death or resignation of the current MP for that area. They can happen at any time.

Cabinet a committee of the 20 or so most senior government ministers who meet once a week to support the Prime Minister in running the country.

Cabinet meeting is a meeting of the senior government ministers that happens once a week. During the meeting they may discuss the creation of new policies and laws. **Parliamentary Committee/ Subcommittee** is a smaller more focused group of politicians and civil servants who meet to discuss potential new policies. They may have more time and more knowledge of the issue than the Cabinet, if they think the policy is needed they may move to the next stage of policy creation which is called a Green Paper. **Draft** is a term used when a policy is not yet in its final form and might be subject to change after further discussion and debate.

Civil law is the area of British law that is concerned with the private affairs of citizens, such as marriage and property ownership.

Civilianisation is the process of freeing up public service personnel by employing civilians to do non-operational work. Reserve forces are volunteer troops who may be called up in time of conflict, but have a normal civilian life and do their military training in their spare time.

Coalition government is a government where no single party has a majority and so they have to team up to form an alliance in order to ensure decisions can be made and legislation is passed. However, because different parties are involved they often disagree on how best to do things and this can lead to instability.

Cold War is a term applied to the relationship between the US and USSR from the 1950s to the 1980s. The two superpowers were openly hostile and the threat of nuclear conflict was ever present. The situation improved dramatically with the fall from power of the communist Soviet regime and the disintegration of the USSR. Russia is now considered to be a friendly nation to NATO and no longer a military threat to Western nations.

Collective conscience is the feeling of people in a group of what is right and wrong; a group of people sharing the same morals and values with similar views of deviant behaviour.

Community orders are a range of punishments given to an offender to serve in the community.

Compliance is to act in accordance with a wish or command.

Constituency is a geographical area that has an elected representative in Parliament.

Corrupt means to be without morals; to be influenced by bribery or fraudulent activity. Corruption is usually motivated by greed

Crime trends are increases or decreases in crime over a period of time.

Criminal law is the area of British law that deals with crimes and their punishment.

Debrief is the process of gathering information about the success of a task or activity after it has been completed. This helps improve the planning process for next time.

Democratic leadership is a style of leadership where the leader maintains control of the group, but team members' opinions and views are encouraged and the leader informs the team about issues which may affect them.

Deviance is often defined as a behaviour that is not normal and goes against morals and values.

Devolution means to pass governmental powers to a lower-level elected body.

Diaphysis is the straight, middle part of the bone.

DNA is the abbreviation for de-oxyribonucleic acid, the molecule that carries the genetic information in the cells of organisms.

Ego is the rational, logical part of us, governed by reality. It is the part of the **id** that has been modified by the world around us. It tries to satisfy the id in a socially acceptable way. The **super-ego** is the moral part of our personality that judges things as right or wrong, good or bad. It develops around the age of 5 years old, and is effectively what we call our conscience.

Epiphysis is the rounded, end part of the long bone.

Evaluation is a process used to gather information to determine whether or not the team has been successful and achievement of its aims has occurred.

Exercise (military sense) is another word for a real-life simulation, it's a chance for the public services to practise their skills and knowledge in a simulated battle or emergency situation.

Fartlek training (fartlek is Swedish for 'speed play') is a combination of both long slow distance and interval training. It involves changing speed, but at varying levels such as walking, sprinting and jogging.

Fight or flight is an instinctive response to a threatening situation which prepares you to resist or run.

Fixed penalty notice refers to a notice issued for a minor offence of a fixed amount of cash that must be paid or the offender will be taken to court.

General election is where all of the seats in the House of Commons come up for election at the same time. General elections are called by the serving Prime Minister and must happen five years and three weeks apart or less.

Hierarchy is a system in which grades or classes of authority are ranked one above the other.

Humanitarian aid is the provision of food, shelter or medical supplies to areas of the world which are in a conflict situation or have been affected by a disaster. It can also include specialist personnel such as doctors or engineers.

Id is the demanding and child-like side of a person, which responds directly to instincts such as hunger, thirst and the need for sexual gratification. The id does not respond to social norms and values, and according to Freud is the part that must be repressed.

Initiative means a new venture.

Instigate means to bring about or make something happen by persuasion or urging someone to do something.

Intelligence is information about crimes and offenders that the police and other authorities can use to reduce crime.

Labelling is the process of giving people a 'label' based on their behaviour. This can be both positive and negative and can greatly influence how you are treated by others.

Laissez-faire leadership is a hands-off approach to leadership, where the group are trusted to complete the task by the leader.

Legislation refers to the laws that have been made. To legislate means to make laws.

Maximal treadmill protocol is a common test used to estimate maximal oxygen uptake in athletes. Oxygen uptake is linked to an athletes capacity to perform sustained activity.

Maximum heart rate (MHR) is calculated as 220 minus your age. It is important to know this so you can plan your cardiovascular training to work your heart hard enough to get some benefit, but not so hard that it might be dangerous.

Mediator is a person who is trained to liaise between different parties in order to resolve conflict fairly and peaceably.

Metabolic rate is the rate that your body uses energy from food.

Minister usually an MP appointed by the Prime Minister to take charge of a government office such as Defence, or the Home Office.

Morale is also known in the services as 'esprit de corps' and it refers to the spirit and enthusiasm of a team and their belief and confidence in their purpose and success.

NACRO stands for National Association for the Care and Resettlement of Offenders.

National Census is a count of people and households that provides statistical data on the population of the UK. This happens every 10 years. The next one is due on 27 March 2011 and will involve around 25 million households.

Obedience means carrying out the command of some authority, doing what you are told to do.

Offender is a person who has committed a crime.

Opposition refers to the members of parliament from those parties who do not form the current government.

People-orientated leadership style focuses on participation of all team members, clear communication and supporting and developing the individual in order to improve skills.

Periosteum is the skin of a bone.

Pilates is an exercise system which focuses on developing core strength by using low impact stretching and conditioning exercises.

Plyometrics is a training technique designed to enhance power. It involves stretching a muscle and then immediately contracting it. An example would be a hill sprint or squats.

Post custody licence is a legal document giving you official permission to leave custody under strict guidelines about re-offending.

Post-traumatic stress disorder (PTSD) is a severe anxiety disorder that can develop after a person experiences a traumatic event.

Primary aim is the key objective of the team, the task or goal that must be achieved.

Prime Minister is the leader of the political party with most seats in the House of Commons.

Pyramid training is just one way to lift weights or engage in any strength building activity and involves changing your reps and weights for each set of each exercise. In other words, you'll start light and end heavy or start heavy and end light.

Referendum is a public vote on whether to pass a law. Usually laws are made and passed in Parliament, but in a referendum the public make a direct decision.

Regional government is a form of government where the decisions about what happens in a particular region are made at local level.

Repeat victimisation refers to a person being the victim of the same crime on more than one different occasions.

Sampling frame is a list of all the people who are eligible to take part in your survey.

Sarcasm is the use of irony to mock someone or something. **Irony** is a statement that, when taken in context, may actually mean the opposite of what is written or said.

Seats are places in an elected parliament (especially in the House of Commons).

Segregation is the separation of people by race, culture or custom. Sometimes it happens in law such as in the US prior to the 1960s and in South Africa up to the 1990s, and sometimes it is based on custom, tradition or choice.

Sentence is the punishment that is given to a person who is found guilty by a criminal court.

State is often described as a geographical area in which a government operates without outside interference.

Statutory licence supervision is a legal document giving official permission for the probation service to supervise your movements.

Stress is the emotional and physical reaction our body shows to meet a challenge, this can be harmful and/or beneficial.

Super-ego see **ego**.

Tabloid newspaper is one that tends to report news that is sensational rather than serious, which means they often focus on entertainment, celebrity scandals or crime. Examples include the *Sun, Daily Mirror* and *Daily Star*. They are called tabloids because the page size is smaller than the traditional broadsheets (such as *The Times* and *Telegraph*) but nowadays some broadsheet newspapers are tabloid-sized.

Task-orientated leadership style is about getting the job done. The completion of the task rather than the needs of the team is the key goal.

Third sector organisations are non-governmental organisations such as voluntary and community organisations and charities.

Transactional leadership is a very direct style of leadership and uses rewards and punishments to motivate the team.

Transformational leadership style is a form of leadership style that focuses on team performance as a whole by encouraging team members to think of the group rather than themselves. It is about moving forward as a team rather than individuals who just happen to be on the same project.

Treaty is a written agreement made between two or more nations that is legally binding. It is like a contract between countries about a particular issue such as trade, conflict or territory.

Veto is the power to stop a piece of legislation or an action in its tracks.

Victim is a person who has been targeted in a crime.

Warsaw Pact was the Eastern European version of The NATO Treaty. It was a military treaty that bound together the USSR and its allies such as Albania, Poland and Czechoslovakia to come to the aid of each other if they were attacked.

Witness is someone who saw what happened, i.e. was present when a crime occurred. All people can be vulnerable to crime but an elderly person can be more vulnerable to certain types of crime such as mugging or burglary.

YOT stands for Youth Offending Team.

Index